THE LEGAL ASPECTS OF HEALTH CARE BUSINESS TRANSACTIONS

A COMPLETE GUIDE TO THE LAW GOVERNING HEALTH INDUSTRY BUSINESS ORGANIZATION, FINANCING, TRANSACTIONS, AND GOVERNANCE

2023 EDITION

THE LEGAL ASPECTS OF HEALTH CARE BUSINESS TRANSACTIONS

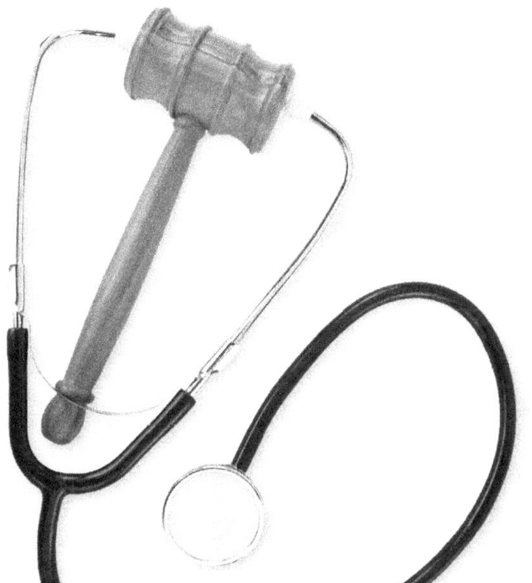

A COMPLETE GUIDE TO THE LAW GOVERNING HEALTH INDUSTRY BUSINESS ORGANIZATION, FINANCING, TRANSACTIONS, AND GOVERNANCE

2023 EDITION

THOMAS WILLIAM BAKER, M.B.A, J.D.

Legal Aspects of Health Care Business Transactions:
A Complete Guide to the Law Governing the Business of Health
Industry Business Organization, Financing, Transactions, and Governance
2023 Edition

For information about this title or to order other books and/or electronic media, contact the publisher:

Thomas William Baker, Esq.
Coronat Services, LLC
(404) 276-1337 (Telephone)
www.coronatservices.com
tom.baker@coronatservices.com

ISBNs:
978-1-7326694-8-2 (print)
978-1-7326694-9-9 (eBook)

Printed in the United States of America

Cover and Interior design: 1106 Design

TABLE OF CONTENTS

CHAPTER 1

OVERVIEW OF THE HEALTH CARE ECONOMY AND THE EFFECT OF STATUTES AND REGULATIONS ON HEALTH CARE BUSINESS TRANSACTIONS

I. WHAT IS THE LAW?

A. **United States Constitution.** The United States Constitution defines federal and state powers and generally incorporates English common law as the law of the land. Everything not defined in the Constitution as a federal power is left to the states. The Constitution also divides power among the legislative, judicial, and executive branches of government. In addition, the "Commerce Clause" in the Constitution permits the Congress of the United States to pass laws that regulate commerce between the states, and federal courts have broadly construed and interpreted what constitutes "interstate commerce" for purposes of federal legislation. Also, the Patient Protection and Affordable Care Act of 2010 (the "Affordable Care Act" or "ACA", which is sometimes referred to as "Obamacare") was declared constitutional because the statute is, in effect, a tax. Therefore, the federal government taxing powers are very broad.

B. **Federal Statutes and Regulations.** The United States Congress passes federal laws, which apply equally to all of the United States. For example, the Medicare program was created by a federal law, and the Affordable Care Act is a federal law with far reaching ramifications for not only the health industry but the United States economy as a whole.

1. **Federal Regulations.** Federal laws, like the laws governing the Medicare program and the ACA, are implemented by federal regulations. Regulations are substantially more detailed than the statutes they implement.

2. **Administrative Procedures Act.** Federal regulations are implemented in accordance with the Administrative Procedures Act, which generally requires publication of proposed regulations

in the Federal Register and opportunity for public comment. Once federal regulations pass through the notice and comment period, they are published in the Federal Register as "final rules" and have the full force and effect of law. Sometimes, however, federal laws are passed but never become effective because federal regulations in accordance with the Administrative Procedures Act are never implemented.

C. **Federal Courts.** The federal courts have jurisdiction over all cases regarding the United States Constitution and federal laws. The Supreme Court of the United States is the final arbiter for issues arising under the United States Constitution. The federal courts can also have jurisdiction over claims between citizens of different states (called "diversity of citizenship"), and, in "diversity" cases, the federal courts are required to make their rulings in accordance with the governing state law.

D. **Federal Manuals.** Federal agencies such as the Department of Defense and the Department of Health and Human Services ("DHHS"), through its agency, the Centers for Medicare and Medicaid Services ("CMS"), have the power to publish manuals that interpret the federal regulations. Although the manuals do not have the force and effect of law, they are given "great deference" by the courts, and their provisions are sometimes treated like laws and regulations for other purposes (such as application of the federal False Claims Act).

E. **The Common Law.** The "common law" generally governs relationships between private parties (property, torts, and contracts). Each state's law is generally based on common law principles. There is some federal common law, but its application is very limited. Even though federal common law is quite limited, one important place where it applies in the health industry is under the privacy rules promulgated under the Health Insurance Portability and Accountability Act of 1996 (commonly referred to as "HIPAA"): HIPAA "covered entities" (which includes virtually all federal reimbursement program certified providers and suppliers) are responsible for HIPAA privacy and security law breaches of their "business associates" under the federal common law principles of "agency."

F. **State Statutes and Regulations.** The states similarly pass laws and implement state laws through state rules and regulations, some of which either codify or modify common law principles. Most business regulation is accomplished through state laws. When the states have a common interest in uniform laws, each state can separately enact a law that is virtually identical in all states. Examples of uniform laws include the Uniform Commercial Code and the Uniform Trade Secrets Act.

G. **State Courts.** The state courts interpret the common law and state legislation. For example, most contract disputes and professional liability claims are resolved by state courts.

H. **Federal Law Preemption of State Law.** Some federal laws completely "preempt" or supersede state laws, but some bodies of federal law address the same areas as state laws. For example, prior to 1976, there were two bodies of copyright law: federal and state. However, under the power of the United States Constitution "commerce clause," the United States Congress passed the Copyright Act of 1976, which preempts all state law. Consequently, copyright law is now uniformly applied in all of the United States. Similarly, federal patent law preempts state law. By contrast, there continue to be two bodies of trademark law: the United States trademark law does not preempt state trademark laws. Examples of other bodies of law covered in this textbook that affect business transactions and are enforced under both federal and state law are securities law involving issuance of investment instruments and antitrust law.

I. **How Has the Law Evolved?** In modern times, a substantial portion of the law involves the relationship of citizens with government and its agencies, not other citizens. Virtually every business enterprise is required to comply with some body of federal law that imposes potential civil or criminal sanctions, and sometimes both. Notable examples include federal securities law, government contracts law, tax law, participation in the Medicare and Medicaid programs, and environmental law. There are also less obvious bodies of law, such as intentional violation of copyright law and Racketeer Influenced Corrupt Organization ("RICO") claims arising from conducting a "criminal enterprise" that are sometimes brought against nursing homes and health care delivery systems. Also, tax exempt organizations are potentially exposed to allegations of violation of Internal Revenue Code provisions governing charitable organizations.

II. WHAT MAKES THE HEALTH CARE INDUSTRY UNIQUE?

A. **Prominence of the Health Care Economy.** The health industry comprises approximately 18% of the gross domestic product. Presently, United States annual health care spending is over $4 trillion, an amount equal to the entire German economy. Also, the United States gross domestic product health care spending percentage is the highest in the world. The next highest is Sweden at 12%. Consequently, it is apparent that the health industry in the United States is an inefficient economy. Also, the health industry does not follow normal economic trends because of the importance of investment by governmental reimbursement programs in the delivery of health care services as well as the regulations that evolve from laws like the ACA and other health care and tax reform legislation.

B. **The Role of Federal Law in Health Care Business Transactions.** Today, approximately 40% of all direct spending on health care comes from governmental reimbursement programs. Like it or not, Medicare has historically been the engine that drives the health industry, and it is important to understand the role of governmental reimbursement program spending in the context of health care business transactions because it is a primary source of health industry operating capital. The industry is now facing the great mystery of how federal health care and tax reform will change economic conditions. Because of this substantial investment of federal funds, there are many federal statutes and regulations that are intended to protect the public fisc, and business investments and arrangements that are perfectly legal in any other industry can lead to criminal indictments in the health industry.

C. **Economic Evolution and Its Effect on Federal Law.** Historically, the federal reimbursement programs as well as the general health care economy have been based on a "fee for service" economy under which providers, in essence, receive more revenue if they perform or order more procedures, items, and services. In fact, traditional Medicare may be the last bastion of pure "indemnity insurance." Therefore, one critical purpose of the statutes and regulations described in this chapter is to prevent overutilization of health care services and procedures. However, any economy based on the number of services or items provided or ordered cannot be sustained interminably, and both public and private payors are moving toward implementation of "coordinated care" payment models in "value-based arrangements" (for example, bundling, capitation, medical home systems, pay for performance, and similar models). Under some of these models, such as the payment systems imposed under the Medicare Access and CHIP Reauthorization Act ("MACRA") that shift traditional Medicare payment for physician services to a performance based compensation system and Accountable Care Organization participation in the Medicare Shared Savings Program ("MSSP"), the paradigm shifts toward preventing underutilization of services.

D. **How Are the Federal Fraud and Abuse Laws Applied In a Coordinated Care Economy?** In the fee for service economy, the focus of the federal fraud and abuse laws is to prevent improper financial incentive to overutilize health care items and services. In a coordinated care economy, the focus is on managing health care within a finite amount of resources and effecting cost savings through proper utilization of health care items and services. The first significant movement by CMS to a coordinated care payment model was the Medicare Shared Savings Program created under the ACA, which permits "Accountable Care Organizations" or "ACOs" to share in savings achieved in providing care to a defined population of Medicare beneficiaries. The stated objective of the MSSP is to accomplish the "triple aim" of (1) better quality of care for individuals, (2) better health for populations, and (3) lower growth in Medicare Part A and Part B expenditures. There are now many more examples. Because providers need to operate within both economic models and creation of new and innovative joint ventures and structures as required for competing in a coordinated care economy may be at odds with the federal fraud and abuse laws, the federal agencies needed to reconcile the two economic models. The first attempt to reconcile fee for service rules for application in a coordinated care economy was in October, 2015, when CMS and the OIG issued final rules for granting waivers from application of the three principal federal and abuse laws to joint ventures entered into by ACOs that participate in the Medicare Shared Savings Program. The laws addressed in the waivers included the federal Anti-Kickback Statute, the Stark Law, and the Beneficiary Inducements Civil Monetary Penalties Law, and they opened the door to development of joint ventures and other contractual arrangements that might otherwise violate those laws. However, on December 2, 2020, CMS and the OIG jointly promulgated new "value-based arrangement" rules that complement the initial ACO "waivers" and apply to all federal government coordinated care payment programs.

E. **Two Bodies of Regulatory Law.** Consequently, we now have two bodies of regulatory law: the legacy body that is intended to prevent overutilization; and the coordinated care body that focuses on permitting cost sharing and value-based arrangements and is intended to prevent underutilization.

III. WHAT IS "STARK" (OR THE "PHYSICIAN SELF-REFERRAL PROHIBITION")?

A. **Stark I.** Enacted in 1989, the federal Ethics in Patient Referrals Act, commonly referred to as "Stark I," prohibits physicians from referring Medicare covered services to any clinical laboratory with which physicians (or their immediate family members) have a financial relationship, unless a specific statutory or regulatory Stark exception applies. Stark I became effective January 1, 1992.

B. **Stark II.** Stark I was amended by the Omnibus Budget Reconciliation Act of 1993, commonly referred to as "Stark II," which became effective January 1, 1995. Stark II broadened the physician self-referral prohibitions set forth in Stark I to include self-referrals for additional "designated health services" (sometimes referred to as "DHS"), including the following: physical therapy services; outpatient speech-language pathology services; occupational therapy services; radiology services and certain other imaging services, including professional and technical components of any diagnostic test or procedure using X-rays, ultrasound, or other imaging services, computerized axial tomography, and magnetic resonance imaging; radiation therapy services and supplies, including X-ray, radium, and radioactive isotope therapy and materials and services of technicians (including nuclear medicine); durable medical equipment and supplies; parenteral and enteral nutrients, equipment, and supplies; prosthetics, orthotics, and prosthetic devices and supplies; home health services; outpatient prescription drugs; and inpatient and outpatient hospital services. Without limitation on the expansive effect of Stark II, this made every arrangement between physicians or physician organizations and hospitals or healthcare delivery systems subject to Stark regulatory scrutiny. It is important to understand that application of the Stark Law is limited to this list of "designated health services." In other words, the Stark Law does not apply to any health service that is not expressly defined as a "designated health service."

C. **Stark Regulations and Modifications.** Since 1995, when the first Stark I final regulations were promulgated, CMS has engaged in promulgation of a series of regulations to implement the Stark Law. The Stark II regulations have come in waves commonly referred to as "Phases" that are also usually referred to by number (Phase I, Phase II, and Phase III). Also, the Stark Law and its regulations are continually being modified in other ways, such as the annual Medicare fee schedule regulation and laws such as the ACA and its implementing regulations. Since promulgation of the Stark II, Phase III rules, the most significant change in the Stark rules came with the "value-based arrangement" rules promulgated by CMS that became effective in January, 2021, which not only create new rules for a coordinated care economy but also modify and clarify many aspects of the legacy "fee for service" rules. What follows in this Chapter 1, Section III is an explanation of the legacy "fee for service" rules, which still apply to the traditional Medicare indemnity insurance model program even though the number of Medicare beneficiaries enrolled in Medicare Part C (called "Medicare Advantage"), a coordinated care model that operates somewhat like a "health maintenance organization" (HMO) under which CMS compensates the plan on a capitation basis, is increasing and it is expected that CMS will offer additional coordinated care payment models. The Stark "value-based arrangement" rules for the coordinated care economy are separately addressed in Chapter 1, Section IV.

D. **What Is the General Rule Under Stark?** All physician referrals for Stark "designated health services" to any entity with which the physician or a member of a physician's immediate family has a "financial relationship" are absolutely prohibited unless the referral falls within a specific statutory or regulatory exception. Stark is a strictly enforced, black and white law; referrals for "designated health services" are either prohibited or they are not. There is no mercy under Stark.

E. **How Do You Determine Whether a Referral Implicates Stark?** There are five basic questions health care providers should ask in determining whether a referral implicates Stark:

1. **Is There a Physician Involved?** Stark applies only if a physician or a member of the physician's "immediate family" has a financial relationship with a DHS entity. "Immediate family member" or "member of a physician's immediate family" means husband or wife; birth or adoptive parent, child, or sibling; stepparent, stepchild, stepbrother, or stepsister; father-in-law, mother-in-law, son-in-law, daughter-in-law, brother-in-law, or sister-in-law; grandparent or grandchild; and spouse of a grandparent or grandchild. Every time the term "physician" is used in a Stark analysis, it incorporates and applies equally to a physician's immediate family members.

2. **Is There a "Designated Health Service" ("DHS") Involved?** Stark applies only to physician referrals for specifically identified "designated health services." Under the express terms of the Stark regulations, DHS means only DHS payable, in whole or in part, by Medicare. However, a federal law was passed to extend Stark to Medicaid (for which there are no implementing regulations), and several False Claims Act cases alleging violations of Stark based on submission of claims for payment under Medicaid have survived motions to dismiss. Therefore, even if not expressly stated in the regulations, we need to assume that Stark applies to both Medicare and Medicaid covered DHS. DHS do not include services that are reimbursed by

Medicare or Medicaid as part of a composite rate (for example, radiological imaging that is a component of an ambulatory surgical center service or physical therapy that is a component of a skilled nursing facility Part A payment) unless the service is specifically defined as a DHS (such as inpatient and outpatient hospital services). Conversely, if the item or service is not included in the list of "designated health services," Stark does not apply. Examples of items or services excluded from Stark include ambulatory surgery, cardiac monitoring, and lithotripsy (if it is not provided as a hospital outpatient service).

3. **Is There a "Referral"?** A referral under Stark occurs when a physician orders or requests any item or service from a designated health service provider for which payment may be made under Medicare or Medicaid. "Referral" does not include services personally performed by the referring physician. For example, there is a "referral" when a physician admits a Medicare or Medicaid covered patient to a hospital because inpatient and outpatient hospital services are included in the definition of "designated health services."

4. **Is There a "Financial Relationship"?** The physician referral for DHS must be to the entity with which the physician has a financial relationship. If the physician does not have a financial relationship with the entity to which the physician is making the referral, then Stark does not apply. A financial relationship can be in the form of either an ownership or investment interest or a compensation arrangement, each of which is a specifically defined term.

    a. **What Is an "Ownership or Investment Interest"?** An "ownership or investment interest" includes both equity interests, such as stock, a membership interest in a limited liability company, or a partnership interest, and debt instruments, loans, bonds, or other financial instruments secured by an entity's property or revenue. However, interests in retirement plans or stock options are not ownership or investment interests. Indirect ownership or investment is sufficient to constitute a financial relationship when:

        i. an "unbroken" chain of persons or entities with ownership or investment interests between them exists; and

        ii. the DHS provider knows, recklessly disregards, or deliberately ignores the fact that the referring physician has some ownership or investment interest in the provider of designated health services.

    b. **What Is a "Compensation Arrangement"?** "Compensation arrangement" is broadly defined and includes any arrangement involving any remuneration, direct or indirect, between a physician and an entity that furnishes DHS. An arrangement for indirect compensation exists when:

i. there is an "unbroken" chain of persons or entities with each link having an ownership/investment interest or compensation arrangement with the preceding link;

ii. the referring physician receives compensation from a DHS provider (with which the physician has a financial relationship) that takes into account the volume or value of referrals or other business brought in by the physician for the DHS provider;

iii. the individual unit of compensation received by the physician is either not fair market value for items or services actually provided, includes the physician's referrals to the DHS furnishing entity as a variable resulting in an increase or decrease in the physician's compensation that positively correlates to the number or value of the physician's referrals to the DHS entity, or includes other business generated by the physician for the DHS furnishing entity that positively correlates with the physician's generation of other business for the DHS entity; and

iv. the DHS provider knows, recklessly disregards, or deliberately ignores that the referring physician receives compensation as a result of the financial relationship.

c. **What Does "Stand in the Shoes" Mean?** The Stark II, Phase III regulations promulgated in September, 2007, adopted the "stand in the shoes" concept as applied to compensation arrangements involving physicians, their group medical practices, and independent contractor physicians who provide services to the group. Under this concept, with respect to a compensation arrangement between a DHS entity (such as a hospital) and a "physician organization," a physician associated with the physician organization is deemed to have a direct compensation arrangement with that DHS entity if the "only intervening entity" between the DHS entity and the physician is the "physician organization."

5. **Does the Financial Relationship Qualify as One of the Specified Exceptions Under Stark?** If your arrangement falls within the first four elements that implicate Stark, then referrals by the physician to the DHS provider with which the physician has a financial relationship are absolutely prohibited unless a statutory or regulatory exception applies. Conversely, if even one of the elements is not present, then Stark does not apply, and the analysis should then proceed under other statutes and regulations, such as the federal Anti-Kickback Statute. There are many Stark exceptions, but this book focuses only on the exceptions that apply to standard business transactions.

F. **What Exceptions Are Available for Ownership Interests?** There are very few ownership interest exceptions. In addition to the "in-office ancillary services exception" described below, which applies to both ownership interests and compensation arrangements, the principal exceptions are as follows:

1. **Publicly Traded Securities.** Investments in publicly traded companies that have in excess of $75 million in stockholder equity.

2. **Rural Provider Exception.** Investments in entities located outside of a Metropolitan Statistical Area if at least 75% of the DHS are provided to residents in the rural area, subject to the limitations imposed by the ACA described below.

3. **The "Whole Hospital" Exception.** Subject to the limitations imposed by the ACA described below, this exception permits physician investment in the hospital as a whole and not a division or profit center of the hospital.

4. **ACA Limitation on Hospital Ownership.** The ACA placed strict limitations on availability of the "rural provider" and "whole hospital" ownership or investment exceptions for physician ownership of hospitals. To qualify for the "rural provider" and "whole hospital" exceptions to the Stark hospital ownership or investment referral prohibitions, the hospital must have issued the ownership or investment interest by March 23, 2010, and the hospital must have been a Medicare enrolled provider before December 31, 2010. The hospital must also submit annual reports and have procedures in place to require any referring physician owner or investor to disclose the ownership interest of the referring and treating physicians to the patient being referred. The hospitals may not condition any ownership or investment interests on the physicians' making or influencing referrals or otherwise generating business for the hospital and must disclose the fact that the hospital is partially owned or invested in by physicians on its website and in any other advertising. If the physician ownership interest was issued as of March 23, 2010, it can be sold to other physicians who were not owners on that date. The 2016 Medicare Physician Fee Schedule Rule clarified that the baseline *bona fide* physician investment amount as of March 23, 2010 includes both referring and non-referring physicians. Consequently, interests owned directly or indirectly by non-referring physicians are included in determining compliance with the "whole hospital exception" as modified by the ACA.

5. **Indirect Ownership Interests and "Under Arrangements" Joint Ventures.** Before promulgation of the Stark II, Phase III regulations, some physicians and hospitals formed joint ventures, such as cardiac catheterization labs and outpatient surgery centers, which sold the performed service to the hospital so the hospital could bill payors, including Medicare, for the acquired service. The 2009 Final Inpatient Prospective Payment Rule published

on August 19, 2008 provided that, as of October 1, 2009, the "under arrangements" provider would be characterized as the provider that "performs" the service. Therefore, since most "under arrangements" services were ultimately billed as hospital outpatient services, the physician referral to an "under arrangements" entity in which the physician had an ownership interest is permissible only if it falls within one of the ownership exceptions to Stark. This, in effect, killed most under arrangements joint ventures involving hospital outpatient services unless the rural exception applied, and now that exception has been limited by the ACA.

6. **Special Scrutiny of Specialty Hospitals.** Physician ownership of "specialty hospitals" (primarily heart and orthopedic hospitals) is permissible under the "whole hospital" exception, but, even before imposition of the ACA limitations described above, physician ownership of specialty hospitals was under substantial scrutiny. In August of 2006, CMS delivered a final report to Congress regarding specialty hospitals as required by the Deficit Reduction Act of 2005 (the "DRA"). The DRA defines "specialty hospital" as a hospital primarily engaged in treating cardiac patients, orthopedic patients, or patients receiving a surgical procedure. If Stark permits physician ownership in a specialty hospital, then CMS expects (but the law does not absolutely require) the following:

   a. disclosure of the financial interest by the physician;

   b. some non-physician investment;

   c. an expressed intent not to induce referrals of items or services payable by Medicare or Medicaid, and a provision stating that the entity will be reorganized if it is ever determined otherwise;

   d. no "cherry picking" of patients covered by the best insurance coverage;

   e. no threat to the well-being of individual patients;

   f. no threat to competing health care delivery systems;

   g. proportionate returns based on investment (and not on actual or expected referrals); and

   h. *bona fide* investment of real capital that the investor puts at risk.

   Investment interests in specialty hospitals are also viewed favorably if they offer a new service that is not otherwise available in the community. Again, the CMS report on specialty hospitals does not establish any legal requirements. However, it is a good guideline for determining whether a hospital ownership structure, or any other structure that complies with the Stark Law but does not fall into a federal Anti-Kickback Statute "safe harbor" as described below, is legally compliant.

G. **What Are the Elements of the In-Office Ancillary Services Exception?** This exception applies to both ownership or investment interests and compensation arrangements for DHS provided by both group and sole practitioner medical practices. It is the only Stark Law exception that applies to both ownership interests and compensation arrangements. In other words, it applies to physicians who have both an ownership interest in and a compensation arrangement with a medical practice. Although the Stark statute and the Stark regulations appeared to state that the Stark "in-office ancillary services exception" was available only to "group medical practices," CMS has provided guidance that a sole practitioner can qualify for the in-office ancillary services exception as long as the supervision, location, and billing requirements described below are satisfied. The essential elements of this exception are as follows:

1. **Persons Who Can Provide Services.** The services are furnished personally by one of the following individuals:

    a. the referring physician;

    b. a physician who is a member of the same group practice as the referring physician (including owners and employees of the practice but not independent contractor physicians); or

    c. individuals who are supervised by the referring physician or a physician who is in the same group practice as the referring physician, provided that the supervision otherwise complies with applicable Medicare law. Physician "in the group practice" means a member of the group practice as well as an independent contractor physician during the time the independent contractor is furnishing patient care services to the group practice under a contractual arrangement with the group practice provided that the independent contractor physician's services are provided on the group medical practice's premises. The independent contractor agreement must contain the same restrictions on compensation that apply to members of the group practice (which prevents payment for services based on volume or value of referrals) or must comply with the "personal services agreement" exception under Stark. Also, the comments to the Stark II, Phase III final regulations clearly state that the independent contractor's arrangement with the group practice must comply with the reassignment rules in the Medicare Claims Processing Manual. Also, Stark II, Phase III made it clear that the independent contractor must contract directly with the group practice, not through an intervening entity.

2. **Location.** They are furnished in one of the following locations:

   a. the "same building," but not necessarily in the same space or the same part of the building, in which the referring physician, or a member of the referring physician's group practice, furnishes substantial physician services unrelated to the furnishing of designated health services payable by any payor;

   b. a building that is used by the group practice for the provision of some or all of the group's clinical laboratory services; or

   c. a building that is used for the centralized provision of the group's designated health services (other than clinical laboratory services).

3. **Billing.** They are billed by one of the following:

   a. the physician performing or supervising the service;

   b. the group practice of which the performing or supervising physician is a either "member" or "in the group practice" under a billing number assigned to the group practice; or

   c. an entity that is wholly owned by the physician or the physician's group practice.

4. **ACA Disclosure Requirements.** Effective January 1, 2011, physicians that furnish MRI, CT, or PET tests in their offices pursuant to the "in-office ancillary services exception" to Stark self-referral prohibitions are required to provide patients with written notice at the time of the referral informing the patient that the patient is not required to receive the diagnostic service in the physician's office. The notice must also include a list of suppliers who furnish such services in the area where the patient resides. The legislation also allows the Department of Health and Human Services to require the notice for additional designated health services, but, to date, the notice requirement is limited to MRI, CT, and PET scans.

H. **What Exceptions Are Available for Compensation Arrangements?** There are over twenty separate Stark "compensation arrangement" exceptions, and the following are the exceptions that most commonly arise in the context of health care business transactions.

1. ***Bona fide* Employment Relationships.** Referrals from physicians who are "*bona fide* employees" in accordance with the Internal Revenue Service test for determining employment status described in Chapter 3, including *bona fide* physician employees of academic medical centers, are excepted provided that:

a. the services are identifiable;

b. remuneration is at fair market value;

c. volume or value of referrals is not considered in determining compensation;

d. the agreement would be deemed reasonable if no referrals were actually made; and

e. bonuses are based on services rendered personally by the physician and not volume or value of referrals. Note that the *bona fide* employment exception does not require that compensation be "set in advance." Also, the employment agreement is not required to be in writing.

2. **Personal Services Arrangements.** Designated health service providers are allowed to compensate a physician or group practice under an independent contractor personal services arrangement and accept referrals if the arrangement is set forth in an agreement that meets the following conditions:

a. the agreement is in writing, signed by the parties, and covers only services that are specified in the agreement;

b. the arrangement covers all of the services to be furnished by the physician to the DHS entity;

c. the services contracted for are reasonable and necessary for legitimate business purposes;

d. the duration of the arrangement is at least one year and, if terminated during the first year, the parties cannot enter into a new contract for the remainder of that year;

e. compensation is "set in advance," is consistent with fair market value, and, except for physician incentive plans, is not determined in a manner that takes into account the volume or value of referrals; and

f. the services do not involve an unlawful business arrangement or other activity.

3. **Physician Incentive Plan Exception.** "Physician incentive plan" means any compensation arrangement between an entity (or downstream contractor) and a physician or physician group that may directly or indirectly have the effect of reducing or limiting services furnished to individual patients enrolled with the entity. In other words, arrangements that are found

in the coordinated care economy and not the traditional fee for service economy. Physician incentive plan compensation may be determined in any manner (through a withhold, capitation, bonus, or otherwise) that takes into account the volume or value of referrals or other business generated between the parties if the plan meets the following requirements:

a. no specific payment is made directly or indirectly under the plan to a physician or a physician group as an inducement to reduce or limit medically necessary services furnished with respect to a specific individual enrolled with the entity;

b. if an incentive plan places a physician or a physician group at substantial financial risk as defined in applicable regulations, the entity or any downstream contractor (or both) complies with certain other requirements concerning physician incentive plans; and

c. upon request, the entity provides CMS with access to information regarding the plan.

4. **Indirect Compensation Arrangements.** There is a Stark exception for indirect compensation arrangements if all of the following conditions are satisfied:

a. the compensation received by the referring physician is fair market value for the services and items actually provided and not determined in any manner that takes into account the volume or value of referrals or other business generated by the referring physician for the entity furnishing DHS;

b. the compensation arrangement is set out in writing, signed by the parties, and specifies the services covered by the arrangement, except in the case of a *bona fide* employment relationship between an employer and an employee, in which case the arrangement need not be set out in writing, but must be for identifiable services and be commercially reasonable even if no referrals are made to the employer;

c. if the indirect compensation arrangement involves space or equipment rental, compensation for the rental of office space or equipment may not be determined using a formula based on either (i) a percentage of the revenue raised, earned, billed, collected, or otherwise attributable to the services performed or business generated in the office space or to the services performed on or business generated through the use of the equipment or (ii) per-unit of service rental charges to the extent that such charges reflect services provided to patients referred by the lessor to the lessee; and

d. the compensation arrangement does not violate the federal Anti-Kickback Statute or any federal or state law or regulation governing billing or claims submission.

5. **Non-Monetary Compensation.** In the interest of making it easier for DHS providers to make certain benefits available to referring physicians, DHS providers may give non-monetary compensation to referring physicians that has a value of up to $300 per year (which is subject to "cost of living" increases each year and is now over $400 per year). As long as the non-monetary compensation is not (a) in any way based on the volume or value of referrals or other business generated by the referring physician, (b) is not solicited by the referring physician or any member of the physician's practice, and (c) does not violate the federal Anti-Kickback Statute, it is excepted from the Stark prohibitions.

6. **Limited Physician Remuneration Exception.** Remuneration from a DHS entity to a physician for the provision of items or services provided by the physician to the entity that does not exceed an aggregate of $5,000 per calendar year, as adjusted for inflation, is excepted under the Stark Law if all of the following conditions are satisfied:

   a. the compensation is not determined in any manner that takes into account the volume or value of referrals or other business generated by the physician;

   b. the compensation does not exceed the fair market value of the items or services;

   c. the arrangement would be commercially reasonable even if no referrals were made between the parties;

   d. compensation for the lease of office space or equipment is not determined using a formula based on a percentage of the revenue raised, earned, billed, collected, or otherwise attributable to the services performed or business generated in the office space or to the services performed on or business generated through the use of the equipment or per-unit of service rental charges if such charges reflect services provided to patients referred by the lessor to the lessee;

   e. compensation for the use of premises or equipment is not determined using a formula based on a percentage of the revenue raised, earned, billed, collected, or otherwise attributable to the services provided while using the premises or equipment covered by the arrangement or per-unit of service fees that are not time-based if such fees reflect services provided to patients referred by the party granting permission to use the premises or equipment covered by the arrangement to the party to which the permission is granted; and

   f. the arrangement would be commercially reasonable even if no referrals were made between the parties.

7. **Fair Market Value Compensation ("Catch All Exception").** Exceptions are made for compensation arrangements when the compensation received or paid by the physician is "set in advance" and reflects fair market value for the services rendered or goods purchased, or space or equipment leased, and the following conditions are met:

   a. the agreement is put in writing, signed by all parties, and specifically refers to the services to be provided or space or requipment to be leased;

   b. the agreement is for a specified time frame;

   c. the compensation does not take into account the volume or value of referrals or business otherwise generated between the parties;

   d. the agreement involves a commercially reasonable transaction and furthers the legitimate business purposes of the parties;

   e. the agreement does not violate the federal Anti-Kickback Statute or any other law or regulation that governs billing or claims submission; and

   f. the services specified in the agreement do not involve the counseling or promotion of any business activity that violates state or federal law.

8. **Space and Equipment Leases.** Stark provides exceptions for space and equipment leases provided that such leases meet the following conditions:

   a. the lease is in writing, signed by the parties, and specifies the space or equipment covered by the lease;

   b. the space or equipment rented or leased does not exceed what is reasonable and necessary for the legitimate business purposes of the lease or rental (except that space leases may include appropriately prorated payments for common areas), and, when used by the lessee, is done so exclusively;

   c. the rental or lease term is at least one year;

   d. the rental charges over the term of the lease are "set in advance," consistent with fair market value, and not determined in a manner that takes into account the volume or value of any referrals or other business generated between the parties;

e. compensation for the rental of office space or equipment may not be determined using a formula based on either (i) a percentage of the revenue raised, earned, billed, collected, or otherwise attributable to the services performed or business generated in the office space or to the services performed on or business generated through the use of the equipment or (ii) per-unit of service rental charges to the extent that such charges reflect services provided to patients referred by the lessor to the lessee; and

f. the lease would be commercially reasonable even if there were no referrals between the parties.

9. **Isolated Transactions.** An isolated transaction, such as a one-time sale of property or a medical practice, is not considered to be a "compensation arrangement" for purposes of the Stark referral prohibition if the following conditions are met:

   a. the amount of remuneration for the transaction is consistent with fair market value and is not determined, directly or indirectly, in a manner that takes into account the volume or value of referrals;

   b. the remuneration is provided in accordance with an agreement that would be commercially reasonable even if no referrals were made to the entity; and

   c. the transaction meets any other requirements that the Secretary of the Department of Health and Human Services may impose by regulation as needed to protect against program or patient abuse.

   Installment payments can qualify as isolated transactions as long as the total aggregate payment (1) is set before the first payment is made and (2) does not take into account, directly or indirectly, referrals or other business generated by the referring physician. Also, payments must be immediately negotiable or guaranteed by a third party, secured by a negotiable promissory note, or subject to a similar mechanism to insure payment in the event of a default by the purchaser. Typical post-closing adjustments are permitted if they are made within six months of the date of the transaction.

10. **Physician Recruitment.** Compensation paid by a hospital to recruit a physician that is paid directly to the physician and is intended to induce the physician to relocate his or her medical practice to the geographic area served by the hospital in order to become a member of the hospital's medical staff if the following conditions are met:

a. the agreement is in writing and signed by the parties;

b. the arrangement is not conditioned on referrals to the hospital;

c. compensation is not based on the value or volume of actual or anticipated referrals;

d. the physician is allowed to establish privileges at any hospital;

e. the physician is relocating his or her practice from outside the geographic area served by the hospital; and

f. many other criteria that may apply to specific arrangements.

11. **Guidance on What Constitutes a "Signed, Written Agreement".** Several of the Stark exceptions require a signed and written agreement. Because Stark is a black and white law, technical violations might arise, if, for example, the parties exchange several documents which, taken together, contain all of the elements of a compensation arrangement exception but the parties fail to enter into one integrated, formal contract. Because many such situations occur, and many providers used the Stark Self Disclosure Protocol when deficiencies were discovered, CMS decided in the 2016 Medicare Physician Fee Schedule Rule to clarify its policy regarding what CMS considers to be a Stark compliant signed and written agreement. That rule was codified and became a direct part of the Stark Law through the Bipartisan Budget Act of 2018. First, a collection of documents evidencing the course of conduct may be sufficient to constitute a "written" agreement if the available contemporaneous documents permit a reasonable person to verify compliance with the "writing" requirement. Also, when relying on a "collection" of documents, not every document must be signed by each party as long as the signature of each party is on at least one document and it is clear that the documents are interrelated.

12. **Holdover Arrangements.** Also, a technical Stark violation may occur, if, for example, a contract between a hospital and a physician expires but the physician continues to provide services and receive compensation. Before promulgation of the 2016 Medicare Physician Fee Schedule Rule, CMS permitted a "holdover" for space and equipment leases as well as personal services arrangements for up to six (6) months if a compliant arrangement of at least one year expired but continued on the same terms and conditions. In the 2016 Medicare Physician Fee Schedule Rule, CMS amended the holdover rule to permit indefinite holdover provided that (a) the holdover continues on the same terms and conditions as the original arrangement and (b) compensation continues to be consistent with and not exceed fair market value. Like the "written agreement" rule,

the holdover value was codified and became a direct part of the Stark Law under the Bipartisan Budget Act of 2018.

13. **Temporary Noncompliance With Signature Requirements.** Under the 2016 Medicare Physician Fee Schedule Rule, if parties fail to comply with the signature requirement for any of the compensation arrangement exceptions, the parties have ninety (90) days from the date the arrangement commences to obtain the signatures. This rule was also codified through the Bipartisan Budget Act of 2018.

I. **How Is "Fair Market Value" Determined?** For purposes of the Stark Law, "fair market value" means the value in arm's-length transactions, consistent with the "general market value," and the definition is subdivided into terms and conditions for determining fair market value and general market value for physician compensation arrangements, asset purchases, and rental of office space or equipment.

1. **How Is Compensation Arrangement Fair Market Value Determined?** For physician compensation arrangements, which are the most common form of physician-hospital financial relationship, general market value is defined as the compensation that would be paid at the time the parties enter into the services arrangement as the result of *bona fide* bargaining between well-informed parties to the agreement who are not otherwise in a position to generate business for the other party. The most common physician compensation arrangement valuation method is comparison of the compensation to market survey data such as the survey compiled by the Medical Group Management Association ("MGMA"), with most hospitals and health care delivery systems attempting to compensate physicians in a range from the 25th to 75th percentile of the survey data. In fact, many hospitals and health care delivery systems are reluctant to enter into physician compensation arrangements above the 75th percentile of the survey data. However, CMS states that reliance on survey data alone may not be sufficient to determine fair market value. For example, a "superstar" physician may receive compensation greater than the survey data might otherwise suggest. Also, if cost of living is low and quality of life is high for some arrangements, the survey data may be too high. In other words, while an independent appraisal is typically obtained for virtually all hospital-physician compensation arrangements, reliance on the appraisal alone may be insufficient to protect the parties from allegations that the compensation does not constitute fair market value.

2. **How Is Asset Purchase Fair Market Value Determined?** The market has seen an increasing number of hospital acquisitions of medical practices that are typically structured as asset purchases. For asset purchases, general market value means the price that an asset would bring on the acquisition date as the result of *bona fide* bargaining between well-informed

buyers and sellers who are not otherwise in a position to generate business for the other party. Usually, the fair market price is the price at which *bona fide* sales have been consummated for assets of like type, quality, and quantity in a particular market at the time of acquisition.

3. **How Is Office Space Rental Fair Market Value Determined?** For rental of office space, fair market value is the value in an arm's-length transaction of rental property for general commercial purposes (not taking into account its intended use), without adjustment to reflect the additional value the prospective lessee or lessor would attribute to the proximity or convenience to the lessor where the lessor is a potential source of patient referrals to the lessee. The arrangement must also be consistent with space lease general market value, defined as the price that rental property would bring at the time the parties enter into the rental arrangement as the result of *bona fide* bargaining between a well-informed lessor and lessee that are not otherwise in a position to generate business for each other.

4. **How Is Equipment Rental Fair Market Value Determined?** For equipment rental, fair market value is the value in an arm's-length transaction of rental property for general commercial purposes (not taking into account its intended use), consistent with general market value which, like space rental, is defined as the price that rental property would bring at the time the parties enter into the rental arrangement as the result of *bona fide* bargaining between a well-informed lessor and lessee that are not otherwise in a position to generate business for each other.

J. **What Is "Commercial Reasonableness"?** Virtually all of the Stark compensation arrangement exceptions require that, in addition to payment of "fair market value" compensation, the arrangement must also be "commercially reasonable." In particular the "commercial reasonableness" requirements left physician-hospital compensation arrangements particularly vulnerable to False Claims Act whistleblower actions alleging that physician compensation was excessive and did not reflect fair market value if the hospital's medical practice operated at a loss, which implied that part of the compensation was intended to induce referrals for lucrative inpatient and outpatient hospital services. However, in 2020 CMS modified the definition of "commercial reasonableness" to mean that "the particular arrangement furthers a legitimate business purpose of the parties to the arrangement and is sensible, considering the characteristics of the parties, including their size, type, scope, and specialty. An arrangement may be commercially reasonable even if it does not result in profit for one or more of the parties." Also, an arrangement may be commercially unreasonable even if the compensation constitutes fair market value. For example, if a contract has an unreasonable term (such as ten years when similar contracts have shorter terms), is not terminable by the DHS provider under any circumstances, or has a compensation escalation clause that will eventually push the compensation above fair market value, then the agreement violates Stark because it is "commercially unreasonable." Many Stark enforcement actions, and specifically including hospital-physician employment agreements, have been based on "commercial reasonableness," often alleging that, because the hospital is losing money on the compensation, it is, by definition "commercially unreasonable." However, CMS has consistently asserted that it does not support that theory. CMS has promulgated a proposed Stark regulation to codify that position, but that rule has not yet been finalized.

K. **What Does "Set in Advance" Mean?** Most Stark compensation arrangement exceptions require that the compensation must be "set in advance." Compensation is deemed to be "set in advance" if the aggregate compensation, a time-based or per-unit of service-based (whether per-use or per-service) amount, or a specific formula for calculating the compensation is set out in writing before the furnishing of the items, services, office space, or equipment for which the compensation is to be paid. The formula for determining the compensation must be described in sufficient detail to permit objective verification. For example, even if the total amount paid per month or per year cannot be set in advance in a Medical Director Agreement that compensates a physician on an hourly basis, as long as the amount paid per hour is fixed in the contract the compensation is "set in advance." While this is clearly understandable, what happens if the parties want to change the compensation structure after performance commences? The Stark rules directly address this issue. Physician compensation, or the formula for determining compensation, may be modified at any time during the course of a compensation arrangement and satisfy the requirement that it is "set in advance" if all of the following conditions are met: (1) the arrangement complies with one of the compensation arrangement exceptions (such as the personal services agreement or space or equipment lease exceptions) on the effective date of the modified compensation or formula; (2) the modified compensation or formula is determined before the furnishing of the items, services, office space, or equipment for which the modified compensation is to be paid; and (3) the modified physician compensation or formula is set forth in writing in sufficient detail so it can be objectively verified. The keys to Stark compliance are: payment of fair market value compensation; and not changing compensation as an overt or covert way to reflect the volume or value of referrals from the physician to the DHS entity.

L. **What Are the "Volume or Value of Referrals" and "Volume or Value of Other Business Generated" Standards?** Last, most Stark compensation arrangement exceptions provide that the compensation may not be based on the "volume or value of referrals" or "volume or value of other business generated" between the parties. While the Stark rules do not expressly define what "volume or value" of either "referrals" or "other business generated" means, in the 2021 Stark rules CMS provided examples of arrangements for both compensation to a physician and compensation from a physician that are affirmatively considered to take into account the "volume or value of referrals" or "volume or value other business generated." Prior to promulgation of the 2021 rules many False Claims Act whistleblower cases were brought on grounds that physician compensation inferred the volume or value of referrals to, or other business generated for, hospitals and health care delivery systems if, for example, the hospital-based medical practice alone operated at a financial loss. The 2021 rule protects many arrangements that might have previously been challenged.

1. **Compensation to a Physician That Takes Into Account Volume or Value of Referrals or Other Business Generated.** Compensation from a DHS entity (like a hospital) to a physician takes into account the volume or value of referrals or other business generated only if the formula used to calculate the physician's compensation includes the physician's referrals to or other business generated by the physician for the DHS entity as a variable, resulting in an increase or decrease in the physician's compensation that positively correlates with the number or value of the physician's referrals to or the generation of other business for the DHS entity.

2. **Compensation From a Physician That Takes Into Account Volume or Value of Other Business Generated.** Compensation from a physician to a DHS entity (like a hospital) takes into account the volume or value of referrals or other business generated only if the formula used to calculate the DHS entity's compensation includes the physician's referrals to the entity as a variable, resulting in an increase or decrease in the entity's compensation that negatively correlates with the number or value of the physician's referrals to the DHS entity.

3. **Positive Correlation Required.** For purposes of applying each of these standards, a positive correlation between two variables exists when one variable decreases as the other variable decreases, or one variable increases as the other variable increases. This is a very strict standard that eliminates the "inferred referrals" whistleblower theory.

M. **What Are "Directed Referrals" and When Are They Permitted?** There are arrangements under which a physician can be required to make referrals to a specific DHS entity. This is called "directed referrals." For example, every employment agreement between a physician and a hospital or health care delivery system provides that the physician is required to make referrals, including referrals for designated health services such as inpatient and outpatient hospital services, to the employing hospital or health care delivery system. Directed referrals are permitted under the Stark Law, but the Stark rules also impose limitations on directed referral obligations. Specifically, each of the following Stark compensation arrangement exceptions provides that the exception applies only if the arrangement otherwise complies with the Stark "directed referral" requirements: *bona fide* employment agreement exception; personal services agreement exception, including: the physician incentive plan exception; indirect compensation arrangement exception; limited physician remuneration exception; and fair market value exception. Directed referral provisions are permitted if the arrangement otherwise qualifies for a Stark compensation arrangement exception and the contract also includes the following:

1. **Written Referral Requirement.** The directed referral requirement is in writing and signed by the parties. Even though the *bona fide* employment agreement exception does not require a written agreement, if employment obligations include "directed referrals" the contract must be in writing for Stark compliance purposes.

2. **Relationship to Physician's Services.** The directed referrals relate solely to the physician's services performed within the scope of the employment, personal service arrangement, or managed care contract, and the directed referral requirement is reasonably necessary to effectuate the legitimate business purposes of the compensation arrangement. In no event may the physician be required to make directed referrals that relate to services that are not provided by the physician within the scope of his or her employment, personal service arrangement, or managed care contract.

3. **Volume or Value Requirements.** Neither the existence of the compensation arrangement nor the amount of the compensation is contingent on the number or value of the physician's referrals to the particular provider, practitioner, or supplier. However, the requirement to make referrals to a particular provider, practitioner, or supplier may require that the physician refer an established percentage or ratio of the physician's referrals to a particular provider, practitioner, or supplier.

4. **Exceptions to the Directed Referral Requirement.** There are three exceptions to any directed referral requirement that must be stated in every physician compensation arrangement that includes a directed referral provision: (a) the patient chooses another provider or supplier; (b) the patient's insurer determines the provider or supplier to whom referrals can be made; and (c) the directed referral is not in the patient's best medical interests in the physician's judgment. In other words: (i) a physician must always defer to patient choice; (ii) if the directed referral is "out of network," the physician must make an "in network" referral; and (iii) if in the physician's sole medical judgement the referral is not in the patient's best interest, such as when a physician refers a patient to the Mayo Clinic for highly specialized treatment that may not be adequately provided by the DHS entity to which the physician is directed to refer.

N. **What Sanctions Arise from Violation of Stark?** Stark is not a criminal law: you cannot go to jail for violating Stark. Stark violations are punishable by a wide range of civil sanctions, including the following:

1. **Claim Denial.** A claim for payment in violation of Stark can be denied.

2. **Refund.** If a provider receives payment on a claim submitted in violation of Stark, it must be refunded promptly.

3. **Civil Monetary Penalties.** Civil monetary penalties of approximately $30,000 per claim and up to almost $200,000 for each illegal arrangement may be imposed.

4. **Exclusion.** Submission of a claim for payment in violation of Stark may result in a five year exclusion from participation in governmental reimbursement programs.

5. **False Claims Act.** A Stark violation may be used as the foundation for a False Claims Act case, which could expose a violator to payments in the amount of up to approximately $22,000 per claim plus three times the amount claimed. In practice, this is the most significant risk of non-compliance with Stark.

O. **What Should a Provider Do If a Stark Violation is Discovered?** CMS has promulgated a protocol for self-disclosure of Stark violations to CMS that must be followed if a Stark violation is discovered. Also, the Affordable Care Act provides that any federal reimbursement program overpayment that is identified by a provider must be repaid within sixty (60) days from the date the overpayment is identified. When the Stark self-disclosure protocol is used, the sixty (60) day repayment obligation is tolled until CMS resolves the matter with the disclosure provider, which may take years. Therefore, unless there is a specific exception in the Stark regulations, even technical errors must be promptly reported to CMS.

IV. WHAT ARE THE STARK LAW VALUE-BASED ARRANGEMENT RULES?

A. **Need for Value-Based Arrangement Rules.** To summarize the learning objectives presented thus far, the legacy Medicare program is based on a "fee for service" health care economy and is the last bastion of pure "indemnity insurance." The core of the fee for service economy is physician referrals: no health care item or service is ordered or performed without a physician referral. When the Medicare program originated in 1965, because of concerns that Medicare beneficiaries would be treated by physicians like pariahs, the United States Department of Health and Services paid Medicare claims without question based on DHHS's trust that physicians would order only medically necessary items and services. By 1995, that position changed. The Medicare program announced that it no longer trusted physician judgment and that it would no longer "pay and chase" for Medicare covered services. Not only would physician referrals be governed by the federal Anti-Kickback Statute with its potential criminal sanctions but by the Stark Law and its civil sanctions. However, no economy based only on the number of health care items or services ordered or performed can exist in perpetuity, and the Medicare program needed to shift to a coordinated care payment model. The economic shift started with Medicare Part C, known as "Medicare Advantage," which operates similar to a health maintenance organization capitation model. That beginning was supplemented by the Medicare Shared Savings Program and now many innovative coordinated care payment models. However, coordinated care payment models cause the fraud and abuse concern to shift from overutilization in the fee for service model to underutilization. Also, instead of restricting patient referrals, effective coordinated care models require collaboration between health care service providers such as physicians and hospitals including mandated referrals. This put the legacy AKS and Stark Law rules on a collision course with effective coordinated care payment models. This was first recognized in AKS and Stark Law "waiver rules" for Accountable Care Organizations that participated in the Medicare Shared Savings Program. The MSSP waiver rules have now been superseded by AKS and Stark Law "value-based arrangement" rules which apply to all "value-based arrangements," not just the MSSP. An overview of the Stark Law value-based arrangement regulations follows. DHHS expects these value-based arrangement exceptions to provide incentives to move toward coordinated care payment models while also ensuring strong Medicare program integrity safeguards to prevent the potential risks of "value-based" models such as underutilization, cherry-picking (choosing to care only for patients who require less medical care), lemon-dropping (denying care to undesirable patients), and manipulation or falsification of data used to verify outcomes. While similar, because Stark is a "black and white" law under which referrals are either prohibited or not, the Stark "value-based" exceptions are broader than the AKS "value-based" safe harbor regulations as described in Chapter 1, Section VI.

B. **Overview of the Stark Value-Based Arrangement Exceptions.** First, the Stark value-based arrangement rules apply only to "compensation arrangements," not "ownership interests." In that regard, the value-based arrangement rules eliminate many requirements that apply to legacy fee for service compensation arrangement exceptions. Specifically, the value-based arrangement exceptions do not require that compensation be "set in advance," consistent with fair market value, or determined in manner that does not take into account the volume or value of the physician's referrals or other business generated by the physician. However, the compensation must be "commercially reasonable." Also, the compensation must arise from value-based activities for patients who are in the target patient population covered by the value-based arrangement. If the remuneration is "in-kind," it must be necessary and may not simply duplicate technology or infrastructure that is already owned by the physician organization. The Stark value-based arrangement exceptions apply regardless of whether the arrangement includes care furnished to Medicare beneficiaries, non-Medicare patients, or a combination of both. Last, "value-based arrangements" already in place as of January, 2021, the effective date of the "value-based" rules, that comply with the prior rules are not required to use one of the new exceptions. As long as the arrangement satisfies all elements of an applicable exception, the arrangement is permitted under the physician self-referral law. Therefore, all arrangements that comply with the Medicare Shared Savings Program "waiver rules" for Accountable Care Organizations do not need to be terminated, even if the arrangements do not comply with the value-based arrangement rules.

C. **Value-Based Arrangement Definitions.** The "value-based" rules require learning an entirely new regulatory vocabulary with intertwining definitions.

1. **What Is a "Value-Based Activity"?** The definition of value-based activity is intentionally broad and non-specific because CMS believes that creating a definitive list will unintentionally limit innovation and inhibit robust participation in "value-based" health care delivery and payment systems. "Value-based activity" means any activity that is reasonably designed to achieve at least one value-based purpose of the value-based enterprise and may constitute

either (a) the provision of an item or service, (b) the taking of an action, or (c) the refraining from taking an action.

2. **What Is a "Value-Based Arrangement"?** "Value-based arrangement" means an arrangement for the provision of at least one value-based activity for a target patient population to which the only parties are either a value-based enterprise and value-based participants or value-based participants in the same value-based enterprise.

3. **What Is a "Value-Based Enterprise" (VBE)?** A VBE is any enterprise which has (a) two or more value-based participants who collaborate to achieve at least one value-based purpose and are parties to a value-based arrangement, (b) an accountable body or person responsible for financial and operational oversight, and (c) a governing document that describes the VBE and how the value-based participants intend to achieve the VBE's value-based purpose. In practice, this is a provider network such as an Accountable Care Organization that participates in the Medicare Shared Savings Program or a Clinically Integrated Network ("CIN"), the characteristics of which are described in detail in Chapter 8, that agrees to collaborate regarding provision of health care services to a target patient population in a manner that is focused on "patient centered care" including care coordination, improving efficiencies in the delivery of care, and improving patient care outcomes.

4. **What Is a "Value-Based Purpose"?** A "value-based purpose" means any of the following: (a) coordinating and managing the care of a target patient population; (b) improving the quality of care for a target patient population; (c) appropriately reducing the costs to or growth in expenditures of payors without reducing the quality of care for a target patient population; or (d) transitioning from health care delivery and payment mechanisms based on the volume of items and services provided (in other words, "fee for service") to mechanisms based on the quality of care and control of costs of care for a target patient population (in other words, "coordinated care"). There is no requirement that the value-based purpose must actually be achieved, but there must be a rational connection between either providing or refraining from providing an item or service and a "value-based purpose."

5. **Who Is a "Value-Based Participant"?** A "value-based participant" means a person or entity that engages in at least one value-based activity as part of a value-based enterprise. CMS considered excluding the following as qualified value-based participants but did not: clinical laboratories; durable medical equipment, prosthetics, orthotics and supplies ("DMEPOS") suppliers, pharmaceutical manufacturers; manufacturers and distributors of DMEPOS; pharmacy benefit managers (PBMs); wholesalers; and distributors. Unlike the corresponding federal Anti-Kickback Statute "value-based" safe harbor regulations described in Section VI

of this Chapter 1, virtually any entity qualifies as a value-based participant under the Stark rules. This is expected because Stark is a black and white, strictly applied law while the federal Anti-Kickback Statute is not.

6. **What Is a "Target Patient Population"?** "Target patient population" means an identified patient population selected by a value-based enterprise or its value-based participants based on legitimate and verifiable criteria that (a) are set out in writing in advance of commencement of the value-based arrangement and (b) further the value-based enterprise's value-based purposes. For purposes of identifying a target patient population, CMS advises that "legitimate and verifiable criteria" may include medical or health characteristics (for example, patients undergoing knee replacement surgery or patients with newly diagnosed type 2 diabetes), geographic characteristics (for example, all patients in an identified county or set of zip codes), payor status (for example, all patients with a particular health insurance plan or payor), or other defining characteristics. However, selecting a target patient population consisting of only lucrative or compliant patients (cherry-picking) and avoiding costly or noncompliant patients (lemon-dropping) is impermissible under most circumstances. Again, a clear example of a target patient population is the body of Medicare beneficiaries attributed to an Accountable Care Organization that participates in the Medicare Shared Savings Program.

D. **What Exceptions Are Available for Value-Based Compensation Arrangements?** There are three "value-based" Stark Law exceptions, all of which apply to value-based compensation arrangements. It bears repeating that the Stark Law absolutely prohibits "referrals" for "designated health services" to entities with which the physician has a "financial relationship" unless the arrangement falls within a specific statutory or regulatory "exception," and the most important category of "designated health services" is inpatient and outpatient hospital services, which implicates all physician-hospital compensation arrangements. In other words, a physician can enter into a compensation arrangement with a hospital that involves referrals for designated health services including inpatient and outpatient hospital services and comply with the Stark Law if the value-based compensation arrangements fall within one of the value-based arrangement exceptions.

E. **What Is the "Full Financial Risk" Exception?** The "full financial risk" exception applies to value-based arrangements between value-based participants in a value-based enterprise that has assumed "full financial risk" on a prospective basis for the cost of all patient care items and services covered by the applicable payor for each patient in the target patient population for a specified time period. Examples include but are not limited to capitation (per member-per month) payments and global budget payments from a payor. Full financial risk arrangements receive the least scrutiny because physicians are truly at financial risk. While there is no "writing" requirement, the arrangement is typically described in an agreement between a payor and a provider network with physician participants. Full financial risk requires the following:

1. **Duration of the Risk.** The value-based enterprise must be at full financial risk during the entire duration of the value-based arrangement.

2. **Remuneration.** The remuneration can be monetary or non-monetary as long as it arises from the value-based activities undertaken by the recipient for "the target patient population." Remuneration cannot be conditioned on referrals of patients who are not part of the target patient population or business not covered under the value-based arrangement.

3. **Directed Referral Requirement.** Recognizing the importance of protecting patient choice, if the remuneration paid to the physician is conditioned on "directed referrals" to a particular provider, practitioner, or supplier, the directed referral requirement must be set out in writing and signed by the parties. Like the legacy Stark rules, a directed referral requirement will not apply if the patient expresses preference for another provider, practitioner, or supplier, the patient's insurer makes the determination, or the referral is not in the patient's best medical interest in the physician's judgment. If the arrangement is structured in a way that leads to a reduction in medically necessary services, it is considered inherently suspect and implicates potential civil monetary penalties. This reveals the thin line between accomplishing the value-based purpose of reducing health care costs by excluding unnecessary and duplicative tests or suggesting therapy instead of a procedure and denying a patient medically necessary care when the financial incentive is to decrease, not increase, ordering of health care items or services.

F. **What is the "Meaningful Downside Financial Risk" Exception?** The "meaningful downside financial risk" exception protects remuneration paid under a value-based arrangement when the physician is at meaningful downside financial risk for failure to achieve the value-based purpose of the value-based enterprise. To qualify as "meaningful" the "downside risk" assumed by the physician must be at least ten percent (10%) of the total value of remuneration the physician receives under the value-based arrangement. The nature and extent of the physician's downside financial risk must be set forth in writing. The same limitations on remuneration and directed referrals that apply to the full financial risk exception also apply to the meaningful downside financial risk exception.

G. **What is the "Value-Based Arrangements" Exception?** The "value-based arrangements" exception includes all compensation arrangements that qualify as value-based arrangements, regardless of the level of risk undertaken by the value-based enterprise or any of its value-based participants. Because physicians are undertaking less risk, the value-based arrangement exception includes additional compliance safeguards.

1. **Signed, Written Agreement.** Unlike the other two value-based arrangement exceptions, the value-based arrangement exception requires, a signed, written agreement that describes the value-based activities, how the arrangement is expected to further the purposes of the

value-based enterprise, the target patient population, the type or nature of remuneration, the methodology used to determine the remuneration, and outcome measures against which the recipient of the remuneration is assessed, if any.

2. **What Are "Outcome Measures" for "Value-Based Arrangements"?** If used to evaluate value-based arrangements, "outcome measure" means a benchmark that quantifies: (a) improvements in or maintenance of the quality of patient care; or (b) reductions in the costs to or growth of expenditures of payors while maintaining or improving the quality of patient care. Only outcome measures that are objective, measurable, and selected based on clinical evidence or credible medical support should be used to assess the recipient of remuneration in a value-based arrangement. CMS recognizes that outcome measures may not be applicable to all value-based arrangements. As an example, an arrangement under which a hospital provides necessary infrastructure to a physician in the same value-based enterprise may not require the physician to meet specific outcome measures to receive or maintain the infrastructure items or services.

3. **How Is a "Value-Based Enterprise" Expected to Monitor Value-Based Arrangements?** While CMS does not prescribe exactly how value-based enterprises and physicians should monitor their value-based arrangements, VBEs are expected to design their monitoring and other compliance efforts in a manner suitable for the particular value-based arrangement. Either annually or at least once during the term of arrangements lasting less than one year the value-based enterprise must assess: (a) whether the parties have furnished the value-based activities required under the value-based arrangement; (b) whether and how continuation of the value-based activities is expected to accomplish the value-based purposes of the arrangement and proceed toward attainment of outcome measures, if any, against which the recipient of remuneration is assessed. If monitoring indicates that a value-based activity is ineffective at accomplishing the purposes of the value-based enterprise, either the arrangement must be terminated within thirty days after completion of the monitoring or the parties must modify the arrangement within ninety days after completion of the monitoring assessment to terminate the ineffective value-based activity.

4. **Commercial Reasonableness.** The value-based arrangement to which the exception applies must be "commercially reasonable." "Commercially reasonable" means that the arrangement furthers a legitimate business purpose and is sensible, considering the characteristics of the parties, including their size, type, scope, and specialty as more particularly described above.

5. **Remuneration and Directed Referral Requirements.** The same limitations on remuneration and directed referrals that apply to the full financial risk and meaningful downside financial risk exceptions also apply to the value-based arrangement exception.

H. **To What Indirect Compensation Arrangements Do the Value-Based Arrangement Exceptions Apply?** The value-based arrangement exceptions protect the physician's referrals to the entity that provides "designated health services" when an indirect compensation arrangement includes a value-based arrangement to which the physician (or the physician organization in whose shoes the physician stands) is a direct party. For the value-based arrangement exceptions, the link closest to the physician may not be an ownership interest; it must be a compensation arrangement that meets the definition of value-based arrangement. VBE parties should first determine if an indirect compensation arrangement exists. If it does, then the parties determine whether the compensation arrangement to which the physician (or the physician organization in whose shoes the physician stands) is a direct party qualifies as a value-based arrangement and satisfies the requirements of a value-based arrangement exception. If it does satisfy an applicable exception, then the physician's referrals to the entity with which the physician has the indirect compensation arrangement are permitted. However, if the entity with which the physician has an indirect compensation arrangement is not a Managed Care Organization or Independent Provider Association, the exception for risk-sharing arrangements is not applicable to the indirect compensation arrangement.

V. WHAT IS THE FEDERAL ANTI-KICKBACK STATUTE AND HOW IS IT DISTINGUISHED FROM STARK?

A. **How Is the Federal Anti-Kickback Statute Applied?** The federal Anti-Kickback Statute provides for sanctions against individuals or entities that knowingly and willfully offer, pay, solicit, or receive remuneration (or anything of value, whether direct or indirect, overt or covert, in cash or in kind) in return for or to induce the referral of items or services reimbursable by Medicare, Medicaid, or any other federal reimbursement program. Simply stated, the federal Anti-Kickback Statute is implicated when referrals for items or services payable by any governmental reimbursement program run in one direction and remuneration runs in the opposite direction. Consequently, application of the federal Anti-Kickback Statute is very broad, and it can apply whenever any person or entity receives remuneration in exchange for access to referrals for items or services covered by a governmental reimbursement program. When analyzing any set of facts, ask these questions:

- Is there a referral of any item or service that is covered by any federal governmental reimbursement program?

- Did any party receive any benefit or transfer of value of any nature that was intended, for at least one of its purposes, to induce or arrange for the referrals?

The Stark Law differs from and is independent of the federal Anti-Kickback Statute, even though violations of each law may arise from the same set of facts and circumstances. The essential aspects of the federal Anti-Kickback Statute are as follows:

1. **The Role of the OIG.** The Anti-Kickback Statute is administered by the Department of Health and Human Services, Office of the Inspector General ("OIG"), which is the agency that polices Medicare and Medicaid fraud and abuse. Stark, which is strictly a payment statute, is administered by CMS.

2. **Criminal Sanctions.** The Anti-Kickback Statute is a criminal statute. You can be imprisoned for violating the federal Anti-Kickback Statute, but not Stark.

3. **Intent.** Prior to enactment of the ACA, violation of the federal Anti-Kickback Statute required intent to violate law. The ACA relaxed the "specific intent" requirement. Now, an Anti-Kickback Statute violation can be asserted without showing that an individual knew of the Statute's proscriptions and intended to violate the Statute. Therefore, violation can be founded upon intent to engage in the conduct and not on specific intent to violate the law.

4. **One Purpose.** If only one purpose of the arrangement is to induce prohibited referrals, the AKS is violated.

5. **The Anti-Kickback Statute Is Not Limited to Physicians.** The Anti-Kickback Statute applies to all referral sources and prohibits other conduct such as arranging for or recommending items, services, or facilities. Stark applies only to physician self-referral.

6. **The Anti-Kickback Statute Is a Two Way Street: It Applies to Both the Party Providing the Prohibited Remuneration and the Party Receiving the Prohibited Remuneration.** Unlike Stark, in which sanctions are principally applied to the provider that submits a claim for payment pursuant to a prohibited financial relationship, the Anti-Kickback Statute sanctions are imposed against both the party that makes the alleged "kickback" and the party receiving it. For example, if a hospital provides illegal remuneration to induce referrals from physicians, then both the hospital and the physician violate the Anti-Kickback Statute. Also, the United States Department of Justice (DOJ) erased all doubt that individuals are being targeted for acts of both civil and criminal corporate fraud when, on September 9, 2015, Sally Quillian Yates, then the DOJ Deputy Attorney General, issued a directive to DOJ division leaders and United States Attorneys to combat corporate fraud by seeking individual accountability for corporate wrongdoing in what is referred to as the "Yates Memo." According to the Yates Memo, which remains in effect and is more fully described in Chapter 11, the DOJ intends to fully leverage its resources to identify culpable individuals at all levels in corporate cases.

7. **Civil Monetary Penalties.** The Anti-Kickback Statute subjects violators of the statute to civil money penalties or program exclusion, remedies that are also available under Stark.

8. **Direct Link to False Claims Act.** The ACA provides that a claim submitted for items or services in violation of the federal Anti-Kickback Statute is "false" under the federal False Claims Act and certain other false claims statutes.

B. **Safe Harbors.** The OIG has promulgated a series of "safe harbor regulations" that describe arrangements that are safe from criminal prosecution under the federal Anti-Kickback Statute and will not serve as a basis for governmental reimbursement program exclusion. However, the safe harbors are narrowly drawn, and they merely describe arrangements that are "safe." The safe harbor regulations do not describe the universe of acceptable business arrangements. Conduct that falls outside of a safe harbor puts the parties "at risk" but does not necessarily violate the Anti-Kickback Statute. This makes the federal Anti-Kickback Statute safe harbor regulations different from the Stark exceptions. Stark is a black and white statute: a referral is either prohibited or it is not because of a specific statutory or regulatory exception to the general self-referral prohibition. The more broad Anti-Kickback Statute has some narrowly drawn safe harbor regulations, but arrangements that fall outside of the safe harbor regulations are not necessarily illegal.

C. **Legacy Fee For Service Safe Harbor Regulations.** Like the Stark Law, the original intent of the federal Anti-Kickback Statute was to prevent overutilization of items or services covered by federal health care programs in the legacy "fee for service" economy. Also like the Stark Law, the OIG promulgated "value-based arrangement" rules that became effective in January, 2021 and mirror but do not always precisely dovetail with the CMS "value-based arrangement" rules under the Stark Law. What follows in this Chapter 1, Section V is an explanation of the legacy federal Anti-Kickback Statute "fee for service" rules, which still apply to traditional Medicare. "Value-based arrangement" federal Anti-Kickback Statute rules are separately addressed in Chapter 1, Section VI. The following are legacy safe harbors that arose under the traditional Medicare fee for service compensation model which remain relevant because the fee for service model is not dead:

1. **Small Investment Interests.** If the entity has investment interests that are held by either active or passive investors, all of the following eight applicable standards must be met:

a. no more than 40% of the value of the investment interests of each class of investment interest may be held in the previous fiscal year or previous 12-month period by investors who are in a position to make or influence referrals to the entity;

b. the terms of the investment interest must be the same for all passive investors;

c. the terms of the investment interest must not be based on expected volume or value of referrals, items or services furnished, or the amount of business otherwise generated from the investor to the entity;

d. there must be no requirement that the passive investor make or influence referrals to the entity;

e. neither the entity nor the investor may market or furnish the entity's items or services to passive investors differently than to non-investors;

f. no more than 40% of the entity's gross revenue related to the delivery of health care items and services in the previous fiscal year or 12-month period may come from referrals or business otherwise generated by investors;

g. neither the entity nor any investor may loan funds to or guarantee a loan for an investor who is in a position to influence referrals to the entity; and

h. the amount of payment to an investor must be in proportion to the amount of the investor's investment.

2. **Publicly Traded Securities.** Like Stark, there is an exception for investment interests in publicly traded securities. This safe harbor regulation applies only to investment interests in entities having more than $50,000,000 in undepreciated net tangible assets related to the furnishing of health care items and services and all of the following five conditions are met:

   a. the equity security must be registered with the Securities and Exchange Commission;

   b. the investment interest must be obtained on terms (including direct or indirect transferability restrictions) and at a price equally available to the public when traded on a registered securities exchange such as the NYSE or in accordance with the National Association of Securities Dealers Automated Quotation System (NASDAQ);

   c. the entity or any investor must not market or furnish the entity's items or services (or those of another entity as part of a cross referral agreement) to passive investors differently than to non-investors;

   d. the entity or any investor must not loan funds to or guarantee a loan for an investor who is in a position to make or influence referrals to furnish items or services to, or otherwise generate business for, the entity if the investor uses any part of such loan to obtain the investment interest; and

   e. the amount of payment to an investor in return for the investment interest must be directly proportional to the amount of the capital investment of that investor.

3. **Investments in Medically Underserved Areas (MUAs).** This safe harbor is like the small investment interest safe harbor, but it requires ownership of no more than 50% of the entity by investors in a position to make or influence referrals and at least 75% of the services are provided to a medically underserved population (MUP).

4. **Space Rental.** Remuneration under the federal Anti-Kickback Statute does not include any payment made by a lessee to a lessor for the use of premises so long as the following six standards are met:

   a. the lease agreement is in writing and signed by each of the parties;

   b. the lease covers all of the premises leased between the parties for the term of the lease and specifies the premises covered by the lease;

   c. if the lease is intended to provide periodic access to the lessee, the lease must specify exactly the schedule of the interval, its precise length, and exact rent amount;

   d. the term of the lease is for not less than one year;

   e. the rental charge is set in advance and consistent with fair market value in arm's length's transactions and not determined in consideration of the volume or value of any referrals; and

   f. the aggregate space rented does not exceed that which is reasonably necessary to accomplish the commercially reasonable business purpose of the rental.

5. **Equipment Rental.** Remuneration under the federal Anti-Kickback Statute does not include any payment made by a lessee of equipment to the lessor of the equipment for the use of the equipment, as long as six standards are met. These standards are substantially the same as those listed above for "space rental."

6. **Personal Services and Management Contracts.** Remuneration under the federal Anti-Kickback Statute does not include any payment made by a principal to an agent as compensation for the services of the agent, as long as the following standards are met:

   a. the agency agreement is set out in writing and signed by the parties;

   b. the agency agreement covers all of the services the agent provides to the principal for the term of the agreement and specifies the services to be provided by the agent;

c. the term of the agreement is for not less than one year;

d. the methodology for determining compensation paid to the agent over the term of the agreement is "set in advance," is consistent with fair market value in arms-length transactions, and is not determined in a manner that takes into account value or volume of referrals;

e. the services performed under the agreement do not involve the counseling or promotion of a business arrangement or other activity that violates any state or federal law; and

f. the aggregate services contracted for do not exceed those which are reasonably necessary to accomplish the commercially reasonable business purpose of the services.

7. **Outcomes-Based Payment Arrangements.** The legacy personal services and management agreement safe harbor was modified when the value-based arrangement safe harbors were promulgated by adding a safe harbor for outcomes-based payment arrangements involving independent contractors. This recent safe harbor introduces terms and conditions that apply not only to this safe harbor but to other value-based safe harbor regulations. "Outcomes-based" payments are limited to payments that either reward the independent contractor for successfully achieving an "outcome measure" or recoup from or reduce payment to the independent contractor recipient for failure to achieve an "outcome measure." "Outcome measure" means achieving one or more legitimate outcome measures that are selected based on clinical evidence or credible medical support and have benchmarks that are used to quantify improvements in quality of patient care, a material reduction in costs to or growth in expenditures of payors while maintaining or improving quality of care, or both. However, outcomes-based payments specifically exclude payments made directly or indirectly by any of the following: a pharmaceutical company; pharmacy benefit manager; clinical laboratory company; compounding pharmacy; medical device and supply manufacturers; entities that sell or rent durable medical equipment, prosthetic, or orthotics covered by a federal health care program; and a medical device distributor or wholesaler that is not the device manufacturer ("Excluded Value-Based Participants"). This exclusion appears in several value-based arrangement safe harbor regulations described in Chapter 1, Section VI. The OIG is unwilling to give a free pass from criminal and exclusion sanctions to Excluded Value-Based Participants because, in the OIG's view, they are more likely to be sources of misconduct. Again, all safe harbor regulations merely describe what is "safe," not the universe of compliant arrangements. Payments related solely to the achievement of internal cost savings or based solely on patient satisfaction or patient convenience measures are also excluded from the definition of outcomes-based payments. Remuneration for purposes of AKS enforcement does not include any payment made for independent contractor services as long as the following standards are met:

a. the methodology for determining aggregate compensation (including outcomes-based payments) is set in advance, commercially reasonable, consistent with fair market value, and not determined in a manner that directly takes into account the volume or value of any referrals or business otherwise generated between the parties (all of which have express meanings described elsewhere in Chapter 1) for which payment may be made in whole or in part by a federal health care program;

b. the agreement is in writing and signed by the parties in advance of, or contemporaneously with, the commencement of the outcomes-based payment arrangement and includes a general description of the services to be performed, the outcome measures that must be achieved to receive an outcomes-based payment, the clinical evidence or credible medical support relied upon by the parties to select the outcome measures, and the schedule for regularly monitoring and assessing the outcome measures;

c. the term of the agreement is not less than one year;

d. the agreement neither limits any party's ability to make decisions in their patients' best interest nor induces any party to reduce or limit medically necessary items or services;

e. for each outcome measure under the agreement, the parties (i) regularly monitor and assess the independent contractor's performance, including the impact of the outcomes-based payment arrangement on patient quality of care and (ii) periodically assess, and as necessary revise, benchmarks and remuneration under the arrangement to ensure that the remuneration is consistent with fair market value in an arm's length transaction; and

f. The principal has policies and procedures to promptly address and correct identified material performance failures or material deficiencies in quality of care resulting from the outcomes-based payment arrangement.

8. **Ambulatory Surgery Centers.** There is a series of safe harbor regulations that permit physician investment in four categories of ambulatory surgery center ("ASC") ventures: surgeon-owned ASCs; single specialty ASCs; multi-specialty ASCs; and hospital-physician ASCs. In general, the ASC safe harbor regulations are based on the premise that performance of surgical procedures in the ASC is an "extension of the physician's practice." Therefore, unlike other safe harbor regulations, the ASC safe harbors require the physician investor to actively perform surgical services. The ASC safe harbor does not extend to passive investment interests. Because there are four separate ASC categories described in the safe harbor regulations, they do not have identical terms, and the following describes some of the more important elements:

a. the terms on which an investment interest is offered to an investor must not be related to the previous or expected volume of referrals, services furnished, or the amount of business otherwise generated from the investor to the entity;

b. for all ASC investments except investment in a hospital-physician joint venture ASC, at least one-third of each physician investor's medical practice from all sources for the previous fiscal year or previous twelve month period must be derived from the physician's performance of "procedures," defined as any procedure on the list of Medicare covered ambulatory surgical center procedures in regulations promulgated by CMS;

c. for the multi-specialty ASC safe harbor only, at least one-third of the procedures performed by each physician investor for the previous fiscal year or previous twelve month period must be performed at the multi-specialty ASC;

d. the entity or any investor (including, for example an ASC developer) must not loan funds to or guaranty a loan for a physician to permit the physician to acquire an ownership interest in the ASC;

e. payments to investors must be directly proportional to the amount of capital investment;

f. all ancillary services (such as radiological imaging) must be directly and integrally related to primary procedures performed at the ASC and none may be separately billed to Medicare or any other federal reimbursement program; and

g. the ASC and physician investors must treat Medicare and Medicaid covered patients in a non-discriminatory manner.

The most important elements of the ASC safe harbor are the "one-third" tests, which require at least one-third of the investor's income to be derived from the performance of surgical procedures for surgeon-owned, single specialty, ASCs, and multi-specialty ASCs and at least one-third of the procedures by each physician investor must be performed at the ASC for multispecialty ASCs. Because the ASC safe harbor regulations are based on active performance of procedures by physicians, most ASC ventures include provisions that permit dissociation of a physician from an ASC venture when the physician's practice no longer qualifies under the "one-third" tests or the physician otherwise is not actively performing surgery at the ASC.

9. **Sale of Practice from One Practitioner to Another.** Remuneration under the federal Anti-Kickback Statute does not include any payment made to a selling practitioner by a purchasing

practitioner when (a) the period from the date of the first agreement to the sale and the completion of the sale is not more than one year and (b) the selling practitioner will not be in a position to make referrals for the benefit of the purchasing practitioner after one year from the date of the first agreement.

10. **Sale of Practice to a Hospital.** Similarly, remuneration does not include payments to a practitioner from a purchasing hospital as long as the following four standards are met:

The period from the date of the first agreement to the sale and completion of the sale is not more than three years;

a. the selling practitioner will not be in a position to make or influence referrals covered by the federal reimbursement programs to the purchasing hospital;

b. the practice is located in a Health Professional Shortage Area; and

c. commencing at the time of the first agreement pertaining to the sale, the purchasing hospital and selling practitioner must diligently and in good faith engage in commercially reasonable recruitment activities to recruit a new practitioner for the acquired practice within one year.

11. ***Bona fide* Employment Relationships.** Like Stark, the federal Anti-Kickback Statute has an exception for *bona fide* employment relationships as well as a safe harbor regulation covering employment relationships that uses the Internal Revenue Service test for determining employment status.

12. **Physician Recruitment.** Remuneration for purposes of the Anti-Kickback Statute does not include any payment or exchange by a hospital to induce a physician who has been practicing for less than one year to locate, or for any other physician to relocate, the physician's practice into a health professional shortage area if certain standards are met. The safe harbor regulation is so narrow it has little applicability to customary physician recruitment transactions. Because the Stark Law is a "black and white" statute that applies to all compensation arrangements between a hospital and a physician, the Stark rules are significantly more important when analyzing recruitment transactions.

VI. WHAT ARE THE FEDERAL ANTI-KICKBACK STATUTE VALUE-BASED ARRANGEMENT RULES?

A. **Need for Value-Based Arrangement Rules.** The fundamental need for federal Anti-Kickback Statute safe harbor regulations for value-based arrangements is the same as the need for Stark Law value-based arrangement rules: new rules are required to reflect the shift from government reimbursement program investment in the health industry from a "fee for service" economy to a "coordinated care" economy as described in the introduction to the Stark Law value-based arrangement rules. On the same day that the DHHS Centers for Medicare and Medicaid Services promulgated the Stark Law value-based rules, the DHHS Office of the Inspector General promulgated federal Anti-Kickback Statute value-based arrangement safe harbor regulations. While similar, because Stark is a black and white, civil payment law under which referrals are either prohibited or not while the AKS is a criminal statute with safe harbors that are more narrowly drafted to describe what is "safe" from prosecution but not the universe of compliant arrangements, the AKS value-based safe harbor regulations are not as specific as the Stark Law value-based exceptions and leave arrangements that fall outside of the AKS safe harbors to a compliance "risk assessment." While it is always best for an arrangement to fall within an AKS safe harbor regulation to the extent possible, it is not absolutely required for regulatory compliance. Also, while the AKS safe harbors are narrower, it is difficult to believe that any arrangement that complies with the Stark Law value-based arrangement exceptions will be alleged to violate the AKS, even if the arrangement falls outside of an AKS safe harbor.

B. **Overview of the Anti-Kickback Statute Value-Based Arrangement Safe Harbor Regulations.** Fundamentally, the federal Anti-Kickback Statute is implicated when remuneration, whether direct or indirect, overt or covert, in cash or in kind, runs in one direction and referrals, or arranging for referrals, of items or services covered by any governmental reimbursement program run in the opposite direction. When the AKS is implicated, it is necessary to analyze the arrangement to determine whether it is subject to regulatory enforcement risk. As initially conceived the AKS was intended to protect governmental reimbursement programs from overutilization of items or services. In a coordinated care economy, the paradigm shifts to protecting covered beneficiaries from underutilization of items or services. There is an old saying that "fraud follows the money." In the fee for service economy, the OIG believes that physician ordering of items and services is suspect because revenue increases with increased referrals. In a coordinated care economy, the OIG believes that health care services will be withheld to increase revenue. The AKS value-based safe harbors protect a wide range of arrangements dependent on the nature of the remuneration, the financial risk undertaken in the arrangement, and the nature of AKS compliance safeguards implemented. Also, like the Stark Law, value-based arrangements already in place as of January, 2021, the effective date of the value-based rules, that rely on prior rules such as the "waiver rules" issued by the OIG that apply to Accountable Care Organizations that participate in the Medicare Shared Savings Program do not need to be terminated, even if the arrangements do not comply with the value-based arrangement rules.

C. **Value-Based AKS Safe Harbor Definitions.** Like the Stark Law, the AKS value-based rules require learning an entirely new regulatory vocabulary with intertwining definitions. While the AKS rules define many of the same terms as the Stark Law value-based rules and the definitions are substantially similar and materially aligned, they are not identical.

1. **What Is a "Value-Based Activity"?** Similar to the Stark Law rules, "value-based activity" is broadly defined to mean any activity that is reasonably designed to achieve at least one "value-based purpose" of the "value-based enterprise" and may constitute either (a) the provision of an item or service, (b) the taking of an action, or (c) the refraining from taking an action. Actual achievement of a value-based purpose is not required. However, unlike the parallel Stark Law definition, the AKS value-based activity definition specifically excludes the mere making of a "referral" for purposes of satisfying the safe harbors without more related to the referral such as coordinating care by multiple providers for a target patient population. The OIG provides the following examples of value-based activities: (a) offering health technology to track patient data, (b) working with a care coordinator, and (c) refraining from ordering certain items and services in accordance with a medically appropriate care protocol

2. **What Is a "Value-Based Arrangement"?** "Value-based arrangement" means an arrangement for the provision of at least one value-based activity for a target patient population to which the only parties are a value-based enterprise (sometimes referred to as a "VBE") and one or more value-based participants or between value-based participants in the same value-based enterprise. While there is no universal value-based arrangement safe harbor regulation like the Stark Law value-based arrangement self-referral exception, only an arrangement that meets the AKS definition of a value-based arrangement is eligible for protection under the value-based AKS safe harbors.

3. **What Is a "Value-Based Enterprise" (VBE)?** The Stark Law and AKS safe harbor definitions of VBE are identical. A VBE is any enterprise which has (a) two or more value-based participants who collaborate to achieve at least one value-based purpose and are parties to a value-based arrangement, (b) an accountable body or person responsible for financial and operational oversight, and (c) a governing document that describes the VBE and how the value-based participants intend to achieve the VBE's value-based purpose. As stated in the Stark Law section, in practice this is a provider network such as an Accountable Care Organization that participates in the Medicare Shared Savings Program or a clinically integrated network that agrees to collaborate regarding provision of health care services to a target patient population in a manner that is focused on patient centered care including care coordination, improving efficiencies in the delivery of care, and improving patient care outcomes.

4. **What Is a "Value-Based Purpose"?** The Stark Law and AKS safe harbor definitions of value-based purpose are also identical. A "value-based purpose" means any of the following: (a)

coordinating and managing the care of a target patient population; (b) improving the quality of care for a target patient population; (c) appropriately reducing the costs to or growth in expenditures of payors without reducing the quality of care for a target patient population; or (d) transitioning from health care delivery and payment mechanisms based on the volume of items and services provided (in other words, fee for service) to mechanisms based on the quality of care and control of costs of care for a target patient population (in other word, coordinated care). There is no requirement that the value-based purpose must actually be achieved, but there must be a rational connection between either providing or refraining from providing an item or service a value-based purpose.

5. **Who Is a "Value-Based Participant"?** A "value-based participant" means a person or entity that engages in at least one value-based activity as part of a value-based enterprise. While this definition is broad on its face, the AKS value-based rules described below exclude remuneration involving some potential value-based participants from safe harbor protection.

6. **What Is a "Target Patient Population"?** The Stark and AKS safe harbor meanings of "target patient population" are also identical: an identified patient population selected by a value-based enterprise or its value-based participants based on legitimate and verifiable criteria that (a) are set out in writing in advance of the commencement of the value-based arrangement and (b) further the value-based enterprise's value-based purposes. For purposes of identifying a target patient population, legitimate and verifiable criteria may include "medical or health characteristics (for example, patients undergoing knee replacement surgery or patients with newly diagnosed type 2 diabetes), geographic characteristics (for example, all patients in an identified county or set of zip codes), payor status (for example, all patients with a particular health insurance plan or payor), or other defining characteristics. However, selecting a target patient population consisting of only lucrative or compliant patients (cherry-picking) and avoiding costly or noncompliant patients (lemon-dropping) is impermissible under most circumstances. Again, a clear example of a target patient population is the body of Medicare beneficiaries attributed to an Accountable Care Organization that participates in the Medicare Shared Savings Program.

7. **What AKS Safe Harbors Are Available for Value-Based Compensation Arrangements?** There are three new value-based AKS safe harbors plus several related new safe harbors intended to promote coordination of patient care and participation in CMS sponsored Medicare payment models.

D. **What Is the "Full Financial Risk" Safe Harbor?** The full financial risk safe harbor provides the most flexibility because its application requires undertaking of the most risk. "Full financial risk" is defined as prospective responsibility for the cost of all items and services covered by a payor for each patient in the target patient populations for a term of at least one year. Remuneration for purposes of AKS enforcement (remember, the AKS is implicated when remuneration runs in one direction and referrals of items or services covered by a governmental reimbursement program run in the opposite direction) does not include all forms of remuneration, whether monetary or in kind, between a VBE and a value-based participant in a full financial risk arrangement if all of the following standards met:

1. **Written Agreement.** The VBE's agreement to undertake full financial risk is memorialized in a written agreement signed by the parties that specifies the value-based activities and has a term of at least one year.

2. **Restrictions on Claims for Payment.** Unless the value-based participant is a payor, the value based participant does not independently claim any form of payment from a payor for items or services covered in the VBE full financial risk contract.

3. **Nature and Sources of Remuneration.** The remuneration can be monetary or non-monetary as long as it (a) is directly connected to at least one value-based purpose, (b) does not include an ownership or investment interest or any distributions related to an ownership interest or investment, and (c) is not exchanged for marketing items or services furnished by a VBE or value-based participants to patients or patient recruitment.

4. **Prohibited Limitations Regarding Patient Care.** The arrangement does not induce parties to reduce or limit medically necessary items or services for any patient in the target population. If the arrangement is structured in a way that leads to a reduction in medically necessary services, it is considered inherently suspect and implicates potential civil monetary penalties. Once again this defines the thin line between accomplishing the value-based purpose of reducing health care costs by excluding unnecessary and duplicative tests or suggesting therapy instead of a procedure and denying a patient medically necessary care when the financial incentive is to decrease, not increase, ordering of health care items or services.

5. **Volume or Value of Referrals.** Payment of the remuneration does not take into account the volume or value of referrals or condition remuneration on (a) referrals that do not involve the target patient population or (b) business not covered by the value-based arrangement.

6. **Quality Assurance Program.** The VBE implements a quality assurance program for services provided to the target patient population that (a) protects against underutilization and (b) assesses quality of care provided to the target patient population.

7. **Excluded Value-Based Participants.** The remuneration is not exchanged by an Excluded Value-Based Participant as defined in the outcomes-based payment arrangement safe

harbor. This is a clear deviation from the corresponding Stark Law exception which has no limitations on the nature of the value-based participant. As stated elsewhere in this Chapter, the OIG is unwilling to give a free pass from criminal and exclusion sanctions to Excluded Value-Based Participants because, in the OIG's view, they are more likely to be sources of misconduct. Also, this rule merely describes what is "safe," not the universe of compliant arrangements, so remuneration involving Excluded Value-Based Participants may be compliant with the AKS even if the arrangement does not fall within the safe harbor.

8. **Recordkeeping.** The VBE must maintain documentation sufficient to support compliance with the safe harbor for a period of six years.

E. **What Is the "Substantial Downside Financial Risk" Safe Harbor?** The substantial downside risk safe harbor is the OIG's version of the Stark meaningful downside financial risk exception and tracks the essential elements of the full financial risk safe harbor. "Substantial financial risk" has three alternative definitions depending in the terms and conditions of the value-based arrangement. Remuneration for purposes of AKS enforcement does not include all forms of remuneration, whether monetary or in kind, between a VBE and a value-based participant in a substantial downside risk arrangement if all of the following standards met:

1. **Substantial Downside Financial Risk for Value-Based Shared Savings Arrangements.** When losses and savings are calculated by comparing current expenditures by a payor for all items and services furnished to a target patient population to a *bona fide* benchmark that reasonably determines the expected cost of such care, "substantial financial risk" is defined as prospective downside financial risk equal to at least 30% of any loss.

2. **Substantial Downside Financial Risk for Global Payment Arrangements.** When the value-based arrangement is based on episodic or bundled payments calculated by comparing current expenditures by a payor for all items and services furnished to a target patient population to a *bona fide* benchmark that reasonably determines the expected cost of such care for the defined clinical episode of care and the parties design the clinical episode of care to cover items and services collectively furnished in more than one care setting, "substantial financial risk" is defined as prospective downside financial risk equal to at least 20% of any loss.

3. **Substantial Downside Financial Risk for Capitation Arrangements.** There is "substantial financial risk" when the VBE receives from the payor a prospective, per patient payment that is designed to produce material savings and paid on a monthly, quarterly, or annual basis for providing a predefined set of items and services to the target patient population.

4. **Value-Base Participants Must Share in the Financial Risk.** The value-based participant (unless the value-based participant is the payor from which the VBE is assuming risk) is at risk for a meaningful share of the VBE's substantial downside financial risk for providing or arranging for the provision of items and services for the target patient population. "Meaningful share" means either (a) 5% of the amount for which the value-based enterprise is at risk under its agreement with a payor or (b) the remuneration is based on a partial or full capitation model.

5. **Restrictions on Claims for Payment.** Unless the value-based participant is a payor, the value based participant does not independently claim any form of payment from a payor for items or services covered in the VBE substantial downside financial risk contract.

6. **Nature and Sources of Remuneration.** The remuneration can be monetary or non-monetary as long as it (a) is directly connected to at least one value-based purpose, (b) does not include an ownership or investment interest or any distributions related to an ownership or investment interest, and (c) is not exchanged for marketing items or services furnished by a VBE or value-based participants to patients or patient recruitment.

7. **Prohibited Limitations Regarding Patient Care.** The value-based arrangement does not induce parties to reduce or limit medically necessary items or services for any patient in the target population. If the arrangement is structured in a way that leads to a reduction in medically necessary services, it is considered inherently suspect and implicates potential civil monetary penalties. This is yet another example of the thin line between accomplishing the value-based purpose of reducing health care costs by excluding unnecessary and duplicative tests or suggesting therapy instead of a procedure and denying a patient medically necessary care when the financial incentive is to decrease, not increase, ordering of health care items or services.

8. **Volume or Value of Referrals.** Payment of the remuneration does not take into account the volume or value of referrals or condition remuneration on (a) referrals that do not involve the target patient population or (b) business not covered by the value-based arrangement.

9. **Quality Assurance Program.** The VBE implements a quality assurance program for services provided to the target patient population that (a) protects against underutilization and (b) assesses quality of care provided to the target patient population.

10. **Excluded Value-Based Participants.** The remuneration is not exchanged by or with Excluded Value-Based Participants.

11. **Written Agreement.** The VBE's agreement to undertake substantial downside financial risk is memorialized in a written agreement signed by the parties that specifies the value-based activities and has a term of at least one year.

12. **Recordkeeping.** The VBE must maintain documentation sufficient to support compliance with the safe harbor for a period of six years.

F. **What Is the "Care Coordination Agreement" Safe Harbor?** The care coordination arrangement safe harbor applies to arrangements that improve quality of care, health outcomes, and efficiency but protects only "in-kind" remuneration. While the value-based participants are not required to assume any payment risk, to qualify for the safe harbor the value-based arrangement must include at least one evidence-based outcome measure and have the following essential elements:

1. **Limitations on Nature and Use of the In-Kind Remuneration.** The property: (a) is used predominantly to engage in value-based activities that are directly connected to the coordination and management of care for the target patient population, does not result in more than incidental benefits to persons outside of the target patient population; and is not exchanged or used than incidentally for the recipient's billing or financial management services or for marketing items or services. The OIG describes a health information technology tool that enables both remote patient monitoring and two-way telehealth capabilities as an example of "in-kind" remuneration that is protected under the safe harbor.

2. **Required Recipient Contribution.** The recipient pays at least 15 percent of the offeror's cost for the remuneration using any reasonable accounting methodology or the fair market value of the in-kind remuneration.

3. **What Are "Outcome Measures" for Purposes of the Care Coordination Agreement Safe Harbor?** For purposes of the care coordination agreement safe harbor, the parties to the value-based arrangement establish legitimate outcome or process measures that: (a) the parties reasonably anticipate will advance the coordination and management of care for the target patient population based on clinical evidence or credible medical or health sciences support; (b) include benchmarks that are related to improving or maintaining improvements in the coordination and management of care for the target patient population; (c) are monitored, periodically assessed, and prospectively revised as necessary to ensure that the measure and its benchmark continue to advance the coordination and management of care of the target patient population; (d) relate to the remuneration exchanged under the value-based arrangement; and (e) are not based solely on patient satisfaction or patient convenience.

4. **How Is a Value-Based Enterprise Expected to Monitor Care Coordination Requirements?** The parties to the value-based arrangement must monitor and assess the following no less frequently than annually: (a) the coordination and management of care for the target patient population in the value-based arrangement; (b) any deficiencies in the delivery of quality care under the value-based arrangement; and (c) progress toward achieving the legitimate outcome or process measures in the value-based arrangement.

5. **Volume or Value of Referrals.** Payment of the remuneration does not take into account the volume or value of referrals or condition remuneration on (a) referrals that do not involve the target patient population or (b) business not covered by the value-based arrangement.

6. **Directed Referrals.** Directed referrals are permitted only as described in the Stark Law value-based arrangement exception.

7. **Excluded Value-Based Participants.** The remuneration is not exchanged by or with Excluded Value-Based Participants as defined in the outcome based payment arrangements safe harbor.

8. **Commercial Reasonableness.** The value-based arrangement to which the safe harbor applies is commercially reasonable.

9. **Signed, Written Agreement.** The terms of the value-based arrangement are set forth in writing and signed by the parties in advance of, or contemporaneous with, the commencement of the value-based arrangement and describe at a minimum: (a) the value-based purpose; (b) the value-based activities to be undertaken by the parties to the value-based arrangement; (c) the term of the arrangement; (d) the target patient population; (e) a description of the remuneration; (f) the cost or fair market value of the property; (g) the percentage and amount contributed to the recipient of the remuneration; and (h) the arrangement's outcome or process measures expected to be accomplished by the recipient.

10. **Recordkeeping.** The VBE must maintain documentation sufficient to support compliance with the safe harbor for a period of six years.

G. **What Is the Patient Engagement and Support Safe Harbor?** This safe harbor protects provision of items or services by value-based enterprise participants to target population patients who need the specific items or services to adhere to treatment regimens. The need for incentives to motivate patient engagement became readily apparent in the early days of the Medicare Shared Savings Program because achievement of "savings" required chronic care management and, because the follow-up visits also required the Medicare beneficiary to be personally responsible for the copayment amount, the Medicare beneficiaries were reluctant to appear for chronic care management appointments. Many ACOs lobbied for a waiver of chronic care management copayments, but the OIG did not want to follow that path. Instead, the OIG developed a safe harbor regulation that applies to almost all non-cash or cash equivalent items or services that promote chronic care management and coordination of care. Remuneration for purposes of AKS enforcement does not include a "patient engagement tool or support" furnished by a VBE participant to a target population patient if the following conditions are met:

1. **In-Kind, Non-Cash Remuneration.** The patient engagement tool or support is an in-kind item, good, or service that has a direct connection to the coordination and management of care of the target patient population, does not include any cash or cash equivalent (such as gift cards), does not result in medically unnecessary or inappropriate items or services reimbursed in whole or in part by a federal health care program, and is recommended by the patient's licensed health care professional.

2. **Relationship to Patient Care.** The patient engagement tool or support advances adherence to a treatment regimen, adherence to a drug regimen, adherence to a follow-up care plan, prevents or manages a disease or condition, or ensures patient safety.

3. **Funding Restrictions.** The patient engagement tool or support is not funded or contributed by a party outside the value-based arrangement or an Excluded Value-Based Participant.

4. **Monetary Limit.** The aggregate retail value of patient engagement tools and supports furnished to a patient by a value-based participant does not exceed $500 annually, provided that this amount is subject to an annual Consumer Price Index adjustment.

5. **Marketing Prohibition.** The value-based participant does not use the patient engagement tools or supports to market other reimbursable items or services or for patient recruitment.

6. **Insurance Coverage Cannot Be Considered.** Availability of a tool or support is not determined in a manner that takes into account the type of insurance coverage of the patient.

7. **No Excluded Value-Based Participants.** The VBE participant is not an Excluded Value-Based Participant

8. **Recordkeeping Requirement.** The VBE participant maintains records of compliance with these conditions for six years.

H. **What Is the CMS-Sponsored Model Arrangements Safe Harbor?** Although CMS did not promulgate a specific value-based exception for participation in a CMS-sponsored payment model (such as the MSSP), the OIG did promulgate two safe harbors related to participation in CMS-sponsored payment models. These CMS-sponsored model safe harbors supersede and replace the OIG's initial MSSP waiver rules and extend to all CMS-sponsored models, although arrangements implemented under the superseded waiver rules can remain in place. The new rules are more restrictive than the waiver rules, which provided only that an MSSP Accountable Care Organization governing body determine that the subject arrangement was reasonably related to the purposes of the Medicare Shared Savings Program. Also, neither excludes "cash equivalents" such as gift cards like the general patient engagement safe harbor does, but application of each requires CMS to independently determine that the arrangement qualifies for AKS safe harbor protection. Remuneration for purposes of AKS enforcement does not include an exchange of anything of value between or among CMS-sponsored model parties under a CMS-sponsored model arrangement if all of the following conditions are met:

1. **Advancement of CMS-Sponsored Model Goals.** The participants reasonably determine that the arrangement advances at least one goal of the CMS-sponsored model.

2. **Medical Necessity.** The value exchange does not induce providers or suppliers to furnish medically unnecessary items or services or reduce or limit medically necessary items or services furnished to any patient.

3. **Influence on Referrals Outside of the CMS-Sponsored Model.** The participants do not offer, pay, solicit, or receive remuneration in return for, or to induce or reward, any federal health care program referrals or other federal health care program business generated outside of the CMS-sponsored model.

4. **Written Agreement.** The terms are memorialized in a signed writing specifying the activities of the CMS-sponsored model parties and the nature of the remuneration to be exchanged under the CMS-sponsored model arrangement.

5. **Recordkeeping.** The parties make available to CMS records sufficient to establish whether the remuneration was exchanged in accordance with the safe harbor.

6. **Compliance with CMS Requirements.** The CMS-sponsored model parties satisfy requirements imposed by CMS in connection with the use of this safe harbor.

I. **What Is the CMS-Sponsored Model Patient Incentives Safe Harbor?** In addition to the CMS-sponsored arrangements safe harbor, the OIG promulgated a safe harbor for CMS-sponsored model patient incentives that is similar to the patient engagement and support safe harbor but whose application requires a CMS determination that the safe harbor applies to the arrangement.

"Remuneration" for purposes of AKS enforcement does not include a CMS-sponsored model patient incentive if all of the following conditions are met:

1. **Advancement of CMS-Sponsored Model Goals.** The participants reasonably determine that the CMS-sponsored model patient incentive advances one or more goals of the CMS-sponsored model.

2. **Direct Connection to Patient Health Care.** The CMS-sponsored model patient incentive has a direct connection to the patient's health care unless the participation documentation expressly specifies a different standard (but does not include a restriction on whether the exchange can be in cash or a cash equivalent).

3. **Source of Patient Incentive.** The patient incentive is furnished by a CMS-sponsored model participant or its agent unless otherwise specified by the participation documentation.

4. **Recordkeeping.** The parties make available to CMS records sufficient to establish whether the remuneration was exchanged in accordance with the safe harbor.

5. **Compliance with CMS Requirements.** The CMS-sponsored model parties satisfy requirements imposed by CMS in connection with the use of this safe harbor.

VII. WHAT DOES THE OIG CLASSIFY AS A "SUSPECT CONTRACTUAL JOINT VENTURE"?

A. **Application to Ancillary Services Provided by a Physician Organization or Medical Practice.** Ancillary services transactions, and especially contractual arrangements involving the provision of therapy, pathology, imaging, durable medical equipment, anesthesia, or other ancillary services by a physician organization, medical practice, or other provider, must be analyzed to determine whether the arrangement falls within the OIG definition of "suspect contractual joint venture" under the federal Anti-Kickback Statute as described in the OIG's April 2003 Advisory Bulletin on Contractual Joint Ventures, the link to which is oig.hhs.gov/fraud/docs/alertsandbulletins/042303SABJointVentures.pdf. What the OIG regards as a "suspect contractual joint venture" is described in the following OIG Advisory Opinions: 04–17, regarding pathology labs (http://oig.hhs.gov/fraud/docs/advisoryopinions/2004/ao0417.pdf); 06–02 regarding durable medical equipment (oig.hhs.gov/fraud/docs/advisoryopinions/2006/ao0602.pdf); 11–03 regarding pharmacy services (http://oig.hhs.gov/fraud/docs/advisory opinions/2011/AdvOpn11-03.pdf): and 12–06 regarding anesthesia services at physician-owned ambulatory surgery centers (oig.hhs.gov/fraud/docs/advisoryopinions/2012/AdvOpn12-06.pdf). It is important to understand that the arrangements described in these Advisory Opinions are described as being "suspect," and not necessarily "illegal," arrangements. Nevertheless, caution is required when the facts reveal a "suspect contractual joint venture."

B. **Role of the Promoter/Manager.** The primary focus of the OIG is whether there is a promoter/manager that currently provides ancillary services in the same service area and bills Medicare and other payors directly for the ancillary services. If the promoter/manager falls within this description, then the OIG believes that, by proposing a contractual joint venture, the promoter/manager captures a referral stream without any real financial or business risk to the physician organization or medical practice.

C. **Whether the Promoter/Manager is a "Competitor".** Perhaps the most critical characteristic in what the OIG describes as "suspect contractual joint ventures" is that the "Manager/Supplier is a would-be competitor of the Owner's new line of business and would normally compete for the captive referrals. It has the capacity to provide virtually identical services in its own right and bill insurers and patients for them in its name." For example, each suspect contractual joint venture OIG Advisory Opinion involves a competitor that proposed to replicate its core business within a physician organization, medical practice, or other provider. Specifically, Advisory Opinion 04–17 involves a proposal by an anatomic pathology lab to create a pathology lab within a physician organization or medical practice, Advisory Opinion 06–02 involves an analogous proposal by a durable medical equipment company, Advisory Opinion 11–03 involves establishment of an institutional pharmacy as part of a long term care facility, and Advisory Opinion 12–06 involves establishment of an anesthesia service for a physician-owned ambulatory surgery center.

D. **Financial Risk.** The OIG will also analyze whether the medical practice undertakes substantial financial risk. If the promoter/manager offers a turn-key operation at little or no financial risk to the medical practice, the arrangement is more likely to be "suspect." The OIG found little physician organization, medical practice, or other provider risk in the proposals described in the OIG Advisory Opinions.

E. **Other Problematic Red Flags.** The OIG has also identified other "red flags" regarding contractual joint ventures as follows: (1) attempting to carve out commercial payor and private pay patients from items or services provided to federal health care program beneficiaries; (2) percentage of revenue contracts that compensate the manager/supplier based on the volume or value of referrals; and (3) arrangements under which a manager/supplier provides "management" or similar services related to the manager/supplier's goods or services.

VIII. WHAT SPECIAL RULES GOVERN BUSINESS TRANSACTIONS BY TAX EXEMPT ORGANIZATIONS?

A. **Community Benefit.** To maintain tax exempt status, a tax exempt organization must meet certain community benefit standards. Conversely, the tax exempt organization must not engage in arrangements that result in "private inurement" or "private benefit."

1. **Definition of "Inurement".** "Inurement" means transfer of an ownership interest in the tax exempt organization's assets to an "insider." The most common type of inurement is excessive or unreasonable compensation, and medical staff physicians may be considered to be "insiders."

2. **Definition of "Private Benefit".** "Private benefit" occurs when a tax exempt organization is used for the benefit of a private entity. For example, private benefit must be considered when a tax exempt organization enters into a management agreement with a private company.

3. **Revenue Procedure 2016–44.** For health care delivery systems that have issued tax exempt bonds, the Internal Revenue Service has issued Revenue Procedure 2016–44, which sets forth requirements for management agreements to avoid "private benefit" allegations. These standards apply, for example, to Co-Management Agreements between physicians and hospitals for management of hospital clinical service lines. In essence, there are limitations on the term of such management agreements. For example, payment cannot be based on the tax exempt organization's net profits, and a service provider cannot be responsible for a tax exempt organization's net losses.

B. **What Sanctions Arise from Violation of Tax Exempt Organizations Laws?**

1. **Disqualification.** Even a minimal amount of inurement can result in disqualification for tax exempt status.

2. **Intermediate Sanctions.** Monetary penalties in the form of excise taxes can be assessed against individuals and entities engaged in private inurement or private benefit transactions.

C. **Link With Anti-Kickback Statute.** In December, 1991, the IRS issued a General Counsel Memorandum which established a direct link between the Internal Revenue Code and the federal Anti-Kickback Statute in policing health industry business arrangements. The IRS emphasized that the hospital's anticipated benefits from any business arrangement of increased operating efficiency and a better competitive position through increased referrals will not be regarded by the IRS as serving the tax exempt hospital's charitable purpose. If the hospital's charitable purpose is not served, the arrangement could violate the federal Anti-Kickback Statute. The IRS appears to have adopted the OIG's expansive interpretation of the federal Anti-Kickback Statute: the Statute is violated if only one purpose of the arrangement is to induce referrals, regardless of whether there are additional, valid purposes underlying the arrangement.

D. **Audit Guidelines.** The IRS Exempt Organizations Examination Guidelines Handbook sets forth audit guidelines for evaluating hospital-physician business arrangements. The guidelines specifically require IRS auditors to determine whether an arrangement may violate the federal Anti-Kickback Statute and instruct auditors to detect unreasonable compensation in physician arrangements by looking for the following:

1. **Space Leases.** No or low rent agreements.

2. **Practice Management Services.** Less than fair market value practice management services.

3. **Income Guaranties.** Private practice income guaranties. Income guaranties are not necessarily illegal, but they should be made in the form of a physician loan as described below.

4. **Cash Payments.** Cash payments to secure or retain services.

E. **Physician Loans.** Every hospital financed physician recruitment includes a loan to a physician or medical practice. The audit guidelines set forth a specific test for determining whether loans made to a physician by a hospital or health care delivery system, in general, are reasonable. The elements of the test are as follows:

1. **Interest.** The loan must specify a reasonable rate of interest (prime plus 1% or 2%) and include adequate security.

2. **Approval.** The proposed loan should be reviewed by the hospital or health care delivery system governing Board and should include consideration of the history of payment by the physician on prior loans.

3. **Terms Must Be Reasonable.** Even if determined reasonable, any variance in the terms of the loan from what the borrower could obtain from a typical lending institution must be treated as compensation.

4. **Forgiveness.** Most loans provide repayment "forgiveness" if a physician remains in practice in the hospital's community for a specific period of time. If the physician leaves before the time period expires, the entire outstanding balance may become due and payable.

F. **Responsibility for Downside Risk By a Tax Exempt Organization Hospital That Participates in a CMS Sponsored Coordinated Care Payment Program.** Although there are clear Stark Law exceptions and federal Anti-Kickback Statute safe harbor regulations for value-based arrangements, the law governing tax exempt hospitals and health care delivery systems that participate in downside risk payment models that include independent physicians who make referrals to the hospital or health care delivery system is a bit murkier. In essence, application of the Internal Revenue Code and related rules and regulations governing organizations that are exempt from taxation under Section 501(c)(3) of the Internal Revenue Code to tax exempt organizations that participate in downside risk payment models such as as an ACO in the MSSP is unsettled. While the Internal Revenue Service promulgated "expectations" regarding tax exempt organization compliance for ACOs that participate in the MSSP in 2011, the IRS has not followed up with definitive rules and regulations. Consequently, each situation that involves acceptance of downside risk by a tax exempt hospital or health care delivery system that might benefit referring physicians must be analyzed on its own merits.

IX. WHAT IS THE CIVIL MONETARY PENALTIES LAW AND HOW DOES IT COMPLEMENT STARK AND THE ANTI-KICKBACK STATUTE?

A. **Policing Both Overutilization and Underutilization.** As discussed above, health care fraud might arise from either overutilization or underutilization of health care services. In addition to potential monetary penalties for violation of the Stark Law or the federal Anti-Kickback Statute described above, the federal Civil Monetary Penalties Law exposes providers to sanctions if they are compensated for withholding care to federal reimbursement program beneficiaries. While Stark and the Anti-Kickback Statute address interference with physician judgment leading to potential overutilization of items or services covered by the federal reimbursement programs such as traditional Medicare Part A and Part B, the Civil Monetary Penalties Law applies to coordinated care payment models, such as Medicare Advantage (Part C) and Accountable Care Organizations that participate in the Medicare Shared Savings Program.

B. **Penalties for Improper "Beneficiary Inducements".** The Civil Monetary Penalties Law also provides for monetary penalties arising from improper "beneficiary inducements" including items or services that are provided either free or at reduced costs to induce Medicare beneficiaries to use providers offering the benefits (the "Beneficiary Inducements Civil Monetary Penalties Law"). To provide guidance on what constitutes an impermissible beneficiary inducement, the OIG published a Special Advisory Bulletin titled Offering Gifts and Inducements to Beneficiaries that is published on the OIG website. In general, inexpensive gifts (other than cash or cash equivalents) or services that have a retail value of no more than $15 individually and no more than $75 in the aggregate annually per patient are permissible. Also, more expensive items or services that fit within one of these five statutory exceptions are permissible: cost-sharing waivers based on financial need;

properly disclosed copayment differentials in health plans; incentives to promote the delivery of certain preventive care services (such as vaccinations); any practice that falls within the Anti-Kickback Statute safe harbor regulations; and waivers of hospital outpatient copayments in excess of minimum copayment amounts.

C. **How is the Civil Monetary Penalties Law Applied to Value-Based Arrangements?** The OIG has also promulgated "value-based arrangement" rules regarding application of the Civil Monetary Penalties Law, but those rules are limited to telehealth services for end stage renal disease patients on home dialysis. However, providers can rely on the patient engagement and support and CMS-sponsored model patient incentives federal Anti-Kickback Statute safe harbors for Civil Monetary Penalties Law Compliance.

X. WHAT STATE LAWS GOVERN HEALTH CARE BUSINESS TRANSACTIONS?

A. **Certificate of Need ("CON") Laws.** Some states, primarily east of the Mississippi River, prohibit the development of a new institutional health service or facility or sometimes the sale of a health care facility or new institutional health service without a CON.

B. **State Self-Referral and Kickback Laws.** Some states have enacted all payor self-referral and kick-back laws similar to Stark and the federal Anti-Kickback Statute. Consequently, innovative health care delivery models that are permissible under the Stark Law or the federal Anti-Kickback Statute under, for example, the ACO fraud and abuse waivers, may be prevented from implementation because of potential violations of state health care fraud and abuse laws.

C. **State Fee Splitting Statutes.** Some arrangements may implicate state law prohibitions against physician "fee splitting."

D. **Corporate Practice of Medicine.** The "corporate practice of medicine" doctrine was developed under the law of most states in the nineteenth century and generally holds that a "corporation" cannot practice medicine. All ownership interests in enterprises that engage in the practice of medicine must be scrutinized under the corporate practice of medicine law in each state in which the enterprise will provide services. In some states, such as Florida, the doctrine has completely dissolved while in others, such as California, North Carolina, and New York, it is strictly enforced. There is a more detailed discussion of the corporate practice of medicine in Chapter 4.

XI. HOW DO YOU MANAGE REGULATORY RISK IN HEALTH CARE BUSINESS TRANSACTIONS?

A. **OIG Advisory Opinions.** There is a regulatory process that permits parties to any arrangement that implicates the federal Anti-Kickback Statute to request an advisory opinion regarding whether the arrangement exposes the parties to potential sanctions.

B. **Stark Advisory Opinions.** The Stark advisory opinion process is similar to the OIG advisory opinion process, but the request is made to CMS, not the OIG.

C. **Stark and OIG Self Disclosure Protocols.** Potential Stark or Anti-Kickback Statute violations can be discovered in merger, acquisition, or financing due diligence. Frequently, potential purchasers or capital financing sources require the target company to self-disclose the potential violation in accordance with the protocols established by CMS for Stark violations and the OIG for Anti-Kickback Statute violations. Also, even if the transaction does not proceed, the target company will be compelled to self-disclose under applicable law as described in greater detail in Chapter 11.

D. **Corporate Compliance Plans.** Every organization that is involved in the health industry, regardless of whether the organization is a provider or a supplier of goods and services, should implement a Corporate Compliance and Ethics Plan in accordance with the Federal Sentencing Guidelines. This is no longer discretionary. The ACA requires that, as a condition of enrollment in Medicare or Medicaid, providers and suppliers must establish compliance programs that satisfy requirements to be established by the Secretary of the Department of Health and Human Services in consultation with OIG. Implementation of Corporate Compliance and Ethics Programs is also described in greater detail in Chapter 11.

E. **Risk Factors in Securities Documents.** If your business arrangement implicates the health care regulatory laws, you must disclose the regulatory risk to potential investors, and you can mitigate the risk through the advisory opinion process.

CHAPTER 2

UNDERSTANDING FUNDAMENTAL CONTRACT LAW: CONTRACTS 101

I. UNDERSTANDING CONTRACTUAL RELATIONSHIPS

A. **Life Is a Series of Contractual Arrangements.** Understanding contract law is important because life is a series of contractual arrangements. Contractual terms and conditions are omnipresent and permeate every aspect of our existence. For example, businesses depend on agreements to borrow funds from banks and other lenders; employment and independent contractor agreements to obtain human resources as well as retirement and benefit plans for their personnel; contracts with sources that supply goods and services that are essential for business operations; licensing of intellectual property such as software and copyrightable works; contracts that govern mergers and acquisitions; and many other contractual arrangements. Individuals also have many contractual relationships, such as agreements to purchase a new car, to obtain a credit card, and to obtain a home mortgage. Therefore, although every person can benefit from an understanding of the general law of contracts, it is absolutely essential for business managers and entrepreneurs.

B. **Contracts Create Rights and Obligations.** In essence, contracts create rights, which may or may not be assignable, and obligations or duties, which may or may not be delegable.

II. WHAT LAW IS APPLIED TO CONTRACTUAL ARRANGEMENTS?

A. **Federal Contract Law.** The Congress of the United States has enacted legislation, and the executive branch has adopted implementing regulations, for defense contracts, government contracts, and other contractual arrangements that involve the federal government, such as contracts involving health care providers that participate in the Medicare program. These bodies of law are very specific and beyond the scope of a discussion of general contract law. However, Congress has also enacted other legislation that has more universal application, such as the Magnuson-Moss Warranty Act, which is discussed in more detail below.

B. **State Statutes and Regulations.** Most aspects of contractual relationships are governed by state law.

1. **General Law of Contracts.** In all states, the common law principles of contract law are "codified" into laws enacted by the state legislature. The general law of contracts applies to all contractual arrangements except for specific kinds of contracts that are governed by the Uniform Commercial Code ("UCC").

2. **Uniform Commercial Code ("UCC").** Because state law governs most contractual arrangements, and because the states want to facilitate interstate commerce, a model act called the "Uniform Commercial Code" (referred to as the "UCC") was developed. Article 2 of the UCC, which will be discussed in detail in this chapter, governs the purchase and sale of goods. "Goods" means all things (including specially manufactured goods) that are movable at the time of identification. Each state, except Louisiana, whose state law is not based on the English common law, has enacted a version of the UCC. Louisiana has enacted all parts of the UCC except Article 2, so contracts for the purchase and sale of goods in Louisiana are governed by Louisiana civil laws. In general, UCC Article 2 does not cover contracts for the purchase and sale of services, intangible property rights (such as copyrights, patents, and trademarks), or real property. The UCC also sets forth the primary law regarding negotiable instruments (such as promissory notes) and security interests (which, for example, lenders use to secure payment on money loaned to a person or business), which are described in other chapters.

3. **Two Bodies of Contract Law Exist in Each State.** Therefore, in each state there are two separate and mutually exclusive bodies of contract law: (1) the UCC, which governs the purchase and sale of goods (in each state except Louisiana), the creation and conveyance of negotiable instruments (in all states), and the enforcement of security interests (in all states); and (2) the general law of contracts, which is a code that is usually founded on the principles of the English common law of contracts and governs all other contractual relationships. When the UCC sets forth specific provisions for contracts, the UCC applies. When it does not, the common law of contracts applies. In other words, when the UCC applies, it supersedes the common law of contracts. There is never a situation in which both bodies of law apply: it is either one or the other. Therefore, in any contract analysis, you first must ask: does the UCC apply?

C. **State Courts.** The state courts interpret the general law of contracts and state legislation such as the UCC. Since contracts and contract disputes generally arise under state law, most contract disputes are resolved by state courts, and federal courts are required to apply applicable state law when the federal court has jurisdiction in a diversity of citizenship case.

D. **Contracts Create Private Law.** Within the context of state and applicable federal law, contracts, in essence, create a private "law" that governs a specific transaction or arrangement. The key question to ask when a contract dispute arises is: What was the intent of the parties? Consequently, if a contract dispute arises, the first place to look is within the four corners of the agreement (if it is in writing) or other evidence of the intent of the parties.

III. WHAT IS A CONTRACT?

A. **Enforceable Promise and Risk Allocation Mechanism.** People make promises every day. A contract is an enforceable promise. In other words, one party to a contract can, by getting an order from a court, force the other party to do what they promised. Contracts are also risk allocation mechanisms. There are risks inherent in every contractual arrangement. For example, if a business purchases a piece of equipment, there is a risk that it will malfunction. To mitigate that risk, the purchaser will negotiate a warranty. Therefore, every contract involves a series of "if this happens, then what are the consequences?" questions and answers. However, no matter how experienced the parties are, they may never be able to identify all of the possible risks, and, at the heart of each contractual arrangement, each party must trust the other party.

B. **What Are the Elements of an Enforceable Promise?** In, general, there are three fundamental elements to each contractual arrangement.

1. **Offer.** Each contract requires an offer, which is an expression of willingness to enter into a bargain.

2. **Acceptance.** To form a contract, there must be acceptance of an offer. Acceptance is a manifestation of assent to the terms and conditions of the offer. Therefore, an enforceable contract requires mutual assent to an ascertainable set of terms and conditions.

3. **Consideration.** "Consideration" generally means something of value given in exchange for a promise. Many offers are made, and many are accepted, but, for contracts in the normal course of business, "consideration" distinguishes enforceable promises from unenforceable promises.

IV. MUTUAL ASSENT

A. **Two Components of Mutual Assent.** The two components of mutual assent are offer and acceptance. The "reasonable person" common law standard is applied: would a reasonable and prudent person believe that an offer was made or accepted? The common law term for mutual assent is the "meeting of the minds."

B. **Offer.** An offer occurs when one person confers upon another the power to create contractual relations between them. The offeror creates power of acceptance in the offeree.

1. **Offeror Controls the Offer.** The offeror is the master of offer and can decide what conditions apply.

2. **How Is the Offer Nullified?** The offer will be null, void, and of no further effect upon occurrence of any of the following:

   a. revocation by the offeror at any time prior to acceptance;

   b. an unreasonable lapse of time for acceptance;

   c. the death or incapacity of either party;

   d. rejection by the offeree; or

   e. a counteroffer by the offeree. Since most negotiations involve a series of counteroffers, this is the most common way in which an offer is nullified.

3. **What If the Offer is Ambiguous?** Any ambiguity should be construed against the offeror.

C. **Acceptance.** Acceptance is a manifestation of assent in a manner invited or required by the offer. Once appropriately accepted, an enforceable contract is formed and both parties are bound. Therefore, each offer and counteroffer must be carefully weighed to determine whether there is sufficient mutual gain to make the arrangement acceptable to both parties. Acceptance can be manifested in any manner reasonable under the circumstances.

1. **How Is the Power of Acceptance Terminated?** The power of acceptance may be terminated upon occurrence of any of the following:

   a. rejection or counteroffer by the offeree;

   b. an unreasonable lapse of time;

   c. revocation by the offeror;

d. death or incapacity of either party; or

e. non-occurrence of a condition of acceptance under the terms of the offer.

2. **Who Can Accept an Offer?** Only the person who is invited by the offeror to accept may accept an offer.

3. **What Happens If an "Acceptance" Includes Additional Terms?** If an acceptance adds additional terms that the offeror must accept, then it is not an acceptance, but a counteroffer. This was known in common law as the "mirror image rule."

V. WHAT KINDS OF CONSIDERATION OR SUBSTITUTES FOR CONSIDERATION MAKE A PROMISE ENFORCEABLE?

A. **What Is "Consideration"?** Consideration is a bargained for exchange that has elements of mutual inducement. In general, each party to the contract must promise to provide something of value to the other party.

1. **What Happens If the Consideration is Nominal?** If the consideration is nominal, the courts may find that no consideration was exchanged and the contract is unenforceable. Under the English common law, some parties tried to make agreements enforceable by stating that the consideration for the contractual agreement was an "acorn." However, this would likely be deemed inadequate consideration for an enforceable contractual obligation.

2. **Are Promises to Make Gifts or Charitable Contributions Enforceable?** Generally, oral promises to make gifts or charitable contributions are "gratuitous promises" that lack the essential element of a bargained for exchange and are not enforceable. However, if the pledge is in writing, and the charitable organization proceeds in detrimental reliance on the pledge, the promise may be enforceable.

B. **When Can a Contract Be Enforceable Without Consideration?**

1. **Quasi-Contract or Unjust Enrichment.** Sometimes, a promise plus subsequent benefit can be enforceable. If a party provides a benefit that the other party accepts knowing that the supplying party expects payment, the agreement could be enforceable to prevent "unjust enrichment."

2. **Option Contracts.** A contract providing a party with an option that can be exercised in the future does not require consideration.

3. **Guaranties.** The guaranty of another party's debts or obligations does not require consideration to the guarantor. However, if the underlying contract is unenforceable, there is nothing to guaranty.

VI. WHAT KINDS OF CONTRACTS ARE ENFORCEABLE?

A. **Freedom of Contract.** There is a long line of cases in virtually every jurisdiction that provides that persons who are able to enter into contracts are free to enter into any agreement that is not illegal or otherwise void as against public policy, even if the contract terms seem unfair or onerous.

B. **Folly Is Not Fraud.** Some parties to seemingly unfair or onerous contracts have asserted that the unfairness constitutes "fraud." However, most courts will hold that "folly is not fraud." In other words, even if one could question the complete lack of judgment of one party to a contract, that party's "folly" is not "fraud."

VII. WHAT CONTRACTS MUST BE IN WRITING TO BE ENFORCEABLE?

A. **Are Oral Contracts Enforceable?** Unless the law requires otherwise, oral contracts are enforceable. However, it is more difficult to prove the terms and conditions of an oral contract. In the business context, there is a presumption that the parties intend their oral agreements to be enforceable.

B. **What Contracts Must Be in Writing?** The Statute of Frauds, which traces its roots to a law enacted in England in 1677 and is part of the statutory or common law of virtually all jurisdictions, requires certain contracts to be in writing to be enforceable. Examples include the following:

1. **Real Property.** Contracts for the purchase or sale of real estate.

2. **The "One Year" Rule.** Contracts that cannot be performed within one year.

3. **Surety.** Any contract under which a party agrees to be responsible for the debts or obligations of another party, such as a guaranty of a loan.

4. **UCC Statute of Frauds.** The UCC has its own Statute of Frauds, which, in most jurisdictions, provides that all contracts for the purchase of goods in excess of $500 must be in writing.

VIII. WHAT KINDS OF CONTRACTS ARE UNENFORCEABLE?

A. **Doctrine of Unconscionability.** The doctrine of unconscionability applies when an agreement is unfair on its face. Determination of whether a contract is "unconscionable" is independent of the consideration doctrine.

1. **Substantive Unconscionability.** Substantive unconscionability could apply when there is a disparity in value. Is there a significant difference between the cost of the good or service in the community and the cost in the contract?

2. **Procedural Unconscionability.** Procedural unconscionability arises from an unfair advantage in or abuse of the bargaining process. This is sometimes called "adhesion contracts," meaning that, because of the substantial bargaining power of one party, the other party has no choice but to sign the contract.

3. **Reconciliation With Other Doctrines.** Note that the doctrine of "unconscionability" seems to directly contradict the doctrine of "freedom of contract" and its related maxim in equity that "folly is not fraud." This leads to an important learning point: in contract disputes, there is almost always "another side to the story."

B. **Pre-Existing Duty Rule.** Under the common law, the performance of, or the promise to perform, a pre-existing duty is not consideration. In other words, if there is a pre-existing duty, there can be no "inducement" to enter into a promise.

C. **Illegal Contracts.** Contracts that are contrary to law are illegal and unenforceable. Examples are as follows:

1. **Contract to Perform an Illegal Act.** A contract to perform an illegal act cannot be enforced, even if the act is performed.

2. **Contracts in General Restraint of Trade.** Contracts that generally restrain trade, such as contracts to create a monopoly, are illegal and unenforceable. However, as explained below, contracts in partial restraint of trade may be enforceable if the restraint is "reasonable."

D. **Capacity.** A contract with a person who does not have "capacity" to understand what they are doing is unenforceable. For example, contracts with minors or persons with diminished mental capacity (called "*non compos mentis*") are unenforceable. Contracts entered into during a spell of temporary incapacity, such as intoxication, may be enforceable.

E. **Authority.** To enforce the contractual obligations of an entity such as a corporation, the person who executes the agreement must have the "authority" to enter into the agreement on behalf of the entity. "Actual authority" is authority that is expressly conferred on a person to act on behalf of an entity. "Apparent authority" arises when a person "apparently" has authority to bind an entity to a contractual obligation, even though the person may not have "actual authority." Some persons who have managerial titles such as "President" or "Chief Executive Officer" have apparent authority to bind a corporation to a contractual arrangement, even if the corporation's bylaws prohibit it. For example, the President of a corporation may enter into an agreement to acquire capital equipment for a purchase price of $250,000 without approval of the Board of Directors, but the corporation's bylaws may provide that any capital expenditure in excess of $100,000 requires approval of the Board of Directors. The corporation cannot avoid the contractual obligation on the grounds that the President did not have "actual authority" because the equipment supplier reasonably and detrimentally relied on the President's apparent authority to bind the corporation to the contract.

F. **Agreements to Agree.** Any agreement, even if signed by the parties, that states that it is subject to a more definitive agreement or is otherwise conditioned on a future agreement is generally unenforceable. A common commercial example of an "agreement to agree" is a "Letter of Intent" executed in connection with a proposed merger or acquisition as described in Chapter 7. While the Letter of Intent typically describes the expected financial terms and conditions of the transaction, it also typically states that enforceability of the arrangement is contingent upon execution of a "definitive agreement" for the transaction. This is a clear example of an "agreement to agree," so the terms and conditions of the transaction described in the Letter of Intent are unenforceable.

G. **Conditions Precedent and Conditions Subsequent.** Some contracts require the fulfillment of some condition prior to commencement of a contractual obligation (a "condition precedent"). Also, the occurrence of some condition after a contract is executed but before it is completely performed (a "condition subsequent") may frustrate the purpose of the agreement and render it unenforceable. For example, an employment agreement between a medical practice and a physician may provide that commencement of the agreement is conditioned on the physician obtaining a license in the state where the medical practice is located. This is a "condition precedent." Using the same example, the physician may obtain the license, but the medical practice may be acquired before the employment agreement commences. Since the medical practice no longer exists, the contract is "frustrated" and cannot be enforced. This is a "condition subsequent."

IX. WHAT IF THERE IS A MISTAKE?

A. **What If the Mistake is Mutual?** There is no mutual assent if both parties know that they have attached different meanings to their promises, and the contract can be voided.

B. **What Is a "Mutual Mistake"?** The essential elements of a "mutual mistake" are as follows:

1. **Basic Assumption**. The mistake must relate to a basic assumption on which the contract was made.

2. **Material Effect.** The mistake must have a material effect on the agreed upon exchange.

3. **Risk**. The adversely affected party must not have imposed the risk.

C. **What Is Not a Mutual Mistake?** Assumptions of future events that do not take place are not mutual mistakes. For example, a change in market conditions that makes a contract disadvantageous does not constitute a mutual mistake.

D. **What If the Mistake is Unilateral?** When only one party is mistaken, it is more difficult to avoid the contract. The aggrieved party must also show that the other party had reason to know about the mistake, that the other party somehow caused the mistake, or that forcing the mistaken party to proceed with the contract would be "unconscionable."

E. **What If the Party Was Mistaken Because of a Failure to Read the Contract Carefully?** This is not a mistake that will lead to relief. The courts will generally enforce contracts, even if they appear unbalanced, if they are entered into by competent parties. This is an example of the "freedom of contract" principle.

X. ONCE CREATED, HOW IS A CONTRACT INTERPRETED?

A. **All Contract Interpretation Focuses on the Intent of the Parties.** Since a contract, in essence, creates "private law" for a specific transaction or arrangement, the key purpose to all contract interpretation is ascertaining the intent of the parties.

B. **General Rule: The Contract Speaks for Itself.** In general, if a contract is clear and unambiguous within "the four corners of the agreement," then the agreement is deemed to be "fully integrated," and no other evidence regarding the meaning of the contract is admissible.

C. **What Happens When the Contract Language is Incomplete?**

1. **Parol Evidence Rule.** If the contract is not fully integrated, then the "parol evidence rule" applies, and parties can introduce oral evidence of the missing or incomplete terms.

2. **Strict Construction.** There are some contract provisions that are subject to "strict construction." The contract terms must be clear on the face of the document, and oral testimony regarding intent of the parties will not be admitted. Examples of such clauses are "restrictive covenants" that are in partial restraint of trade and "surety" contracts that require a party to be responsible for a third-party's obligations, including a personal guaranty of a corporate obligation such as a lease or a promissory note.

D. **What Happens When the Contract Language Is Ambiguous?** Generally, courts will construe contracts against the party who drafted the agreement. To mitigate this, some contracts include clauses that state that the parties had equal opportunity to review the contract and, therefore, the contract should not be construed against the drafting party. Also, courts almost always allow outside evidence to clarify ambiguous terms.

E. **Are There Other Ways That Outside Evidence Can Be Introduced to Interpret the Intent of the Parties?** Most courts allow outside testimony or evidence related to the following:

1. **Course of Performance.** Evidence describing how the parties have actually performed under the agreement is admissible.

2. **Course of Dealing.** If the parties have engaged in a series of transactions, then evidence of their course of dealing with each other is admissible.

3. **Custom and Usage in the Industry.** Evidence of custom and usage in the industry is also admissible. For example, "custom and usage" evidence can be entered to define terms commonly used or business practices typically followed in a specific industry.

XI. WHAT TERMS AND CONDITIONS ARE TYPICALLY FOUND IN CONTRACTS?

A. **Substantive Terms and Conditions.** Most contract negotiations are focused on the substantive terms and conditions of the transaction or arrangement. Substantive terms and conditions may include: (1) a description of the goods, services, or other property being provided or conveyed; (2) financial and payment terms; and (3) term and termination of the agreement. For example, a business may enter into an agreement for consulting or management services. If so, the parties are inclined to focus on describing the scope of the services, payment terms, the term of the agreement, and how it may be terminated, and, perhaps, intellectual property rights during the negotiation process.

B. **Special Terms and Conditions.** Many agreements include special terms and conditions. Examples include, without limitation, indemnification, warranty, limitation of liability, liquidated damages, and restraint of trade clauses, each of which merits specific attention.

C. **Indemnification Clauses.**

1. **What Is an Indemnification Clause?** Indemnification clauses are perplexing and among the most difficult provisions to understand and negotiate. In general, "indemnify" means to compensate another party for damages, losses, or expenses they incur. For example, in a construction contract, the owner may require the construction contractor to indemnify the owner for any claims made against the owner by third parties arising from the contractor's negligence. As another example, a hospital that engages the services of a management

company may require the manager to indemnify the hospital for claims made against the hospital arising out of a failure by the management company to perform its services in a manner that complies with the statutes and regulations governing the health industry. As a final example, an entity that enters into a license agreement that permits the use of computer software or other work that may be governed by copyright or patent law may require an indemnification clause that requires the licensor to indemnify the licensee for claims of infringement by third parties arising from use of the computer software. These seem like simple concepts. However, the language used in indemnification clauses is often confusing.

2. **Example of an Indemnification Clause.** This is a sample indemnification clause:

   Indemnification. Each party hereby agrees to indemnify, defend, and hold harmless the other party and its officers, partners, employees, and agents from and against any and all claims, losses, damages, costs, expenses, liabilities, assessments, judgments, or deficiencies of any nature whatsoever, including, without limitation, reasonable attorneys' fees and other costs and expenses incident to any suit, action, or proceeding, which may arise out of, result from, or constitute any breach of any representation, warranty, or covenant contained in this Agreement.

3. **Negotiation of Indemnification Clauses.** As a general rule, parties want to avoid indemnification obligations. Therefore, when confronted with an indemnification clause, the first position to take is to request deletion of all indemnification obligations. If the other party insists on indemnification, then the usual response is to make the indemnification obligations mutual when this makes sense. The clause set forth above is an example of a simple mutual indemnification clause.

4. **Limitations on Indemnification Obligations.** Under the law of most jurisdictions, an indemnification clause cannot apply if the indemnified party is responsible for the costs or damages. In other words, you cannot be indemnified for your own negligent acts or contract breaches. Also, the parties can negotiate limitations on indemnification obligations. For example, in mergers and acquisition contracts, it is typical for the parties to negotiate a threshold "basket" amount that must be reached before there are any indemnification obligations that arise as well as time limitations for asserting indemnification claims.

D. **Warranties.** A "warranty" is, in general, an assurance of some particular matter that is an essential element of the contractual arrangement. Warranties can be express (stated in clear terms in the contract) or implied (not expressly stated but understood by custom and usage in the industry, a course of dealing between the parties, or the nature of the transaction to be an essential part of the contractual arrangement). In general, breach of a warranty will result in damages to the other party.

1. **Warranties in General Contracts.** In many contracts, representations and warranties are expressly made and form the core of the agreement. For example, in contracts for mergers and acquisitions or for capital financing, the seller or borrower is required to make extensive representations and warranties, and a breach would lead to indemnification obligations as described above. For example, a seller or borrower is typically required to represent and warrant that the seller or borrower is not involved in any litigation that might decrease the value of its business or threaten its ability to repay a loan.

2. **Warranties Related to the Purchase and Sale of Goods.** Warranties related to the purchase and sale of goods are governed by the UCC. In addition to any warranties expressly provided in the contract, the UCC also provides implied warranties of merchantability, implied warranties arising from a course of dealing or custom and usage in a trade, and implied warranties of fitness for a specific purpose unless the contract expressly excludes those warranties. Therefore, most contracts for the purchase and sale of goods (to which the UCC applies), and many contracts for the purchase of items to which the UCC may not apply (such as computer software), contain warranty disclaimer provisions.

3. **Warranty Disclaimer Provisions.** One way to exclude warranties is to include an "as is" clause in the contract. Under this provision, the seller agrees to provide the property or services under the contract "as is, where is, and with no further warranties." The UCC also has specific requirements for warranty disclaimers, and clauses that comply with the UCC requirements are sometimes used in contracts to which the UCC does not apply. A typical warranty disclaimer clause is as follows:

   EXCEPT AS PROVIDED IN THE SPECIFIC WARRANTIES SET OUT HEREIN, ALL SERVICES AND PRODUCTS PROVIDED UNDER THIS AGREEMENT ARE PROVIDED ON AN "AS IS" BASIS. NEITHER SELLER NOR ANY OF ITS AFFILIATES, EMPLOYEES, OFFICERS, DIRECTORS, AGENTS, OR LICENSORS WARRANTS THAT THE SERVICES OR PRODUCTS PROVIDED PURSUANT TO THIS AGREEMENT WILL BE DEFECT FREE, NOR DO THEY WARRANT THAT CERTAIN RESULTS MAY BE OBTAINED BY PURCHASER IN CONNECTION WITH SELLER'S RENDERING OF SERVICES OR PROVISION OF PRODUCTS HEREUNDER. SELLER AND ITS AFFILIATES, EMPLOYEES, OFFICERS, DIRECTORS, AGENTS, AND LICENSORS MAKE NO WARRANTY, GUARANTEE, OR REPRESENTATION, EITHER EXPRESS OR IMPLIED, REGARDING THE MERCHANTABILITY, TITLE, OR FITNESS FOR A PARTICULAR PURPOSE OF ANY SERVICES OR PRODUCTS PROVIDED UNDER THIS AGREEMENT.

4. **Magnuson-Moss Warranty Act.** The Magnuson-Moss Warranty Act is a federal consumer protection law that applies to the purchase and sale of consumer products that come with an express written warranty. The Act distinguishes between "full" and "limited" warranties, requires warranties to be presented conspicuously, and provides consumers with remedies for a breach of warranty. The Act does not preempt state law. Therefore, all state laws, including the UCC, also apply to transactions that are regulated by the Magnuson-Moss Warranty Act. Any entity that offers consumer products for sale must obtain a complete understanding of the Magnuson-Moss Warranty Act.

E. **Limitation of Liability.** Contractual provisions that limit liability of the parties are another way to limit the risk of a breach of a warranty. Limitation of liability clauses are found in all types of agreements, but are frequently based on the specific contractual arrangement. There are several ways in which liability may be limited, including limitation on the amount of damages that may be recovered, limitation of the types of damages that may be asserted, and limitation on the time for asserting a claim of breach of contract. For example, a contract between a consultant and business may provide that any damages under the arrangement are limited to the amount that the business paid the consultant for its services and that the claim must be made within a year of the date when services were terminated. Also, the UCC has specific requirements for limitation of liability clauses. A typical limitation of liability clause that complies with the UCC is as follows:

> **NOTWITHSTANDING ANY TERM OR PROVISION CONTAINED IN THIS AGREEMENT, IN NO EVENT SHALL SELLER BE LIABLE TO PURCHASER OR TO ANY OTHER PERSON OR ENTITY, FOR ANY INDIRECT, INCIDENTAL, SPECIAL, CONSEQUENTIAL, EXEMPLARY, OR PUNITIVE DAMAGES, OR OTHER SIMILAR TYPE OF DAMAGES, ARISING OUT OF OR IN ANY WAY RELATED TO THIS AGREEMENT, THE PERFORMANCE THEREOF, THE USE OF THE PRODUCTS PROMISED OR SERVICES DELIVERED PURSUANT TO THIS AGREEMENT OR SELLER'S ALLEGED BREACH OF THIS AGREEMENT, REGARDLESS OF WHETHER SELLER KNEW OR SHOULD HAVE KNOWN OF THE POSSIBILITY OF SUCH DAMAGES IN ADVANCE.**
>
> **UNDER NO CIRCUMSTANCES WHATSOEVER SHALL SELLER BE LIABLE TO PURCHASER OR TO ANY OTHER PERSON OR ENTITY FOR DAMAGES OF ANY KIND ARISING OUT OF OR IN ANY WAY RELATED TO THIS AGREEMENT, THE PERFORMANCE THEREOF, THE PRODUCTS OR SERVICES DELIVERED PURSUANT TO THIS AGREEMENT, OR SELLER'S ALLEGED BREACH OF THIS AGREEMENT, IN ANY AMOUNT OF MONEY WHICH SHALL EXCEED THE AMOUNT OF THE FEE PAID BY PURCHASER TO SELLER WITH RESPECT TO THE PRODUCTS OR SERVICES PROVIDED UNDER THIS AGREEMENT.**

THE LIMITATIONS ON LIABILITY SET FORTH IN THIS SECTION SHALL APPLY TO ALL CAUSES OF ACTION, INCLUDING, WITHOUT LIMITATION, BREACH OF CONTRACT, BREACH OF WARRANTY, STRICT LIABILITY, NEGLIGENT MISREPRESENTATION AND OTHER TORTS, AND LIABILITY BASED UPON THE PROVISIONS OF ANY PART OF THIS AGREEMENT AND ANY FEDERAL, STATE, OR LOCAL LAW/OR ORDINANCE. THE LIMITATIONS ON LIABILITY REPRESENT A FUNDAMENTAL TERM OF THIS AGREEMENT, AND SELLER WOULD NOT HAVE ENTERED INTO THIS AGREEMENT WITHOUT THEIR INCLUSION.

NO ACTION, REGARDLESS OF FORM, ARISING OUT OF THIS AGREEMENT, MAY BE BROUGHT BY PURCHASER AGAINST SELLER MORE THAN ONE YEAR AFTER THE CAUSE OF ACTION HAS ARISEN.

F. **Liquidated Damages.** Sometimes the parties agree in advance to the amount of damages that might arise from a breach and put that specific amount in the contract. This is referred to as a "liquidated damages" clause. A "liquidated damages" clause is appropriate when actual damages will be difficult or impossible to ascertain and the parties agree in advance upon a reasonable amount of damages arising from a breach of contract. For example, a contract may have a restrictive covenant that restrains competition, and the parties may agree that, in the event of a breach, the breaching party will pay the non-breaching party $150,000. Liquidated damages clauses are very common in construction contracts as a means to measure damages arising from construction delays. However, the amount of the liquidated damages cannot be either a penalty or forfeiture, which would be unenforceable. Therefore, there is always some risk that a liquidated damages clause could be challenged as being an illegal penalty.

G. **Agreements in Restraint of Trade.** Agreements in general restraint of trade (such as agreements to create a monopoly) have long been illegal and unenforceable under the common law and general contract law. However, agreements in partial restraint of trade are enforceable if they are "reasonable." Such provisions, also called "restrictive covenants," are commonly found in employment agreements and in mergers and acquisitions agreements. For example, if a business purchases another business, the purchaser does not want the seller to turn around and start a competing business. In general, such clauses are enforceable if they are reasonable as to time, territory, and activity restrained and are also reasonable as to each party and the general public. The law governing agreements in restraint of trade has peculiarities in each state, and such clauses must be closely scrutinized.

H. **"Boilerplate" Contract Terms are Important.** Regardless of the substantive terms and conditions of a contract, virtually all contracts include terms and conditions at the end of the contract that are referred to as "boilerplate" provisions. The term "boilerplate" may lead you to believe that the terms and conditions that are commonly found in virtually all contracts are unimportant. This is a misconception. "Boilerplate" terms and conditions are extremely important for allocating contractual risk, and careful attention to boilerplate clauses can lead to litigation avoidance. Also, there are several different ways in which the "boilerplate" terms may be expressed. A comprehensive, but by no means exhaustive, list of boilerplate contract terms is as follows:

1. **Entire Agreement.** This clause is generally buried at the end of a contract but it may be the most important boilerplate clause. In general, this clause will provide that (a) the agreement constitutes the entire agreement between the parties and (b) all prior representations of the parties, whether written or oral, are merged into the agreement. In other words, if something is not expressed in the agreement, even if the parties discussed it, it is not enforceable. In my experience, I have seen this clause help to avoid many lawsuits. Parties will frequently take the position that, regardless of the terms and conditions of the agreement, the parties had a side deal or separate understanding. This clause can kill those arguments. Every contract should include an "entire agreement" clause.

2. **Amendments.** If the agreement constitutes the entire agreement of the parties, the parties must agree on how the agreement can be amended. In most agreements, amendments must be in writing and signed by the parties. However, there may be items that can be changed without formal amendment of the agreement. Therefore, you may need to consider how to amend the contract.

3. **Waiver of Breach.** Sometimes, one party may be in technical breach of the precise terms and conditions of the agreement, but, if the only remedy available is termination of the agreement, the non-breaching party may want to give the breaching party a second chance and not terminate the agreement. However, the non-breaching party will not want this isolated instance to constitute a waiver of the breaching party's obligations if it happens again. Therefore, you will frequently see a clause that provides that the waiver by either party of a breach or violation of any provision of the agreement shall not operate as or be construed to be a waiver of any subsequent breach of the same or other provisions of the agreement. For example, this clause is very important in construction contracts.

4. **Assignment.** When parties enter into an agreement, they generally intend to do business with each other. Therefore, a typical clause provides that no assignment of the agreement or the rights and obligations under the agreement will be valid without the specific written consent of both parties. However, there are frequently exceptions that need to be considered. For example, one party may be looking forward to a liquidation event in which either all of the party's assets are sold or the party is merged into an acquiring entity, and it is not uncommon to see a clause that permits assignment to an entity that purchases all or substantially all of an entity's assets or an entity into which a party is merged.

5. **Force Majeure.** Sometimes, parties will want to avoid performance if there is an unforeseen event. For example, the events of September 11, 2001 made it impossible for performance of some contracts. Therefore, some agreements provide that neither party shall be liable nor deemed to be in default for any delay or failure in performance under the agreement or other interruption of service resulting directly or indirectly from acts of "force majeure," including acts of God; acts of civil or military authorities; acts of public enemies or war; accidents; fires; explosions; earthquakes; floods; failure of transportation; pandemic disease; strikes or other work interruptions by either party's employees; or any cause beyond the reasonable control of either party.

6. **Governing Law.** When parties are in different states, they may want the agreement to be governed by the law of their own state. If there is not a governing law clause, the governing law will be decided by the principles of "conflicts of laws." Therefore, it is important to include a governing law clause in a contract. However, unless the choice of law is California, New York, or another state that has a complicated statutory and regulatory system, negotiation of the governing law clause should rarely be a deal killer.

7. **Attorneys' Fees.** Under the English legal system, the party that loses in litigation pays the winner's court costs and attorneys' fees. In the United States, however, the general rule is that each party pays its own costs and attorneys' fees, regardless of the outcome. Therefore, to dissuade frivolous litigation, agreements sometimes include a clause providing that, in the event that either party resorts to legal action to enforce the terms and provisions of the agreement, the successful party shall be entitled to recover the costs of such action so incurred including, without limitation, reasonable attorneys' fees.

8. **Third-Party Beneficiaries.** Some agreements intend to provide a specific third party with rights under the agreement, even when the third parties are not direct parties to the agreement. This is known as an "intended third-party beneficiary." Conversely, an "incidental beneficiary" has no rights under the contract. Therefore, it is a good practice to include a clause that identifies intended third-party beneficiaries.

9. **Notices.** Many contracts will provide that the parties are required to provide each other with "notice" to assert certain rights under the agreement. For example, if there is a breach of the agreement, the non-breaching party will need to provide "notice" of the breach to the allegedly breaching party before proceeding with termination or other contractual rights. Therefore, each agreement must have a "notice" clause. It was formerly common practice to allow notice to be given by "certified mail, return receipt requested." However, this is a slow and antiquated method of providing notice. Modern contracts allow notice to be delivered by a reliable overnight delivery service that provides evidence of receipt or, in

some instances, by facsimile or electronic mail. Therefore, careful attention must be given to the notice provision.

10. **Counterparts.** Frequently, the parties are not in the same place when the contract is executed. Also, most states now allow contracts to be executed by electronic signature. In fact, today there are rarely face-to-face closings of agreements, even large merger and acquisition agreements. Therefore, many agreements need a clause providing that the agreement and any amendments thereto may be signed in multiple counterparts and that each counterpart shall be deemed an original, but all counterparts together shall constitute one and the same instrument.

11. **Additional Assurances.** To avoid arguments that the agreement is found in the four corners of the document, it is helpful to include a clause stating the terms and conditions of the agreement are self-operative and shall not require further agreement by the parties except as specifically provided to the contrary.

12. **Severability.** It is common practice to include a clause providing that the terms and conditions of the agreement are severable. A typical clause will provide that, in the event any provision of the agreement is held to be unenforceable for any reason, the unenforceability thereof shall not affect the remainder of the agreement, which shall remain in full force and effect and enforceable in accordance with its terms, unless such would frustrate the original purposes thereof.

13. **Headings.** It is common practice to put headings on sections of the agreement, but they should not be used in interpreting the meaning of the precise terms and conditions of the agreement. A typical clause provides that the articles and other headings contained in the agreement are for reference purposes only and shall not affect in any way the meaning or interpretation of the agreement.

I. **What Contract Provisions Require Particular Scrutiny After the COVID 19 Public Health Emergency?** The economic disruption arising from the COVID public health emergency caused virtually all business enterprises to review contract terms and conditions to mitigate contractual and financial risk. What happens if a supply chain is disrupted because a government or governmental agency closes an economy? For example, what if a critical component like a computer chip is manufactured in a nation that has a "shelter in place" order, causing the chip manufacturer to default on the delivery terms of a supply agreement, in turn causing the chip manufacturer's customer to default on an agreement for delivery of a finished product? What if the inability to conduct business is based on an industry stopping its services because the cost of providing services is greater than the cost of shutting down? For example, what if business operations rely on open air travel, but airlines cancel flights to preserve liquidity? What if a public health emergency causes a business to incur financial losses, making it impossible to fulfill positive and negative covenants in a bank Loan Agreement and to default on payment obligations? Last, since the virus can be transmitted anywhere, what contract terms and conditions cans shield a business from a claim that the virus was transmitted because a business opened to the public but did not implement sufficient safeguards to prevent transmission either to a consumer or from worker to worker? For example, what if a concert venue opens and an infection hotspot can be traced to the concert venue? Many of the risks arising from a public health emergency have always been present, but historically the chances of their coming into play seemed remote. With the exception of the 1918 Spanish Flu, the economy was not materially disrupted by many virus epidemics and pandemics such as polio, Severe Acute Respiratory Syndrome (SARS), Middle Eastern Respiratory Syndrome (MERS), H1N1 Swine Flu, Bird Flu, and other annual flu viruses. However, after COVID 19, the game has changed for every business enterprise. Although it may be difficult or impossible to negotiate terms and conditions that deviate from standard terms and conditions that businesses such as banks and commercial real estate landlords impose in contracts like Loan Agreements, Security Agreements, and Lease Agreements, every person or entity that enters into a post-COVID 19 contract is advised to pay particular attention to the following terms and conditions and consider whether they impose acceptable contract performance risk.

1. ***Force Majeure.*** A review of post-COVID 19 contract risk management begins with "*force majeure*" contract provisions. "*Force majeure*" is a French expression that literally means "superior force." The core purpose of a *force majeure* provision is to avoid contract performance if there is an unforeseen event, and historically the clauses were buried in the contract "boilerplate" provisions without much thought. For example, a *force majeure* clause may provide that neither party shall be liable nor deemed to be in default for any delay or failure in performance under the agreement or other interruption of service resulting directly or indirectly from acts of "*force majeure*," including the following: acts of God; acts of civil or military authorities; acts of public enemies or war; accidents; fires; explosions; earthquakes; floods; failure of transportation; pandemic disease; strikes or other work interruptions by either party's employees; or any cause beyond the reasonable control of either party. Before COVID 19, the last truly disruptive event occurred on September 11, 2001, which, because air travel was stopped, made it impossible for performance of some contracts. While that caused some attention to be directed to *force majeure* provisions, because the disruption was short-lived, so was the focus on *force majeure*. The key contract negotiation issue is reviewing the precise definition of *force majeure*. The sample provided above includes at least three causes that directly relate to the COVID 19 public health emergency: (a) acts of civil or military authorities; (b) pandemic disease; and (c) failure of transportation. Many *force majeure* provisions, however, are not so well defined. For example, some *force majeure* provisions include only "acts of God" and do not include the specific categories described above. The term "act of God" has appeared in contracts going far back to the common law of England and generally means a natural hazard that is beyond human control. In the post-COVID 19 period, there

were many arguments regarding how to define an "act of God" and whether a universally destructive virus such as COVID 19 is itself an "act of God," although a pandemic is a "natural hazard beyond human control." Also, although "acts of civil or military authorities" reasonably includes federal and state Executive Orders including "shelter in place" orders, it might be necessary in a specific situation to embellish on this simple statement. Also, once a *force majeure* event occurs, what are the remedies? While a *force majeure* event generally excuses contract performance, what if the objective is not to nullify the contract terms and conditions but to modify? For example, one health care delivery system whose Physician Employment Agreements did not have a precise *force majeure* definition but did include "acts of God" as excusing contract performance tried to use that provision not to nullify performance but to modify the compensation terms and conditions because of the unexpected financial burden caused by the lockdown and loss of revenue. If that is the desired effect, it is best to describe specific powers the parties will have if there is a *force majeure* event and modifying financial terms is necessary for financial survival.

2. **Waiver and Release.** When you agree to a "waiver and release" you voluntarily give up through a contractual agreement a right that you would otherwise have, typically a right to bring an action in tort for damages. We have all routinely executed waivers and releases in many contexts, such as using a rock climbing wall, attending and outdoor camp, or engaging in other activities when there is some risk of harm. In the COVID 19 context, a contract might state that a party cannot provide absolute assurance that, in accessing a party's premises or engaging with a party's representatives, the person electing to access the premises or engage with a party's representatives will not be exposed to the COVID 19 virus. For example, a skilled nursing home or assisted living facility may require a waiver and release as a condition for admission to the facility.

3. **Assumption of Risk.** The concept of "assumption of risk" also typically arises in the context of tort litigation as a defense that, in essence, provides that a person cannot recover damages for an injury when the person voluntarily engages in the conduct knowing the risk. The knowledge is sometimes expressed in contracts. For example, every ticket to a professional sporting event has small print stating that the bearer of the ticket assumes the risk and danger incidental to the sporting event. In the COVID 19 context, if a facility resident has in the past tested positive for COVID 19 or even passed away in the facility as a resulting of contracting the virus, the admission agreement or a separate acknowledgement accompanying the admission agreement might state with transparency that facility residents have tested positive for COVID 19 and, although the facility will use its best efforts to engage in infection control, there is no guarantee that the admitted resident will not contract COVID 19 in the facility. Assumption of risk is very similar to a waiver and release but perhaps a bit less harsh. Rather than a traditional one-sided waiver of claim release saying "if you do business with me, you

cannot sue me" an assumption of risk acknowledgment says "we all know this is out there, and while we are committed to taking reasonable steps to prevent or slow transmission of a virus or other communicable disease, this may not be possible. If you are expecting perfection or a guarantee of some kind, you need to know we cannot provide that."

4. **Informed Consent.** Informed consent is a variation of waiver and release and assumption of risk and is typically used by health care providers to obtain permission to perform a medical procedure or provide other medical services. It is also a bridge between tort liability and contract law and may have application in the COVID 19 context.

5. **Limitation of Liability.** This is a backstop to the provisions discussed above and provides that, if there is an alleged breach of the contract, liability for damages is limited as explained in greater detail above but may require greater scrutiny in the context of a public health emergency. For example, a party can bargain for limited liability for actual, incidental, or consequential damages if they arise from a public health emergency and are not excused by a *force majeure* provision.

J. **Other Special Terms and Conditions.**

1. **Examples of Other Special Terms and Conditions.** Contracts may include special clauses, such as dispute resolution clauses requiring arbitration or mediation of contract disputes instead of judicial proceedings; representations and warranties that the parties have certain qualifications, certifications, or licenses; clauses requiring compliance with specific laws and regulations; clauses addressing intellectual property rights, including patent, copyright, trademark, and trade secret rights; and clauses that are intended to protect the relationship of the parties, such as exclusive dealing agreements.

2. **"Best Efforts" Clauses.** In general, the common law implies a duty on both parties to use their "best efforts" to fulfill the terms and conditions of the contract. In addition, when a party perceives it may be difficult to accomplish a contractual obligation, the party may want to modify the duty but requiring only that it use its "best efforts" to accomplish the duty. For example, a hospital may enter into a contract with a management company that requires the management company to obtain certain insurance coverage. However, the manager cannot control the insurance markets, and it may be difficult to procure insurance precisely as described. Therefore, the manager will negotiate a clause that provides that the manager will use its "best efforts" to procure the insurance. Some parties try to modify "best efforts" by asking for either a "reasonable best efforts" or "commercially reasonable best efforts" clause under the fear that a court will interpret "best efforts" to mean every possible effort, regardless of cost or consequences, but most courts will imply a "reasonableness" standard

to a best efforts clause, and "commercially reasonable" is generally construed to be the same as "reasonable" best efforts.

XII. WHAT REMEDIES ARE AVAILABLE FOR A BREACH OF CONTRACT?

A. **What Is the General Rule for Breach of Contract Remedies?** The general rule is that the damaged party will be "made whole." In other words, the damaged party will be able to either receive the benefit of the bargain or be put into a position where the damaged party does not suffer any loss.

B. **What Are the General Kinds of Remedies Available?** Two kinds of remedies are generally available: remedies available at law, such as monetary damages; and equitable remedies.

C. **What Remedies Are Available at Law?** Examples of how an aggrieved party can be "made whole" as a matter of law follows:

1. **Compensatory Damages.** A party can recover "compensatory" damages, which means actual monetary damages. Note: compensatory or monetary damages should not be confused with liquidated damages, which are reasonable estimates of damages agreed to in advance.

2. **Liquidated Damages.** As stated above, the parties can agree in advance in the contract to a specific amount of damages for a breach of contract, provided that, when the contract was executed, actual damages would be difficult or impossible to ascertain and the amount of the liquidated damages is a reasonable estimate of the amount of damages that the party would suffer. The courts will not enforce a liquidated damages clause that is, in essence, a penalty.

D. **What Are "Equitable Remedies"?** Equitable remedies are generally applied to prevent something unfair or unjust from happening when there is no adequate remedy at law (in other words, monetary damages alone will not be the appropriate remedy). Some examples are as follows:

1. **Specific Performance.** This requires the breaching party to complete the transaction. It is seen most frequently in contracts for the sale of unique property (such as real property).

2. **Rescission.** Rescission is an equitable remedy, and it means that the contract is nullified and the parties are restored to the positions they had before entering into the contract.

3. **Reformation.** Reformation is an equitable remedy that requests the court to rewrite or correct a contract to make it conform to the original agreement of the parties. Reformation can be used when the parties have reached an agreement but the written contract inaccurately reflects that agreement.

4. **Injunctions and Restraining Orders.** Courts will issue injunctions and restraining orders when there is no adequate remedy at law, there is a likelihood of success of the merits of the case, and the party seeking the relief would otherwise suffer irreparable harm.

E. **What Remedies Are Not Generally Available for Breach of Contract?**

1. **Punitive Damages.** "Punitive damages" are generally assessable only when there is an intentional tort (such as, in the context of contractual arrangements, fraud), and are intended to "punish" the culpable party. Since "punishment" is not a part of contract law, punitive damages are generally not awarded in contract cases.

2. **Costs and Attorneys' Fees.** Costs and attorneys' fees related to breach of contract litigation are generally not recoverable unless the parties agree otherwise in the contract or, in some states, there is an award based on the "stubbornly litigious" conduct of the breaching party.

F. **Mitigation of Damages.** When a contract is breached, the non-breaching party generally has a duty to "mitigate" the potential damages (in other words, to act in a manner that minimizes the damages). For example, if a business contracts with a supplier of widgets and the supplier breaches the contract, the business must try to find another source of widgets to "mitigate" its damages.

XIII. WHAT DEFENSES ARE TYPICALLY RAISED IN BREACH OF CONTRACT CASES?

A. **Illegality.** As stated above, illegal contracts are unenforceable. One ground that may arise in the business context is performance of services without a required license or permit.

B. **Duress.** A contract will not be enforced if a party can show that it was unfairly coerced into entering the contract (for example, threats of violence or imprisonment or the illegal taking of property).

C. **Unconscionability.** As described above, a party may allege that the contract was procedurally or substantively unconscionable. However, whether the agreement is "unconscionable" needs to be balanced against the doctrine of "freedom of contract" and its related maxim in equity, "folly is not fraud."

D. **Impossibility.** The doctrine of impossibility applies if there is either a change in circumstances or the discovery of unknown preexisting circumstances that makes performance of the contract impossible. "Impossibility" has its roots in ancient common law.

E. **Impracticability.** Sometimes intervening events occur that may not make it impossible for the parties to perform but may make it impracticable for a party to perform because of excessive or unreasonable cost. Impracticability is a more difficult defense than impossibility because it is more difficult to prove and also needs to be assessed in the context of "freedom of contract" and "folly is not fraud."

F. **Capacity or Authority.** In a business context, the person who signed the agreement had no actual or apparent authority to bind the party to a contract.

G. **Fraud.** Sometimes a party may allege that it was fraudulently induced into entering into a contractual arrangement. "Fraud" is a tort that is based upon a misrepresentation or concealment of a material fact that induced a party to act in a certain way. Therefore, a tort claim for "fraud" is sometimes alleged in the same complaint that alleges a breach of contract, which opens up the possibility of recovery of punitive damages as well as costs and attorneys' fees, which may be awarded in a tort lawsuit. In a lawsuit alleging "fraud," the plaintiff must specifically and particularly describe the facts upon which the fraud claim is based in the complaint. Also, as stated above, "folly is not fraud."

XIV. CONTRACT DRAFTING

A. **Each Contract Is Unique.** With the possible exception of standardized purchase orders and adhesion contracts, business contracts are like snowflakes. Even when the parties have substantial contract drafting experience, business contracts are rarely identical for many reasons. For example, contracts will reflect the bargaining power of the parties; economic shifts; changes in management, advisors, accountants, and legal counsel; changing laws and regulations; and experience of the parties in identifying potential risks. While it is common practice to begin drafting with an existing contract, most business contracts will evolve over time.

B. **Use Clear, Precise Language.** Contract drafting requires clear, precise, descriptive, and grammatically correct language. While it may be commonly held that attorneys intentionally draft ambiguous contracts, the opposite is true. Each contract must expressly state the intent of the parties. The goal is to produce a fully integrated contract that is easily understood within the "four corners" of the document.

1. **Delete Unnecessary Words.** When drafting a contract, review it carefully. If unnecessary words appear, delete them. Economy of language will be rewarded with certainty of contractual rights and obligations.

2. **Define Terms.** If a contractual phrase or provision will be used throughout the document, create a definition. This will eliminate ambiguity and create a shorter document. This can be done either by defining terms when the contractual phase first appears in the document or creating a definition section that sets forth all of the defined terms in the agreement.

C. **The Danger of Do-It-Yourself Contracting.** Although this may seem like a self-serving statement for the engagement of legal counsel, businesses should avoid trying to prepare their own material contracts. Since contracts are unique, modifying them yourself or combining provisions from multiple documents is fraught with drafting danger. For example, the defined terms in two combined contracts may be different, and the combined language can easily create ambiguities.

XV. CONTRACT NEGOTIATION

A. **Negotiation of Contracts.** Some contracts, known as "adhesion" contracts, must be accepted without negotiation. For example, when you apply for a credit card, you are compelled to accept the terms offered by the credit card company without negotiation, and the credit card company reserves the right to amend the contract without the cardholder's consent. Also, when you purchase a new car, the form includes many provisions on a printed form, and the dealer generally will not deviate from the terms and conditions on the printed form. Many business contracts, however, are negotiable.

B. **Contracts Require Mutual Gain.** The key to concluding contractual negotiations is to find the point where each party receives the benefit of the bargain. Some negotiation experts refer to this as the "mutual gain line," which is the point where each party essentially gets what it wants.

C. **Finding the Mutual Gain Line.** The best way to find the mutual gain line is to discover what the other party wants and then, to the extent possible without compromising the benefit of the bargain for you, giving it to them. This is accomplished by getting information from the other party. When you enter into any contract negotiation, you should prepare a series of questions beginning with the word "what" that are designed to discover what the other party wants. Some experts say that, when negotiating a contract, it is better to get more information than you give.

D. **Discredited Negotiation Strategies.** Although others may debate what might be the most effective negotiation strategy, some strategies are not recommended. For example, in labor law, there was formally a negotiation technique called "Boulwarism," which, in effect, was a "take it or leave it strategy" and refusal to negotiate any terms and conditions. This usually does not work. Similarly, the techniques of "win through intimidation" or "zero sum game" are not terribly effective.

E. **Smart Is Dumb and Dumb Is Smart.** Since the key to negotiation is to get more information than you give, trying to show how knowledgeable or intelligent you are may not be an effective negotiation strategy. When you are confronted with a party that makes a bold or definitive statement with which you may disagree, instead of refuting it, you should say that you do not fully understand and ask the other party to rephrase the question. For some reason, the rephrased statement is never as forceful as the first, and this frequently leads to balanced negotiations.

F. **Keep Your Emotions Under Control.** The party that loses his or her temper is always at a negotiating disadvantage. Keep your emotions under control. When the other party becomes temperamental, you can defuse it by saying: "This seems to make you angry. Tell me why it upsets you."

G. **Playing the "Deal Breaker" Card.** At least once in every negotiation you are likely to reach an impasse on a critical deal point. If it is truly a deal breaker, it is permissible to say so and advise the other party that, if they do not concede, then you will walk away from the table. However, there are two conditions to playing this card. First, you can only play it one time. Second, you have to mean it.

H. **Be Guided by Reasonableness.** Even if you are entirely confident that your contract is inherently fair and clearly articulated, reasonable people may review your work and find ambiguities or place a different meaning on a contractual provision than you intended. It is best to keep an open mind and not get trapped by "pride of authorship."

I. **Read and Understand the Contract.** Last, you need to actually read what you are being asked to sign and clearly understand your rights and obligations. If you do not understand something, ask questions. If there are blanks in the contract, be sure they are filled in before you execute the contract. If a dispute ever arises, the terms and conditions of what you signed govern, and it is up to you to know what you have agreed to do or not to do.

CHAPTER 3

EMPLOYMENT AND INDEPENDENT CONTRACTOR AGREEMENTS

I. WHAT ARE THE ESSENTIAL ELEMENTS OF AN EMPLOYMENT RELATIONSHIP?

A. **Employment Under the Common Law.** Modern employment law is founded on "master-servant" common law principles.

B. **Duties of Loyalty and Confidentiality.** Some duties arise under the common law, even in the absence of a written contract, including the duties of loyalty and confidentiality. In general, the duty of loyalty means that the employee must not engage in conduct that constitutes a "conflict of interest" with the employer. Also, employees are generally required to maintain confidentiality of an employer's trade secrets for all time, regardless of whether the parties have entered into a written employment agreement.

C. **Oral Versus Written Employment Agreements.**

1. **Oral Agreements.** Most employment agreements are oral and are terminable at will by either party.

2. **Written Agreements.** Written employment agreements give both parties more rights and obligations than general law provides.

D. **What Bodies of Law Govern Health Care Employment and Independent Contractor Agreements?**

1. **State Law.** Most aspects of employment and independent contractor agreements are governed by state laws and judicial decisions.

2. **Federal Law.** There is no true federal contracts law, but certain aspects of employment and independent contractor agreements are governed by federal law.

   a. **Stark, Anti-Kickback, and Tax Exempt Organizations Laws.** All health industry employment and independent contractor agreements must be analyzed under Stark and the federal Anti-Kickback Statute, and, if the agreement is with a tax exempt organization such as a "non-profit" health care delivery system, the Internal Revenue Code and the rules and regulations governing tax exempt organizations.

   b. **Whistleblower Protection.** The federal False Claims Act and some state laws protect "whistleblowers" from employment termination and other discipline.

   c. **General Federal Laws.** Some federal laws govern all employment relationships (for example, the Equal Employment Opportunity Act and the Family and Medical Leave Act). However, those laws are beyond the scope of this book.

II. WHAT ARE THE ESSENTIAL ELEMENTS OF A PHYSICIAN EMPLOYMENT AGREEMENT?

A. **Duties**. The employment duties should be described.

   1. **Full Time Employment.** The agreement usually requires full time services.

   2. **Permitted Activities**. If there are any permitted outside activities, they should be clearly described.

   3. **Employer's Right to Possession of Revenue from Medical Services.** Usually, unless otherwise expressly agreed to in writing by the employer or described as a permitted activity, all remuneration related to or arising from the practice of medicine is employer revenue. This might include, for example, revenue received under Medical Director Agreements or hospital clinical service line Co-Management Agreements as well as revenue received from performance of professional medical services.

B. **Physician-Employee Representations and Warranties.** Representations and warranties are important to protect the employer. Typical representations and warranties include the following:

   1. **Licensure.** Physician is licensed to practice medicine, and the license has never been restricted or revoked.

   2. **Controlled Substances Registrations and Licenses.** The physician has all required DEA licenses.

3. **Medical Staff Privileges.** Physician has appropriate staff privileges and has never been disciplined.

4. **Exclusion or Debarment.** The employee is not now, and has never been, excluded from participation in the Medicare program, any state Medicaid program, or any other governmental reimbursement program.

5. **Criminal Misconduct.** The employee has never been convicted of a criminal offense of any nature (except minor traffic violations).

6. **General Conduct.** The employee has not been named as a defendant in any civil action alleging (a) professional negligence, (b) violation of any state or federal statute or regulation governing discrimination or sexual harassment, or (c) any tort for assault or battery related to any alleged harmful or offensive touching of another person.

C. **Reporting Actions Involving the Physician-Employee.** The employee should be required to notify the employer in writing of:

1. **Actions That Limit Ability to Perform Services.** Any action against the employee that results in the reduction, restriction, suspension, revocation, or denial of the ability to provide medical services under any health insurance plan, reimbursement program, or managed care plan.

2. **Disciplinary Notices.** Being notified that any report involving the employee has been filed with the Board of Medical Examiners of any state or with the National Practitioner Data Bank.

3. **Events That Might Create Claims.** Any event that raises a reasonable probability that it will result in a legal claim or action against the employee relating to the practice of medicine.

4. **Communications from Governmental Agencies.** The employee's receipt of any document, communication, or contact from any governmental agency or representative thereof.

D. **Compensation and Benefits.** Physician compensation can take many forms, including the following:

1. **Fixed Salary.** A fixed amount for performance of all services.

2. **Bonus or Productivity Based Compensation.** Many medical practices are moving to productivity incentive compensation, which is subject to some Stark restrictions that are discussed below.

3. **Fringe Benefits.** Typical fringe benefits include health insurance, retirement plan benefits, an automobile allowance, and a cellular phone and personal device with related cellular service.

4. **Relocation and Moving Expenses.** Relocation and moving expense reimbursement is sometimes provided, but it is typically tied to continued employment and possible repayment obligations.

5. **Time Away from the Practice; Continuing Medical Education.** It is generally preferable to lump vacation, sick leave, continuing medical education, and other paid time off together. From an employer's perspective, it is important to provide that time away from the practice will not accrue from year to year, and, upon termination of the employee's employment for any reason, the employee shall not be entitled to payment for any unused time away from the practice. Of course, a physician employee will want the reverse.

6. **Professional Liability Insurance.** Although provision of professional liability insurance during the term of employment is typical, responsibility for tail insurance is sometimes negotiated and made the responsibility of the employee under certain circumstances (such as a termination without cause by the employee or a termination for cause by the employer).

7. **Deferred Compensation and Internal Revenue Code Section 409A Compliance.** In 2004, Congress enacted Internal Revenue Code Section 409A to provide rules regarding the taxation of deferred compensation, including severance pay arrangements. To comply with Section 409A, the time, form, and triggering event for deferred compensation arrangements must be established when the agreement is entered into. Once established, subsequent changes in the form, time of payment, or payment itself are heavily restricted. The stakes are high because non-compliant deferred compensation must be included in the recipient's gross income immediately, even if not paid. All agreements that provide for deferred compensation or severance benefits need to be scrutinized for compliance with Internal Revenue Code Section 409A.

E. **Stark Productivity Bonus and Profit Share Restrictions.** Under Stark, there is a special rule for productivity bonuses and profit shares arising from the provision of Stark designated health services. A physician "in the group" may be paid (1) a share of overall DHS profits of the group or (2) a productivity bonus based on personally performed "incident to" services, provided that the share or bonus is not determined in a manner that is directly related to the volume or value of referrals of Stark DHS by the physician. DHS that may be provided by a group practice include, for example, physical and occupational therapy, diagnostic imaging, clinical laboratory, and chemotherapy.

1. **Overall Profits.** "Overall profits" means the group's entire profits derived from DHS payable by Medicare or Medicaid, or the profits derived from DHS payable by Medicare or Medicaid of any component of the group practice that consists of at least five physicians. Note that, while the Stark definition of "referral" includes only referral for items or services payable under the Medicare program, the definition of "overall profits" includes profits derived from both Medicare and Medicaid. The share of overall profits will not be deemed to relate directly to the volume or value of referrals if one of the following conditions is met:

    a. **Per Capita.** Profits are divided per capita.

    b. **Non-DHS Revenue.** DHS revenues are distributed based on the distribution of the group's revenues attributable to services that are not DHS payable by any federal health care program or private payor.

    c. **Five Percent Rule.** Revenues derived from DHS constitute less than 5% of the group's total revenues, and the allocated portion of those revenues to each physician in the group practice constitutes 5% or less of his or her total compensation from the group.

    d. **Other Methods Not Directly Tied to Volume or Value of Referrals.** Overall profits are divided in a reasonable and verifiable manner that is not directly related to the volume or value of the physician's DHS services.

2. **Productivity Bonuses and "Incident to" Compensation.** A physician may be paid a productivity bonus based upon services the physician personally performs and services "incident to" the physician's services. The Stark II, Phase III regulations clearly confirmed that productivity bonuses based directly on "incident to" services are permissible. However, some Stark DHS, such as diagnostic imaging services, cannot be billed as "incident to" a physician's professional services, so a productivity bonus based on ordered diagnostic services is not permissible. "Incident to" productivity bonuses will be deemed not to relate directly to volume or value of DHS if one of the following conditions is met:

    a. **Patient Encounters or RVUs.** The bonus is based on the physician's total patient encounters or RVUs.

    b. **Non-DHS Revenue.** The bonus is based on the allocation of the physician's compensation attributable to services that are not DHS payable by any federal health care program or private payor.

c. **Five Percent Rule.** Revenues derived from DHS are less than 5% of the group's total practice revenues.

d. **Other Methods Not Directly Tied to Volume and Value of Referrals.** The bonus is calculated in a reasonable and verifiable manner that is not directly related to the volume or value of the physician's referrals of DHS.

F. **Compliance Costs.** Some employment agreements make the employee responsible for any costs incurred by the employer arising from a breach of broadly defined "compliance" obligations, including, for example, illegal billing practices or any conduct that could be alleged to constitute either sexual harassment or misconduct or illegal discrimination.

G. **Medical Records.**

1. **Ownership of Medical Records.** Battles are frequently waged over ownership of medical records, and this should be addressed in the agreement. State law, not federal law, governs ownership of medical records, although the HIPAA privacy regulations grant individual access to medical records, and the HIPAA security regulations include requirements for electronically stored records.

2. **Transfer of Medical Records.** Any transfer of patient medical records requires patient consent because of issues related to compliance with the HIPAA privacy rules. A physician who leaves a medical practice cannot simply take a copy of any patient's medical records.

H. **Term and Termination.**

1. **Term.** The actual term of the contract is not as important as the right to terminate. Most agreements have "evergreen" clauses, which automatically renew from year to year, but some have fixed terms with an expiration date.

2. **Termination.**

a. **Probation Period.** Some agreements have a probationary period, during which the agreement can be terminated at any time and for any reason.

b. **Without Cause.** This can be a fixed period at any time (such as 30, 60, or 90 days) or fixed in relation to the term (for example, if notice is given 90 days before expiration of the term).

c. **Employer's Termination for Cause.** Employers want to be able to terminate for "cause," and "cause" is frequently defined in the agreement. Some examples are as follows: (i) the discovery of conduct by the employee that is harmful to the business of the employer; (ii) the employee's failure to maintain any professional license; (iii) the inability of the employer to obtain malpractice insurance under reasonable terms on behalf of the employee; (iv) the termination of the employee from being a provider under any of the governmental reimbursement programs; (v) the limitation of the employee's medical staff privileges; (vi) if the employee becomes the subject or target of any investigation relating to the governmental reimbursement programs; (vii) the employee's indictment for, conviction of, or pleading no contest to any other criminal offense involving moral turpitude; or (viii) any breach of any material term or condition of the agreement by the employee that is not cured within a reasonable period of time after written notice from the employer specifying the breach and requesting that it be cured.

d. **Employee's Termination for Cause.** The employee may sometimes terminate the employee's employment under the agreement for cause, but these rights are usually very limited. For example, (i) the employer's filing (whether voluntarily or involuntarily) any petition for bankruptcy or (ii) the employer's material breach of the agreement that is not cured within a reasonable period of time after written notice from the employee specifying the breach and requesting that it be cured.

e. **Disability.** Employment agreements may be terminated (subject to federal law) if the employee becomes "disabled," but the definition of "disability" is sometimes heavily negotiated.

I. **Covenants in Partial Restraint of Trade.**

1. **Restrictive Covenant or Noncompetition Agreement.** A traditional "restrictive covenant" or "noncompetition agreement" restrains an employee from competing with the employer for a certain period time in a specific geographic territory. If a hospital provides a physician or a medical group practice with physician recruiting remuneration, Stark provides that the recruited physician's employment agreement may include a restrictive covenant only if the covenant is "reasonable." While Stark does not expressly provide that "reasonableness" will be governed by applicable state law, it is generally believed that covenants that comply with state law will also comply with Stark.

2. **The "Reasonableness" Test.** To be enforceable, the covenant generally must be reasonable to the employee, the employer, and the public; must protect only an employer's legitimate

business interests; and must be reasonable as to time, territory, and activity restrained. Each element of the reasonableness test must be separately analyzed.

3. **Strict Construction.** Agreements in partial restraint of trade are "strictly construed." The restrictions must be precisely clear: oral testimony regarding the intent of the parties is not admissible evidence. An "overly broad" restrictive covenant is "void as against public policy" and therefore unenforceable.

4. **The "Blue Penciling" Rule.** Some states follow a rule that, if an "overly broad" covenant can be made reasonable by striking out a word or phrase (referred to as "blue penciling"), the restrictive covenant is enforceable as modified.

5. **Non-Solicitation of Patients or Customers.** To protect its customer base, an employer may also require an employee to agree that the employee will not divert, solicit, or contact, or attempt to divert, solicit, or contact, any patient or customer for the purpose of having the patient or customer provided with services or products offered by the employer from a competitor. This is an alternative "restrictive covenant" that must pass a "reasonableness" test. Usually, enforcement of a non-solicitation clause requires only a reasonable time restraint.

6. **Non-Solicitation of Employees.** To protect its valuable human resources, an employer may also require an employee to agree that the employee will not hire, solicit, recruit, or induce any employee, consultant, or independent contractor employed or otherwise engaged by the employer to sever his or her relationship with the employer or to be employed or otherwise engaged by any competitor. This type of covenant also generally requires a reasonable time restraint.

7. **Covenant Not to Disclose or Confidentiality Agreement.** There are two types of information that may be subject to a non-disclosure or confidentiality obligation:

    a. **Trade Secrets.** Under the Uniform Trade Secrets Act and the common law, trade secrets as defined under applicable state law are protectable for all time and for so long as they are maintained by the employer as trade secrets, even in the absence of a written contract. A standard definition of trade secrets includes lists of actual or potential customers and referral sources, lists of actual or potential suppliers, technical and non-technical data, formulae, patterns, compilations, programs, devices, methods, techniques, drawings, processes, financial data, financial plans, and product plans, which are known only to the employer and those of its employees in whom the information must be confided for business purposes.

b. **Other Confidential Information.** Otherwise confidential information that does not rise to the level of a "trade secret" may also be subject to a non-disclosure obligation, but some jurisdictions require a written confidentiality agreement with a time limit on the non-disclosure or confidentiality obligation.

8. **Non-Disparagement.** Although not technically a covenant in partial restraint of trade, some employers may ask an employee not to engage in public or private disparagement of the employer or its business methods, operations, programs, or employees, or prepare articles or other written material for publication that specifically negatively refer to, or are critical of, the employer or its business methods, operations, programs, employees, agents, officers, directors, or other representatives after termination of the agreement. However, such provisions are difficult to enforce.

9. **Remedies.** If a restrictive covenant is breached, the typical remedy is a temporary or permanent injunction against the employee prohibiting any further violation of any such covenant. The employer can also seek monetary damages.

J. **Consideration for Ownership and Participation in Ancillary Ventures.** For medical group practices, there is sometimes a clause describing the circumstances under which the employee will be considered for ownership in the employer. Some medical practices also have separately organized ancillary ventures, such as ambulatory surgery centers, and the agreement may also provide conditions for participation in such ventures.

K. **Requirement to Direct Referrals to Employer.** The typical health care delivery system employment agreement requires the employed physician to use the physician's best efforts to make referrals for health care services to the employer health care delivery system unless (1) the use of a different provider is required by the terms of a patient's enrollment or participation in an insurance or other health care plan, (2) the employed physician determines, in the physician's clinical judgement, that the use of a health care delivery system affiliated provider to provide such services is not in the best medical interests of the patient, (3) the patient on the patient's own initiative requests to use a different provider, (4) the health care delivery system affiliated providers do not offer the needed services, or (5) such services are necessary in a medical emergency. Other than this "best efforts" standard, the employed physician will not be obligated or required to use health care delivery system affiliated providers and facilities. Nothing in the employment agreement is to be construed to restrict the employed physician's professional judgment while performing professional services under the employment agreement to refer any patient to any health care facility when necessary or desirable for a patient to obtain proper and appropriate treatment or to comply with the wishes of the patient or patient's family. A provision of this nature is necessary for purposes of compliance with the Stark Law and the federal Anti-Kickback Statute as described in Chapter 1.

L. **Intellectual Property.** Three forms of intellectual property may be relevant to an employment relationship: trade secret; patent; and copyright. Each requires a different contract provision. As stated above, an employer's trade secrets are protected even in the absence of a written contract. Because patent rights arise with the individual and not the employer, patent rights need to be individually assigned by the employee in writing. However, the employer owns the copyright in all copyrightable works produced by the employee within the scope of employment under the "works made for hire" doctrine, and a separate contract clause is unnecessary.

M. **Assignment.** Typically, because the contract is for an employee's personal services, the employee may not assign, transfer, or subcontract the employee's rights and obligations under the agreement to any other person or entity. However, the employer usually wants the right to assign its rights and obligations under the agreement to any legal entity or individual that acquires or otherwise continues the business currently conducted by the employer.

N. **Indemnification.** Under an indemnification obligation, a party is required to defend and hold harmless the other party from and against any and all claims, losses, damages, costs, or expenses, arising out of any breach of any representation, warranty, or covenant contained in the agreement or any claims for damages or injury against the other party that are caused by or result from negligent acts or omissions by the other party in the performance of their respective duties and obligations. Employees frequently object to indemnification clauses in employment agreements. Indemnification may be appropriate in a professional services agreement.

O. **Waiver.** The waiver by either party of a breach or violation of any provision of the agreement shall not operate as or be construed to be a waiver of any subsequent breach hereof.

P. **Notices.** Most contracts provide that the parties must give the other party notice in certain situations. For example, most agreements require notice of termination. Therefore, most contracts describe how to give effective notice to the other party. If a notices clause is added, the procedure must be followed.

Q. **Governing Law.** Typically, the agreement is governed according to the substantive laws of the state of employment without regard to principles of conflicts of law.

R. **Entire Agreement.** It is very important, in any contract, to include a clause stating that the agreement constitutes the entire agreement of the parties regarding the subject matter thereof, that all prior representations of the parties, whether written or oral, are merged therein, and that the agreement may be modified or amended only by a writing executed by both parties.

III. WHAT RISKS ARISE FROM EMPLOYMENT BY A HEALTH CARE DELIVERY SYSTEM?

A. **Stark and Anti-Kickback Laws.** In response to a changing health care economy, many physicians are leaving independent practices and becoming directly employed by hospitals and health care delivery systems. Stark and the federal Anti-Kickback Statute apply to all employment agreements between physicians and hospitals or health care delivery systems. While there is a Stark exception and an Anti-Kickback Statute safe harbor for *bona fide* employment agreements, each requires payment of fair market value compensation. Compensation in excess of fair market value can lead to sanctions under Stark and the federal Anti-Kickback Statute and can also be bootstrapped to form the foundation for an alleged violation of the federal False Claims Act.

B. **Tax Exempt Organizations Law.** The Internal Revenue Service can determine that a hospital or health care delivery system is exempt from federal taxation because the hospital or health care delivery system serves a charitable purpose. To preserve tax exempt status and to avoid liability for intermediate sanctions in the form of excise taxes, every tax exempt organization must avoid arrangements that can be characterized as involving prohibited "inurement" or "private benefit" as described in Chapter 1. Both physician compensation arrangements and health care provider executive compensation arrangements must comply with the laws, rules, and regulations that govern tax exempt organizations. Once again, the key element is fair market value.

C. **Determining Fair Market Value in Hospital-Physician Employment Agreements.** All physician-hospital employment agreements must be reviewed and assessed to obtain assurance of fair market value payments. The safest approach is to engage the services of an independent appraiser. Most appraisers benchmark compensation against published surveys. The Medical Group Management Association (MGMA) survey is most frequently used. Many hospitals and health care delivery systems will not compensate physicians in an amount that exceeds the ninetieth percentile of the MGMA survey in the particular specialty. While this is a conservative approach, some hospitals and health care delivery systems will compensate physicians above that threshold, but physician productivity must be commensurate with the compensation paid. When payments exceed these limits, regulatory risk increases, and the need for continuing compilation of evidence that supports the higher compensation also increases.

D. **IRS Executive Compensation Initiative.** Although Stark and the federal Anti-Kickback Statute do not apply to executive employment agreements with tax exempt hospitals and health care delivery systems, these executive compensation arrangements must withstand scrutiny under the laws that prohibit private inurement and private benefit.

1. **Revised Form 990.** As a result of its recently concluded IRS Executive Compensation Compliance Initiative, the Internal Revenue Service has revised IRS Form 990 (the tax exempt organization tax return form) to include detailed questions regarding executive compensation, the intention of which is to ferret out excessive compensation arrangements that might result in loss of exempt status or intermediate sanctions.

2. **Ethics and Conflicts of Interest Policies.** Every tax exempt organization must implement an ethics and conflicts of interest policy that includes independent oversight of executive compensation.

IV. WHAT ARE THE KEY NEGOTIATION POINTS FOR AN EXECUTIVE EMPLOYMENT AGREEMENT?

A. **Executive Employment Agreement Negotiation.** In general, many of the issues related to physician employment agreements also apply to executive employment agreements. However, executive employment agreements have many unique issues. Since this book is intended for individuals, we will focus on contract negotiation for an individual Executive.

B. **Essential Elements of Executive Employment Negotiation from the Executive's Perspective.** From the Executive's perspective, the essential elements are as follows:

1. **Formal Written Contract.** The Executive's employment terms should be set forth in a formal written contract.

2. **Scope of Responsibilities.** The Executive's responsibilities must be delineated clearly. This is important because a description of responsibilities typically inter-relates with restrictive covenants and "for cause" termination provisions. The Executive should report only to the Board of Directors and should be given reasonable latitude to exercise executive discretion. The Executive may also want to ensure that the Executive has a place on the company's Board of Directors.

3. **Full Time and Efforts Clause.** Employment agreements often require that the Executive devote all of the Executive's productive business time and efforts to the Executive's employment related responsibilities. If the Executive employment agreement includes such a provision, then exceptions must be made for the Executive's outside "permitted activities" such as serving on the Board of Directors of non-competing companies and, perhaps, involvement with civic, charitable, or professional organizations.

4. **Location of Employment.** This needs to be fixed in the contract. Any variation needs the Executive's prior written approval. Reasonably required travel (up to a certain number of weeks per year) can be accepted.

5. **Term of Employment.** Ideally, the term should be indefinite or as long as possible. Avoid short (two to five year) terms. Early termination by the company should only occur (a) if the Executive is terminated "for cause", provided that "cause" is precisely defined, or (b) upon the mutual agreement of the Executive and the company.

6. **Early Termination by the Company.**

   a. **General.** The agreement should clearly specify those circumstances under which the Executive's employment term can be cut short by the company. Ideally, it should occur only if the Executive has been "really bad" or if the parties mutually agree that the Executive's employment should end. The company should not be able to terminate the Executive employment at its whim or discretion (and, in the event that it does, either in accordance with or in breach of the agreement, the Executive should have a very attractive "parachute" package of benefits). In some situations, when the Executive is giving up an established secure position and taking one with a fair amount of associated risk, the Executive might want to negotiate a "free walk" that allows him, after a relatively short period of time (for example, three months), to walk away from the position with no strings attached on either side.

   b. **For "Cause".** The company may want the right to terminate the Executive "for cause." The agreement should clearly delineate an exclusive list of items that will constitute grounds for termination "for cause." The Executive should strongly resist inclusion of the following items as grounds for "cause" termination: (i) fuzzy, unspecific grounds (for example "the company's failure to perform as well as projected") or (ii) performance based grounds (for example "Executive's failure to perform the Executive's duties as required"). The following grounds are generally acceptable: (x) conviction of a felony; (y) material breach by the Executive of certain provisions in the Executive's employment contract (such as a restrictive covenant provision) and failure of the Executive to cure the breach within a reasonable time period; and (z) embezzlement or fraud of the Executive in performing services for the company.

   c. **Death or Total Disability.** Certain termination benefits should flow from such an occurrence. It is important to define "total disability" carefully.

7. **Early Termination by Executive.** The Executive should be able to terminate employment early for "good reason" including the following: (a) the Executive loses the title or managerial position or the Executive's authority is materially undercut (perhaps even if the Executive loses his or her seat on the Board of Directors); (b) the company's executive offices are relocated more than a certain distance from the current location; (c) the company commits a

material breach of the employment contract and does not cure the breach within a certain period of time after being provided notice of the breach; and (d) a "change of control" occurs in the company or if a substantial portion of the company's assets or equity is sold to a third party. Certain severance benefits should flow to the Executive if the Executive terminates for good reason.

8. **Compensation and Benefits.**

   a. **Base Salary.** Consider setting this as a minimum figure (for example, "The Company shall pay Executive an annual cash salary that is no less than $_________"). Also provide that the salary will increase each year in accordance with a cost of living index (CPI).

   b. **Annual Bonus.** "C level" Executives should be entitled to some form of annual incentive cash bonus, regardless of whether other executives are entitled to one. The standards should be as objective as possible, although the Board of Directors should be entitled to pay the Executive an additional bonus based on subjective criteria. Sometimes annual bonuses are paid in the form of stock options, although it is common for executives to get a bonus of both stock and cash.

   c. **Benefit Plans.** The Executive should be given the opportunity to participate in a variety of employee benefit plans such as 401K plans, retirement savings plans, supplemental benefit plans, qualified and non-qualified stock option plans, phantom stock plans, long term incentive plans, disability plans, and life, dental, and disability insurance plans. Most companies have plans such as these already set up for members of senior management. The company should not be able later to cut the Executive out of these plans, and, if it does scale back on any plan, then the Executive should be given the economic equivalent in cash so the Executive is in no worse financial position when compared to the benefits provided when the agreement was executed.

   d. **Stock Ownership.** It is generally advantageous for an Executive to own shares in his or her company. In fact, private equity and venture capital funds usually require Executives to be incentivized by stock ownership. The advantages usually far outweigh the disadvantages, particularly if the Executive can obtain shares on a favorable basis (for example, through stock options, bonus grants, or stock appreciation rights). The first advantage is the power that share ownership brings. An Executive is subject ultimately to the whim of the controlling shareholders; they have the power to elect the Executive to or remove the Executive from the Board of Directors and in some cases to remove the Executive as an officer of the company. Another advantage of share ownership is the ability of the shareholders to profit if the value of the company increases. Ascertaining a value in a small privately-owned company is not as obvious, so the upside for appreciation is not usually discernible until a major corporate opportunity presents itself to the company such as a sale of the company or an opportunity for the company to "go public." There is little downside to owning shares since a shareholder's personal liability for corporate liabilities is generally limited to the amount of the shareholder's investment. Most well run (and well-advised) privately owned companies require their shareholders to enter into shareholder agreements.

e. **Automobile Allowance.** Executives typically receive an automobile allowance.

f. **Expense Reimbursement.** The company should reimburse the Executive for any employment related expenses incurred by the Executive, including reasonable recreational expenses (for example, dinner with clients and prospects). Reasonable entertainment expenses should be reimbursable as well (notwithstanding the decrease in tax benefits that are allowable to companies under recent changes in the Internal Revenue Code).

g. **Vacation.** Four weeks paid vacation is typical. Vacation time should accrue.

h. **Travel Perks.** First class air travel is often negotiated for top line executives.

i. **Club Memberships.** Companies often agree to reimburse executives for executives' private and business club expenses and dues.

j. **Financial Consulting.** Companies often reimburse executives (subject to a cap) for expenses incurred by the executives in connection with financial and tax counseling and tax return preparation.

9. **Deferred Compensation.** As stated above but bears repeating, compensation arrangements that include any deferred compensation or deferred benefits arrangements must be written to comply with strict requirements under Internal Revenue Code Section 409A. Deferred compensation is a legally binding right arising during a taxable year to compensation that, pursuant to the terms of the arrangement, is or may be payable after the end of the taxable year. Failure to conform such arrangements to these strict requirements will result in the executive employee (or independent contractor) immediately paying income tax on the deferred compensation as well as an additional 20% penalty and interest. Some examples of deferred compensation that are typically negotiated in Executive employment agreements include: salary deferral arrangements (but not 401(k) and similar plans); termination or severance payments; and equity compensation arrangements such as discounted stock options and stock appreciation rights, and stock buy-back features at other than fair market value.

10. **Severance Compensation.** The agreement should carefully identify any compensation or benefits that are to be paid to the Executive upon the termination of the Executive's employment, which also must comply with Internal Revenue Code Section 409A. The degree of benefits typically will range from virtually none (other than accrued salary and bonuses) to quite lavish (in the case of a termination by employee for good reason or an arbitrary termination by the company). The following is an example of how severance compensation can be handled:

    a. **"Parachute" Type Payment in the Event of Termination by Executive for Good Reason or by the Company in Breach of the Employment Contract.** The Executive should be entitled to receive the monetary equivalent of his or her salary and benefits (including the minimum amount of any guaranteed bonuses) for a certain period of time after the effective date of termination (two to three years is not uncommon). The vesting for all stock options should accelerate. Office space and executive placement services should be provided by the company. The company has a right to ask for restrictive covenants (for example, no compete covenants) during any period that the Executive is getting parachute type payments. Though it may not be good for tax reasons, getting all projected benefits and continued salary in a single lump sum payment up front would prevent the company from being able to cease paying benefits later.

    b. **Severance in the Event of Executive's Death or Total Disability.** In the event of physical or mental incapacity, death, or permanent disability, the company should continue at least the salary portion of the Executive's compensation package for a certain period of time (for example, two to three years) following the Executive's incapacity, death, or disability. This package is usually less "sweet" than the parachute package.

11. **Restrictive Covenants.** It is commonplace for a company to ask its senior executives to enter into restrictive covenants. The elements for enforceability of an Executive employment agreement restrictive covenant are the same as the elements described previously: the covenant must be reasonable as to time, territory, and activity restrained. The "reasonableness" test must take into account the size of the enterprise (is the company a national enterprise like Microsoft or is it a uniquely regional enterprise?) and the nature of the company's competitor enterprises. In that regard, a covenant that might be considered "overly broad" for a salesman might be reasonable when applied to a "C-suite" Executive. While the Executive should resist onerous post-termination restrictive covenants, it is not reasonable for the Executive to expect to be provided post-termination severance benefits and not to be bound by restrictive covenants, at least during the period of time the Executive receives these severance benefits. That is why accelerating and paying in lump sum severance benefits may be desirable: there is not the same rationale supporting long post-termination restrictive covenants. In the rare

event that the company does not offer the Executive any (or only modest) severance benefits, the Executive should resist being required to sign anything more than minimal restrictive covenants.

12. **Indemnification.** The company should give the Executive maximum indemnification allowed under the laws. The indemnity should cover, for example, losses and liabilities sustained by the Executive in carrying out his express duties at the direction of the Board of Directors. The company's governance documents (for example, by-laws, articles of incorporation or organization, and shareholder agreements) should be scrutinized closely to ensure that the Executive gets maximum protection.

13. **"Most Favored Executive Status".** Any benefits or perks given to any other senior member of management during the Executive's period of employment should also be offered to the Executive on similar terms.

14. **Excessive Compensation Taxes.** Although it is tempting for an Executive to negotiate the highest compensation package possible, the Tax Cuts and Jobs Act of 2018 imposes new taxes on "excessive compensation" for both "for profit" and tax exempt organizations. A publicly held corporation generally may not take a tax deduction for C level employee remuneration in excess of $1 million annually. Tax exempt organizations that compensate C level employees in an amount in excess of $1 million annually are exposed to payment of an excise tax.

V. WHAT IS AN INDEPENDENT CONTRACTOR AGREEMENT?

A. What Distinguishes an Independent Contractor Agreement from an Employment Agreement?

1. **Common Law Test.** For many years, the IRS and the common law used a twenty point test to determine whether a relationship is properly characterized as an "employment" or "independent contractor" relationship.

2. **New Eleven Factor Test.** In 2006, in response to complaints that the twenty factor test was too difficult to interpret and apply, the IRS promulgated a new eleven factor test that consolidates the original twenty factors and organizes the factors into three groups: behavioral control; financial control; and the relationship between the parties. The elements of the eleven point test are set forth on **Attachment 3-A**.

   a. **Behavioral Control.** Behavioral control factors test whether the business has the right to direct and control how the worker performs the task for which the worker was hired, usually through instruction and training.

b. **Financial Control.** Financial control factors test whether the business has a right to control the business aspects related to tasks performed by the worker. The factors consider whether the worker has unreimbursed business expenses, the extent of the worker's investment, the extent to which the worker provides services to others, how the business compensates the worker, and whether the worker can realize a gain or loss.

c. **Relationship Between the Parties.** Factors regarding the relationship between the parties include whether there is a written contract that describes the intentions of the parties, whether the business provides benefits to the worker, whether the relationship is intended to be permanent, and the extent to which the worker's services are a key element of the company's business.

3. **Duties of Loyalty and Confidentiality.** The duty of loyalty arises in employment relationships by law. Therefore, such duties must be expressly addressed in an independent contractor relationship.

4. **Tax Law Issues.** Characterization of the relationship has a direct impact on tax collection. It is easier for the IRS to collect taxes from an employer, which directly pays Social Security and Medicare taxes and is subject to income tax withholding oversight. An independent contractor must file quarterly "estimated tax" returns and pay self-employment tax. An employee gets a W-2 with taxes removed. An independent contractor gets a 1099 with no tax withholding.

5. **The IRS Test Is Directly Linked to Federal Regulatory Tests Regarding *Bona fide* Employment.** The new IRS eleven point test has been adopted by the OIG and the CMS, respectively, for purposes of determining whether a relationship constitutes "*bona fide*" employment under the federal Anti-Kickback Statute safe harbor regulation and the similar exception to the Stark physician self-referral statute.

B. **What Terms and Conditions Are in Independent Contractor Agreements That Are Not in Employment Agreements?** Most terms and conditions are the same. However, in addition to the health care specific issues described below, duties of loyalty and confidentiality need to be specifically addressed because they arise automatically under a *bona fide* employment relationship but must be specifically contracted in an independent contractor relationship. Also, intellectual property laws need to be addressed. Like employment agreements, patent rights need to be assigned. Copyright ownership in works created by the independent contractor must be transferred because the "works made for hire" doctrine does not apply.

C. **How Do Health Care Statutes and Regulations Distinguish Between Employment and Independent Contractor Agreements?**

1. **Stark Exceptions.** There is a specific Stark exception for *bona fide* employees. If the Medical Director is an independent physician, Medical Director Agreements and other independent contractor agreements between physicians and entities to which they may make referrals for DHS must fall within another exception, such as the personal services agreement exception or the "fair market value" exception. Also, the Stark II, Phase III regulations state that the independent contractor relationship between a physician and a medical practice for which the physician provides independent contractor services must be between a medical practice and the individual physician, not the physician's employer. Many independent contractor agreements involve hospitals and physicians, and the definition of DHS includes "inpatient and outpatient hospital services," so every compensation arrangement between a physician and a hospital must be scrutinized under Stark.

2. **Stark Distinction Between "Members of the Group" and "In the Group".**

   a. **Group Practice Definition.** The Stark "in-office ancillary services" exception applies to sole practitioners as well as "group practices" as defined in the regulations. Among other requirements, a group practice must meet the following conditions: (i) it must have at least two physicians who are "members" of the group; (ii) each physician "member" of the group must furnish substantially the full range of patient care services that the physician routinely furnishes; (iii) at least 75% of the total patient care services of the group practice "members" are furnished through the group and billed under a billing number assigned to the group, and the amounts are treated as receipts of the group; and (iv) "members" of the group personally conduct no less than 75% of the physician-patient encounters of the group practice. "Members of the group" include only owners or employees of the practice. Independent contractors are defined by Stark as being "in the group" but are not "members" of the group. Therefore, the impact of independent contractor relationships in medical group practices on Stark compliance with the group practice definition must be closely monitored.

   b. **In-Office Ancillary Services Exception.** To qualify for the in-office ancillary services exception, the DHS must be furnished by the referring physician, a "member" of the referring physician's group practice, or by an individual supervised by a physician "in the group." Therefore, independent contractors can be used to meet the supervision requirements of the in-office ancillary services exception. However, independent contractors must perform their services on the premises of the group medical practice.

   c. **Overall Profit and Productivity Bonuses.** Independent contractors can participate in profit sharing and productivity bonuses of the group related to the provision of Stark designated health services.

d. **Special Clause for "Personal Services Agreement" Exception.** To qualify under this exception, the written agreement must either cross reference all other service contracts between the designated health service provider and the referring physician or reference a master list maintained by the designated health services provider.

3. **Federal Anti-Kickback Safe Harbors.** Like Stark, the federal Anti-Kickback Statute itself, as well as the safe harbor regulations, allows remuneration to W-2 employees, even when "referrals" are involved. Independent contractor agreements must be analyzed under the "personal services and management agreement" safe harbor.

4. **HIPAA Privacy Rules.** Independent contractors who have access to an individual's "protected health information" must execute business associate agreements or, in most Medical Director Agreements, be part of an "organized health care arrangement."

5. **Access to Records.** Federal regulations require a specific "access to records" clause in all independent contractor agreements for the provision of services to institutional providers that file cost reports.

D. What Additional Issues Are Applicable to Medical Director Agreements?

1. **Conditions of Participation.** The conditions of Medicare participation for most institutional providers describe specific duties for medical directors.

2. **Stark and Anti-Kickback Concerns.** Always, the services must be provided at fair market value and must be necessary for the effective operation of the provider.

E. What Regulatory Risks Arise from Independent Contractor Agreements?

1. **Stark and the Federal Anti-Kickback Law.** As always, Stark and federal Anti-Kickback compliance hinges on fair market value.

2. **Call/Coverage Agreements.** While several OIG Advisory Opinions have approved hospital payment to physicians for emergency department call/coverage, the parties must insure that the payments constitute fair market value. An independent appraisal is an advisable practice to avoid a violation of Stark and the federal Anti-Kickback Statute.

ATTACHMENT 3-A

INTERNAL REVENUE SERVICE EMPLOYMENT TEST

1. Compliance with instructions—independent contractors cannot be told when, where, or how to do the job.

2. Training—independent contractors do not go through any type of instructional training period with a more experienced employee to learn how to do the job. Independent contractors specialize in the field in which you have employed them and do not need to be trained.

3. Payment of business or travel expense—an independent contractor is generally responsible for his/her own business or travel expense. If paid by an employer, the employer must include in the independent contractor's 1099, unless the assets are verifiable under the accountable plan rules.

4. Investment in facilities—if the independent contractor maintains an office on the employer's premises, the independent contractor pays a rent or lease payment for the office space as well as overhead.

5. Worker's availability to the general public—an independent contractor makes services available to the public on a regular and consistent basis.

6. Payment by the hour, week, or month—an independent contractor is paid in a lump sum fee basis when the job is done.

7. Risk of profit or loss—independent contractors realize a profit or sustain a loss based on their success in performing the work or service.

8. Written contracts—describe the relationship the parties intend to create.

9. Benefits—an independent contractor is not provided with company benefits.

10. Permanency of the relationship—an independent contractor's relationship does not continue indefinitely with the company.

11. Key services—independent contractors do not provide services that are a key aspect of the company's regular business activity.

CHAPTER 4

FUNDAMENTALS OF BUSINESS ORGANIZATIONS

I. EVOLUTION OF BUSINESS ORGANIZATIONS

A. **History of Business Organizations.** Since the dawn of commerce, business organizations have evolved. The first businesses were financed entirely by their owners. Now it is possible for businesses to be owned by the public. Consequently, as capitalization models evolved, the law of business organizations has evolved with it.

B. **Choice of Entity.** Today businesses have a wide variety of organizational choices. Considerable thought is required to insure the right "choice of entity."

II. SOLE PROPRIETORSHIP

A. **Origin of Business Enterprises.** At the dawn of the common law, the merchants and vendors were individual "sole proprietors," such as the village blacksmith or baker. Consequently, "sole proprietorship" is the oldest and simplest form of doing business. In a sole proprietorship, no organizational or other documents are required to commence and conduct business (with the exception of required permits, licenses, etc.). An individual simply holds himself or herself out to the public as being in business.

B. **Disadvantages of a Sole Proprietorship.** There are two material disadvantages to a sole proprietorship. First, because the sole proprietorship's identity is the same as its owner's, it affords the owner no protection against personal liability. If the customer has a claim against the business, it is the same as having a claim against the individual person, and all of the individual person's assets can be taken if a court enters a judgment arising from operation of the business. In a litigious society, it is virtually never advisable to do business as a sole proprietor because it puts all of the sole proprietor's individual assets at risk. While engaging in a hobby-like business might be suitable for a sole proprietor, if there is any risk of litigation, such as providing professional medical services, a sole proprietorship is not a viable choice of organization. Second, a sole proprietorship can be capitalized only by the individual sole proprietor.

C. **Tax Reporting.** The sole proprietor reports the activities of the business on his or her individual tax return. Under the Tax Cuts and Jobs Act of 2017, sole proprietorships are eligible to receive a 20% deduction on taxable income up to certain income limits, which could stimulate "cottage industry" growth.

III. GENERAL PARTNERSHIPS

A. **Common Law Definition.** A general partnership is formed when two or more persons associate themselves to carry on, as co-owners, a business "for profit". The partnership, therefore, is the second oldest form of doing business and the oldest form of "business organization."

B. **Who Can Form a Partnership?** A general partnership can be formed by individuals, corporations, estates, trusts, or any combination thereof.

C. **How Is a Partnership Formed?** No written documents are required to form a general partnership and, at times, courts have found that a general partnership exists even when the parties did not expressly intend to form one. However, general partnerships are usually governed by either an oral or written partnership agreement, but, since oral agreements are difficult to prove, it is always advisable to enter into a written partnership agreement.

D. **What Terms Are in a Typical Partnership Agreement?**

1. **Purpose.** The purpose is usually clearly stated.

2. **Capital.** The amount of initial capital requirements and how additional capital will be raised.

3. **Distributions.** The manner and method of distributing profits and losses, including the percentage interests held by each partner, should be described.

4. **Governance.** How the partnership will be managed and any limitations on the general rule that any partner can bind the partnership should be described. In general, each partner has an equal vote unless the partnership agreement provides otherwise.

5. **Limitations on Transfer of Partnership Interest.** In general, partnership interests are not conveyable assets. Permitted transfers are specifically described.

6. **Dissolution.** Provisions regarding dissolution and winding up of the partnership's affairs are advisable. Under the common law and partnership laws in most states, a partnership dissolves if one partner dissociates from the partnership unless the partnership agreement provides otherwise. Consequently, a written partnership agreement can, and typically does, provide otherwise.

7. **Confidentiality Agreements and Restrictive Covenants.** These provisions may be included in the partnership agreement to protect the core value of the enterprise. Just like restrictive covenants in employment agreements, to be enforceable, restrictive covenants in partnership agreements must be reasonable as to time, territory, and activity restrained. However, the rules governing enforceability of a restrictive covenant regarding a business ownership interest are more relaxed than the rules governing enforcement of restrictive covenants in employment agreements.

E. What Are the Advantages of a Partnership?

1. **"Pass Through" for Taxation.** The greatest advantage of a partnership is that it allows for "flow through" taxation of gains and losses. Flow through taxation means that there is no tax payable at the entity level, only at the partner level. Also, entities taxed as partnerships provide great flexibility with respect to allocation and distribution of profits and losses. Like a sole proprietorship, a partnership also qualifies for a 20% deduction on taxable income under the Tax Cuts and Jobs Act of 2017.

2. **Simplicity.** Another advantage of a general partnership is that it is simpler and less costly to organize and operate than other forms of business entities. Specifically, a general partnership is purely a creation of private parties and is not created by registering the entity with a state's Secretary of State like other forms of business organizations.

F. What Are the Disadvantages of a Partnership?

1. **General Liability.** The main disadvantage of a general partnership is that each partner is personally liable for both the debts of the general partnership and the acts of other partners acting as agents of the general partnership. Consequently, in a litigious society, doing business as a general partnership is rarely (if ever) recommended because it puts the partners' personal assets at risk like a sole proprietorship. In fact, any business that actively engages in commerce should not be organized as a general partnership. This is particularly applicable to health industry businesses, including medical practices, which are frequently the target of litigation. For example, if a medical practice is organized as a general partnership, and the organization is sued on the grounds that one of the physicians employed by the general

partnership committed medical malpractice, each general partner is exposed to joint and several liability for any costs and damages arising from the litigation. In other words, a plaintiff can recover all of the damages from one general partner if, for example, one partner has attachable assets and one partner does not.

2. **Transferring and Valuing Partnership Interests.** Other disadvantages of the general partnership form are that transferring partnership interests requires more legal and tax analysis than transferring corporate stock or limited liability company membership interests.

3. **Raising Capital.** If an entity needs equity capital, a general partnership is not a suitable organizational form. No sophisticated investor (whether an individual or an institutional investor) will invest funds in an enterprise that exposes their wealth and assets to unlimited personal liability.

IV. CORPORATIONS

A. Brief History of Corporations.

1. **Historic Distrust.** As the common law developed and commerce grew, a need arose for an organizational form that protects the owners from individual liability. However, there was a distrust regarding the creation of non-corporeal "persons" and a fear that wealth and power could be misused.

2. **Creation by Statute.** Therefore, the first corporations could be created only by an act of the king or queen or, in the United States, by state legislation. This method of incorporation was followed by all of the states in the United States through the nineteenth century.

3. **Why Do We Hear So Much About Delaware Corporations?** In the early twentieth century, the small and relatively insignificant State of Delaware saw an opportunity to create a liberal corporations code to attract organization of corporations which could then be taxed based on the number of shares of stock the corporation was authorized to issue. This was very attractive to corporate management. Therefore, many of the oldest and largest corporations are Delaware corporations.

4. **The Race to the Bottom.** The liberal Delaware corporation law touched off the "race to the bottom" as the other states tried to create more liberal corporation codes and make it easier to incorporate. Today, it is very easy to incorporate in almost any state, but Delaware law continues to be the most influential body of business law. Delaware corporation law is regarded to be the most "liberal" because it is perceived to provide the greatest protection of management and management decisions.

5. **Model Business Corporations Act.** The corporations code in most states is based on a uniform act known as the Model Business Corporations Act, but this Act is largely ignored in Delaware as well as California and New York.

B. **What Are the Essential Elements of a Corporation?**

1. **Articles of Incorporation.** A corporation is formed by filing Articles of Incorporation with a state's Secretary of State. Although Articles of Incorporation were formerly required to contain many specific provisions, little information is now required. For example, many states formerly required the Articles to set forth both a specific purpose and a minimum amount of equity capitalization (to protect the public against "thinly capitalized" companies). Now, states rarely require either. The Articles describe the amount and classes of authorized shares of stock. Amendments require the filing of a new document with the Secretary of State. Copies of a corporation's Articles of Incorporation are publicly available.

2. **By-Laws.** The by-laws set forth the general terms and conditions of corporate governance and can usually be revised by resolution of the Board of Directors. In contrast to Articles of Incorporation, by-laws are not recorded with the Secretary of State.

3. **Shares of Stock.** The corporation issues shares of stock to its shareholders. There may be more than one class of shares (for example, common stock and preferred stock), and a class of stock may have different characteristics (such as voting and non-voting common stock).

4. **Governance Structure.** In a corporation, ownership and management are separated. Shareholders elect directors, which have the power to direct the actions of the corporation. Directors in turn elect officers, and the officers manage the day to day affairs of the corporation. In general, the primary duty of the officers is to maximize shareholder wealth. In a closely held corporation, all roles may be filled by the same persons, but a closely held corporation still needs to follow corporate formalities to maintain "corporate integrity" and prevent a "piercing of the corporate veil," which makes individual corporate officers, directors, and shareholders personally liable for corporate obligations.

5. **Shareholders' Agreements.** Shareholders' Agreements generally place restrictions on the transfer of shares and corporate governance and are recommended for closely held corporations with multiple shareholders. Like partnership agreements, Shareholders' Agreements can also include restrictive covenants intended to protect and preserve the corporation.

C. **Who Can Form a Corporation?** Corporations can be formed and owned by either individuals or other corporations, but, as described below, ownership structures are influenced by tax considerations. All corporations are formed in the same way with the Secretary of State, regardless of their tax status. Once formed, a corporation can elect to be taxed under several different chapters of the Internal Revenue Code, the most common of which are subchapter "C" and subchapter "S." These designations merely signify how a corporation is taxed, not how it is organized under state law.

D. **C Corporation.** The C corporation is the traditional form of taxable entity for large, public businesses. The term "C corporation" refers only to how a corporation is taxed, not how it is organized under state law.

1. **What Are the Advantages of a C Corporation?** The C corporation offers several advantages, including limited liability for the owners (shareholders), few limitations on the number and type of shareholders allowed, permissive transfer of ownership interests, and easy access to capital in both the public and private markets. Both individuals and any kind of business organization (such as a corporation, limited partnership, trust, or limited liability company) can own shares of stock in a company that is taxed as a C corporation. The C corporation is also the most established and recognized form of business entity and thus enjoys a wealth of case law interpreting the intricacies of corporate transactions, governance, and operations.

2. **What Are the Disadvantages of a C Corporation?** The major drawback of the C corporation is double taxation. First, the C corporation pays corporate tax on its profits. Second, shareholders are taxed when they receive distributions such as cash dividends. While a smaller corporation may be able to practically eliminate double taxation by paying out profits as reasonable salaries, other taxes such as Social Security, Medicare, and Obamacare taxes must be paid on such salaries, again reducing after-tax return of C corporation shareholders. Third, in order to ensure that the shareholders are insulated from personal liability, corporate formalities should be followed, such as keeping current records of all corporate action taken and having regular meetings of shareholders and directors. Last, because corporations are managed by a Board of Directors elected by the shareholders and officers elected by the Board of Directors, shareholders have no direct authority to manage the affairs of the corporation.

E. **S Corporation.** Again, the term "S corporation" refers to how a corporation is taxed, not how it is organized under state law. Consequently, much of the above analysis with respect to C corporations also applies to S corporations. There are, however, important differences.

1. **What Are the Advantages of an S Corporation?** The "S" in S corporation means that the shareholders have unanimously elected to have the corporation taxed under Subchapter S of the Internal Revenue Code. This election allows the S corporation shareholders to

receive pass-through taxation of profits and losses without taxation of the corporation itself. At the same time, the shareholders of an S corporation enjoy the limited liability of a C corporation. Also, some tax deduction benefits are provided to S corporation shareholders under the Tax Cuts and Jobs Act of 2017, but the S corporation tax deduction is less than the potentially 20% tax deduction for limited liability companies that are taxed as partnerships. Since there are few material differences between limited liability companies taxed as partnerships and S corporations, availability of the tax deduction may cause formation of more limited liability companies.

2. **What Are the Disadvantages of an S Corporation?** An S corporation can have no more than 100 shareholders, no foreign investors, and no more than one class of stock (although voting rights may differ within the class), and shareholders are restricted to individuals, their estates, and certain trusts. In other words, if a corporation's shares of stock are owned by another business organization such as another corporation or limited liability company, the corporation cannot qualify for "S" tax status. Also, the 100 shareholder and no foreign owner limitations prohibit an S corporation from being a publicly traded company.

F. **"Not for Profit" Corporations.** "Not for profit" or "non-profit" corporations make profits, but the profits are retained by the corporation and not distributed to equity owners. Consequently, all "not for profit" corporations are classified as "C corporations" for tax purposes but may be exempt from taxation as described below. This organizational form is appropriate when there is no expectation that the corporation will have profits or when there is no expectation of distribution of proceeds to individuals from the corporation's profits. In other words, all of the corporation's profits are retained by the corporation and taxed to the corporation at that level.

1. **Governance Models.** The Board of Directors has the power to direct the actions of a "not for profit" corporation, and, like "for profit" corporations, the Board of Directors appoints officers to manage the day to day affairs of the "not for profit" corporation. There are two different "not for profit" corporation governance models for election or appointment of a Board of Directors:

a. **Member Model.** The "not for profit" corporation has "members" who, like shareholders, elect directors, and the directors elect officers. The "not for profit" corporation may create several "membership" classes that have different voting or governance rights.

b. **Self-Nominating Board Model.** The by-laws provide for a nominating committee, usually consisting of current directors, which nominates a slate of directors to be voted on by the existing Board of Directors.

2. **Importance of the Articles and By-Laws.** Unlike "for profit" corporations, which typically have standard Articles of Incorporation and by-laws, "non-profit" Articles of Incorporation and by-laws are highly customized because the terms and conditions typically described in a "for profit" corporation shareholders' agreement are described in a "non-profit" corporation's by-laws (because, obviously, a "not for profit" corporation has no shareholders).

3. **Tax Exempt Status.** "Non-profit" corporations are created under state law, and profits of "non-profit" corporations are taxable under state and federal tax laws unless the corporation receives "tax exempt" status under the federal Internal Revenue Code. Tax exempt status is generally available only to entities that qualify under the Internal Revenue Code as "charitable" organizations (which can accept charitable contributions) or social or trade organizations (which cannot accept charitable contributions). Only "not for profit" corporations (or other entities that are organized as being "not for profit") can apply for tax exempt status. To obtain tax exempt status, a "non-profit" corporation must submit IRS Form 1023 and receive a determination letter from the federal Internal Revenue Service that confirms the entity's charitable purpose. Without this, a "non-profit" corporation's profits are taxable to and become earnings of the entity.

4. **Advantages of "Not for Profit" Corporations.** When an organization is not organized for purposes of making a profit and distributing earnings, the "not for profit" corporation is a suitable organizational form. For example, a "not for profit" corporation is suitable for a trade association that has numerous members in the same industry. A "not for profit" corporation may be a suitable organizational structure for any entity that exists more to promote its members or participants than to promote the business of the corporation itself. Also, as stated above, it is also the only kind of corporation that can apply for tax exempt status.

5. **Disadvantages of "Not for Profit" Corporations.** The obvious disadvantage is that all "not for profit" corporation profits are retained by the "not for profit" corporation and taxed at C corporation levels (unless the Internal Revenue Service provides tax-exempt status) and cannot be distributed to the corporation's members or participants.

G. **Professional Corporations.** Although the "race to the bottom" in the late 19th and early 20th centuries took hold early for general business corporations, the states continued to distrust the practice of the "learned professions" through corporations. For example, dating back to the nineteenth century, most states had laws prohibiting the "corporate practice of medicine," which developed in the 19th century and early 20th century in response to the increasing provision of medical care by corporations and the resulting encroachment upon the traditional private physician based practice of medicine. The same rules generally applied to all of the "learned professions," such as medicine, law, accounting, and architecture. However, in the early 1970s, most states began enacting "professional corporations" codes, which allow "learned professionals" to practice in a corporate form. Therefore, in most states, while a profession like the practice of law or medicine cannot be organized as a general corporation, it can be organized as a professional corporation subject to restrictions and limitations that are not imposed on general corporations.

1. **Ownership and Governance Limitations.** Typically, shares of stock in a professional corporation (PC) can be owned only by professionals who are active in the practice; once a professional stops actively practicing the profession, the professional's shares of stock must be redeemed by the corporation or sold to other actively practicing professionals. Also, the President must be an actively practicing professional. However, there are typically no restrictions on who may serve as a director of the professional corporation.

2. **Restrictions on Limited Liability.** Typically, a professional who practices under a professional corporation is still individually responsible for his or her professional services. Therefore, the PC does not provide its shareholders with the same broad limitation on liability as a standard business corporation.

3. **Evolution of Professional Corporations Codes.** Some states, such as Arizona, have revised their professional corporations codes to permit investment interests in a professional corporation by non-professionals, recognizing that the old restrictions may prevent a professional enterprise from raising the capital necessary to compete in a changing economy.

4. **Taxation of Professional Corporations.** Like all business corporations, a professional corporation can be taxed as either a C corporation or an S corporation.

V. LIMITED LIABILITY COMPANIES

A. **Limited Liability Company Acts.** The limited liability company (LLC) is a relatively new form of entity that has quickly gained popularity because of its flexibility. LLCs are organized under state Limited Liability Company Acts. The first LLC statute was enacted in the late 1970s, but many states did not enact LLC statutes until the early 1990s. Today, most closely held ventures are organized as LLCs rather than corporations.

B. **Who Can Form an LLC?** Any person or entity can be a member of an LLC. This instantly makes an LLC more flexible than an S corporation because an organized entity such as a corporation, partnership, or another LLC can acquire an ownership interest in an entity that has the tax pass through benefits of an S corporation plus limited liability for the investors. It is also possible to have a single member LLC.

C. **How Is an LLC Formed?** An LLC is formed by filing Articles of Organization with a state's Secretary of State. While Articles of Organization can include specific and detailed provisions regarding governance and operations of an LLC, most Limited Liability Company Acts also permit LLCs to file "bare bones" Articles of Organization that describe no more than the name, principal place of business, and registered agent for service of process, leaving all details regarding governance and operation of the LLC to its "Operating Agreement" described below. Filing bare bones Articles of Organization is usually preferable because amendments to the Articles of Organization require filing a public document with the state's Secretary of State while amendments to the Operating Agreement are subject only to amendment provisions in the private contract.

D. **How Is an LLC Owned?** The equity owners of an LLC are called "members." This is a somewhat awkward term because, in common parlance, "membership" connotes a voluntary act, such as being a "member" of a country club or church congregation. However, when used by an LLC, its meaning is analogous to "shareholder." "Membership interests" can have almost any desired characteristic without affecting the tax status of the LLC. For example, membership interests may be voting or non-voting for governance purposes or may be merely a "profits interest" that provides an interest in profit distribution but not as "participating" in a liquidation event such as a sale of the LLC's assets or all membership interests.

E. **How Is an LLC Governed?** Unlike a corporation, whose governance structure is dictated by the applicable corporations code, an LLC can be governed in almost any way that it wants. For example, an LLC can be either "member managed" or "manager managed;" managed by a "Board of Directors" or "Board of Managers" like a corporation; or managed by a single "managing member." This list is not exhaustive; there are as many governance variations as imagination permits.

F. **How Is an LLC Operated?** The heart and soul of an LLC is its Operating Agreement (in some states, such as Delaware and Texas, called the "Company Agreement"), which looks substantially similar to a partnership agreement and includes terms and conditions such as the following: qualification for purchase of a membership interest; governance; transferability of membership interests; events of disassociation; and restrictive covenants. Also, most LLC statutes permit an LLC to have an oral Operating Agreement. However, if the members do not enter into a written Operating Agreement, important aspects of the LLC are governed by the default provisions in the LLC code. For example, some written Operating Agreements require either unanimous or super-majority approval of some acts such as a sale of all or substantially all of an LLC's assets, but LLC codes typically provide that all actions of the members can be taken by majority vote of the members unless the Operating Agreement provides otherwise.

G. **How Is an LLC Taxed?** There are several ways that an LLC can be taxed. In general, most LLCs are taxed like partnerships as "pass through" entities. To isolate operating risk, corporations or

LLCs frequently form separate LLCs in which the parent organization is the sole "member." A single member LLC is a "disregarded entity" for tax purposes, so its finances are consolidated with the sole individual member or the parent entity for taxation. The LLC is also a hybrid entity that can, if it so desires, elect to be taxed like either a C corporation or an S corporation. Last, an LLC that is taxed as a partnership qualifies for the 20% tax deduction under the Tax Cuts and Jobs Act of 2017 described above for sole proprietorships and general partnerships. Consequently, organization of an LLC requires consultation with a qualified tax advisor.

H. **What Are the Advantages of a Limited Liability Company?** Advantages include the following: an LLC can be organized for virtually any purpose; an LLC offers investors limited liability and flow through taxation without limited partnership management restrictions described below, S corporation ownership restrictions, and the corporate formalities typically required of S and C corporations; and an LLC provides investors the opportunity to customize a business entity through a detailed Operating Agreement that meets their individual needs without many of the constraints imposed by the previously discussed business entities. In particular, an LLC permits entities like corporations and other LLCs to have tax pass-through advantages that they cannot have in a corporation because S corporation status can be given to corporations that have only individual shareholders.

I. **What Are the Disadvantages of a Limited Liability Company?**

1. **Lack of Legal Precedent.** One disadvantage of the LLC is the lack of precedent interpreting the rules that govern the entity. Because the LLC can be crafted to meet individual needs, there is no typical LLC. This has caused courts to struggle when applying traditional business concepts, like fiduciary duties, power of a member to bind the entity, and choice of law, to LLCs.

2. **Inability to "Go Public".** An additional concern for companies in need of capital is that the LLC is not the form of business entity principally used when seeking private equity or venture capital or in public securities offerings. Even though it is theoretically possible to engage in a public offering of LLC membership interests, there are practical difficulties associated with it, and the general corporation form is highly preferred. This can limit the ability of the company to raise capital and create adverse tax consequences if a switch to the corporate form is made without adequate planning.

J. **Use of LLC for Professional Services Company.** Most state LLC laws provide that the LLC organizational form can be used for any profession covered by the state's professional corporations code. In many states, the LLC law does not include any further specific provisions regarding "professional LLCs," so it appears that a profession such as the practice of law or medicine can organize as an LLC without the PC restrictions on active professional ownership. In some states, this is implied. In others, this is openly acknowledged. Some states, however, have enacted professional limited liability company or PLLC statutes, and these laws include many of the same ownership and governance restrictions as professional corporation codes. Specifically, membership interests in most PLLCs can be owned only by physicians who are active in the practice, which limits equity capital sources and makes a PLLC suitable only for the medical practice and not for any other business venture.

K. **What Is a Low-Profit Limited Liability Company (L3C)?** A low-profit limited liability company (L3C) is a hybrid between a traditional for profit limited liability company and charitable nonprofit organization that is organized for a socially beneficial purposes that itself is not exempt from taxation under Section 501(c)(3) of the Internal Code but can receive program-related investments from tax exempt private foundations. Specifically, a private foundations is required to give away at least 5% of its assets in each year. While this is typically satisfied through grants, it can also be satisfied through "program related investments," defined as an investment whose primary purpose is to accomplish one or more of the foundation's exempt purposes. Only around ten states permit organization of L3Cs, and few exist. However, this organizational form is sometimes used by nonprofit health care delivery systems for organization of affiliated entities that serve the system's core charitable purpose but do not generate internal profits such as a clinically integrated network that includes employed and independent physicians who make referrals to the health care delivery system.

VI. LIMITED PARTNERSHIPS

A. **Uniform Limited Partnership Act.** A limited partnership (LP) is an organizational form that provides limited liability to some of its partners, thereby reducing the investment risk of those "limited" (as opposed to "general") partners. In the evolution of business organizations, the LP form is quite old. The original Uniform Limited Partnership Act ("ULPA") was published in 1916, and it was replaced by the Revised Uniform Limited Partnership Act ("RULPA") in 1976. When it first came into effect, it was the only alternative to either a general partnership or a corporation. ULPA and RULPA have been legislatively tweaked in many states.

B. **How Is a Limited Partnership Organized?** An LP is composed of at least one general partner (usually a corporation) who has unlimited liability for the debts and obligations of the LP and at least one limited partner who enjoys limited liability for partnership debts. The limited partner's risk is limited to the amount of the investment. If the LP fails, the limited partner loses his or her investment money, but the limited partner is not exposed to any other risk related to operation of the LP. While unlimited liability for the general partner can seem daunting to an individual, a corporation can be used as a general partner, resulting in limited liability to its individual shareholders.

C. What Are the Advantages of a Limited Partnership?

1. **"Pass Through Entity".** Like other partnerships, LPs enjoy flow through taxation from the limited partnership to the partners.

2. **Limited Liability.** The limited partners enjoy limited liability but the general partner does not. Only the limited partner's equity investment is at risk. However, in most states, in exchange for limited liability, limited partners cannot participate in the management of the business.

3. **Suitability.** An LP is a suitable organizational form when a general partner with business expertise seeks investment from strategic investors to promote a business concept. For example, many of the early ambulatory surgery center syndications were formed with a corporate general partner and physician limited partners who provided services at the ASC. Also, private equity funds are typically organized as limited partnerships: a corporate general partner with investment expertise raises funds through capital contributions by individual investors. The private equity fund has a duty to maximize the wealth of its investors, but the investors are not involved in the private equity fund's investment decisions.

D. What Are the Disadvantages of a Limited Partnership?

1. **Reliance on the General Partner.** A general partner is permitted to withdraw from the limited partnership at any time. This can leave a limited partner who relied upon the general partner to manage the LP in a precarious situation. The withdrawal of a general partner can also result in dissolution of the LP, which can result in loss of important contracts, strained financial resources, and general uncertainty during critical times. Conversely, it is frequently difficult to remove a general partner who is not meeting performance expectations.

2. **Taxation Limitations.** While general partners may enjoy the benefits of "flow through" taxation, "passive activity" and "at risk" restrictions in the Internal Revenue Code may prevent limited partners from deducting certain losses passed through to them from the LP.

3. **Limited Management Involvement.** As stated above, in most states, limited partners are prohibited from participating in management of the LP: management is controlled entirely by the general partner.

VII. LIMITED LIABILITY PARTNERSHIPS

A. **Use of Limited Liability Partnerships.** The limited liability partnership (LLP) is the newest form of entity and, while rarely used, is most often used by professional entities like medical practices or law firms in which all partners actively participate in the management of the firm. In essence, a partnership that would otherwise be treated as a general partnership can acquire limited liability for its partners by merely filing a document declaring that it is a "limited liability partnership," usually in a state court.

B. **What Are the Advantages of a Limited Liability Partnership?** An LLP combines the tax advantages of a general partnership with the limited liability of a corporation or limited liability company (LLC). In essence, an LLP allows partners to escape the control restrictions of a limited partnership, the ownership restrictions of an S corporation, and the double taxation of a C corporation and is virtually identical to a limited liability company. Because an LLP is virtually the same as an LLC that elects partnership taxation and organization of an LLC is a more formal process, an LLP is rarely used.

C. **What Are the Disadvantages of a Limited Liability Partnership?** Whether the partners truly have limited liability can differ depending on the basis of the claim and the state in which the claim arises. In addition, states vary on whether a partner is personally liable for the contractual debts of the LLP. There is virtually no market for the purchase and sale of partnership interests, and, while perhaps suitable for a professional services organization, an LLP is generally not advisable for a commercial enterprise.

VIII. WHAT FORMS OF OWNERSHIP STRUCTURE ARE RECOMMENDED FOR HEALTH CARE COMPANIES?

A. **Sole Proprietorships and General Partnerships.** Although virtually all medical practices were organized as sole proprietorships or partnerships until the 1970's, no medical practice should be organized as a sole proprietorship or general partnership today principally because of unlimited joint and several liability and difficulty in issues related to governance and continuity of the business.

B. **Corporate Practice of Medicine.** Although the "race to the bottom" took hold early for general business corporations, the states continued to distrust the practice of the "learned professions" through corporations. Specifically, dating back to the nineteenth century, most states had laws prohibiting the "corporate practice of medicine."

1. **Purpose of the Doctrine.** The purpose of the "corporate practice of medicine" doctrine is to prevent unlicensed corporations and other business entities, as well as unlicensed individuals, who may have a profit motive from interfering in the medical decision-making process. The broad public policy goal of the doctrine is to protect consumers of medical care. The corporate practice of medicine doctrine seeks to prevent the commercial exploitation of the

practice of medicine and insure that the loyalty of physicians remains with their patients rather than employers or others to whom they may be financially obligated.

2. **History.** The doctrine developed in the 19th century and early 20th century in response to the increasing provision of medical care by corporations and the resulting encroachment upon the traditional private physician based practice of medicine. Large industrial plants, mines, railroads, lumber companies, and other industries began providing health services onsite to their employees and their families through contracts with physicians or groups of physicians. This was referred to as "contract practice." Of even greater concern were the entrepreneurial businessmen who employed physicians and marketed the physicians' medical services to the general public.

3. **When Is Violation of the Doctrine Asserted?** In most states, "corporate practice of medicine" is a physician licensure matter and is administered and policed by the state Boards of Medicine. The corporate practice of medicine doctrine is most frequently asserted:

   a. as a defense in the course of contract disputes involving fee splitting arrangements between professionals and nonprofessionals;

   b. in disciplinary proceedings brought by state authorities against licensed professionals; and

   c. by individuals who have received medical services as a defense to paying for the services.

4. **Sanctions.** Possible sanctions for violation of these restrictions include, but are not limited to, loss of a physician's license and civil and criminal penalties.

5. **Erosion Over Time.** In many states, the corporate practice of medicine prohibition is alive and well (for example, California, New York, and Texas). In other jurisdictions, however, this prohibition appears to be eroding (for example, Maryland, the District of Columbia, and Georgia). In some jurisdictions, it has been entirely eliminated (for example, Florida).

6. **Current Status of the Doctrine.** Application of the doctrine varies from state to state in terms of both scope of the doctrine and the vigor of enforcement. Some states allow a business to exercise significant management responsibilities over the day-to-day operations of a medical practice, while other states restrict or prohibit such activities. These statutes are often vague or unclear, and the only way to determine whether the doctrine applies in a particular state is to analyze the state's various other statutes, administrative codes, court decisions, attorney general opinions, and regulatory interpretations. In general, however, because of integration requirements in a changing health care economy, the corporate practice of medicine

is eroding across the nation. The primary driver of integration is the ability to survive in a health care economy that is evolving from a purely "fee for service" economy to a coordinated care payment economy and implementation of performance based payment models such as those imposed under the Medicare Access and CHIP Reauthorization Act ("MACRA"). This increases operating risks. Also, medical practices have increasing capital requirements and frequently need equity capital from sources other than the physicians. This creates a collision between the corporate practice of medicine and innovative organizational structures required to compete in a changing health care economy.

C. **Professional Corporations.** In all states professional medical practices can be organized as professional corporations. As stated above, although some states have revised their professional corporations codes to permit investment from more diverse capital sources, in most states only physicians "active in the practice" can own shares of professional corporation stock. Also, a professional corporation is suitable only for the practice of medicine and not for any other purpose. In other words, if an enterprise does not provide professional medical services, it cannot be organized as a professional corporation.

D. **Limited Liability Companies.** A medical practice can organize as a "limited liability company" in virtually all states. As stated above, however, some states have "professional limited liability company" (PLLC) statutes that require the same restrictions on ownership and governance as the professional corporations codes, while some states either expressly or by implication permit a medical practice organized as an LLC to be owned by any person or entity without restrictions.

E. **Limited Liability Partnerships.** This is a viable form of business organization, but the PC and LLC forms are much more widely used.

IX. WHAT ARE THE REQUIREMENTS FOR ORGANIZATION OF A MEDICAL "GROUP PRACTICE" UNDER STARK?

A. **Stark "Group Practice" Definition.**

1. **Single Legal Entity.** The group practice must consist of a single legal entity operating primarily for the purpose of being a physician group practice in any organizational form recognized by the state in which the group practice is organized. The single legal entity may be organized or owned (in whole or in part) by another medical practice, provided that the other medical practice is not an operating physician practice (and regardless of whether the medical practice meets the conditions for a group practice under this section). For purposes of Stark, a single legal entity does not include informal affiliations of physicians formed substantially to share profits from referrals, or separate group practices under common

ownership or control through a physician practice management company, hospital, health system, or other entity or organization.

2. **Ancillary Services Subsidiaries.** A group practice that is otherwise a single legal entity may itself own subsidiary entities. For example, a group practice can form a wholly owned subsidiary for provision of clinical laboratory services.

3. **Range of Care.** Each physician who is a member of the group must furnish substantially the full range of patient care services that the physician routinely furnishes, including medical care, consultation, diagnosis, and treatment, through the joint use of shared office space, facilities, equipment, and personnel.

4. **Patient Care Services.** In general, substantially all of the patient care services of the physicians who are members of the group (that is, at least 75 percent of the total patient care services of the group practice members) must be furnished through the group and billed under a billing number assigned to the group, and the amounts received must be treated as receipts of the group. Patient care services are generally determined based on time. This test does not apply to practices located in Health Professional Shortage Areas (HPSAs) and services provided in HPSAs by physicians in non-HPSA locations. During the "start-up" period (not to exceed 12 months) that begins on the date of the initial formation of a new group practice, a group practice must make a reasonable, good faith effort to ensure that the group practice complies with the "substantially all" test requirement as soon as practicable, but no later than 12 months from the date of the initial formation of the group practice.

5. **Distribution of Expenses and Income.** The overhead expenses of, and income from, the practice must be distributed according to methods that are determined before the receipt of payment for the services giving rise to the overhead expense or producing the income. Nothing in this section prevents a group practice from adjusting its compensation methodology prospectively, subject to other restrictions on the distribution of revenue.

6. **Unified Business.** The group practice must be a unified business having at least the following features: (a) centralized decision-making by a body representative of the group practice that maintains effective control over the group's assets and liabilities (including, but not limited to, budgets, compensation, and salaries); and (b) consolidated billing, accounting, and financial reporting.

7. **Permissibility of Location and Specialty-Based Compensation.** Location and specialty-based compensation practices are permitted with respect to revenues derived from services that are not Stark DHS and may be permitted with respect to revenues derived from DHS from any component of the group practice that consists of at least five physicians.

8. **Physician-Patient Encounters.** Members of the group must personally conduct no less than 75% of the physician-patient encounters of the group practice.

B. **Ability to Provide Ancillary "Designated Health Services".** Compliance with the "group practice" regulations is a prerequisite to being able to "self-refer" for DHS within the group under the Stark "in office ancillary services exception."

X. HOW ARE BUSINESS ORGANIZATIONS USED IN ASSET PROTECTION STRATEGIES?

A. **What Is the General Rule for Asset Protection?** The general rule is that each revenue producing asset should be in a separate limited liability entity.

B. **What Can You Do to Protect Your Personal Assets from Professional Liability Claims?** Many physicians use Delaware Asset Protection Trusts or Family Limited Partnerships (or LLCs) to preserve and protect personal assets.

CHAPTER 5

FUNDAMENTALS OF EQUITY FINANCING

I. HOW ARE BUSINESS VENTURES CAPITALIZED?

A. **How to Finance a Business.** All businesses need capital financing. There are a variety of financing options. The type of capital financing appropriate for the particular business depends in large part on the requirements for implementing a business plan (such as clinical trials and FDA approval for medical devices and biomedical substances) and the company's financial characteristics, such as whether the company has adequate cash flow to service a commercial loan or whether the cash generated by the business must be reinvested to build the business.

B. **What Is a "Security"?** Equity capitalization of any venture except a "not for profit" enterprise involves the purchase and sale of "securities". The following are the common elements involved in defining what a "security" is: (1) the investment of money; (2) in a common enterprise; (3) with an expectation of profits; (4) to be earned through the efforts of others. As interpreted in the federal courts and most state courts, the test is intended to be broadly construed and to meet the economic realities of the investment and business world. As soon as there is an offering of a security, state and federal securities laws are implicated.

C. **Regulation of the Purchase and Sale of Securities.** The federal government, primarily through the Securities Act of 1933 and the Securities Exchange Act of 1934, and all of the states separately regulate the purchase and sale of "securities." The federal laws are administrated by the United States Securities and Exchange Commission (the "SEC"). The state securities regulation laws, commonly referred to as the "Blue Sky Laws," are administered by securities regulators in each state. In other words, securities regulation is an area in which federal and state laws function in parallel: federal law does not preempt state law.

D. **Securities Fraud.** Under federal Securities and Exchange Commission Rule 10b-5, securities fraud arises from the misrepresentation or concealment of a material fact in connection with the offering or sale of a security. Consequently, the securities rules apply as soon as there is an offering of a security, regardless of whether there is acceptance of the offer and a corresponding sale. Therefore, compliance with securities laws relies heavily on disclosure of all material facts and risk factors as soon as there is an offering of a security. This is frequently a challenge for entrepreneurs, who are inclined to characterize businesses in the most favorable manner possible without acknowledging weaknesses in the business plan.

E. **Equity.** Businesses raise equity capital by selling ownership interests in the venture, from which the investors expect a return on investment.

1. **Organization of the Business Entity.** All businesses issue ownership interests when they are organized (for example, shares of stock in a corporation, membership interests in an LLC, or partnership interests in a partnership).

2. **Adequacy of Initial Equity Capitalization.** Virtually no successful business, and especially businesses that have a significant growth strategy, can be completely capitalized with organizational equity contributions. Typically, there is a search for deeper pockets.

F. **Debt.** Equity capital is rarely adequate to entirely fund the enterprise's business plan. The venture will likely need to borrow funds with a promise to repay the debt at some rate of interest. Debt can also be used to leverage a business's profits. Debt is usually the only capital funding that a "not for profit" enterprise (like many health care delivery systems) can obtain.

G. **Hybrids of Debt and Equity.** Some forms of capital investment have features of both equity and debt, such as preferred stock and convertible debentures.

H. **Health Care Regulatory Issues Arising from Capitalization.**

1. **Stark Definition of "Ownership Interest".** The physician self-referral prohibition under Stark can arise from an ownership interest. Stark defines "ownership interest" very broadly. Under Stark "an ownership interest may be through equity, debt, or other means, and includes an ownership interest in an entity that holds an ownership or investment interest in an entity that furnishes DHS." In other words, under Stark, an "ownership interest" can be direct or indirect and is created even if the transaction is in the form of a loan.

2. **Federal Anti-Kickback Statute Definition of "Investment Interest".** "Investment interest" for purposes of the federal Anti-Kickback Statute includes any "security" and may include

shares in stock in a corporation, interests or units in a partnership or limited liability company, bonds, debentures, notes, or other debt instruments.

3. **Cost Report Requirements for Institutional Providers.** All transactions between institutional providers that file Medicare or Medicaid cost reports, such as hospitals, nursing homes, home health agencies, and renal dialysis centers, and persons "related" to the provider must be disclosed and sometimes result in lower payments to the provider. A person or entity can become "related" to the provider through direct or indirect common ownership.

I. **Limitations on Financing of Medical Practices.** State laws governing business organizations can limit capitalization alternatives for medical practices. Under almost all professional corporations codes and states that have enacted professional limited liability company (PLLC) codes, only physicians "active in the practice" can own shares of stock or membership interests in the medical practices. These laws harken back to "corporate practice of medicine" concerns that medicine should not be practiced in a manner that "maximizes shareholder wealth" because that might interfere with professional judgement. This deprives medical practices organized under those laws from access to equity capital that might be used to finance equipment, technology, and other capital items because equity capital can be raised only from the actively practicing physicians. Only a few states have recognized and attempted to address this problem. For example, the Arizona professional corporations code was revised to permit independent ownership of up to 49% of a professional corporation. Some state limited liability company statutes, however, do not restrict independent investor ownership in medical practices, and some states, such as Florida, have no restrictions on capitalization and ownership of entities engaged in the practice of medicine. Consequently, many medical practices are undercapitalized and rely on debt as their principal capital financing source.

J. **Business Plan.** Regardless of whether a company obtains financing through debt or equity, the company will need a business plan designed to "sell" the company to its potential funding sources. The business plan should: describe the company, the product it makes or the services it provides, and the market for its products or services; present a compelling argument for investing in or lending to the company; demonstrate the potential for rapid growth in the business; provide projections of the future financial condition of the company and assumptions to explain how it anticipates achieving the targeted level of growth; assess the risks associated with the business; and explain how the financing will be used and how it will assist the company in meeting its projections. Projections of future financial condition based on historical financial statements that have been audited will enhance the credibility of the projections, but start-up enterprises rarely have audited financial statements. One key to any successful business plan is to determine how the goods or services will be distributed. While private equity and venture capital companies frequently say that a unique and scalable product or service and effective management are more important in making investment decisions than the business plan, every well-organized entrepreneurial enterprise needs a well prepared business plan.

II. WHAT ARE THE TYPICAL EQUITY CAPITAL SOURCES?

A. **Founders.** Typically, most business enterprises are initially capitalized by having the founders invest their own resources. As a general rule, the more capital invested by the founders, the more likely other sources of capital will invest in or loan funds to the company.

B. **Friends and Family.** The next likely source of investment capital is "friends and family." Warning: be sure to document the investment correctly if you expect to preserve your relationship and protect your company against claims in the future if the company prospers and grows.

C. **Crowdfunding.** A relatively new way to raise equity capital, "crowdfunding" means getting small amounts of capital from a large number of individuals, usually through Internet based networks and social media. Crowdfunding provides start-ups with an alternative to the traditional sources of equity capital. Entrepreneurs and early stage start-ups that are unable to undertake traditional methods of capital financing may choose to take advantage of using crowdfunding to reach an expansive group of investors through a seemingly user-friendly access point: the Internet. However, the extensive reporting requirements and regulatory restrictions, as well as the practical difficulties associated with having numerous minority investors, are likely to make crowdfunding an expensive and time-consuming exercise for both issuers and intermediary funding portals. Also, it is frequently advantageous for emerging companies to obtain equity capital from strategic investors who can help the enterprise implement its business plan, which is sometimes referred to as "smart money." Crowdfunding cannot be characterized as "smart money."

D. **Incubators.** In many places, either local government or academic institutions sponsor and promote "incubators" which may provide space for the business and consulting advice as well as access to capital for business start-ups.

E. **Private Placement of Securities to Outside Investors.** If the company is not sufficiently capitalized by the initial equity capital and commercial loans, the next step up the investment line is the private offering of securities (which are offerings made solely by the issuer). At this stage, there are three typical financing sources.

1. **Angel Investors.** An "angel" investor is typically a high net worth individual who provides capital for early stage businesses or business concepts, usually in exchange for stock or

equity ownership but sometimes for convertible debt. While statistics show that the average angel investment is around $500,000, the range may run from several thousand dollars to several million dollars. Angel investors usually do not get involved in management of the venture. In some areas, angel investors have organized into networks and groups, and a business can make a presentation to several potential investors at one time at an angel network meeting.

2. **Venture Capital.** Venture capitalists invest in start-up and early stage companies, typically in the technology industry, in amounts typically less than $10,000,000. While venture capital investors are typically not involved in day to day management, the funds expect representation on the target company's Board of Directors.

3. **Private Equity Funds.** A private equity fund raises capital from a series of investors and then looks for investments to make that capital grow. Typically organized as limited partnerships, the funds are intended to exist for a limited period of time (typically ten years). If successful, the private equity company will raise new funds every three to five years. A typical private equity fund looks to put at least $10,000,000 but frequently $100,000,000 or more to work in each target company either at the closing or within two years after the closing with the expectation that the capital will be used for substantial target company growth. Generally, the private equity fund looks for a proven business concept that has generated actual revenue. Unlike angel investors and venture capital investments, private equity funds are rarely interested in early stage or start-up businesses. At this investment level, the private equity company will impose restrictions on the target company's ability to raise equity and debt capital from other sources.

F. **Public Offering of Securities.** The last source in the equity capital chain is the public offering of securities, after which the securities can be traded on a public exchange. Public capital is expensive, and it exposes the company to a wide array of securities regulation, including reporting requirements under the federal Securities Acts and responsibility requirements under Sarbanes-Oxley. The rules governing public offering of securities are beyond the scope of this work.

III. WHAT ARE THE FUNDAMENTALS OF EQUITY CAPITAL INVESTMENT?

A. **Partnerships and Limited Partnerships.**

1. **General Partnerships.** Ownership structures in general partnerships can be designed and implemented in almost any manner. However, as stated in Chapter 4, general partnerships are rarely used and in fact are unsuitable for any commercial enterprise, especially an enterprise with a growth strategy.

2. **Limited Partnerships.** Limited partnerships have passive limited partners and an active general partner but are funded almost entirely by monetary contributions of the limited partners. Typically, the general partner is a special purpose entity, usually a corporation, formed by the developer or promoter of an enterprise, that brings a core expertise or asset to the limited partnership as its contribution. As described in Chapter 4, the limited partnership interests give investors an interest in the profits of the enterprise but no governance rights.

B. **Shares of Stock in a Corporation.** One very common investment interest is shares of stock in a corporation. In general there are two types of stock: common stock and preferred stock.

1. **Common Stock.** Holders of common stock are pure equity holders and, as such, bear the greatest risk of loss. In a liquidation of the company, common stockholders will be paid only after debt and preferred equity is paid in full. On the other hand, if the business is successful, common stock will generally appreciate faster than the other types of investment securities.

a. **Return on Investment.** A stockholder receives a return on investment in two ways: (i) appreciation of the value of the stock as the company grows; and (ii) dividends. The appreciation of the value of the stock can only be realized upon a liquidity event (sale of the stock or the business), and the gain may be taxed at favorable capital gains rates if the stock is held for a year or more. Dividends are subject to double taxation (after tax profits of the corporation are distributed to the shareholders, and the shareholders pay tax at their individual tax rates). Growth company stock ownership focuses on stock value appreciation, not dividends.

b. **Voting and Non-Voting Common Stock.** The common stock shareholders have the power to elect the directors of the corporation. A corporation can also issue non-voting common stock for governance purposes. Any corporation that issues more than one class of stock with differing rights to distributions and liquidation proceeds cannot qualify for S corporation status, but shares of stock can have different voting rights without exposing the corporation to loss of "S" tax status.

c. **Tracking Stock.** Stock can be issued that "tracks" the performance of a separate division of a business enterprise.

2. **Preferred Stock.** Holders of preferred stock receive dividend and liquidation priority over holders of common stock. There are three characteristics attributable to preferred stock: (a) cumulative, noncumulative, or partially cumulative dividend payment obligations based

on a percentage "coupon rate"; (b) convertible or nonconvertible, usually into shares of common stock; and (c) participating or nonparticipating in the proceeds of a liquidation event involving the sale of the company's assets or stock. This is the most utilized investment vehicle for private equity funds and venture capitalists.

C. **Membership Interests in Limited Liability Companies.** Equity ownership interests in limited liability companies are called "membership interests," and the owners are called "members." This can be confusing because the common meaning of the word "member" does not connote "ownership." In other words, the term "member" when used in the context of limited liability companies is analogous to the term "shareholder" in the context of corporations. However, LLCs have substantially more flexibility in defining rights of membership interests as opposed to shares of stock in a corporation. As stated in Chapter 4, LLC membership interests can have any characteristics that the LLC desires. For example, some LLCs find it beneficial to issue "profits interests" in the LLC or a division of the LLC that require no capital contribution and have no rights upon liquidation of the enterprise to reward key management personnel.

D. **Convertible Debentures.** A convertible debenture is a debt instrument that may be changed or converted into another form of security (often common stock but can be membership interests in a limited liability company) generally at the insistence of the investor. It is typically evidenced by a promissory note or bond and is generally unsecured, being backed simply by the full faith and credit of the company. Convertible debentures are very similar to preferred stock and are also commonly used for early stage and venture capital investment.

E. **Warrants.** A warrant is a contractual right to purchase a certain number of shares of a particular class of stock or membership interests in a limited liability company at a stated price, known as the "strike price." Warrants are often issued in connection with debt financing as a means of inducing lenders to accept terms which would otherwise be unacceptable to such lenders. The "strike price" is usually higher than market value at the time of issuance and is an inducement to create a long term relationship. A warrant provides considerable upside to the holder if the company is successful. Accordingly, a company that issues warrants in connection with debt financing may be able to negotiate for lower financing costs up front, either on a loan with its commercial lender or on a debenture.

F. **Options.** An option is a contract in which one party agrees to sell stock or membership interests in a limited liability company for a specified price at a specified time in the future. An option to buy is a "call;" an option to sell is a "put." A warrant is a type of option.

IV. WHAT RULES GOVERN PRIVATE PLACEMENT OF SECURITIES?

A. **What Laws Govern the Purchase and Sale of Securities?** The sale of securities is regulated by both federal and state law. Federal and state securities laws focus on three primary variables: (1) the security itself; (2) the persons selling the security; and (3) the disclosures made to investors about the security. In general terms, every sale of a security in the United States must either be registered with the Securities and Exchange Commission and the securities regulators of each state where investors reside or qualify for an exemption from such registration requirements.

B. **Exemptions From Registration.** Registration of the sale of a security with the SEC is an expensive and time-consuming process. Therefore, an exemption from registration is often critical, especially for start-up and emerging companies. Two of the most important exemptions from the registration requirements of the federal securities laws are the *private placement exemption* contained in Section 4(a)(2) of the Securities Act of 1933, as amended (the "Act"), and the safe harbor thereunder provided by SEC Rule 506 of Regulation D.

1. **The 4(a)(2) Private Placement Exemption.** Section 4(a)(2) of the Act exempts from the registration requirements of the Act "transactions by an issuer not involving any public offering." This section usually is referred to as the "private placement exemption," but the statute does not define what constitutes a "non-public offering." The SEC and the courts have interpreted the exemption to be available for offerings involving sophisticated offerees and purchasers who have access to or are provided the same kind of information that a registered offering would provide and who are able to "fend for themselves" as knowledgeable investors, and when the offerings are conducted in a non-public manner. Section 4(a)(2) also provides that the sophistication level of both the offerees and the purchasers are important in determining the availability of the exemption.

2. **Regulation D Offerings.** Because of the great uncertainty in determining when the private placement exemption was available under Section 4(a)(2), the SEC adopted Rule 506 of Regulation D, which provides a "safe harbor" under Section 4(a)(2). Section 4(a)(2) is sometimes used when an offering is made to a small number of sophisticated investors. However, most issuers attempt to employ the Rule 506 exemption and use the Section 4(a)(2) exemption as a back-up in the event one of the conditions of the Rule is not met.

3. **Impact of the JOBS Act on Private Placement of Securities.** The Jumpstart Our Business Start-ups Act of 2012 (the "JOBS Act") included material changes to the law governing private placement of securities. The intended purpose of the JOBS Act is to stimulate job growth in small companies and "start-up" enterprises by relaxing regulatory burdens on raising capital. The JOBS Act both (a) modified the rules governing private

placements under Rule 506 and (b) created a new exemption from registrations for "crowdfunding" transactions.

C. **What Are the Limitations on the Manner of a Rule 506 Offering?** Prior to enactment of the JOBS Act, neither the issuer of the securities nor any person acting on its behalf could offer or sell the securities by any form of general solicitation or advertising, including any advertisement, article, press release, mass mailing, notice or other communication published in a newspaper, magazine, or similar media or broadcast over television or radio. The JOBS Act, however, included a radical departure from prior law regarding solicitation of investors in private placements that rely on the exemption from securities registration under Rule 506.

1. **Permissible General Solicitation Under Rule 506(c).** Rule 506 (b) offerings are limited to persons with whom the issuer has an existing relationship. General solicitation is impermissible. After the JOBS Act, issuers can elect to rely on Rule 506(c), which permits general solicitation and advertising of securities offering under certain circumstances. Under Rule 506(c), issuers are free to advertise securities offerings in any medium provided that the ultimate purchasers are "accredited investors", which requires issuers to take "reasonable steps" to verify that the purchasers are accredited investors. The intention of Rule 506(c) is to provide an issuer with access to a deeper pool of accredited investors. While Rule 506(c) offers a flexible approach to permit an issuer to ascertain whether an investor is "accredited," issuers will need to maintain adequate documentation of the verification process to carry the burden of proving that the issuer is entitled to the Rule 506(c) registration exemption. To receive the relaxed solicitation benefits, the issuer will need to indicate on Securities and Exchange Commission Form D that the offering is being made under Rule 506(c).

2. **What If the Issuer Does Not Elect to Proceed Under Rule 506(c)?** If the issuer does not select Rule 506(c), then the old non-solicitation rules apply. In practice, Rule 506(c) and the broader solicitation rights are rarely used. Most offerings continue to rely on the old Rule 506. To maintain the Rule 506 registration exemption when Rule 506(c) does not apply, the issuer must control the number and kind of offerees to be able to show that no general solicitation occurred. Practical steps include a determination that (a) the prospective investor is an "accredited investor," or otherwise meets the standards established by the issuer and (b) investment in the securities would be suitable investment for the prospective investor. Ideally, each prospective investor should have a pre-existing relationship with the issuer and its officers, directors, or affiliates of sufficient contact to determine suitability.

D. **How Many Offerees and Purchasers May There Be?** Rule 506 places no limitation on the number of persons to which the issuer may offer the securities. However, offers to a significant number of persons may be deemed a prohibited general solicitation. Rule 506 does restrict the number of purchasers. The issuer must reasonably believe that no more than 35 "sophisticated" investors (as discussed in more detail below), plus a theoretically unlimited number of "accredited investors," become purchasers. However, some transactions are structured for sale only to accredited investors because certain additional protections from potential liability are obtained thereby and requirements with respect to the information that must be provided to investors are more flexible.

E. **Who Is an "Accredited Investor"?** "Accredited investor" means any person who comes within any of the following categories or who the issuer reasonably believes comes within any of the following categories at the time of the sale of the securities to that person:

1. **Directors, Executive Officers, and General Partners.** Any director, executive officer, or general partner of the issuer of the securities being offered or sold, or any director, executive officer, or general partner of a general partner of that issuer (if the issuer is a limited partnership).

2. **High Net Worth Individuals.** Any natural person whose individual net worth or joint net worth with that person's spouse or spousal equivalent, at the time of purchase, exceeds $1,000,000, or has assets under management in the amount of $1,000,000 or more, excluding the value of the person's primary residence. Also, any amount of indebtedness secured by the primary residence that is in excess of the residence's value is to be considered a liability and deducted from the investor's net worth accordingly. Net worth of a spouse or spousal equivalent may be included even when the property is held solely by that spouse or spousal equivalent. Partnerships, corporations, or other entities may not take advantage of this category. The term "spousal equivalent" means a cohabitant occupying a relationship generally equivalent to that of a spouse.

3. **Income Test.** Any natural person who had an individual income in excess of $200,000 in each of the two most recent years or joint income with that person's spouse or spousal equivalent in excess of $300,000 in each of those years and who reasonably expects at least the same income level in the year of purchase.

4. **Limited Liability Companies.** Limited liability companies that have total assets in excess of $5 million and were not formed for the specific purpose of acquiring the securities being offered.

5. **Other Entities Meeting an Investments-Owned Test.** Any entity that holds investments in excess of $5 million that is not formed for the specific purpose of acquiring the securities being offered.

6. **Certain Family Offices and Family Clients.** A "family office" as defined under the Investment Advisers Act "family office rule" if (a) such family office has at least $5 million in assets under management, (b) such family office is not formed for the specific purpose of acquiring the securities offered, and (c) the prospective investment is directed by a person who has such knowledge and experience in financial and business matters that such family office is capable of evaluating the merits and risks of the prospective investment, including any "family clients" (as defined in the family office rule) of a family office that meets the requirements stated above, whose prospective investment in the issuer is directed by such family office. "Family offices" are generally investment funds managed for high net worth families and individuals.

7. **Registered Investment Advisers.** Investment advisers registered under the Investment Advisers Act, the laws of the various states, or exempt from such registration.

8. **Rural Business Investment Companies.** Rural Business Investment Companies as defined in the Consolidated Farm and Rural Development Act.

9. **Employee Benefit Plans.** An employee benefit plan as defined in the Employee Retirement Income Security Act if a bank, insurance company, or registered investment adviser makes the investment decisions, or if the plan has total assets in excess of $5 million.

10. **Professional Certifications.** Individuals qualify as accredited investors based on possession of certain professional certifications, designations, or other credentials that demonstrate a background and understanding in the areas of securities and investing regardless of their personal net worth or annual income. In particular holders of SEC General Securities Representative, Private Securities Offerings Representative, and Licensed Investment Adviser Representative licenses qualify as accredited investors. The SEC has authority to evaluate and adjust the professional certifications, designations, and credentials that confer accredited investor status on an ongoing basis.

11. **Knowledgeable Employees.** Knowledgeable employees of a private fund (or its investment manager) qualify as accredited investors. "Knowledgeable employees" include, without limitation, (a) an executive officer, director, general partner, trustee, and advisory board member, or persons serving in a similar capacity, of a private investment fund or an affiliated person of the fund that oversees the fund's investments and (b) employees or affiliated persons of the private fund (excluding employees who perform solely clerical, secretarial, or administrative functions) who, in connection with their regular functions or duties, have participated in the investment activities of such private fund or its affiliated adviser for at least 12 months.

12. **Certain Institutional Investors.** Generally applies to banks, registered investment companies, broker-dealers, insurance companies, and other financial institutions.

13. **Tax Exempt Organization With Total Assets in Excess of $5,000,000.** Any organization described in Section 501(c)(3) of the Internal Revenue Code (dealing with tax-exempt organizations), any corporation, Massachusetts or similar business trust, or partnership not formed for the specific purpose of acquiring the securities offered, with total assets in excess of $5,000,000. Any corporation, whether publicly or privately held, will be accredited under this section if it has total assets (not net worth) in excess of $5,000,000.

14. **Certain Trusts.** Any trust with total assets in excess of $5,000,000 not formed for the specific purpose of acquiring the securities offered whose purchase is directed by a sophisticated person.

15. **Entities Made Up of Accredited Investors.** Any entity in which all of the equity owners are accredited investors.

F. **What Information Must Be Disclosed?** If the issuer is not relying on Rule 506(c) and securities are sold to non-accredited investors, certain specified information (similar to that contained in a registration statement) must be delivered to such purchasers, usually in the form of a Private Placement Memorandum (PPM). Offerings in which securities are sold exclusively to accredited investors allow significant flexibility in the form of offering documentation to be used in the offering. Theoretically, it is not necessary to provide a PPM if all of the investors are "accredited," but it is a "best practice."

1. **Material Information.** State and federal securities laws require the issuer to provide the purchasers with full, fair, and complete disclosure of all "material" facts about the offering and the issuer, its management, business, operations, finances, and most importantly, the risks associated with the offering. Information is deemed "material" if a reasonable investor would consider the information important in making an investment decision. Omissions of material facts, even if inadvertent, can lead to liability for "securities fraud."

2. **Ability to Ask Questions.** Last, all purchasers must be given the opportunity to ask questions and receive answers about the offering and to obtain information reasonably obtainable by the issuer to verify the information furnished.

G. **What Sophistication Must the Purchasers Possess?** If the issuer is not relying on Rule 506(c) and the purchaser is not an accredited investor, the issuer must reasonably believe immediately prior to making any sale that each purchaser (except for accredited investors), either alone or with a purchaser representative, has such knowledge and experience in financial and business matters that the investor is capable of evaluating the merits and risks of the prospective investment.

H. **How Does the Issuer Determine That a Prospective Purchaser That Is Not an Accredited Investor Is Capable of Evaluating the Merits and Risks of the Investment?** A commonly used approach is to require that the prospective investor complete a questionnaire that elicits responses concerning education, investment background, net worth, investment experience, and other matters. Only after review of the completed questionnaire and a determination that the person qualifies as being "sophisticated" is the person accepted as a purchaser.

I. **What Limitations Are Imposed on Resale of the Securities?** Securities acquired in a transaction under Rule 506 must be acquired for investment purposes only and may not be resold for an indefinite period, which for persons not closely associated with the issuer is generally not less than two years. These securities will be deemed restricted and cannot be resold without registration under the Act or an exemption therefrom. The issuer must exercise reasonable care to assure that the purchasers of the securities do not intend to immediately redistribute the securities acquired. Such reasonable care includes, but is not limited to, an inquiry as to whether the purchaser is acquiring the securities for his or her own account; written disclosure to each purchaser prior to the sale that the securities have not been registered under the Act and therefore cannot be resold unless they are registered under the Act or unless an exemption is available; and the placement of a legend on any certificate or document that evidences the security stating that the security has not been registered under the Act and setting forth the restriction on transferability and sale of the securities.

J. **What SEC Filings Are Necessary for a Regulation D Offering?** The issuer should file with the SEC five copies of a notice on Form D no later than 15 days after the first sale of securities in a Regulation D offering, although the failure to file the Form D on time may not affect the availability of the exemption.

K. **What Is the "Crowdfunding" Exemption to Securities Registration?** The JOBS Act created a new exemption from securities registration for "crowdfunded" offerings under a new Section 4(6) to the Securities Act of 1933 and the SEC adopted final crowdfunding rules in 2015. The final rules provide that securities issued pursuant to the crowdfunding exemption are restricted securities that must be held for at least one year and are not be required to be registered with any state securities commission. The following are the criteria of the SEC's crowdfunding regulation:

1. **Crowdfunding Issuer Requirements.** Issuers who intend to use the crowdfunding exemption must meet the following requirements:

a. The issuer must be a United States company;

b. The issuer must not be either a company that is required to submit reports to the Securities Exchange Act of 1934 or an investment company; and

c. The issuer is limited to selling a maximum of $1,000,000 in crowdfunded securities in a twelve month period.

2. **Crowdfunding Investor Requirements.** The following restrictions are imposed on the amount the issuer can raise from any individual investor.

a. Investors with an annual income or net worth below $100,000 may only invest, in the aggregate, the greater of $2,000 or 5% of such investor's annual income or net worth; and

b. Investors with both an annual income and net worth greater than $100,000 may only invest 10% of such investor's annual income or net worth, with a maximum aggregate investment through all crowdfunding offerings capped at $100,000.

3. **Crowdfunding Information and Disclosure Requirements.** Crowdfunding issuers are registered to both file certain information with the Securities and Exchange Commission and provide the same information to potential investors and intermediaries or funding portals, the requirements for which are as follows:

a. The initial filing with the SEC must contain basic information related to the issuer, including: the issuer's business; the officers, directors, and significant holders of the company's securities; financial information; and the size and scope of the offering.

b. Offerings of $100,000 or less require financial statements certified by the company's principal financial officer; offerings of $100,000 to $500,000 require financial statements reviewed by an auditor when relying on the crowdfunding exemption for the first time (if audited financial statements are unavailable) and audited financial statements thereafter; and audited financial statements for offerings from $500,000 to $1,000,000.

c. At least once per year, the issuer must file with the SEC and provide to investors financial statements and reports of results of operations as the SEC deems appropriate.

4. **Restrictions on Crowdfunding Issuers.** Issuers are subject to the following restrictions.

   a. Issuers are prohibited from advertising the terms of the offering except for directing investors to the funding portal or broker that is managing the offering;

   b. Issuers may not compensate any third party promoter of the offering unless the compensation is disclosed to the investors; and

   c. Issuers may be subject to liability for misleading communications to investors as well as for misrepresentation or concealment of material facts under Rule 10b-5.

5. **Intermediaries or Funding Portals.** Crowdfunding transactions can be funded only through a qualified broker or "funding portal" that is registered with the SEC. Under the JOBS Act, a "funding portal" is defined as any person acting as an intermediary in a transaction involving the offer or sale of crowdfunded securities for the account of others. Intermediaries of crowdfunding transactions have significant responsibilities under the JOBS Act, including providing certain disclosures regarding the offering and undertaking actions both to prevent fraud and to ensure investor and issuer compliance. Funding portals are subject to the following requirements:

   a. Funding portals may not offer investment advice or recommendations;

   b. Funding portals are restricted from soliciting purchases, sales, or offers to buy the securities offered or displayed on its web site or portal;

   c. Funding portals may not compensate employees, agents, or other persons based on the sole securities displayed or referenced on its web site or portal;

   d. Funding portals may not hold, manage, possess, or otherwise handle investor funds or securities; and

   e. Funding portals must otherwise comply with SEC regulatory requirements.

L. **What Are the State Securities Laws Considerations?** An exemption from federal registration pursuant to Rule 506 does not generally exempt offerings from the qualification requirements of state Blue Sky Laws. The Blue Sky Laws of every state where the securities are being offered must be reviewed to determine the effect and applicability of such laws on the transaction.

M. Broker-Dealer Issues.

1. **Registration of Broker-Dealers.** Persons or entities selling the issuer's securities, and particularly when a commission or compensation is received in connection therewith, may be required to register as "brokers," "dealers," or "agents" under federal or state securities laws. However, if the issuer is going to sell the stock without a broker-dealer, then the issuer and related individuals may fall within a federal exemption and avoid having to register as "brokers," "dealers," or "agents."

2. **Exemption from Broker-Dealer Registration for Directors and Officers.** Directors and officers of the issuer may qualify for an exemption from broker-dealer registration if they: (a) have not relied on the issuer exemption in the preceding twelve months; (b) are not subject to a "statutory disqualification;" (c) are not compensated (directly or indirectly) by paying commissions or other compensation based on sales of the securities; and (d) are not at the time of the sales of the securities an "associated person of a broker or dealer," nor were they "a broker or dealer, or an associated person of the broker or dealer" within the prior 12 months, all as defined under applicable SEC rules.

V. HOW ARE VENTURE CAPITAL AND PRIVATE EQUITY FUND TRANSACTIONS NEGOTIATED?

A. Overview of the Venture Capital and Private Equity Industry.

1. **General Description of Venture Capital and Private Equity Funding.** "Venture capital" and "private equity" funds are sometimes confused because each invests in companies that are projected to grow with an expectation of receiving an internal rate of return of at least 20% in a liquidity event that may involve a refinancing take-out, sale of all or substantially all of the portfolio company's assets, or a public offering of the portfolio company's equity securities (typically common stock). Also, each of venture capital and private equity funds are typically organized as limited partnerships in which the passive investor limited partners are high net worth individuals, institutional funds, or other accredited investors who rely on a general partner with investment expertise to make investments in growth companies. Venture capitalists and private equity funds may be generalist or specialist investors depending on their investment strategy. In the current economy it is sometimes extremely difficult to distinguish between private equity and venture capital investment. It is also sometimes difficult to draw a precise line between "angel investors" and "venture capital investors" since both typically enter the target company growth cycle at the same early point, and sometimes angel investors form "angel funds" that, in essence, are a source of venture capital. While "venture capital" and "private equity funds" have many similarities, and while the lines

between the two sometimes blur, private equity and venture capital investments typically differ in the following ways: portfolio company business plan phase; portfolio company industry; amount and nature of the investment; percentage of ownership interests; and involvement in management or governance of the enterprise.

2. **What Are the Characteristics of Venture Capital Investment?** Venture capital investments generally have the following characteristics:

   a. Target investments are generally in start-up or early stage emerging growth companies that have been organized for two years or less but have potential for rapid growth, sometimes called the "hockey stick curve:" flat when the investment is made but increasing at an increasing rate if the business plan succeeds. Naturally, the venture capital investors dilute ownership of the founding entrepreneurs and expect a voice in corporate governance, but the emerging company does not otherwise have access to capital markets. If a venture capitalist invests in only one or two venture stage companies, there is a substantial likelihood that the venture capitalist will suffer a total loss because the odds of success are so low. Consequently, venture capital funds spread the risk by investing in many enterprises with hopes of one skyrocket return.

   b. Venture capital is usually associated with investments in technology, biotechnology, and biomedical companies.

   c. For tax reporting reasons, venture capital generally takes a less than 50% equity interest in a portfolio company.

   d. While typically requiring a place on the portfolio company governing board so the company has the benefit of the venture capitalist's knowledge and experience, venture capitalists do not want to assume active management of the portfolio company.

   e. Venture capital sources generally invest $10,000,000 or less in their high risk portfolio companies to mitigate investment risk. However, as stated above, these are not strict rules, and some venture funds are willing to take early stage risk with investments of $100,000,000 or more.

3. **What Are the Characteristics of Private Equity Funds?** Fundamentally, "private equity" is any investment in an enterprise whose shares are not publicly traded. Approximately 25% of the economy is financed with all forms of private equity investment, but that 25% represents approximately 98% of all business enterprises. In the past a company frequently turned to a public offering of securities when substantial capital was required to implement a business

plan. However, public capital is expensive capital and requires compliance with complex federal laws and regulations and administration by the federal Securities and Exchange Commission. Today the private capital market has matured to offer sufficient capital to be a viable alternative to public securities offerings. Private equity fund investments generally have the following characteristics:

a. Target investments are generally mature companies that have a flattened growth curve arising from poor management or business decisions that need a capital infusion and a management change to return to a growth strategy.

b. Private equity does not focus on any industry: any mature company with growth potential qualifies. For example, a supply chain company is just as attractive as a technology company provided that the private equity fund believes that financial goals can be accomplished.

c. Private equity generally acquires a 100% ownership interest in the portfolio company and assumes managerial control, but, in any event, will not take a less than 50% equity interest in the portfolio company. At one time private equity was seen as a ruthless, short vision industry run by high profile "corporate raiders" that purchased undervalued mature companies then broke them apart to recover the investment as portrayed in the iconic 1980s movie Wall Street, but today private equity is viewed more favorably. In general, private equity funds are expected to purchase, grow, and then sell portfolio companies because the funds, usually financed by high net worth individuals or financial institutions, are expected to provide earnings multiples from liquidity events for the investors.

d. 25% of all private equity transactions involve between a $25,000,000 and $100,000,000 investment, but many sources use $100,000,000 as a standard private equity deal and $10,000,000 as the absolute private equity minimum investment.

e. The investment typically involves both debt and equity to mitigate investment risk.

4. **What Is the Typical Target Company?** The usual target of both venture capital and private equity investment has some unique, core asset or service that is frequently protected by intellectual property (patent, trade secret, copyright, or trademark).

5. **Types of Venture Capital and Private Equity Fund Firms.** The most common type of venture capital or private equity fund is an independent firm that has no affiliation with any other financial institution. However, venture capital and private equity funds may also be

affiliates or subsidiaries of a commercial bank, investment bank, or insurance company and may make investments on behalf of outside investors such as high net worth individuals. Still others may be subsidiaries of non-financial, institutional companies that want to provide incubator capital to enterprises that are a good strategic fit with the institution. These latter firms typically are referred to as "strategic investors" or "corporate venture investors."

B. **Uniform Venture Capital and Private Equity Investment Documents.** To reduce legal fees and facilitate venture capital and private equity fund transactions, many funds require use of publicly available model documents developed for the National Venture Capital Association found at https://nvca.org/resources/model-legal-documents/ as a starting point. The forms are annotated with substantive footnotes that describe alternative terms and conditions, many of which are mutually exclusive, and include the following documents that are common to virtually every venture capital or private equity fund transaction:

- Term Sheet;
- Stock Purchase Agreement;
- Voting Agreement;
- Investor Rights Agreement;
- Right of First Refusal and Co-Sale Agreement;
- Indemnification Agreement; and
- Amended and Restated Certificate of Incorporation.

C. **Guidelines and Checklists for Entrepreneurs.**

1. **Evaluating Project Risks.** An entrepreneur should understand and be able to address the project's risks before approaching a venture capitalist or private equity fund. These risks should be clearly articulated in the company's business plan. Venture capitalists and private equity funds typically will review the following four risks of a target company's business plan before investing in it. Thus, if a target company understands and addresses these risks up front, financial backing is much easier to obtain.

a. **Market Risk.** What problem is this product solving? This helps equity funds and venture capitalists determine whether the product or technology addresses a significant problem in the marketplace, what the competitive alternatives are, and whether the market is large enough to yield a significant return on the investment.

b. **Technology Risk.** Who owns the idea and has it been effectively protected? Considering this risk requires investors to evaluate the proprietary aspects of the technology, including trade secrets; patent position and ownership; further development work needed to produce the first product or service; manufacturability; whether regulatory approvals such as Food and Drug Administration ("FDA") clearance is required for the product to be distributed; and the potential breadth of the protected technology's application.

c. **Financial Risk.** How much money will it take? The investors will evaluate the amount of capital needed to achieve a sustainable market position, the potential sources of capital required by the project in addition to initial capital investments, and the possible investment withdrawals that may occur.

d. **Management Risk.** Can the market opportunity be exploited? The investors will assess the strengths and weaknesses of the entrepreneur or founding management team, whether management should be replaced or whether additional management assistance is needed, whether effective working relationships can be established, and whether the commercial objectives and expectations of the entrepreneur and the venture capitalist or private equity investor match.

2. **The Entrepreneur's Checklist.** The following is a checklist for approaching a venture capitalist or private equity fund.

a. **Type of Security.** Companies typically convey convertible preferred stock to investors, which provides a preference payment to the preferred stockholder if the company is acquired or otherwise liquidated and other preferences over the common stock held by the founders. These preferences help justify a much higher price for the preferred stock than the price paid by founders for the common stock.

b. **Price/Valuation.** Investors use a number of different methods to determine a company's value and the price they will pay for their investment, from a discounted revenue stream approach based on business plan projections, to a more arbitrary figure based on a desire to own a predetermined percentage of the company in return for the anticipated level of funding needed to achieve a certain milestone.

c. **Liquidation Preference.** Upon liquidation of the company, the preferred stock will receive a certain fixed amount before any assets are distributed to the common stock.

A "participating preferred" stock will not only receive this fixed amount, but then also will participate in some manner with the common stock in further distributions.

d. **Dividend Preference.** Generally, a dividend must be paid to the preferred stockholder before any dividend is paid to the common stockholders. This dividend may be non-cumulative and discretionary, or it may be cumulative so that it accrues from year to year until paid in full.

e. **Redemption.** Preferred stock may be redeemable, either at the option of the company or the investors or mandatorily on a certain date, perhaps at some premium over the initial purchase price of the stock.

f. **Conversion Rights.** Preferred stock will be convertible into common stock at some conversion ratio, which is typically expressed as the initial purchase price of the preferred stock divided by a "conversion price" which initially equals the purchase price but is subject to adjustment upon the occurrence of certain events. Conversion is generally available at any time at the option of the stockholder and may be automatically triggered by certain occurrences, such as an initial public offering.

g. **Anti-Dilution Protection.** The conversion price of the preferred stock will be subject to adjustment for diluting events, such as stock splits or stock dividends, and will probably also be subject to "price protection," which is adjustment upon future sales of stock at prices below the conversion price. Price protection can take many forms, from an extreme "ratchet" protection which lowers the conversion price to the price at which any new stock is sold, regardless of the number of shares, to a broad-based "weighted average" protection which adjusts the conversion price based on a formula incorporating both the number of new shares being issued and their price. The issuance of a certain number of shares is generally excepted from this protection to cover anticipated issuances to key employees, consultants, and directors. Price protection is sometimes subject to a "pay-to-play" provision, which makes the continuation of such protection for a given investor contingent on that investor purchasing at least its pro-rata share of any future issuances priced below the conversion price.

h. **Voting Rights.** On general matters, preferred stock usually votes along with common stock and has a number of votes equal to the number of shares of common stock into which it is convertible. The preferred stock also typically has special voting rights, such as the right to elect one or more of the company's directors or to approve certain types of corporate actions, such as amendments of the articles of incorporation, mergers, or creation of a new series of preferred stock.

i. **Right of First Refusal.** Holders of preferred stock generally will have a right to participate, usually at up to an investor's current aggregate ownership percentage, in any future issuance of securities by the company.

j. **Co-Sale Right.** Preferred investors often will require founders to enter into a co-sale agreement. A co-sale right provides some protection against founders selling their interest in the company to a third party by giving investors the right to sell a portion of their stock as part of any such sale.

k. **Registration Rights.** Preferred investors generally will receive registration rights as a part of their investment. These rights provide liquidity to investors by allowing them to require the company to register their shares for sale to the public, either as part of an offering already contemplated by the company ("piggy-back rights") or in a separate offering initiated at the investors' request ("demand rights").

l. **Vesting on Founders' Stock.** As a protection against founders leaving the company after the investment money is in, investors generally insist on some sort of "vesting" on founders' stock, so that a percentage of such stock, decreasing over time, is subject to repurchase by the company at cost if a founder terminates his or her employment.

CHAPTER 6

FUNDAMENTALS OF DEBT FINANCING

I. WHAT LAWS GOVERN DEBT FINANCING TRANSACTIONS?

A. **Debt Financing.** While the previous chapter describes the general role of debt financing in a capital plan, this chapter covers the specifics of debt financing. Virtually every commercial debt transaction includes the following documents: Loan Agreement; Promissory Note; Security Agreement; and Guaranty Agreement. Some forms of debt financing, such as bond financing, include additional agreements.

B. **Debt Financing Is Governed by Both the State Law of Contracts and the Uniform Commercial Code.** Unlike contracts for the purchase and sale of "goods," which are governed entirely by Article 2 of the Uniform Commercial Code (UCC), debt financing transactions are governed by a combination of the general state law of contracts as well as Article 3 of the UCC, which governs "commercial paper," and Article 9 of the UCC, which governs "secured transactions."

C. **Medical Practice Debt Financing.** Because the only available source of equity financing for medical practices organized as either professional corporations or professional limited liability companies (and, in fact most medical practices) is the physicians who are active in the practice themselves, most medical practices are undercapitalized by equity capital funding and rely principally on debt financing. Consequently, many medical practices are highly leveraged.

II. WHAT ARE THE TYPES OF DEBT TRANSACTIONS?

A. **Term Loans.** A term loan is generally a longer term form of financing, typically three to five years, which is amortized over the term of the loan, often at a fixed interest rate.

1. **What Is the Purpose of a Term Loan?** Term loans generally provide capital asset financing for the borrower such as to purchase or develop real estate or to purchase equipment or other fixed assets, but also may be used to provide operating capital. As a fundamental part of an enterprise's capital plan, term loan debt can be used as "leverage" to enhance the value of the enterprise's stock or other ownership interests.

2. **What Is the Cost of a Term Loan?** Although term loans can have a variable interest rate, they typically have a fixed rate of interest that reflects the credit worthiness of the borrower and market rates. Sometimes the interest rate is based on an objective rate such as the bank's "prime rate" (the rate available to the bank's best customers) or the Intercontinental Exchange London Interbank Offered Rate, commonly referred to as "LIBOR."

3. **How Is a Term Loan Secured?** Term loans are generally senior loans secured by real estate, equipment, or other fixed assets, but can also be secured by additional types of collateral, including accounts receivable, personal property, and intellectual property.

B. **Revolving Credit Loans.** Revolving credit loans are usually made by commercial banks and provide short-term financing for a company to meet its working capital requirements. A revolving credit loan is a line of credit that may be drawn down, paid back, and drawn down again, but is generally not intended to provide long-term capital financing. Most revolving loans also require a zero balance for some period of time during each year, typically 30 days. Most revolving credit loans have a one year term that is renewable at the election of the lender from year to year.

1. **What Is the Purpose of a Revolving Credit Loan?** A revolving credit loan is used when a business has short term working capital needs. For example, if a business pays its employees every two weeks, occasionally there is a month in which the business has three payrolls but does not have available cash. Having a revolving credit loan can fill this short term working capital deficiency. Also, working capital loans can support a business's purchase of inventory needed for the business to produce its goods or services or help to carry accounts receivable until they are paid.

2. **What Is the Cost of a Revolving Credit Loan?** The interest rate for a revolving credit loan is generally a floating interest rate set at a certain percentage above the lender's prime rate. Lenders generally also require that the borrower pay a quarterly commitment fee which is a percentage of the amount of the revolving credit facility not used by the borrower.

3. **How Is a Revolving Loan Secured?** A revolving credit facility may be secured solely by the borrower's accounts receivable, inventory, or equipment, in which event the lender will generally lend up to the lesser of the commitment or a borrowing base, which is generally

a percentage of eligible accounts receivable, inventory, or equipment. Alternatively, a line of credit may be secured by all the assets of the business and may not be tied to a specific borrowing base.

C. **SBA Financing.** Banks and other financial institutions are common sources of debt financing. However, banks in the current economy have tight credit requirements, and, without substantial collateral, it may be difficult for early stage enterprises to obtain commercial bank financing. The United States Small Business Administration (the "SBA"), a governmental agency that is dedicated to the growth of entrepreneurial businesses, assists start-up and early stage enterprises that may not qualify for a loan under a bank's typical credit standards to obtain loans by guaranteeing repayment of the loan, which reduces the bank's lending risk. Thus SBA guaranteed loans may provide start-up and early stage enterprises with a path to debt financing that might otherwise be available.

D. **HUD and Other Federal Loan Programs.** The United States Department of Housing and Urban Development (HUD) has special loan programs for financing assisted living facilities, senior care facilities, skilled nursing facilities, continuing care retirement centers, memory care facilities, rehabilitation hospitals, and similar enterprises. Both "for profit" and "not for profit" enterprises can qualify for HUD loans. Similarly, other federal government departments, such as the United States Department of Agriculture through its Rural Development Loan program, can be sources of debt financing.

E. **Tax Exempt and Industrial Revenue Bonds.** By definition, "not for profit" corporations do not have equity investors. Consequently, the only way that "not for profit" corporations can raise capital is through debt financing transactions. "Not for profit" corporations that have qualified as "tax exempt" under Section 501(c)(3) of the Internal Revenue Code can borrow from the issuance of the tax exempt bonds issued by or on behalf of a state or local governmental unit. Similarly, Industrial Revenue Bonds (IRBs) are tax-exempt loans issued by state or local governments to finance private company projects, particularly those with the prospect of stimulating the local economy and creating jobs for local residents.

1. **What Are the Characteristics of Bond Financing?** Bond financing is usually amortized over a longer period of time than commercial term loans, with most having terms of ten, twenty, or thirty years.

2. **How Are Bond Financings Managed?** In addition to fundamental loan documents including a Loan Agreement, Promissory Note, and Security and Mortgage Agreements, bond financing also requires a "Trust Indenture" or "Trust Agreement" that appoints a "Trustee," usually a division of a commercial bank, to manage the flow of funds related to the borrower's

operations and obligations to repay the bonds. Under the terms of a bond financing Loan Agreement, the borrower pledges all of its revenue to be transferred to the Trustee. The Trustee is obligated to establish a series of internal funds, including, for example, a Revenue Fund, Debt Services Reserve Fund, Operating and Maintenance Fund, Renewal and Replacement Fund, and Depreciation Reserve Fund. The Trustee then manages the revenue received from the borrower in accordance with a prescribed "flow of funds."

3. **How Are Bond Financings Secured?** Bond financings are typically secured in every manner possible. Not only are all gross revenues transferred to the Trustee, security will include accounts receivable, furniture, fixtures, equipment, and all other personal property that can be secured under UCC Article 9 as well as mortgage security interests in any borrower owned real property.

III. WHAT ARE THE FUNDAMENTAL TERMS OF LOAN AGREEMENTS?

A. **Nature of Loan Agreements.** A commercial lender will require execution of a Loan Agreement in connection with a credit facility. The Loan Agreement is a private contract that is governed by the state law of contracts. Many commercial Loan Agreements are form documents prepared by a commercial lender. You must read them carefully to ensure that they fit your entity. Loan Agreements typically include the provisions described below.

B. **Positive Covenants.** One purpose of positive covenants is to require that the borrower provide the lender financial and other information in the future. For example, the borrower may be required to deliver to the lender quarterly and annual financial statements. In order to remain informed about the borrower's condition, the lender may require that the borrower give it notice of certain events such as the threat of litigation or instigation of a governmental investigation. Otherwise, positive covenants are a list of borrower's promises to take such actions as: maintain its corporate or other existence; pay all its debts when due; keep proper records; maintain adequate insurance; and comply with laws.

C. **Negative Covenants.** Negative covenants are the most heavily negotiated provisions of a Loan Agreement. It is through negative covenants that the lender imposes on the borrower restrictions that protect the lender's interest in being paid but may interfere with the borrower's unfettered conduct of its business and may not be clearly understood when an enterprise executes a bank's standard form of loan agreement. The lender reasonably wants to ensure that its loan is paid and the borrower reasonably wants to conduct its business in a manner that results in a successful enterprise. Sometimes these positions, although each may be "reasonable," clash. Standard negative covenants for a borrower to make to a lender include the following: not to merge, consolidate, liquidate, or dissolve itself without lender prior written permission (often excepting mergers of, into, or among wholly-owned subsidiaries); not to enter into a new business without the lender's prior permission; not to sell assets without using the proceeds to pay down the principal amount of the loan; not to sell stock or other ownership interests; not to pay dividends (possibly qualified by whether or not the borrower maintains certain financial ratios); not to increase executive compensation; and other promises tailored to particular borrowers.

D. **Financial Covenants.** Financial covenants generally cause borrowers the most headaches. The lender wants to ensure that the borrower maintains substantially the same financial condition as it had when the Loan Agreement was executed, produce substantially the same results of operations in the future as it had produced in the past, or some combination of both. Lenders frequently require that borrowers maintain certain financial ratios to ensure these results.

E. **Financial Representations and Warranties.** Any credit facility, whether a term loan or revolving loan, will have a representations and warranties section that describes a borrower at a particular moment in time. For example, the borrower represents and warrants that the financial statements provided to the lender are true and accurate, prepared in accordance with GAAP, and fairly represent the financial condition of the company. There will generally also be a representation that no material adverse event has occurred since the date of the financial statements.

F. **Non-Financial Representations and Warranties.** The non-financial representations and warranties usually include statements that the borrower is a validly formed corporation (or other entity), is engaged in a specific business, and does not engage in some other types of businesses. The borrower will have to list all of its subsidiaries and make statements about what types of entities they are and where they are validly formed. The lender is probably going to ask the borrower to make statements about some or all of the following: litigation; labor matters; compliance with ERISA; compliance with environmental laws; payment of taxes; and ownership of property (whether real, personal, or intellectual property).

G. **Regulatory Representations and Warranties.** Most loan agreements involving health care businesses require representations and warranties regarding compliance with all health care statutes and regulations.

1. **Fraud and Abuse Laws.** Expect representations regarding compliance with fraud and abuse laws, including Stark and the federal Anti-Kickback Statute.

2. **Regulatory Approvals.** The borrower will represent and warrant that the business has all approvals necessary to carry on the business, such as licensure, certification, and certificates of need.

3. **Claims for Payment.** Lenders will expect a representation that all claims for payment have been correctly submitted.

H. **How Do You Manage the Risk of Potential Breach of Warranty?**

1. **Knowledge.** Try to precisely define "knowledge" to actual, not constructive, knowledge, and try to limit knowledge to specific borrower representatives.

2. **Material Adverse Effect (MAE).** Limit representations and disclosures to those that have a material adverse effect.

3. **Time Limit.** Limit the duration of the representation.

4. **Schedules.** Schedules to the Loan Agreement disclose exceptions to the representations and warranties.

I. **Events of Default.** "Events of Default" typically include not only failure to make timely payment but also a breach of the other terms and conditions of the Loan Agreement (such as representations and warranties, positive and negative covenants, and other contract terms), insolvency of the borrower, and any false statement made to induce the lender to make the loan. That is why reading the bank's standard form of Loan Agreement is so important: Loan Agreements sometimes include representations and warranties that it is impossible for the borrower to make because it is difficult to force a "one size fits all" document into applying to individual borrower circumstances.

J. **Relationship of Loan Agreements to Health Care Fraud Investigations.** When an organization is investigated for potential health care fraud, investigations frequently look at loan applications and agreements for false statements.

IV. WHAT IS A PROMISSORY NOTE?

A. **History of "Commercial Paper".** A promissory note is a form of "commercial paper" that is governed by the UCC Article 3 and is referred to in law as a "negotiable instrument." As the commercial common law developed in the 17th and 18th centuries, while the courts would enforce "bills of exchange" (analogous to modern "checks"), the courts did not enforce notes that promised payment in the future. However, a law was passed in England in 1704 that made promissory notes enforceable, and the modern law of negotiable instruments is based on English law developments after that enactment. Today every state, including Louisiana, has enacted a form of UCC Article 3.

B. **Definition of Promissory Note.** A "Promissory Note" is defined in Article 3 of the UCC to be a written document in which a borrower unconditionally promises to pay to the order of a specific person or to the bearer a certain sum to a lender on demand or at a definite time, usually with interest accruing on the outstanding principal amount. It is more than mere acknowledgment of a debt like an "I.O.U." A Promissory Note is actually a separate agreement from other loan documents that in many ways stands on its own.

C. **What Makes a Promissory Note a "Negotiable Instrument"?** To be "negotiable," an instrument must (1) be in writing, (2) be signed by the maker, (3) contain an unconditional promise to pay a fixed sum of money on demand or at a definite time, (4) contain "words of negotiability," and (5) be free from unauthorized promises (like conditioning payment on the delivery of goods or services, which makes the agreement a simple contract, not a negotiable instrument). A negotiable instrument can be enforced by a "holder in due course." In other words, it can be transferred from the original holder to a successor holder. For example, a bank that is the "holder" of a Promissory Note payable over a long period of time, such as five or more years, can sell the note to a "holder in due course" for a discounted present value, exchanging payout over time for present cash. This is the foundation for the 2008 financial collapse. Mortgage lenders "securitized" mortgage loan instruments by bundling many Promissory Notes into one security and then selling an interest in that security to the public. However, when the underlying mortgage loans began going into default, the bundled loan securities lost their value.

D. **What Are the Typical Provisions in a Promissory Note?** Promissory Notes generally have the following terms:

1. **Financial Terms.** The principal amount, interest, and term.

2. **Payment Terms.** The payment schedule (for example monthly or annual installments) and how payments will be allocated to the loan amortization (typically first to interest and then to principal). If permitted under the terms of the Promissory Note, payments in an amount greater than the required interest and principal payment are allocated to unpaid principal, which results in faster repayment of the loan.

3. **Prepayment Penalty.** While most Promissory Notes permit prepayment at any time without penalty, some require a prepayment "penalty" to compensate the lender for expected interest income and some do not permit prepayment at all.

4. **Late Charges.** Promissory Notes typically charge a late payment fee which might be either a percentage of the unpaid amount or a flat fee.

5. **Interest After Default.** Upon a default, interest will increase substantially, sometimes to as much as 21%.

6. **Events of Default.** In addition to nonpayment, commercial Promissory Notes sometimes permit a lender to declare a default on less objective grounds, such as (a) the occurrence

of a material adverse change in the financial condition of the borrower or a guarantor or (b) the lender in good faith believes itself insecure regarding repayment of the Promissory Note.

7. **Lender's Rights Upon Default.** When a Promissory Note is in default, commercial Promissory Notes typically provide lenders with an array of assertible rights, all of which a lender can pursue without exclusion (provided that, as with any contract action, the lender's remedies end when the lender is "made whole," meaning that the lender makes a full financial recovery under the terms of the Promissory Note). Rights and remedies available to a commercial lender upon default typically include the following: (a) accelerate full payment of the outstanding principal and interest plus attorneys' fees, costs, expenses, and other fees and charges (such as late fees and default interest) permitted under the Promissory Note; (b) if the borrower has more than one loan or credit facility with the lender, declare all other loans and obligations in default, even if there is no independent default on those loans; (c) proceed directly against guarantors of the Promissory Note; and (d) take such action as may be permitted under a related Security Agreement. These same rights are also typically described in the Loan Agreement.

8. **Attorneys' Fees.** Commercial Promissory Notes typically require a defaulting borrower to be responsible for the lender's attorneys' fees that accrue as soon as the Promissory Note is referred to an attorney for collection. Because this may be a relatively open-ended financial risk, borrowers may want to negotiate for a cap on potential attorneys' fees, such as a percentage of the outstanding principal amount or a fixed monetary cap.

9. **Collateral.** The collateral for the Promissory Note is generally described in the Promissory Note but more particularly described in the Security Agreement.

E. **How Is a Promissory Note Enforced?** With the possible exception of "fraud," which requires evidence of a factually specific misrepresentation or concealment of a material fact, if the signature on a Promissory Note is authentic, there is virtually no defense to a lawsuit to enforce payment on a Promissory Note. Once the authenticity of the signature is proved, the holder can get a judgment against a maker in default. Note: Whenever a transaction involves a Promissory Note, the maker should sign only one original. While it is customary to have several originally executed transaction documents so each party has a set of originals, that practice does not apply to Promissory Notes.

F. **What Happens When a Promissory Note Is Fully Paid?** When a Promissory Note is fully paid, the original Promissory Note should be returned to the borrower marked "SATISFIED."

V. WHAT IS A "SECURED TRANSACTION" AND WHAT IS THE IMPORTANCE OF A SECURITY AGREEMENT?

A. **What Is a "Secured Transaction"?** A Security Agreement makes a Loan Agreement a "secured transaction." Consequently, the word "security" is relevant to both equity capital and debt capital transactions, but with completely different meanings. In the context of equity financing, a "security" is an investment interest in which the investor expects to profit from the efforts of others. In a debt capital transaction, the meaning of the word "security" is closer to its common dictionary usage: it refers to making the lender more "secure" when loaning money to an enterprise. A promise to repay the loan as embodied in the Promissory Note is typically not enough to induce a bank or other lender to make a loan because the only remedy the lender has for repayment is to file a lawsuit and go through the entire judicial process to obtain a judgment against the defaulting borrower. However, if the borrower already cannot repay the loan, judicial proceedings are useless and futile. The lender wants other ways to be "made whole" in the event of a loan default. In other words, the lender wants to enter into a "secured transaction," meaning that the lender takes a "security interest" in the borrower's "personal" (as opposed to "real") property, including, for example, accounts receivable, furniture, fixtures, equipment, inventory, and any other moveable good such as a motor vehicle as well as "intangible" property such as patents, copyrights, and trademark goodwill.

B. **What Law Governs Secured Transactions?** Secured transactions are governed by Article 9 of the UCC, which has been enacted in all of the states. Security interests in real property through a real property "mortgage" are governed by state real property law and are not covered in this discussion of "secured transactions."

C. **What Is a "Security Interest"?** A "security interest" is a consensual "lien" granted by a borrower to a lender in specifically identifiable personal property that secures payment or performance of a contracted obligation.

D. **What Is a Security Agreement?** A "Security Agreement" is a contract between a lender and borrower that states that the lender can repossess the property a person has offered as collateral if the loan is not paid as agreed. After acquiring security interests through the Security Agreement, the lender must "perfect" the security interest. It is important to understand that, without proper security, a lender is unlikely to make a loan. This makes it particularly difficult for a start-up enterprise with no accounts receivable or other valuable assets to obtain debt financing.

E. **What Are the Typical Provisions in a Security Agreement?** Security Agreements generally have the following terms:

1. **Grant of the Security Interest.** The Security Agreement must grant a security interest in specifically described collateral as required for perfection of the security interest. Without limitation, as described elsewhere in this chapter, the security interest governed by Article 9 of the UCC may be granted in the following personal property: accounts receivable; inventory; furniture; fixtures; equipment; intellectual property and other intangible property; bank accounts and cash; and borrower books and records.

2. **Representations and Warranties.** Like the Loan Agreement, a Security Agreement typically includes representations and warranties on which the lender relies, including, for example, that the borrower:

    a. Has clean title to the collateral;

    b. Has not granted another security interest that has higher priority than the security interest granted under the Security Agreement; and

    c. Has not stored the collateral at any location not disclosed to the lender.

3. **Covenants.** Again like the Loan Agreement, the Security Agreement includes positive covenants that focus on protection and preservation of the collateral, including, for example, that the borrower will:

    a. Not change its principal office or locations where the collateral is maintained without the lender's prior written consent;

    b. Keep and maintain satisfactory books and records related to the collateral and make them available to the lender on request;

    c. Keep and secure goods and inventory in a careful, secure, and commercially reasonable manner;

    d. Not transfer the collateral except as permitted in the Loan Agreement;

    e. Maintain the collateral free of all other liens, claims, and encumbrances;

    f. Pay all taxes, assessments, and fees related to ownership and use of the collateral as and when due;

    g. Maintain the collateral in good condition and repair and replace it when necessary;

h. Procure and maintain suitable insurance on the collateral; and

i. Execute all documents required to perfect security interests in the collateral upon the lender's request.

4. **Default and Remedies.** Upon occurrence of an Event of Default as defined in the Loan Agreement, the Security Agreement sets forth specific remedies related to the security interest in the collateral, such as stating that the lender can:

a. Require the borrower to assemble and send the collateral to the lender;

b. Enter the defaulting borrower's premises and take possession of the collateral;

c. Ask a court to appoint a receiver to take possession of or manage the collateral;

d. Sell the collateral; and

e. Have the borrower's power of attorney to, in essence, take over all management of the collateral, to which the borrower is powerless to object.

F. **How Are Rights in a Security Interest Perfected?** After a security interest is granted in a Security Agreement, the creditor such as a commercial bank needs to take certain actions to "perfect" the creditor's lien on the collateral.

1. **UCC-1 Financing Statements.** Perfecting security interests in collateral governed by UCC Article 9 requires the filing of financing statements either centrally (with the Secretary of State) or locally (for example, in a county Superior Court) for security interests in property that is not characterized as real property, including the following: furniture; fixtures; equipment; accounts receivable; general intangible property, such as copyrights, patents, and trademarks; and inventory. UCC-1 financing statement have terms of five years and need to be periodically renewed.

2. **Real Estate as Collateral.** If the lender is taking real estate as collateral, the lender will also require the following:

a. deed to secure debt or mortgage;

b. UCC-2 notice filing in order to perfect a security interest in fixtures;

c. mortgagee title insurance policy;

d. appraisal; and

e. survey.

3. **Perfecting a Security Interest in Cash.** The only way to perfect a security interest in cash is by possession. Consequently, commercial bank loans typically require the borrower to maintain its bank accounts with the lending bank and provide the bank with the power to seize the funds in the borrower's bank account upon an Event of Default.

4. **What Other Capital Financing Transactions Are Governed by Article 9 of the UCC?** Some businesses raise capital by selling certain assets that can potentially be liquidated into cash proceeds, like accounts receivable and promissory notes, and such transactions are governed by Article 9 of the UCC. For example, an enterprise may have substantial accounts receivable but may not expect to receive payment of the accounts receivable in a manner that meets the enterprise's cash flow needs. Rather than borrowing funds granting a security interest in accounts receivable, an enterprise can sell its accounts receivable to an independent purchaser at a discount. This is commonly called "factoring" accounts receivable. The advantage to factoring is that it provides ready cash with no corresponding liability. The disadvantage is that factoring discount rates are typically higher than commercial loan interest rates. As discussed above, the holder of the promissory note can also sell the note to a "holder in due course" at a discounted rate, which might also be a cash source. Since virtually all enterprises have accounts receivable, factoring is a commonly used capital financing method.

VI. WHAT IS A GUARANTY AGREEMENT?

A. **Definition of a Guaranty.** A "guaranty" is an independent party's agreement to be responsible for the payment obligations of a third party and, in the context of debt financing, is manifested in a Guaranty Agreement. For example, commercial lenders typically require individual owners of a borrower to "guaranty" the borrower's payment obligations and performance under a Loan Agreement and Promissory Note.

B. **What Special Laws Govern Guaranty Agreements?** First, a guaranty is a form of "surety" agreement, and, under the Statute of Frauds, must be in writing to be enforceable. Second, Guaranty Agreements are "strictly construed," which means that the language of the guaranty and how it can be enforced must be precisely and unambiguously described.

C. **What Are Typical Provisions in a Guaranty Agreement?** Some provisions are relatively standard and found in virtually all Guaranty Agreements, while some provisions may be customized to fit the specific facts underlying the guaranty obligation.

1. **Description of the Guaranty Obligations.** Typically, the guaranty is tied specifically to a borrower's indebtedness.

2. **Joint, Several, and Solidary Liability With the Borrower.** Guaranty Agreements typically provide that the guarantor's obligations and liability are "solidary" or "joint and several" with the borrower to the same degree and extent as if the guarantor is a co-borrower or co-signer on the core indebtedness.

3. **Joint, Several, and Solidary Liability With Other Guarantors.** There are two ways that a guarantor can be obligated. One way is to have "joint and several" liability with all guarantors. This means that, if there is more than one guarantor, each guarantor guaranties the borrower's entire indebtedness, permitting, for example, a lender to proceed against only one guarantor for the entire amount due to the lender from the borrower. However, multiple guarantors can negotiate to guaranty only a portion of the borrower's indebtedness. For example, a limited liability company with four members might negotiate to have each member guaranty only a pro rata portion of the borrowing LLC's indebtedness.

4. **Cancellation or Termination of Guaranty Obligation.** Most Guaranty Agreements provide that the guaranty obligation remains in effect until the underlying borrower has paid the debt in full and cannot be terminated except by the lender. This can lead to difficulties when a co-guarantor of the borrower's debt is no longer involved with the borrower. For example, a medical practice may have four physician-owners, each of whom guaranties the medical practices debt. Even if one physician leaves the medical practice, the guaranty obligation continues unless the lender, at the lender's sole discretion, releases the guarantor from the Guaranty Agreement.

5. **Bank Deposit Accounts.** The commercial lender may require the guarantor to maintain personal bank accounts with the lender against which the lender may proceed to confiscate the amounts in the bank accounts if there is an event of default.

VII. WHAT OTHER FORMS OF SECURITY MAY BE REQUIRED BY A LENDER?

A. **Stock or Other Ownership Interest Pledge.** The guaranties of individual owners might be enhanced by a pledge of the individual owner's stock or other ownership interest in the borrowing entity. This is another way to make individuals responsible for the debts of the borrowing entity.

B. **Commercial Lender Bank Accounts.** As stated above, commercial bank lenders frequently require borrowers to maintain bank accounts at the lending brank and take a security interest in the bank account deposits.

VIII. LENDER REMEDIES WHEN A LOAN IS IN DEFAULT

A. **Choice of Remedies.** As stated above, typically, upon occurrence of an Event of Default, the lender may: accelerate payment of the loan in full plus principal, interest, costs, expenses, and attorneys' fees; file a collection lawsuit against the borrower; file a lawsuit against a guarantor; and proceed to seize collateral and exercise all rights under the Security Agreement. It is important to understand that the remedies are not mutually exclusive and the lender has the right to take whatever action sit wants to exercise the lender's rights under the loan documents.

B. **"Work Out" of Loan Default.** In practice, lenders typically do not go directly to court or proceed to seize collateral: a loan in default is assigned to the lender's "work out" department. For example, even if the lender secures a loan through a stock pledge upon an Event of Default, the lender is unlikely to exercise its rights and assume ownership and operation of a business. A lender would rather find a way to receive money and mitigate its monetary damages. However, when in a "work out" situation, borrower's management typically loses virtually all control and authority over business operations, and the additional costs of the "work out" will be allocated to the borrower under the loan documents.

IX. OVERVIEW OF BANKRUPTCY LAW

A. **Bankruptcy Court Protection.** When a borrower goes into default under a Loan Agreement and the borrower is insolvent, the borrower may consider filing a petition with the United States Bankruptcy Court for protection to prevent the lender from exercising all of the lender's rights under the loan documents. "Insolvency" generally means either the inability for an entity to pay its debts as they become due or an entity's liabilities are greater than its assets. This is called "voluntary bankruptcy." Under certain circumstances, creditors can force an insolvent business into "involuntary bankruptcy."

B. **What Law Governs Bankruptcy?** Bankruptcy is governed by the federal Bankruptcy Code. There are no state bankruptcy courts, although it is possible for an entity to go into "receivership" under state law. Nevertheless, the most common way that an insolvent entity seeks protection from creditors is through the federal Bankruptcy Code.

C. **What Forms of Bankruptcy Code Protection Are Available to Insolvent Entities?** There are two forms of Bankruptcy Court relief that are used more commonly than others: petitions filed under Chapter 7 and Chapter 11 of the Bankruptcy Code.

   1. **Chapter 7 Bankruptcy Petitions.** Chapter 7 is used for a complete liquidation of the debtor's assets, with net proceeds being distributed first to secured creditors and then, if there are any funds remaining, to unsecured creditors.

2. **Chapter 11 Bankruptcy Petitions.** Chapter 11 protection permits an insolvent entity to "reorganize" under the protection of the Bankruptcy Court and emerge as an enterprise that has an opportunity to continue its operations. In the typical situation, debts are reduced or sometimes eliminated, so, even if a lender may believe it is fully secured, the lender may not receive payment in full. Chapter 11 requires Bankruptcy Court approval of a "plan of reorganization" that involves input from creditors, but the Court can force the creditors to accept a plan even if the creditors do not approve.

3. **The Automatic Stay: a Potential Lifeline for an Insolvent Enterprise.** When an enterprise is not making timely payments on its obligations, it is likely to be sued by its creditors. Virtually all litigation is time consuming and expensive. The last thing an insolvent company wants to do is pay attorneys to defend the company in litigation. A bankruptcy petition can throw the insolvent enterprise a lifeline through the "automatic stay," which immediately stays virtually all creditor collection activities, including without limitation, the following:

    a. any attempt to collect on a debt, including phone calls and letters;

    b. any lawsuit to collect a debt;

    c. repossession of the debtor's assets; and

    d. any attempt to perfect a security interest.

5. **When Should a Debtor Consider Seeking Bankruptcy Court Protection?** As long as an enterprise is able to work out its debt obligations outside of the Bankruptcy Court, it is not in an enterprise's best interest to seek Bankruptcy Court protection. However, when the enterprise starts getting sued, survival may require filing a petition in bankruptcy to obtain the benefits of the automatic stay.

X. WHAT SPECIAL RULES APPLY TO GOVERNMENT HEALTH CARE ACCOUNTS RECEIVABLE FINANCING?

A. **Anti-Factoring Laws.** Soon after the Medicare program commenced, concerns regarding "factoring" agreements arose. In essence, the government perceived that there was substantial risk of fraud and abuse if providers could convey their receivables to third parties. The result was the passage and implementation of anti-factoring statutes and regulations that limit the provision of government health care receivables (including both Medicaid and Medicare accounts receivables) as collateral for any loan. The key to the anti-factoring laws is that payment may be made by the government reimbursement programs only to an account under the provider's or supplier's control.

B. **Medicare Claims Processing Manual Procedure for Making Payments to a Bank.** The Medicare program will make payments to a bank (or similar financial institution) for deposit in the provider/supplier's account so long as the following requirements are met:

1. **Waiver of Offset.** The bank in which the deposit is made must state in writing, in the loan agreement, that it waives its right of offset. Therefore, the bank may have a lending relationship with the provider/supplier and may also be the depository for Medicare receivables, provided that the bank waives any offset rights.

2. **The Account Is in the Provider's Name.** The bank account is in the provider/supplier's name and only the provider/supplier may issue instructions on that account. The bank shall be bound by only the provider/supplier's instructions. No other agreement that the provider/supplier has with a third party shall have any influence on the account. In other words, if a bank is under a standing order from the provider/supplier to transfer funds from the provider/supplier's account to the account of a financing entity in the same or another bank and the provider/supplier rescinds that order, the bank must honor this rescission regardless of whether it is a breach of the provider/supplier's agreement with the financing entity.

3. **Prohibition Against a "Purchase" of Government Reimbursement Program Receivables.** Irrespective of the language in any agreement that a provider/supplier has with a third party that is providing financing, that third party cannot purchase the provider/supplier's Medicare receivables.

C. **Sweep Accounts.** Once the proceeds are deposited into an account in accordance with these requirements, the proceeds can be "swept" into other general accounts. Lenders to providers usually set up two accounts: one for government receivables, and the other for general commercial receivables.

D. **Payments Pursuant to a Court Order.** Notwithstanding the above restrictions, if a court of competent jurisdiction orders the assignment or reassignment of Medicare payments, Medicare will follow that order if a certified copy of the court order and the executed assignment or reassignment (if it was necessary to execute one) is filed with the contractor responsible for processing the claim and the assignment or reassignment (1) applies to all Medicare benefits payable to a particular person or entity during a specified or indefinite time period or (2) specifies a particular amount of money, payable to a particular person or entity by the particular contractor. In all other instances, the Medicare program will make payments subject to the restrictions listed above. For example, even if a court order directed to a provider/supplier limits the provider/supplier's ability to breach its financial agreement with a third party, the bank is bound by instructions from the provider/supplier.

CHAPTER 7

FUNDAMENTALS OF MERGERS AND ACQUISITIONS

I. BAKER'S RULES OF BUSINESS TRANSACTIONS

A. **Most Deals Don't Happen.** Inertia is against consummation of transactions, particularly complex transactions. Multiple parties with multiple advisors need to be looking in the same direction at the same time. Therefore, we need to be aware of the inertia and remove obstacles that might prevent completion of the transaction.

B. **All Transactions Take More Time Than Intended or Desired by the Parties.** Time is a constant enemy. Also, there is a direct correlation between time and cost of closing the deal because delays almost always result in higher legal, accounting, and consulting fees.

II. WHAT ARE THE TYPICAL ACQUISITION FORMS?

A. **Generally Used Forms.** Although there are numerous forms that negotiated acquisitions can take, they are generally accomplished by means of one or more of the following methods: (1) a stock or limited liability company membership interest purchase; (2) an asset purchase; or (3) a merger under state law (including subsidiary mergers and other variations). For purposes of this material, the symbol "T" will be used to denote the acquired or target company; the symbol "P" will be used to denote the acquiring or parent company; and the symbol "S" will be used to denote a subsidiary of P, the parent company. Also, this chapter will refer only to transactions involving corporations and limited liability companies since these are the most common forms of business organization, and these materials assume that there are no restrictions on transfer of stock or membership interests in the entity's organizational documents.

B. **Stock or Limited Liability Company Membership Interest Purchases.** The stock or membership interest purchase is probably the simplest method of acquisition. P purchases the stock or membership interests of T from its shareholders or members, each of whom makes his or her own decision whether to sell. P can acquire all or less than all of the outstanding T stock or membership interests. Following the acquisition, T will continue in existence as a subsidiary of P. P will pay the purchase price directly to T's shareholders. As a general rule, stock or membership interest purchases are favored by sellers because of potentially favorable capital gains tax treatment and few post-closing issues. However, purchasers generally may not prefer ownership interest acquisition because the liabilities of the selling entity are assumed by the purchaser and the purchaser will not receive a "stepped up basis" on the assets of the selling entity for purposes of depreciation.

C. **Asset Purchases.** Rather than acquire T's business by purchasing its outstanding stock or membership interests, P could instead purchase all or substantially all of T's assets. In contrast to an ownership interest purchase, the purchaser does not acquire the liabilities and other obligations of the seller unless they are specifically identified and assumed, and an asset purchase will provide the purchaser with a "stepped up basis" in the assets of the target company, which creates value for the purchaser through the ability to depreciate the acquired assets at their purchase price. Although T continues in existence as a corporation or limited liability company, this transaction differs from the stock or membership interest purchase in at least two important respects.

1. **Continued Existence of the Target Company.** First, T does not become a subsidiary of P; it is still owned by its shareholders or members. Similarly, what had formerly been T's assets are now owned directly by P, which is also now responsible for those liabilities and obligations of T assumed by it. T, by contrast, no longer holds what had been its assets or (to the extent P has agreed to take them) its liabilities, absent third party releases. However, T generally will remain liable for its obligations, with rights against P if P fails to discharge the liabilities assumed by P.

2. **Payment of the Purchase Price to the Target Company.** Second, the purchase price has been paid to T, not to its shareholders or members, who, in order to receive such consideration, will have either to (a) liquidate T or have T declare a dividend on its outstanding stock if T is a corporation or (b) distribute the proceeds through the Operating Agreement if T is a limited liability company.

D. **Mergers.** Mergers are creatures of, and governed in large part by, the laws of the states of incorporation of the companies that are to be merged (often referred to as the "constituent organizations") and by the charters and by-laws or Operating Agreements of such constituent organizations. Thus, the ability of two companies to merge is entirely dependent on a statutory enabling provision. In these materials, we are assuming that the merging entities are corporations, but the same principles generally apply to a merger involving limited liability companies.

1. **Direct Merger.** As a matter of law, the merger of T into P results in P automatically succeeding to all of the assets and liabilities of T, which disappears into P. At the corporate level, therefore, a merger is similar to a sale of all of T's assets to P and P's assumption of all of T's liabilities, although in the latter case T remains in existence, still owned by its former shareholders. At the shareholder level, however, the merger operates more like a stock purchase in which T's shareholders all participate (except to the extent that any such shareholder exercises in the merger any available dissenters' appraisal rights). As a result of the merger, the T stock held by T's shareholders is converted automatically into the consideration to be paid by P in the transaction. Under the law of most states, this consideration can be securities, cash, or other property. Both of the constituent corporations are parties to the acquisition agreement.

2. **Three-Party Mergers.** Two important variations on the direct merger transaction are the "forward subsidiary merger" and the "reverse subsidiary merger."

   a. **Forward Subsidiary Merger.** In a forward subsidiary merger, T merges into S, a wholly-owned subsidiary of P. S succeeds to all of T's assets and liabilities, T goes out of existence, and the T stock formerly held by T shareholders is converted into the same consideration which the T shareholders would have obtained pursuant to a merger of T directly into P. The only structural difference between a direct and a forward subsidiary merger (although an important one) is that, following consummation, the assets and, particularly, the liabilities of T have been assumed by a subsidiary of P, not by P itself. This procedure permits P to acquire T using the merger technique for tax or other reasons without having to obtain the vote of P's shareholders or triggering dissenters' rights in those holders, while largely preserving the historical attributes of T.

   b. **Reverse Subsidiary Merger.** If a forward subsidiary merger is similar at the corporate level to an asset acquisition by S and at the shareholder level to a stock sale, a reverse subsidiary merger is similar from both the corporate and shareholder viewpoints to a stock purchase of T by P. In a reverse subsidiary merger, S merges into T (S, rather than T, ceasing to exist), and T succeeds to all of S's assets and liabilities. If, as is often the case, S were a newly created shell corporation with no assets or liabilities, then after the merger T would be the same entity practically as well as legally as T pre-merger. The outstanding shares of the common stock of S are converted into shares of common stock of T; accordingly, T becomes a wholly-owned subsidiary of P, and the T stock held by the former shareholders of T is converted into the acquisition consideration. The effect is the same as a purchase by P of all of the outstanding stock of T from its shareholders. This procedure may make possible a merger without the risk of having the transaction treated as an "assignment" which may be prohibited by various contracts and licenses to which T is a party, which is frequently important in the health industry.

3. **Short-Form Mergers.** In order to simplify those transactions where T is entirely, or almost entirely, owned by P, states have adopted so-called "short-form" merger statutes. Short-form mergers can be accomplished between parents and subsidiaries without the approval of the Board of Directors or a vote by shareholders of the subsidiary being acquired if (a) P owns at least a specified percentage (90% in most jurisdictions) of the outstanding shares of each class of T and (b) the Board of Directors of P adopts a resolution approving the merger. Parent shareholder approval is generally not required.

E. **Board or Management Approval.**

1. **Corporate Board Approval.** Generally speaking, every corporation that is a party to the acquisition agreement must obtain the approval of the transaction its Board of Directors. This will be required either specifically by statute or by the bylaws of the corporation.

2. **Limited Liability Company Management Approval.** In the absence of a modifying provision in the Operating Agreement, any fundamental organizational change, such as a merger or acquisition, will require approval by a majority of the members as described below. However, many Operating Agreements have customized approval processes, such as delegating approval of a transaction to either a single managing member or to a management committee.

F. **Shareholder or Member Approval.** The question of whether shareholder or member approval is required in a particular acquisition is significantly more complicated than the issue of Board approval. For corporations, whether such approval is required and, if so, what the requisite vote will be varies from jurisdiction to jurisdiction and depends to a significant degree on the method of acquisition. Indeed, the issue of shareholder approval (or, rather, a desire to avoid the need to obtain such approval) often helps determine the method of acquisition. For limited liability companies, as stated above, the approval process may be customized. As a general rule, in the absence of an Operating Agreement provision to the contrary, majority member approval is required for a fundamental organizational change such as a merger or acquisition. However, some Operating Agreements require super-majority member approval. Therefore, you will always need to review the terms and conditions of the Operating Agreement.

1. **Stock or Membership Interest Purchases.** Stock or membership interest purchase acquisitions are the easiest transactions to consummate. In the absence of restrictive provisions in a Shareholders' Agreement or Operating Agreement, no vote by the shareholders or members of T is required since T is not engaged in any transaction. The acquiror is viewed as purchasing assets (from the viewpoint of the acquiror, stock of the target is really just another asset) and, except where the acquiror's securities are listed or quoted on a stock exchange or association and their rules provide otherwise, no shareholder or member vote is necessary. As always, this general rule can be modified by the agreement of the shareholders or members.

2. **Mergers.** The general rule is that, except for statutory short-form mergers, the shareholders or members of both constituent organizations in a merger must approve the transaction. In most jurisdictions, the required vote is a majority of the outstanding shares, but this can be modified by agreement of the shareholders or members.

3. **Asset Sales.** If a target company is selling all or substantially all of its assets, approval by its shareholders or members is required in virtually all jurisdictions. In most of these jurisdictions, the required vote is a majority of the outstanding shares or membership interests. The critical, and often very difficult, question is determining when a sale is of "substantially all" of the entity's assets. The acquiror's shareholders or members are rarely given a statutory right to vote on acquisitions of assets from another entity (even when they constitute all or substantially all of its assets), regardless of the form of consideration paid by the purchaser.

4. **Dissenters' Rights.** As a general rule, when shareholder or member approval is required for a transaction, shareholders or members who do not give their approval and who follow the statutory procedures are generally entitled to claim dissenters' rights of appraisal and receive in cash the value of their shares in lieu of participating in the transaction. Under the normal statutory provisions, shareholders or members who exercise such rights must vote against, or fail to vote for, the transaction and claim their rights in a timely fashion.

    a. **No Dissenters' Rights in Stock or Membership Interest Transactions.** Dissenters' rights are not available to target company shareholders or members in connection with a straight stock or membership purchase. A target company shareholder or member who does not wish to sell remains as a shareholder or member in the target.

    b. **Shareholders or Members of the Acquiror.** Shareholders or members of the acquiror are generally not entitled to appraisal rights except in connection with a direct merger of the target into the acquiror, although in many jurisdictions, shareholders or members of the acquiror will not be entitled to appraisal rights with respect to a transaction in which they were not entitled to vote.

    c. **Market Exception.** Many states create an exception to appraisal rights with respect to shares or other equity interests listed on a national securities exchange or held of record by more than a statutorily prescribed minimum number of shareholders or members subject, in certain instances, to the satisfaction of other conditions.

5. **Shareholder Protections in the Absence of Dissenters' Rights.** If, under general corporate law, shareholders have no dissenters' rights in a stock transaction, how can shareholders be protected from an unfair transaction or squeeze out?

a. **Co-Sale Rights.** As discussed in connection with venture capital funding, to protect the venture capitalist as a minority investor, the venture capitalist requires execution of a Co-Sale Agreement that provides the venture capitalist with the right to sell its minority interest on the same terms as the selling majority shareholder. Co-Sale rights are also called "tag along rights."

b. **Drag Along Rights.** Conversely, "drag along rights" provide a majority shareholder with the right to "drag" minority shareholders along in a majority interest stock sale transaction in a manner that provides minority shareholders with the same economic benefits under the same terms and conditions as the majority shareholder.

G. **Other Structuring Issues.** In addition to the differences in board approval requirements and shareholder or member voting and appraisal rights discussed above, there are other important aspects of structuring a transaction that may influence the nature of the transaction.

1. **Third Party Consents.** The ability of the target to retain the benefits of a material agreement to which it is a party is often an important consideration in an acquisition. This issue normally arises where the consent of the other party to the contract is required to waive a provision that prohibits its assignment by the target. A purchase of all of the outstanding stock of the target, whether by a negotiated stock purchase or pursuant to a share exchange, if permitted under the target's (and acquiror's) jurisdictions of incorporation, does not constitute a transfer of any assets of the target; accordingly, any non-assignment provision would not be violated and no consent or waiver would be required. A sale of assets by the target, however, would constitute an assignment of the contract and would require the consent of the other party to the contract. This is critically important for managed care contracts, which virtually always provide that they are not assignable without the written consent of the payor. Given that the parties may lose very favorable payment rates if an existing managed care contract is terminated, requiring renegotiation with the payor, obtaining third party consents is a material aspect of all acquisitions of existing health care providers.

2. **Governmental Consents.** Whether any particular consent, approval, or filing with a governmental or regulatory body is required in connection with a given structure depends, as with third party consents, on the exact wording of the particular statutory provision or regulation.

III. HOW DOES THE ACQUISITION PROCESS USUALLY FLOW?

A. **Initial Discussions.** The first step in any acquisition is a realization by the parties that there may be a deal to be made. Sometimes investment bankers for one or both parties are involved at this stage; sometimes not. Lawyers are generally not involved at this stage except, perhaps, to give some advice about the process to their clients or to draft or negotiate an appropriate confidentiality agreement. The steps outlined below are fairly typical of many transactions in terms of "what happens when" and "who does what." Obviously, significant variations can (and often do) occur in any particular transaction.

B. **Confidentiality Agreement.** When parties begin discussions, it is advisable to enter into a simple confidentiality agreement to create a fiduciary relationship and preserve certain rights, such as trade secret and patent rights. Health care providers also have to consider compliance with HIPAA privacy regulations. The parties usually commence their business and legal due diligence during this period, the scope of which will vary from deal to deal.

C. **Term Sheet.** As the parties continue to negotiate, it is sometimes advisable to develop a term sheet that outlines the fundamental terms and conditions of the transaction. One benefit of a term sheet is that it may describe fundamental terms and conditions that lead to an early decision not to proceed with the transaction, which may save the parties substantial time and resources.

D. **Memorandum of Understanding.** The term sheet may evolve into a detailed memorandum of understanding of the transaction. Again, preparation of a memorandum of understanding is not absolutely necessary, but it may reveal material issues that lead to an early decision not to proceed with the transaction.

E. **Letter of Intent.** The parties also might, but need not, enter into a letter of intent or agreement in principle. There is some dispute among practitioners as to whether a letter of intent is a desirable document in an acquisition transaction and, if so, what its provisions should be. Whether the execution of such a document may be beneficial in a given factual setting cannot be definitively answered in the abstract.

1. **Advantages to Executing a Letter of Intent.**

a. **Facilitating a "Meeting of the Minds".** The process of preparing and executing a letter of intent makes it possible for the parties to determine, at least in broad outline, whether in fact there is a basic agreement as to the terms and structure of a transaction. This consideration may be of particular significance in transactions in which (i) one party (or both) is relatively inexperienced in these types of transactions and, therefore, may more easily misunderstand some of the consequences of the process or (ii) there are particularly complex or intricate elements to the transaction that may lead to mutually inconsistent interpretations in the absence of a written statement.

b. **Obtaining Some Binding Agreements.** Second, it may be the desire of one party or the other that at least some elements of the preliminary understanding are to be binding.

In such a situation, a written agreement is obviously necessary to reflect those understandings, and the other party is unlikely to agree to a separate written agreement unless there is at least an expression of the parties' understanding of the principal terms of the acquisition itself. Examples include "no shop" clauses (which restrict the target company from "shopping" the transaction to other potential purchasers), confidentiality (if not subject to a separate confidentiality agreement), earnest money and its application, and matters related to the due diligence process.

c. **Initiating Regulatory Approvals.** Third, required regulatory approvals for the transaction can delay the transaction and can be initiated at an earlier stage if a letter of intent, memorandum of understanding, or some comparable writing has been executed. In this context, execution of such a document may mean that proceedings seeking the required approval and negotiation of the definitive agreement can proceed along parallel tracks, thus reducing the total elapsed time until consummation of the transaction.

d. **Facilitating Public Disclosure.** Finally, if other factors compel the conclusion that public disclosure of the proposed transaction is appropriate, either or both of the parties may be more willing to make that disclosure if the transaction is sufficiently firm that the parties are willing to sign the letter of intent.

2. **Disadvantages of a Letter of Intent.**

a. **Obligations Arising From Execution of a Formal Letter of Intent.** A letter of intent may have sufficient elements of a contract to bind the parties and will almost certainly obligate them to carry on further negotiations in good faith. Furthermore, with a publicly-held entity on one side or the other of the transaction, the execution and announcement of a letter of intent will bring to bear significant pressures to complete the transaction. Given that there are always significant variables that cannot be resolved at the letter of intent stage and that will be thoroughly negotiated in connection with a definitive agreement, it is not unusual for a party to refuse to commit to a transaction until a full definitive agreement is in a form acceptable for execution.

b. **Potential for Wasted Time and Effort.** The second principal disadvantage is related to the first. In a transaction with complex elements, trying adequately to define them in a letter of intent may prove counterproductive to the total effort. The letter of intent may itself become a lengthy, involved document that tries to do too much. In such an environment, negotiations over the letter of intent may make the entire process more, rather than less, cumbersome and may unnecessarily jeopardize the ability of the parties to negotiate a definitive agreement.

F. **Due Diligence.** "Due diligence" is the part of the negotiation process during which each party is able to analyze non-public and sometimes confidential or proprietary information about the other party that is material to closing the transaction. There is no absolutely fixed place where due diligence fits into the transaction process. However, due diligence generally begins with an analysis of fundamental target company information by the purchaser after execution of the confidentiality agreement, and it will continue in earnest after execution of a memorandum of understanding or letter of intent (if any) and the definitive agreement.

1. **Stock Purchase Due Diligence.** Because a stock purchase requires the purchaser to assume all of the actual and contingent liabilities of the seller, stock purchase due diligence can be expected to be detailed and time consuming.

2. **Asset Purchase Due Diligence.** Since an asset purchase is focused on the assets acquired and liabilities assumed, due diligence is generally more focused and streamlined from stock purchase due diligence.

G. **Execution of the Definitive Agreement.** Regardless of whether a letter of intent has been executed, the next step in the acquisition process is the negotiation, approval, and execution of a definitive acquisition agreement. During the course of negotiating and finalizing the acquisition agreement, the parties will be continuing and, in most cases, essentially completing their due diligence. When the agreement is fully negotiated, or almost finalized, the parties will usually obtain the necessary board approvals. Fairness opinions, if a part of the transaction, will typically be delivered at the board meeting at which the execution of the definitive agreement is approved.

H. **Closing the Transaction.**

1. **Execution Date and Closing Date.** Although it is possible to have a "sign and close" transaction when execution of the definitive agreement and the closing occur simultaneously, more frequently the closing occurs after the execution of the definitive agreement on a "Closing Date" described in the definitive agreement.

2. **The Post-Signing/Pre-Closing Period.** The length of this time period will often primarily be a function of many factors, some of which are described as follows:

   a. **Due Diligence.** Each party will complete the due diligence process to fulfill any conditions to closing set forth in the definitive agreement.

   b. **Preparation of Schedules.** Every acquisition agreement, and especially an asset purchase agreement, will require the seller to complete numerous schedules to the definitive agreement. For example, the seller will be required to complete schedules describing insurance, real and personal property leases, pending litigation, retirement and benefit plans, and many other items, most of which relate to the covenants, representations, and warranties set forth in the definitive agreement. An asset purchase agreement will include a detailed description of the assets being acquired and the liabilities being assumed by the purchaser. This can be a painstaking and time consuming process.

c. **State Corporations or LLC Law Requirements.** There likely will be an additional waiting period under state corporate or limited liability company law if a vote is required by shareholders or LLC members on a merger or a sale of all or substantially all of a corporation's or limited liability company's assets. At the end of the applicable period, the shareholders' or members' meeting will be held and the vote taken. By contrast, if the transaction is a stock or membership interest purchase, then (subject to the time necessary to allow shareholders or members to review any necessary disclosure document) no additional time is needed.

d. **Securities Law Requirements.** If the buyer is required to register securities under the Securities Act of 1933 or if the target is required to file a proxy or consent statement with the SEC pursuant to the Securities and Exchange Act of 1934 (the "1934 Act") in connection with obtaining shareholder approval of the sale, the period between signing and closing could be substantial. It could easily take up to 20 days or longer to prepare the registration statement or proxy statement to be filed with the SEC and an additional 30 to 60 days to complete the SEC review process and mail to shareholders.

e. **Hart-Scott-Rodino Act Notification Requirements.** Another time variable is the Hart-Scott-Rodino Act, which, if applicable to the acquisition, will require a waiting period of 30 days (15 days in the case of a stock purchase by cash tender offer rather than a privately negotiated stock purchase asset acquisition or merger) from the filing of the requisite forms before the transaction can be consummated. If the Federal Trade Commission ("FTC") or the Antitrust Division of the Department of Justice (the "Justice Department") requests additional information before the expiration of the waiting period, the period will be extended until 20 days (10 days in the case of a cash tender offer) following "substantial compliance" by the parties with the request for additional information. If the FTC or Justice Department has concerns about the anti-competitive effects of the transaction, they will often ask the parties to voluntarily extend the waiting period beyond the statutory limits; failure to voluntarily extend the waiting period could result in the commencement of litigation by the applicable government agency.

f. **Request for Audited Financial Statements.** The period of time necessary between signing and closing also may be significantly affected by the pre-signing status of financial statements of the business being acquired. If the statements are unaudited, the buyer or its financing source may well demand that an audit be performed prior to closing, sometimes accompanied by a physical inventory.

3. **Conditions to Closing.** Consequently most definitive agreements provide a list of "conditions to closing" that must occur for the deal to close. For example, closing may be conditioned on obtaining regulatory approvals. Also, closing may be conditioned on approvals by the purchaser's Board of Directors or completion of due diligence to the purchaser's satisfaction. As you can see, such provisions can provide an easy escape for the purchaser from closing the deal.

4. **Closing.** At the closing, the buyer will purchase the selling shareholders' stock (in a stock purchase transaction), the selling company's assets (in an asset purchase transaction), or effect the merger (in a merger transaction). Whatever documents of transfer are needed (in the first two cases) or are to be filed in the appropriate Secretary of State's office (in the merger situation) to accomplish the transaction will be delivered or filed at closing as well as any officers' certificates, opinions of counsel, and accountant's letters required by the acquisition agreement. The closing will usually occur as soon as possible. In many transactions, this will mean as soon as practicable after the expiration of the Hart-Scott-Rodino Act waiting period and the obtaining of all requisite shareholder and regulatory approvals. Following the closing, a press release will be issued in many transactions.

5. **Electronic Closings.** In the past transaction closings were ceremonial and done in person followed by a closing dinner and celebration. Today virtually all closings are accomplished by electronic signature exchange followed by an electronic flow of funds.

IV. WHAT ARE THE TYPICAL TERMS AND CONDITIONS OF DEFINITIVE ACQUISITION AGREEMENTS?

A. **Typical Terms and Conditions in the Definitive Agreement.** The definitive agreement is typically a lengthy document replete with representations, warranties, other protective mechanisms, conditions to the closing (because the closing usually will occur after the signing of the definitive agreement), and the like. With the exception of the first portion of the agreement, which will generally set forth the basic economics and form of the transaction and identity of the parties, acquisition agreements are generally very similar in structure regardless of whether they are for an asset purchase, a stock purchase, or a merger.

B. **Description of the Transaction.** The initial provisions of the definitive agreement will generally describe the deal.

1. **Stock Sale Description.** If it is a stock purchase, they will describe the stock being transferred. If there are numerous shareholders, the purchaser may request appointment of a "shareholders representative" who will have power of attorney to execute documents on behalf of all of the shareholders.

2. **Asset Sale Description.** If it is an asset sale, the definitive agreement will describe the assets being transferred as well as specifically excluded assets. Also, the definitive agreement will describe any liabilities to be assumed by the purchaser.

C. **Consideration.** Of course, the consideration and payment provisions are critically important. These provisions may be simple, as is usually the case in a simple stock purchase agreement for a fixed cash amount, or very complicated, as, for example, in a cash election merger or a transaction that includes an "earn-out" that provides future consideration depending on the post-closing performance of the business enterprise or a closing balance sheet adjustment. Although it is impossible to describe every possible permutation, the consideration and payment provisions might include the following:

1. **Purchase Price.** The overall purchase price will be described, which may include cash, stock, or other consideration. Frequently, however, the total purchase price is not paid at the closing. In general, a hospital or health care delivery system cannot offer an ownership interest as part of the consideration for the sale (either because the hospital or health care delivery system is a nonprofit, tax exempt organization or because ownership interests in the hospital are not offered through any kind of syndication), but ownership interests in such ancillary ventures such as a physician-hospital joint venture ambulatory surgery center may be part of the consideration.

2. **Purchase Price Escrow.** A portion of the purchase price may be held in escrow or paid in installments, with the amount held in reserve used for payment of indemnification claims as described below. This protects the purchaser from undisclosed liabilities and other unforeseen circumstances. If the parties negotiate a formal escrow arrangement, the transaction documents will include a separate Escrow Agreement.

3. **Earn-Out.** An "earn-out" provision permits the seller to obtain additional consideration if, after the closing, the target company achieves certain performance objectives. Although

this may seem appealing to a seller, many sellers experience difficulty in achieving the goals once the company is under control of the purchaser. Therefore, in most situations, a seller is well advised to determine whether the transaction is acceptable based on the purchase price paid at closing and not on contingent consideration like an earn-out. Also, in a transaction involving the sale of a medical practice to a hospital or health care delivery system, payment of an "earn-out" based on future performance by the selling physicians is problematic under the statutes and regulations governing the health industry and will likely not be part of the proposed transaction.

4. **Employment Agreements.** Continuing employment of the seller's principal management is usually a critical deal point. Consequently, formal Employment Agreements and Restrictive Covenant Agreements are typically executed as part of the transaction documents. If a medical practice is selling to a hospital or health care delivery system, the Compensation Plan that will become part of the Employment Agreement is also a critical transaction document, understanding that the Compensation Plan will need to comply with Stark and the federal Anti-Kickback Statute.

D. **Representations and Warranties.** Each party to the agreement makes representations concerning its business and the effect of the transaction on it. Representations and warranties are statements made by a party about itself or the company it owns. Representations can cover such matters as the due incorporation of a party; its qualifications to conduct business; its authorization of the transaction; receipt of any regulatory approvals or third party consents it must obtain prior to consummation; compliance with generally accepted accounting principles with respect to its financial statements; the absence of material adverse changes in its business; compliance with the statutes and regulations governing the health industry; and many other matters.

1. **Responding to Representations and Warranties Through a Disclosure Schedule.** Typically, the representations and warranties will provide, for example, that "except as otherwise provided in the Disclosure Schedule to this Agreement, the seller is not involved in any litigation." If the seller is involved in litigation, it needs to be disclosed on the Disclosure Schedule. Therefore, the Disclosure Schedule becomes the heart and soul of the acquisition agreement and forms the foundation for determining what the purchaser is acquiring.

2. **The Seller Typically Carries the Burden of Substantial Representations and Warranties.** Usually, and almost certainly in a cash transaction, the seller's representations and warranties will be lengthy and all-inclusive while the purchaser's representations will be relatively few and limited in nature. If the purchaser is paying cash, the only concern the

seller should have is whether it will be prevented from keeping the cash (i.e., whether there are any potential claims that the transaction or the payment of the consideration was improper). If a significant part of the consideration consists of debt or equity securities of the purchaser, additional representations may be appropriate; when the quantity of equity securities being issued is such as to make it unclear who is "acquiring" whom, there is good reason to argue for parallel representations and warranties from each party to the other.

3. **Responsibility for Accuracy of the Representations and Warranties.** Once all of the representations and warranties have been negotiated and included in the agreement, the questions become who is liable for them, for what period of time, how are damages to be measured, and what security is to be provided to ensure payment. These questions can create significant obstacles to the completion of an acquisition, and some of the questions that are raised may not be easily resolved.

4. **Managing Risks Related to Representations and Warranties.** Like loan agreements, risk arising from representations and warranties can be mitigated by the following:

    a. **Knowledge.** Trying to precisely define "knowledge" to actual, not constructive, knowledge, and try to limit knowledge to specific seller representatives.

    b. **Material Adverse Effect (MAE).** Limiting representations and disclosures to those that have a material adverse effect.

    c. **Time Limit.** Limiting the duration of the representation.

    d. **Disclosure Schedule.** Paying careful attention to preparation of the Disclosure Schedule.

5. **What Happens When There is a False Representation?** If a representation is false when made (for example, when the agreement is executed), the representing party may be liable for damages regardless of whether the transaction closes. If any representation becomes false by the time of the closing, the other party will generally be allowed to refuse to close. This is the crucial "bring-down" condition. If the representation is false at closing and this is not disclosed to the other party and the acquisition is consummated, the other party might be entitled to indemnification for losses or damages as a result.

E. **Example of Health Care Representations and Warranties.** Health care businesses can expect to be asked to provide specific health care representations and warranties. The following is an example from an actual transaction document:

Fraud and Abuse. Physician Group and, to the best knowledge of Physician Group, Physician Group's officers and directors, and persons and entities providing professional services for Physician Group, have not engaged in any activities which are prohibited under U.S.C. Section 1320a-7b, or the regulations promulgated thereunder pursuant to such statutes, or related state or local statutes or regulations, or which are prohibited by rules of professional conduct, including but not limited to the following: (i) knowingly and willfully making or causing to be made a false statement or representation of a material fact in any application for any benefit or payment; (ii) knowingly and willfully making or causing to be made any false statement or representation of a material fact for use in determining rights to any benefit or payment; (iii) failure to disclose knowledge by a claimant of the occurrence of any event affecting the initial or continued right to any benefit or payment on its own behalf or on behalf of another, with the intent to fraudulently secure such payment or benefit; and (iv) knowingly and willfully soliciting or receiving any remuneration (including any kick-back, bribe, or rebate), directly or indirectly, overtly or covertly, in cash or in kind, or offering to pay or receive such remuneration (A) in return for referring an individual to a person for the furnishing or arranging for the furnishing of any item or service for which payment is made in whole or in part by Medicare or Medicaid, or (B) in return for purchasing, leasing, or ordering or arranging for or recommending purchasing, leasing, or ordering any goods, facility, service, or item for which payment may be made in whole or in part by Medicare or Medicaid.

Except as listed in the **Disclosure Schedule**, (i) neither Physician Group's right nor, to the best knowledge of Physician Group, the right of any licensed professional or other individual affiliated with Physician Group to receive reimbursements pursuant to any Government or Private Program has been terminated or otherwise adversely affected as a result of any investigation or action whether by any federal or state government or regulatory authority or by a third party, (ii) neither Physician Group nor, to the best knowledge of Physician Group, any rights of professional or other individuals affiliated with Physician Group has, during the past three years, been the subject of any inspection, investigation, survey, audit, monitoring, or other form of review by any government or regulatory entity, trade association, professional review organization, accrediting organization, or certifying agency for the purpose of any alleged improper activity on the part of such individual, nor has Physician Group received any notice of deficiency in connection with its operations, (iii) there are not presently, and at the Effective Date there will not be, any outstanding deficiencies or work orders of any government authority having jurisdiction over Physician Group, or other third party, requiring conformity to any applicable agreement, statute, regulation, ordinance or bylaw, including but not limited to, the Government and Private Programs, and (iv) there is no notice of any claim, requirement, or demand of any licensing or certifying agency or other third party supervising or having authority over Physician Group or its operations to rework or design any part thereof or to provide additional furniture, fixtures, equipment, appliances, or inventory so as to conform to or comply with any existing law, code, rule, regulation, or standard. Attached as part of the Disclosure Schedule are copies of all reports, correspondence, notices, and other documents relating to any matter described or referenced therein.

F. **Restrictive Covenants.** Purchase agreements typically restrain the selling entity, if an asset transaction, and the owners of the target enterprise in both asset and stock purchase transactions, from competing with the purchasing enterprise. Like restrictive covenants in employment agreements described in Chapter 3, restrictive covenants in acquisition agreements must be reasonable as to time, territory, and activity restrained. However, it is generally easier to enforce a restrictive covenant in an acquisition agreement than an employment agreement, and the restrictions are typically more broad. For example, while the time restraint in an employment agreement is usually one or two years, the time restraint in an acquisition agreement is typically five years.

G. **Other Covenants.** Just as representations and warranties serve to establish the condition of the entity when the acquisition agreement is executed and, frequently, at the time of the closing if they are reaffirmed then, covenants establish what the owner of the business will do between execution of the definitive agreement and the closing and, sometimes, after the closing. At least as to the pre-closing covenants, the goal is usually to create a contractual obligation on the part of the seller to preserve the business, operations, and conditions of the entity substantially as they were at the time of execution of the agreement and to preclude actions that would adversely affect the buyer (such as paying dividends, redeeming stock, increasing salaries, issuing warrants or options, or committing to material obligations). These obligations are particularly important when there are elements of the transaction that could be affected by activities of the seller between execution of the agreement and closing.

H. **Conditions to Closing.** As stated above, the conditions to close determine whether a party must consummate the transaction. These conditions may include receipt of any necessary shareholder, member, or Board of Director approval; satisfaction with detailed due diligence; delivery of the opinions of opposing counsel as to various matters; receipt of a tax ruling or opinion; receipt of an accountant's letter; third party and governmental consents and approvals; availability of financing; absence of litigation; in non-cash transactions, conditions relating to securities and stock exchange matters; satisfactory completion of due diligence; and reaffirming representations and warranties at the closing as though made again at that time.

I. **Indemnification.** Most acquisition agreements provide for indemnification. These provisions grant either party (particularly, the purchaser) the right to recover post-closing for misrepresentations and noncompliance with covenants by the other party. Because these provisions have real economic substance, they are among the most highly negotiated aspects of the agreement.

1. **Liability.** Liability arises from a breach of a representation, warranty, or covenant.

2. **Limitation of Exposure.** There are several aspects of indemnification clauses that should be vigorously negotiated. First, negotiate a "basket," which is a minimum amount in indemnification claims that must accrue before a claim is made. Second, negotiate a time limit for survival of the representations and warranties and indemnification claims. Third, negotiate a precise procedure for making an indemnification claim.

3. **The Danger of "Materiality Scrapes".** Increasingly, purchasers are preparing agreements that, in essence, remove "materiality" qualifications in representations and warranties for purposes of indemnification, under the theory that the seller is protected from material claims by the "basket." This "scrapes" materiality qualifications from the agreement, resulting in more exposure to the seller. Therefore, if the purchaser insists on a materiality scrape, the seller needs to increase the "basket."

4. **Representation and Warranty Insurance.** Increasingly, especially in larger transactions, purchaser representation and warranty indemnification insurance is leading to walkaway transactions with no indemnification obligations, leaving all reliance on the insurance. For example, it is estimated that 50% to 60% of all private equity transactions use representation and warranty insurance. A sell side transaction request for proposal might say that proposals that include representation and warranty insurance in the purchase price will be favored or sometimes even require representation and warranty insurance for the bid. In practice, escrow of 10% of the purchase price for a year or two is relatively standard. When the buyer has representation and warranty insurance, the escrow amount can be reduced to 1% or less or sometimes entirely eliminated. However, representation and warranty insurance is relatively expensive. It is rarely seen under the level of private equity fund mergers and acquisitions, the floor for which is typically $10,000,000, and is more prevalent in transactions of $100,000,000 or more. Also, there is usually some buyer "retention" that is similar to a "basket" for indemnification obligations: indemnification insurance does not kick in until some threshold amount of indemnification obligations is reached. Retention is determined by enterprise value, so it can be quite high. Because liabilities travel with stock and membership interest transactions, representation and warranty insurance is more useful in stock transactions. The key to whether representation and warranty insurance is appropriate for health care transactions is what is excluded in the insurance policy. For example, fraud and abuse might be excluded. If so, then the value in a health industry transaction is diminished. To underwrite the insurance, the insurer will conduct its own due diligence to ascertain indemnification risk. For example, the insurer may either perform its own chart review or require the seller to perform an internal chart

review that is reported to the insurer to ascertain False Claims Act risk, which might lead to mandated disclosure of overpayments under the "60-day-rule" described in Chapter 11 and possible death of the deal.

J. **Miscellaneous Matters.** The concluding sections of the agreement typically deal with a number of miscellaneous matters, including choice of law, consent to jurisdiction, termination rights, and, not infrequently, "lock-up" options, "bust-up" fees, "no-shop," and "go shop" covenants, and expense reimbursement, all of which latter provisions will, if challenged, be closely scrutinized by the courts and should be agreed to only after the most careful and deliberate consideration by target directors. The agreement will also include many of the "boilerplate" provisions described in Chapter 2, which must not be overlooked in your contract negotiations.

V. WHAT SPECIAL PROCEDURES ARE REQUIRED FOR HEALTH CARE BUSINESS TRANSACTIONS?

A. **Regulatory Scrutiny of Health Care Business Transactions.** Consideration paid in a health care business transaction implicates the statutes and regulations that govern the health industry, particularly Stark and the federal Anti-Kickback Statute and, if the purchaser is a nonprofit entity, the Internal Revenue Code provisions governing tax exempt organizations if the purchaser is in a position to receive referrals for items or services payable by a governmental reimbursement program post-closing. By contrast, purchasers that are not in a position to receive referrals from the acquired medical practice, such as a private equity capitalized or publicly traded company, have significantly less regulatory exposure.

1. **Application of the Stark Law to Health Care Business Transactions.** To reiterate, the Stark physician self-referral law prohibits the referral of certain "designated health services" or "DHS" payable by the Medicare or Medicaid program to any entity with which the physician has a "financial relationship," including a "compensation arrangement," unless there is a specific statutory or regulatory exception that applies to the financial relationship. Hospital inpatient and outpatient services fall within the definition of "designated health services." For example, the sale of a medical practice to a hospital or health system, which is becoming more and more prevalent in a consolidating health care economy, implicates Stark because the physicians are receiving compensation from the hospital. In such a transaction, referrals by the physicians to the purchasing hospital or health care delivery system are prohibited unless the law provides a specific exception. Fortunately, the Stark Law includes an exception for one-time "isolated financial transactions." The self-referral prohibition does not apply to isolated financial transactions, such as a one-time sale of real property or a physician's medical practice, provided that the following criteria are fulfilled:

a. **Aggregate Fixed Payment.** Total aggregate payment is fixed before the first payment is made and does not take into account the volume or value of referrals or other business generated by the selling physicians for the purchasing hospital. As stated in Chapter 1, compensation takes into account volume or value of referrals or other business generated only if the formula used to calculate the physician's compensation includes the physician's referrals to or other business generated by the physician for the DHS entity as a variable, resulting in an increase or decrease in the physician's compensation that positively correlates with the number or value of the physician's referrals to or the generation of other business for the DHS entity. For medical practice-hospital acquisitions, this means that the purchase price cannot be expressed in the form of an earn-out based on a stream of future referrals. The purchase price of medical practice-hospital acquisitions must be definitively stated in the purchase agreement.

b. **Fair Market Value.** The consideration paid is consistent with fair market value.

c. **No Accounting for Referrals of Other Business Generated.** The consideration paid is not determined in a manner that takes into account (directly or indirectly) the volume or value of referrals by the selling physicians to the purchasing hospital or other business generated by the selling physicians for the hospital. As stated in Chapter 1, compensation takes into account volume or value of referrals or other business generated only if the formula used to calculate the physician's compensation includes the physician's referrals to or other business generated by the physician for the DHS entity as a variable, resulting in an increase or decrease in the physician's compensation that positively correlates with the number or value of the physician's referrals to or the generation of other business for the DHS entity. For medical practice-hospital acquisitions, this means that the purchase price must be definitively stated in the purchase agreement and cannot be expressed in the form of an earn-out based on a stream of future referrals.

d. **Commercial Reasonableness.** The consideration is paid pursuant to an agreement that is commercially reasonable even if no referrals were made by the physician to the purchaser.

e. **Limitation on Additional Transactions.** There are no additional transactions between the parties for six months after the isolated financial transaction except for transactions that either fall within other Stark Law exceptions or are commercially reasonable post-closing adjustments. In the typical hospital-medical practice transaction the selling physicians enter into employment agreements with an affiliate of the purchasing hospital in addition to the separate practice sale. The employment compensation arrangement must be analyzed on its own merits because it does not fall within the "one-time" definition required for application of the isolated financial transaction exception. DHS referrals from the selling physicians to the purchasing hospital are not prohibited under the post-transaction closing employment compensation arrangement if it falls within the *bona fide* employee Stark exception as described in Chapter 1. Also, independent contractor arrangements can fall within the personal services agreement Stark exception.

f. **Payments.** The purchase price in the isolated financial transaction can be either a single payment at closing (which is by far the most common payment method) or installment payments provided that the installment payments are either guaranteed by a third party, secured by a negotiable promissory note, or subject to a similar mechanism to insure payment in the event of default by the purchaser. In other words, any installment payment arrangement needs to be secured in a commercially reasonable manner.

2. **Application of the Anti-Kickback Statute to Health Care Business Transactions.** To reiterate, the federal Anti-Kickback Statute prohibits any remuneration any kind, whether direct or indirect, overt or covert, in cash or in kind, that is intended for at least one of its purposes to induce the referral of items or services payable by any governmental reimbursement program. Also, the federal Anti-Kickback Statute is not limited to physicians, and it has severe criminal and civil sanctions. Therefore, if a hospital or health care delivery system acquires a medical practice, the federal Anti-Kickback Statute is implicated because the referral of items or services payable by governmental reimbursement programs runs in one direction and remuneration from an entity that benefits from the referrals runs in the other direction. However, at least one appellate court has recognized that the mere hope for or expectation of referrals collateral to a legitimate motive for the financial arrangement does not rise to the level of an improper purpose.

a. **"Goodwill" as a Form of Illegal Remuneration.** In a letter dated December 22, 1992, D. McCarty Thornton, the OIG's then Associate General Counsel, created a firestorm when he stated that the sale by a medical practice to a hospital or health care delivery system of the "goodwill" or other intangible property (such as covenants not to compete, going business concern value, patient lists, and exclusive dealing arrangements) of the practice, especially when the selling physicians remained in a position to make referrals to the purchaser, raised "grave questions of compliance with the anti-kickback statute." These arrangements, he indicated, may be "merely sophisticated disguises to share profits of business at a hospital with referring physicians, in order to induce physicians to steer referrals to the hospital." Strenuous objections were immediately raised to this broad interpretation of the federal Anti-Kickback

Statute, and the OIG, over time, has retreated from this extreme position. Today, it is generally believed that payment for some form of "goodwill" by hospitals may be appropriate, as long as the amount paid is not in excess of the fair market value of the practice as a going concern (without regard to the value of existing or future referrals from the seller to the buyer).

b. **Enforcement Actions Arising From Overpayment by a Hospital for a Medical Practice.** There have been several enforcement proceedings in which hospitals have been accused of overpaying for medical practices, resulting in a violation of the federal Anti-Kickback Statute. For example, in 2002, McLeod Regional Medical Center in Florence, South Carolina agreed to pay over $15,000,000 to settle an enforcement proceeding that arose from allegations that McLeod overpaid for the acquisition of medical practices.

c. **Safe Harbor Regulation for Acquisition of Medical Practices.** There is an Anti-Kickback Statute safe harbor regulation that applies generally to the sale of a medical practice, but this safe harbor is extremely narrow. It protects only the sale of a practice by one practitioner to another practitioner and requires that the practitioner who is selling his or her practice will not be in a position to make referrals or otherwise generate business for the purchasing practitioner after one year from the date of sale. Thus, as a practical matter, this safe harbor is only available if the selling practitioner is retiring or leaving the service area. In 1999, the OIG expanded safe harbor protection to include the sale of a practice by a practitioner in an underserved area to a hospital. For payments made to a practitioner by a hospital to qualify under the safe harbor and not be treated as remuneration: (a) the sale must be completed within three years; (b) the selling practitioner must not be in a position to make referrals to or generate business for the purchasing hospital or entity after the sale; (c) the practice must be located in a Health Professional Shortage Area (HPSA) for the practitioner's particular specialty; and (d) the hospital or other purchasing entity must, in good faith, engage in recruitment activities to find a new practitioner to take over the acquired practice.

3. **Internal Revenue Code Compliance for Tax Exempt Organizations.** Hospitals and health care delivery systems that are tax exempt organizations are subject to yet another layer of statutory and regulatory scrutiny.

a. **Private Benefit.** A tax exempt organization must serve public rather than private interests. There is a presumption that, when a medical practice is acquired by a tax exempt hospital, a private benefit flows to the physicians either because of the acquisition itself or the continuing relationship with the hospital. However, this is only a presumption, and the organization may serve private interests as long as the private benefit is incidental to the organization's exempt purpose. The IRS has explained that private benefit is "incidental" if it is: (a) a "necessary concomitant" of the public activity; and (b) insubstantial in relation to the public benefit resulting from the activity. For example, a tax exempt hospital may benefit a physician who is employed by the hospital after the hospital acquires the physician's practice as long as that benefit is incidental to the public benefit provided by the hospital.

b. **Private Inurement.** The net earnings of a tax exempt organization may not "inure in whole or in part to the benefit of private shareholders or individuals." This is different from private benefit in that the inurement proscription applies only to "insiders" but, unlike private benefit, there is no *de minimis* exception to the inurement proscription. The inurement proscription is applied to "insiders" who have a personal and private interest in the organization's activities and could cause the organization to confer a prohibited private benefit. The IRS's Exempt Organizations Handbook focuses on whether an individual possesses control over the organization to determine whether an individual is an "insider". The IRS has stated that the private benefit prohibition applies "to all physicians, either individually or as part of a medical group that sells assets to a tax exempt organization and all physicians who subsequently perform services for the exempt organization," and notes that benefits to the physicians from such arrangements must be balanced against benefits to the public.

c. **Acquisition of Practices.** To avoid inurement or private benefit, a tax exempt hospital that acquires for-profit private practices from physicians and thereafter employs those physicians must: (a) obtain an appraisal to show that the purchase price does not exceed fair market value; (b) enter into employment or independent contractor agreements with all or most of the selling physicians in order to retain the goodwill value of the practices; (c) pay the selling physicians on the same compensation scale (adjusted for experience and specialty) as the other physicians employed by the hospital (or affiliate) and, if necessary, provide evidence that the selling physician's reputation and experience justify a higher salary; (d) if necessary, enter into fair market value leases with the physicians for any assets retained by them (although the IRS prefers that the hospital (or affiliate) purchase all of the assets to clearly establish the hospital's control over the practice and the selling physician's lack of control); and (e) if tax-exempt bonds are used to finance practice acquisitions, complete an extensive questionnaire. The IRS has revoked the tax exempt status of hospitals that overvalued acquired physician medical practices and paid unreasonably high physician compensation to the acquired physicians.

B. **The Importance of Obtaining an Independent Determination of Fair Market Value.** Therefore, the Stark exception and the Internal Revenue Code (if the entity is tax exempt organization) absolutely require fair market value consideration for a hospital or health care delivery system purchase of a medical practice, and any such purchase, even if it falls within the Stark exception, is characterized as "at risk" under the federal Anti-Kickback Statute because it does not fall within any safe harbor regulation. To both comply with Stark and, if applicable, the Internal Revenue Code, and to negate any inference that the purchase price includes payment for referrals under the federal Anti-Kickback Statute, the value of intangibles related to the sale of a medical practice to a hospital or health care delivery system should be determined by an independent valuator or appraiser using recognized valuation methodologies based on reasonable economic and market assumptions.

1. **Stark Definition of "Fair Market Value."** As described in Chapter 1, "fair market value" for purposes of the Stark Law means value in arms-length transactions, consistent with general market value. General market value, in turn, means the price that an asset would bring as a result of *bona fide* bargaining between well-informed buyers and sellers who are not otherwise in a position to generate business for the other party on the date of acquisition of the asset. Usually the fair market price is the price at which *bona fide* sales have been consummated for assets of like type, quality, and quantity in a particular market at the time of the acquisition where the price has not been determined in any manner that takes into account the volume or value of anticipated or actual referrals.

2. **Anti-Kickback Statute Definition of "Fair Market Value".** The Anti-Kickback Statute does not define or specify any standard for valuing transactions to avoid an adverse inference that the transaction may be intended to induce referrals. In OIG advisory opinions, however, the OIG has generally looked favorably upon independent appraisals of "fair market value in arm's length transactions." See, e.g., OIG Advisory Opinion 03–15 (OIG approves reintegration of medical group and hospital where transfer of assets to hospital and price paid by hospital for real estate were pursuant to independent appraisals of fair market value in arm's length transactions).

3. **Internal Revenue Service Definition of Fair Market Value.** The IRS generally defines "fair market value" as the price at which the property would change hands between a willing buyer and a willing seller, neither being under any compulsion to buy or to sell and both having reasonable knowledge of relevant facts.

4. **Appraisal Methods for Determining Fair Market Value.** The definition of "fair market value" generally used for valuation purposes by appraisers and accountants is the following: "The price, expressed in terms of cash equivalents, at which property would change hands between a hypothetical willing and able buyer and a hypothetical willing and able seller, acting at

arms-length in an open and unrestricted market, when neither is under any compulsion to buy or sell and when both have reasonable knowledge of the relevant facts."

C. **Valuation Methods.** There are three basic approaches to valuation of on-going businesses: income approach; "asset approach;" and market approach.

1. **Income Approach.** The income approach is a general way of determining value using one or more methods that convert anticipated economic benefits into a present single amount. The income approach may involve either a discounted cash flow approach, which combines the organization's estimated free cash flows, terminal value, and the value of assets not required for operations (for example, cash and short-term investments) or a discounted earnings approach, which takes debt-free earnings for a given number of years and capitalizes them to estimate the current value of the organization. The discounted cash flow or earnings are multiplied by a capitalization rate (a market multiple) that reflects the relative risk of the business as a going concern.

a. **Regulatory Issues Related to Income Approach.** The principal issue with the income approach is how to value future cash flows without taking into account in an impermissible way the volume or value of existing and future referrals between the seller and the buyer when the seller is in a position to refer to the buyer post-transaction.

b. **Typical Non-Regulatory Issues Related to the Income Approach.** Undercoding or overcoding will affect valuation. A coding review is required in virtually every hospital or private equity medical practice acquisition. Also, if the seller is a practitioner who will be employed by the buyer post-transaction, then the available cash flow to the purchaser will be reduced by the amount of the seller's on-going compensation and will reduce the value of the transaction. Payment for a restrictive covenant or non-compete provision may double count cash flow since the income approach already assumes that cash flow will remain with the purchased practice. Revenue growth rate assumptions can have a significant impact on the valuation, especially when the future of the entire government reimbursement program is uncertain. In addition, the need for capital investment (for example, for information technology, communications systems, or new space or equipment) will reduce value under an income approach. Last, small practices are inherently riskier than large practices because they are dependent on the health, availability, and performance of only a few practitioners who have fewer resources to respond to market conditions and so, in general, will command a lower market multiple.

2. **Asset Approach.** The asset-based approach uses one or more methods based on the value of the assets net of liabilities. This approach may involve an estimate of the value of property

and equipment based on replacement cost new, less depreciation, an estimate of the value of current assets and liabilities at book values, and calculation of the adjusted debt-free net asset value of the organization based on individual asset values and non-interest bearing liabilities.

3. **Market Approach.** The market approach determines value by using one or more methods that compare the target business to similar businesses or business ownership interests that have actually been sold. This approach involves looking for comparable transactions. However, it is sometimes difficult to define precisely what is "comparable" because of, for example, different geographic regions and payor mix, and there is no ready market for the stock or ownership interests of small medical practices. Therefore, many appraisers rely on the published lists that show the "goodwill" paid in health care business transactions since this is a sensitive issue under the statutes and regulations that govern the health industry.

D. **Sales of Clinical Laboratory or Other Designated Health Service.** The Stark isolated transaction exception will not protect the sale by a medical group of a clinical laboratory, imaging center, or other DHS service to a hospital if the value of the DHS service is based upon the anticipated continuing referral volume from the selling medical group. As stated in Chapter 1, the legality of such a sale under Stark will be governed by the "stand in the shoes" concept. Under this concept, with respect to a compensation arrangement between a DHS entity (such as a hospital) and a "physician organization," a physician associated with the physician's organization is deemed to have a direct compensation arrangement with that DHS entity if the "only intervening entity" between the DHS entity and the physician is the "physician organization." Therefore, the parties will need to find an appropriate direct compensation exception under Stark. The only available exception appears to be the "fair market value" exception. Exceptions are made for compensation arrangements when the compensation received or paid by the physician is "set in advance" and reflects fair market value for the services rendered or goods purchased, and the following conditions are met: (a) the agreement is in writing, signed by all parties, and specifically refers to the services to be provided; (b) the agreement is for a specified time frame; (c) the agreement involves a commercially reasonable transaction and furthers the legitimate business purposes of the parties; (d) the agreement does not violate the federal Anti-Kickback Statute or any other law or regulation that governs billing or claims submission; and (e) the services specified in the agreement do not involve the counseling or promotion of any business activity that violates state or federal law.

E. **HIPAA Privacy Regulations.** A seller that is a "covered entity" for HIPAA purposes is permitted under the HIPAA privacy regulations to share patient identifying information (protected health information or "PHI") with a buyer as part of the covered entity's "health care operations." Medical group practices are "covered entities." "Health care operations" include "Business management and general administrative operations of the entity, including, but not limited to... the sale, transfer, merger, or consolidation of all or part of the covered entity with another covered entity, or an entity that following such activity will become a covered entity and due diligence related to such entity."

F. **Corporate Practice of Medicine.** In some states, acquisition of a medical practice by any entity may violate the state "corporate practice of medicine" doctrine as described in Chapter 4.

G. **Change of Ownership Issues May Influence Choice of Acquisition Structure.** A sale of stock, or a reverse subsidiary merger in which the provider is the surviving entity, is not a "change of ownership" ("CHOW") under Medicare law and under the CON and licensure laws of most states. However, a minority of the states characterize stock transactions as CHOWs. All asset transactions are CHOWs under both federal and state law. Most states follow a similar rule for purposes of state licensure, but some do not. However, in virtually all states, a sale of assets of a licensed health care provider requires advance notice to the licensure agency.

H. **Health Care Successor Liability Issues.** For institutional health care providers such as hospitals, nursing homes, ambulatory surgery centers, home health agencies, and hospices, actual and contingent liability to the government reimbursement programs runs with the provider agreement or provider number, even when the transaction is characterized as an asset sale. Starting with the 1994 Fifth Circuit Court of Appeals case of United States v. Vernon Home Health, Inc., which held that the actual and contingent payment liabilities attach to and run with an assigned provider agreement or provider number, the law has evolved to make a successor who takes assignment of a provider agreement liable for both civil monetary penalties and allegations under the federal False Claims Act. Therefore, any purchaser of an institutional provider needs to perform substantial due diligence before accepting assignment of a provider agreement or provider number. Depending on what is found, at a minimum, a purchaser will want to escrow part of the purchase price until the purchaser is satisfied that there is little likelihood of an overpayment allegation followed by recoupment of funds by the Medicare program because an indemnification provision alone may not be sufficient to make the purchaser whole if a claim against the purchaser for the seller's acts arises.

VI. WHAT ARE THE FUNDAMENTAL ASPECTS OF PRIVATE EQUITY ACQUISITION OF MEDICAL PRACTICES?

A. **Emergence of Physician Practice Management ("PPM") Companies.** The advent of "managed care" in the 1990s created a wave of medical practice acquisitions by not only hospitals and health care delivery systems but "physician practice management" ("PPM") companies including private equity funded companies with a view toward public offering of securities, such as Medpartners, Phycor, Phymatrix, and many others. The structure used by every PPM was virtually the same: the medical practice sold its non-clinical assets including furniture, fixtures, equipment, and goodwill to the PPM for cash or a combination of cash and ownership interests in the PPM company; the

PPM entered into a long term management services agreement (twenty to forty years); physicians were required to continue to work for an extended period of time (at least five years) at reduced compensation to permit the PPM to receive a return on its investment with "claw back" payment required from the physicians if they did not serve the full term of the employment agreement; the physicians were bound by restrictive covenants to protect the PPM investment; and the PPM consolidated disparate practices under one tax identification number so the practice could collectively negotiate price terms of managed care agreements in compliance with antitrust law.

B. **Failure of the 1990s PPM Industry.** The 1990s PPM equity model failed for a variety of reasons, including the following:

1. **The Market Myth.** Many medical practices entered into PPM arrangements based on the expectation that stock in the PPM would grow in valuing, giving the selling physicians consideration multiples. Unfortunately, the PPM promise of substantial wealth created by the stock market was mythical. The market values growth. The PPMs grew only through acquisitions. When acquisition opportunities diminish, the PPM must grow internally to sustain market value, but the PPMs did not implement effective internal growth strategies. The PPMs were unable to sustain high earnings multiples when they were required to rely more heavily on internal growth.

2. **The Management Myth.** PPMs would have physicians believe that PPMs can be better managers of medical practices than physicians. That did not happen. Because the PPM management had fiduciary duty to maximize shareholder wealth, the PPM managers were frequently more interested in creating wealth for investors than in the practice of medicine. Many managerial decisions interfered with physician judgment. For example, PPM managers may oppose acquisition of state of the art equipment on the grounds that the return on investment is inadequate when the physicians say that the need the state of the art equipment for effective patient care. In the 1990s it became apparent that PPMs managed money, not medical practices.

3. **The Capital Myth.** PPMs attempted to persuade physicians that physicians could not compete without a substantial capital partner. However, in practice it became apparent that PPMs, and especially publicly traded PPMs, were an expensive source of capital, and the physicians could more economically finance needed growth through other capital sources.

4. **The Restrictive Covenant Foundation.** A critical element of continuing viability of a PPM management agreement is enforcement of restrictive covenants in physician contracts that prevent sometimes the best physicians in the community from practicing in that area if the employment agreement is terminated. To be enforceable, covenants must be reasonable as to time, territory, and the activity restrained, and they must further be reasonable

as to the employer, the employee, and the public. It is unlikely that public policy will support the removal of the best physicians from any community only to serve the interests of Wall Street investors. Already in a minority of the states all restrictive covenants in physician contracts are void as against public policy because they unduly interfere with the physician—patient relationship. There is likely to be further erosion of restrictive covenants in physician contracts.

5. **Control Over the Practice of Medicine.** Physicians love to control their destinies. In PPM arrangements, virtually all control was relinquished to the PPM. Eventually, physicians naturally wanted to reassert control.

C. **New Wave of PPM Medical Practice Acquisitions.** The last decade saw a resurgence of PPM transactions but with slightly different structures based on lessons learned from the first wave. However, the elements and issues remain the same.

D. **What Questions Must a Medical Practice Ask When Considering a Private Equity Acquisition?** When considering a PPM transaction, physicians should consider the following:

1. **Market Questions.** Physicians should ask: What percentage of the PPM's growth is attributable to acquisitions? What internal rate of growth has the PPM achieved for the practices it presently manages? If the PPM is growing primarily by acquisitions, its value is sure to drop when acquisition opportunities diminish.

2. **Management Questions.** Physicians should ask: What can the PPM do to enhance revenue or reduce costs that the practice is not doing already? In many instances, the answer is "nothing."

3. **Capital Questions.** Physicians should ask: How much capital does a successful practice need? How much capital is invested in revenue producing assets? What is the relative cost of the capital?

4. **Restrictive Covenant Questions.** Physicians should ask: Will the restrictive covenant be enforced if my employment is terminated by the PPM without cause? Will the restrictive covenant last beyond the initial term and the PPM has recovered its investment? Can I avoid the restrictive covenant if the PPM does not fulfill specific representations and warranties?

5. **Control Questions.** Physicians should ask: What protocols are in place to insure that there is no interference with clinical decision-making? At what point does maximizing PPM shareholder wealth deviate from the provision of the highest quality medical services?

6. **Other Questions.** It may be tempting to cash out while the market is hot, but physicians should ask: Is this decision best for the delivery of health care services? Is this the legacy I want to leave to the public and the next generation of physicians?

E. **Corporate Practice of Medicine Issues.** The structure of a PPM transaction is influenced by the applicable state corporate practice of medicine doctrine. In states where the doctrine is not enforced, the acquisition can be made directly by the PPM. In states that have strict professional corporation or professional limited liability company codes where the medical practice can be owned only by physicians active in the practice, PPMs use the "friendly physician" model under which a physician "friendly" to the PPM owns 100% of the medical practice, permitting the PPM effectively to control the practice. However, the "friendly physician" model has been successfully challenged as violating the corporate practice medicine in several states.

VII. WHAT OTHER STRUCTURING ISSUES MUST BE CONSIDERED?

A. **Allocation of Purchase Price.** Asset transfers require an allocation of purchase price among the various assets or types of assets being sold. This is critical for obtaining a stepped up basis for purposes of depreciation. Both parties must agree on the allocation of the purchase price and report it to the IRS in the same manner.

B. **Bulk Sales of Assets.** Asset transfers have other complications. Virtually all states have enacted what are known as "bulk sales" laws which require the purchaser of a "major portion" of the inventory of a seller whose principal business consists of the sale of inventory to give advance notice of the sale to each creditor of the seller and, in some jurisdictions, to ensure that the proceeds of sale are used by the seller to pay its existing debts.

CHAPTER 8

UNDERSTANDING FUNDAMENTAL ANTITRUST LAW AND OTHER LAWS GOVERNING CLINICAL AND FINANCIAL INTEGRATION

I. WHAT IS "ANTITRUST LAW"?

A. **Common Law Foundation.** Antitrust, like many bodies of law, has its foundation in the English common law, under which contracts in general restraint of trade are unenforceable. For example, contracts that create a monopoly are unenforceable under the common law because they constitute a general restraint of trade. However, contracts in partial restraint of trade may be enforceable under the common law if they are "reasonable." Consequently, a core principle of the United States legal system, stretching far back into its common law roots, is promotion of "free trade."

B. **What Is the Purpose of Antitrust Law?** In general, the purpose of antitrust law is to protect economic competition for the benefit of the public under the theory that unfettered competition is in general the best system for allocation of scarce economic resources. The United States Supreme Court has consistently held that the antitrust laws protect individual consumer welfare by promoting lower prices, higher output, higher quality, efficiency in production and distribution, innovation, and consumer choice. Antitrust law does not protect competitors from each other; antitrust law operates for the benefit of consumers, not to insure that competitors such as small businesses remain in the market.

C. **What Conduct is "Anticompetitive"?** There are several schools of antitrust thought. The more populist "liberal school," in general, takes the position that "big is bad" and favors possible governmental regimentation of some portions of the economy. If size leads to squeezing out competition and thereby increasing prices, decreasing quality, or both, big can certainly be bad. However, sometimes larger size leads to economies of scale that permit distribution of goods and services at lower prices and higher quality. The more conservative "Chicago school" (named because of prominent economists at the University of Chicago) promotes incentives to compete and provide the best products or services at the lowest cost to consumers based on the belief that unfettered competition leads to market efficiency. In either case, there are no clear lines for determining whether conduct is anticompetitive. Consequently, antitrust law is difficult to understand and at some point becomes counterintuitive.

D. **The Role of Economics.** Antitrust law and economics are intimately intertwined: you cannot understand antitrust law without understanding economics because, in essence, antitrust law is applied microeconomics and industrial economic theory. In most markets, there are no market dominant forces so there is open competition. Other markets, however, constitute an oligopoly in which there are five or six enterprises that control the market. When there are fewer competitors, concerns regarding potential anticompetitive conduct increase. When only one enterprise is market dominant it can be alleged to have a "monopoly." However, simply having monopoly power alone may not be illegal, but the manner in which monopoly power was obtained may be impermissibly anticompetitive. Therefore, antitrust law compliance requires economic analysis, and legal proceedings alleging antitrust law violations require expert witness testimony from economists.

E. **Federal Antitrust Law.** The federal government has enacted a series of laws intended to prevent unfair restraints on competition. The general purpose of the federal antitrust laws is to prevent conduct that weakens or destroys competition in the marketplace. Generally stated, federal antitrust law prohibits (a) agreements or actions that unnecessarily restrain trade or commerce and (b) unilateral monopolistic activity. Federal antitrust laws do not preempt state antitrust laws, but most antitrust enforcement arises under federal antitrust law.

F. **What Are the Three Principal Federal Antitrust Laws?** There are three principal federal antitrust laws: the Sherman Act; the Clayton Act; and the Federal Trade Commission Act. There are other federal laws that have antitrust-related provisions, such as the Robinson-Patman Act that makes certain forms of price discrimination illegal, but for purposes of obtaining a fundamental understanding of the impact of the federal antitrust law on business transactions we will focus on the three principal antitrust laws:

1. **The Sherman Act.** The Sherman Act prohibits (a) contracts, combinations, or conspiracies in restraint of trade and (b) monopolization, attempts to monopolize, and conspiracies to monopolize.

2. **The Clayton Act.** The Clayton Act prohibits (a) mergers, acquisitions, and the formation of joint ventures which may substantially lessen competition and (b) certain types of exclusive and conditional dealing.

3. **The Federal Trade Commission Act.** The Federal Trade Commission Act prohibits unfair methods of competition and unfair or deceptive trade practices. Actions that violate the

Sherman Act also violate the Federal Trade Commission Act, but the Federal Trade Commission Act includes other prohibitions.

G. **What Federal Agencies Enforce Federal Antitrust Law?** There are two principal federal enforcement agencies: the Federal Trade Commission (FTC) and the Antitrust Division of the Department of Justice (DOJ). This leads to some confusion regarding whether the FTC or DOJ is responsible for any specific arrangement, but the agencies have historically cooperated in their enforcement activities.

H. **State Antitrust Laws.** Most states have enacted antitrust laws that generally codify the common law principles regarding restraint of trade. While state laws generally follow federal antitrust law precedent, some state law is particular to the governing state. State antitrust laws may provide broader remedies for anticompetitive behavior than the common law does and are primarily enforced by state attorneys general.

II. WHAT ARE THE ESSENTIAL CONCEPTS FOR UNDERSTANDING AND APPLYING ANTITRUST LAW?

A. **Federal Law Regulates Interstate Commerce.** As stated in Chapter 1, the "Commerce Clause" in the United States Constitution permits Congress to pass laws that regulate commerce between the states. The federal antitrust laws rely on the Commerce Clause for their passage. For the federal antitrust laws to apply, the subject conduct must either be in interstate commerce or substantially affect interstate commerce. Conduct that is entirely intrastate is subject only to state antitrust laws, and the federal antitrust laws do not apply. However, in modern commerce it is difficult to find commercial conduct that does not at least substantially affect interstate commerce.

B. **The Importance of Market Power.** Virtually all antitrust analysis is focused on two kinds of "market power." First, the most familiar is "seller market power" that gives a seller (or, through collusion, a group of sellers) the ability to raise prices above those that would exist in a competitive market. Seller market power depends on an organization's market share in the "relevant market" and the number of alternative sources of goods or services available to consumers. "Monopoly power" is a high degree of market power but does not necessarily mean a 100% market dominance. Second, there is the less familiar "buyer market power" (sometimes called "monopsony power") gives a buyer (or group of buyers) the power to reduce the amount they pay for a good or service below the competitive price by a significant amount.

C. **What Is the "Relevant Market"?** Before determining market share, you need to define the "relevant market." "Relevant market" has two components: the "relevant product market;" and the "relevant geographic market." Therefore, two fundamental questions must be answered. First, what is the product or service in question? Second, what is the geographic area in which the subject product or service is provided? Each question has the same purpose: to identify significant competitors. Businesses tend to see the "relevant market" very broadly, while regulators frequently see a much more narrow market. Determination of the "relevant market" frequently requires the expert testimony of economists.

1. **How Is "Relevant Product Market" Determined?** In general, the scope of the relevant product market includes all firms selling, from the consumer's perspective, "reasonably interchangeable" products or services that are good substitutes for one another from the consumer's perspective. That can be difficult to define because the regulatory agencies need to present the perspective of the "reasonable consumer." Again, commercial enterprises will define the product or service as broadly as possible. For example, the FTC or DOJ might allege that a merger of orthopedic medical practices in a particular market is anticompetitive based only on an assessment of medical practices that are presented as practicing orthopedic medicine. However, the orthopedic medical practices might counter by asserting that the service is much broader and includes podiatrists (which perform orthopedic procedures in a specific area of the body), neurosurgeons who perform spine surgery such as spinal fusion, and physical therapists, chiropractors, or acupuncturists who provide alternative treatments to orthopedic procedures. Nevertheless, the FTC and DOJ use the "smallest market principle" in determining relevant product market, which seeks to define competitors that, by themselves, would restrain the selling enterprise in question from raising prices.

2. **How Is "Relevant Geographic Market" Determined?** In general, relevant geographic market is the area in which the enterprise in question operates and to which its customers could practicably turn to obtain the relevant product or service. It is impossible define the relevant geographic market without first defining the relevant product or service market. The FTC and DOJ also apply the "smallest market principle" for determining relevant geographic market using the "hypothetical monopolist" methodology. The smallest market in which the subject enterprise as a "hypothetical monopolist" could profitably raise prices above competitive levels is a "relevant geographic market." If, however, consumers would react to increased prices by purchasing products or services from outside the region, then the geographic market expands. Therefore, determining relevant market is an iterative process, starting with the smallest market and expanding outward as the hypothetical monopolist methodology is applied. For example, in a hospital merger, a health care delivery system took the position that the relevant geographic market should be as far as the hospital's emergency helicopter service flies, which naturally was an expansive area. The FTC and DOJ, however, took a different approach and applied the "smallest market principle" to determine whether the merger might be anticompetitive.

D. **What Are "Horizontal" and "Vertical" Integration?** Under universally accepted economic theory, inefficient markets consolidate, requiring development of integration strategies in the pursuit of market efficiency. Business plans may follow either a "horizontal" or "vertical" integration strategy (or both), each of which has antitrust implications.

1. **What Is Horizontal Integration?** "Horizontal integration" refers to market consolidation of enterprises that are in the same relevant product or service market in order to gain market strength, which may, in some instances lead to monopoly power and anticompetitive conduct. The merger of oligopoly telecommunications enterprises Sprint and T-Mobile is an example of a horizontal merger.

2. **What Is Vertical Integration?** "Vertical integration" refers to market consolidation of enterprises in different but interrelated product or service markets. For example, "vertical integration" may involve acquisition of a supplier to assure a source of materials for producing a consumer product or service or by a hospital system of physicians and other ancillary service providers. Vertical integration can also result in increased prices, decreased quality, or other conduct that is harmful to consumers.

III. WHAT ARE THE ESSENTIAL CHARACTERISTICS OF THE SHERMAN ACT?

A. **What Is the Purpose of the Sherman Act?** With the advent of the Industrial Revolution in the 19th century and the evolution from an agrarian to a manufacturing economy, commerce, and in particular commerce among the states of the United States, changed. Steel, coal, and soon automobile and other manufacturing that required substantial amounts of capital became dominant. It was an era of "trusts" and business or capital "combinations" organized and developed to control markets and suppress competition in the marketing of goods and services, leading to enterprises attaining monopoly power in manners that were not previously of collective public concern. It was perceived that this anticompetitive conduct placed an undue burden on free competition in interstate commerce, but there were no federal laws to address the problem. That changed with the passage of the Sherman Antitrust Act in 1890. As stated in the United States Supreme Court decision in *Apex Hosiery Co. v. Leader*, the goal of the Sherman Act was to prevent restraints of free competition in business and commercial transactions that tended to restrict production, raise prices, and otherwise control the market to the detriment of consumers of goods and services. Note that the Sherman Act, at its core, prohibits unreasonable "restraint of trade," a concept that was well developed under the common law.

B. **What Are the Fundamental Elements of the Sherman Act?** There are two core parts of the Sherman Act: (1) Section 1 declares illegal every "contract, combination, or conspiracy in restraint of trade;" and (2) Section 2 provides sanctions for "monopolization" or attempts at monopolizing any aspect of interstate trade or commerce.

C. **What Are the Fundamental Elements of Sherman Act Section 1?** As stated above, Section 1 of the Sherman Act prohibits contracts, combinations, and conspiracies that unreasonably restrain trade or commerce and is the antitrust statute that is used most frequently in enforcement proceedings.

1. **What Is an "Agreement" Under the Sherman Act?** Although there is some legal authority to the contrary, in general the terms "contract," "combination," and "conspiracy" are synonymous, meaning merely an "agreement," "understanding," or "concerted action." "Agreement" is very broadly defined and construed. An "agreement" under the Sherman Act does not have to be an explicit, formal agreement and does not have to be written. It is not necessary that there have been a handshake or even a knowing wink. An "agreement" can be an informal, loose knit arrangement. However, the existence of the agreement must be supported by factual evidence, and the agreement must unreasonably restrain trade.

2. **An Agreement Can Be Implied Based on Facts and Circumstances.** An "agreement" can be, and frequently is, implied from all the facts and circumstances. It has been found that there was a "meeting of the minds" as to concert of action sufficient to constitute an "agreement" when competitors, in the course of a meeting, on the golf course, at a reception, or at a trade association meeting, have discussed that "prices are too low," or that "cost increases in the industry certainly justify a price increase," or, with respect to purchasing, that "prices are too high," or that "it would be foolish to purchase from a manufacturer that does not offer a five year warranty," or similar statements and have thereafter acted consistently with the views expressed. In such cases, "agreements" for purposes of antitrust enforcement have been found, despite the presentation of evidence that the pricing or other actions were taken for sound business and market reasons. Consequently, every trade association meeting or gathering of competitors leads to antitrust sensitivity.

3. **Internal Agreements Are Not "Agreements" for Purposes of Sherman Act Enforcement.** There must be two or more parties in an agreement to support a violation of Sherman Act Section 1. For example, agreements between an organization and its employees or between a parent organization and its subsidiaries cannot violate Section 1 of the Act. Also, arrangements between corporations or other entities and their stockholders or other equity owners, directors, officers, and employees generally are not "agreements" for purposes of Sherman Act Section 1, although a Sherman Act violation may be alleged if an individual otherwise has an "independent personal stake" in the organizational action.

4. **Unilateral or Independent Acts Are Not "Agreements" or "Conspiracies" for Purposes of Sherman Act Enforcement.** Sometimes, competitors in a relevant product or service market take actions that are substantially identical. We have all seen consumer gasoline prices rise and fall in near unison in geographic markets. However, "conscious parallelism" in which,

for example, competitors raise prices because they believe their competitors will do so, standing alone, is a unilateral act that does not constitute an impermissible conspiracy. Inference of a "conspiracy" requires evidence of certain "plus factors" that indicate that behavior was collective and not unilateral, including that the organizations involved (a) had a motive to conspire, (b) had an opportunity to conspire, (c) acted in a manner that was unlikely absent an agreement, (d) can offer no legitimate explanation or procompetitive business justification for the action, or (e) presented only pretextual justifications for their actions. Consequently, proving whether there was an impermissible conspiracy is very fact specific and difficult to prove with certainty.

5. **What Kind of Conduct Violates Sherman Act Section 1?** There are generally two types of violations of the Sherman Act: (a) *per se* violations; and (b) conduct that constitutes an "unreasonable" restraint of trade under the "Rule of Reason." However, the courts also apply a third rule, the "Quick Look Rule of Reason," which is an intermediate standard somewhere between the *Per Se Rule* and the Rule of Reason on the enforcement spectrum.

6. **What Are *Per Se* Violations of Sherman Act Section 1?** A *per se* violation of a law requires only that the prohibited conduct occur: the intent of the parties is not taken into consideration. Certain arrangements are considered to be so indefensible under any circumstances that they are presumed to be "unreasonable restraints of trade" and, therefore, illegal. *Per se* violations of the Sherman Act include the following:

   a. **Price Fixing.** Any agreement or understanding between competitors to raise, lower, or stabilize prices is illegal. Price fixing applies to the price at which goods or services will be purchased, as well as the price at which they will be sold. Agreements that affect price or an element of price are also illegal (for example, agreements on terms of sale, credit terms, price changes, profit margins, warranties, discounts, or rebates). An agreement or understanding between a supplier and customer as to the price at which the customer will resell the goods purchased from the supplier is also illegal. Such an agreement is commonly referred to as vertical price fixing or resale price maintenance.

   b. **Limitation of Supply or Demand.** An agreement or understanding between competitors to restrict the volume of goods or services they will produce or make available for sale or to restrict the amount of a product or raw material which they will purchase is illegal.

   c. **Allocation of Business.** An agreement or understanding between competitors that each will confine its business to a different geographic area, to a different line of products or services, or to different customers or classes of customers is illegal. Such an agreement is sometimes called market division or customer allocation.

d. **Boycotts.** An agreement or understanding between competitors that they will not sell to a particular customer or purchase from a given supplier or that in some manner they will not deal with another is generally illegal, although many boycotts are now treated under the Rule of Reason.

e. **Tying Arrangements.** An arrangement in which a customer is required to purchase an unwanted product or service in order to obtain a desired product or service is illegal if the seller controls a substantial part of the market for the desired product or service.

7. **What Kind of Conduct Violates the "Rule of Reason"?** Numerous types of business conduct other than *per se* conduct may become "unreasonable" restraints of trade in light of surrounding facts and circumstances. For example:

a. **Refusal to Deal.** A supplier or purchaser of goods or services generally may determine with whom it will or will not do business. However, a supplier may not cut off a customer in furtherance of a *per se* violation such as price fixing.

b. **Reciprocity.** The practice of purchasing goods from another on condition that the other purchase different goods from you may be an antitrust offense. It is more likely to be condemned if done systematically and enforced through coercion.

c. **Exclusive Dealing.** An agreement to purchase from only one supplier or sell to only one customer may be illegal if it has a substantial adverse impact on competition. However, exclusivity may also be procompetitive under certain circumstances.

d. **Other Non-Price Vertical Restraints.** This category includes practices such as territorial and customer restraints on dealers. Such restraints may be illegal if they have a substantial adverse impact on competition.

D. **What Is the "Quick Look Rule of Reason" for Enforcement of Sherman Act Section 1?** As stated above, antitrust law is difficult to apply and is very fact specific. In that regard, the *Per Se* Rule and the Rule of Reason for determining what constitutes an "unreasonable restraint of trade" sit on opposite ends of the enforcement spectrum. Over time, the "Quick Look Rule of Reason" has emerged as an intermediate standard. The Quick Look Rule of Reason provides that certain actions involving competitors that directly affect price or output are conclusively presumed to have anticompetitive effects, but the courts permit the competitors to rebut the presumption by producing evidence of plausible procompetitive justification for the agreement that is allegedly in restraint of trade.

E. **What Are the Fundamental Elements of Sherman Act Section 2?** Section 2 of the Sherman Act prohibits monopolization, attempts to monopolize, and conspiracy to monopolize. Contrary to Sherman Act Section 1, no "agreement" is required to find a Sherman Act Section 2 violation: a single legal entity can engage in conduct that violates Sherman Act Section 2. In general, Section 2's monopolization and attempted monopolization provisions apply to "exclusionary" or "predatory" conduct exercised by organizations with substantial market power.

1. **What Is "Monopolization"?** Monopolization has two separate elements. First, monopolization requires "monopoly power." However, monopoly power alone does not constitute illegal monopolization. More is required. Second, monopolization requires "predatory," "unreasonably exclusionary," or "anticompetitive" conduct resulting in willful acquisition or maintenance of monopoly power as distinguished from legitimate reasons for attaining monopoly power such as a superior product or service, business acumen, or historically fortuitous circumstances and a deliberateness in the acquisition, use, or preservation of such power.

a. **What Is "Monopoly Power"?** The legal definition of "monopoly power" is the power to control prices or exclude others from the market. This definition is broad and imprecise. Rationally, an organization cannot control prices unless others are excluded from the market. However, mere ability to exclude competition, without more, is not sufficient to give an organization monopoly power. In essence, "monopoly power" is a substantial degree of "market power." "Market share" is often used as a shorthand for market power. Control of 65% or more of the market is generally enough to constitute "monopoly power."

b. **What Is "Predatory," "Unreasonably Exclusionary," and "Anticompetitive" Conduct for Purposes of Constituting "Monopolization"?** This element of monopolization focuses on how an organization interacts with competitors, not consumers, and is an area in which antitrust analysis becomes obtuse. It defies definition. For example, it is difficult to distinguish aggressive, but procompetitive, conduct from predatory or unreasonably exclusionary anticompetitive conduct. For purposes a fundamental understanding, conduct is "predatory" for purposes of Sherman Act Section 2 if (a) it has exclusionary effect on an organization's competitors and contributes significantly to an organization's ability to maintain market power but generates none of the benefits of competition, such as lower prices, greater productivity, more choice, increased market access, innovation, and efficiency in production or distribution and (b) there is no legitimate business interest that renders the conduct non-predatory. In other words, "predatory" conduct is fact specific and difficult to define, but one type of conduct typically found to constitute predatory conduct is "predatory pricing," which results when an organization (i) charges a price below its cost of market production for a significant period of time to drive its competitors from the market and (ii) can recoup its losses after competitors are driven from the market by charging higher prices.

c. **Refusals to Deal With Competitors.** A predominant amount of Sherman Act Section 2 cases involve an organization with substantial market power refusing to deal in some form with its competitors who allegedly need the organization's cooperation to compete effectively against the organization. However, there is no clear duty for a market dominant organization to deal with competitors, so there are no bright lines for determining monopolization.

2. **What Is an "Attempt to Monopolize"?** An attempt to monopolize requires a specific intent to monopolize, predatory conduct pursuant to that intent, and a "dangerous probability" that the attempt will succeed if the predatory conduct continues. The only difference between "monopolization" and "attempt to monopolize" is the necessary share of the perpetrator's market share.

a. **What Is the Meaning of "Specific Intent to Monopolize"?** This element is typically satisfied by an organization engaging in "predatory conduct," and thus this element is typically collapsed unto the "predatory conduct" element.

b. **What Is the Meaning of "Predatory Conduct"?** The definition of "predatory conduct" for attempts to monopolize is the same as for "monopolization."

c. **What Is the Meaning of "Dangerous Probability of Actual Monopolization"?** Even if an organization has a specific intent to monopolize and has engaged in predatory conduct, Section 2 of the Sherman Act is not violated unless the conduct results in a dangerous probability of actual monopolization, given the market's structural characteristics and the type of alleged predatory conduct. The critical criteria for this element of the test is the perpetrating organization's market share. While there is no specific market share percentage for purposes of the test for an attempt to monopolize, it is generally agreed that a market share of at least 40% to 50% is sufficient to support a violation.

3. **What Is a "Conspiracy to Monopolize"?** A conspiracy to monopolize has three essential elements: (a) a conspiracy; (b) two or more concerns acting with the specific intent to monopolize;

and (c) an overt act in furtherance of the conspiracy. Like Section 1 of the Sherman Act, a "conspiracy" requires two different entities that are not financially integrated. In reality, any alleged "conspiracy to monopolize" under Section 2 can be alleged as a violation of Section 1, under which claims are more commonly made.

IV. WHAT ARE THE ESSENTIAL CHARACTERISTICS OF THE CLAYTON ACT?

A. **What Is the Purpose of the Clayton Act?** As the Industrial Revolution progressed, large organizations continued to develop in the United States economy, and, even after passage of the Sherman Antitrust Act in 1890, there were concerns regarding the anticompetitive impact of large enterprises on interstate commerce. While the Sherman Act provided sanctions for conduct that restrained trade, that presupposes that the arrangement exists. So the question was posed: what can be done to prevent anticompetitive conduct? From those concerns, Congress enacted the Clayton Antitrust Act of 1914. Instead of policing existing organizations and arrangements, the Clayton Act, as a supplement to the Sherman Act, attempts to thwart anticompetitive conduct in its incipiency by prohibiting certain anticompetitive conduct.

B. **What Is the Clayton Act Prohibition of Arrangements that May Have Anticompetitive Effects?** Section 7 of the Clayton Act provides that no person engaged in any activity affecting interstate commerce shall acquire, directly or indirectly, the ownership interests or assets of another person in any line of commerce in any geographic area if a reasonable probability of such acquisition may be to lessen competition or to tend to create a monopoly. In essence, Chapter 7 of the Clayton Act prohibits arrangements that *may* have significant anticompetitive effects, including, without limitation, mergers, acquisitions, joint ventures, leases, licenses, partial acquisitions, and even employment. No actual lessening of competition is required to violate the Clayton Act: only reasonable probability of an adverse effect on competition, and doubts are resolved against the arrangement.

1. **What Are the Market Thresholds for Applying the Clayton Act?** If a merger, acquisition, or other consolidation results in an organization having a "high market share" or "high market concentration," there is a rebuttable presumption that the transaction will be anticompetitive, and it is *prima facie* unlawful. The general rule is that the rebuttable presumption applies if the merging firms have a post-merger market share that is 30% or more. If that threshold is reached, then the burden shifts to the organization to introduce evidence that the merger, acquisition, or consolidation is not anticompetitive.

2. **How Are Clayton Act Merger Challenge·Actions Brought?** Although private plaintiffs may challenge mergers, almost all merger challenges are enforcement actions brought by the FTC or DOJ Antitrust Division as pre-transaction injunctions to block the transaction, which requires prediction of the post-transaction anticompetitive effects.

3. **Pre-Merger Notification Requirements.** Acquisitions, mergers, and formations of joint ventures which exceed certain "size of the transaction" and "size of the parties" thresholds are subject to reporting requirements to both the FTC and the DOJ Antitrust Division under the Hart-Scott-Rodino (HSR) Act, which amended the Clayton Act, to enable the FTC and DOJ to examine the legality of the transaction before it is consummated. The thresholds required to trigger the HSR filing requirement are quite substantial: the size of the transaction must be greater than $80,000,000.00; and, alternatively under the size of the parties test, one party to the transaction must have assets or annual revenues of at least $170,000,000.00 and the other party must have assets or annual revenues of at least $17,000,000.00. Consequently, only the largest transactions require HSR pre-transaction notification; most transactions do not.

C. **What Is the Clayton Act Prohibition on Exclusive Dealing?** Section 3 of the Clayton Act prohibits exclusive dealing arrangements, requirements contracts, and tying arrangements if the effect of the arrangement may be to substantially lessen competition or tend to create a monopoly.

D. **What Is the Clayton Act Prohibition of Interlocking Officers and Directors?** Section 8 of the Clayton Act prohibits any person from simultaneously serving as an officer or on the Board of Directors of competing organizations, commonly referred to as "interlocking" relationships, if the organizations are engaged in interstate commerce and exceed certain capital, surplus, and profits thresholds as established and annually revised by the FTC. Like HSR reporting, the "interlocking" relationships thresholds are quite substantial. In general, the Clayton Section 8 prohibitions apply if each of the interlocking organizations has capital, surplus, and undivided profits in excess of $35,000,000 and the competitive sales of each organization are greater than $3,500,000. The actual thresholds are greater, and they increase annually. Even without application of Clayton Act Section 8, as explained in the Chapter on Corporate Governance and Fiduciary Duty, officers and directors cannot engage in conflicts of interest arrangements, cannot usurp corporate opportunities for their own benefit, and must maintain confidentiality of an organization's trade secret and otherwise proprietary information. Therefore, "interlocking" relationships are dangerous regardless of whether they violate the Clayton Act.

V. WHAT ARE THE ESSENTIAL CHARACTERISTICS OF THE FEDERAL TRADE COMMISSION ACT?

A. **What Is the Purpose of the Federal Trade Commission Act?** Again during the early days of the Industrial Revolution, the need for a federal agency that could police anticompetitive conduct became apparent. Consequently, in the same year that the Clayton Act was enacted, Congress passed the Federal Trade Commission Act of 1914, through which the FTC was created.

B. **What Conduct Does the Federal Trade Commission Act Cover?** In general, the Federal Trade Commission Act prohibits unfair methods of competition and deceptive acts or trade practices. For example, the FTC has been actively involved in investigating trade associations such as independent physician associations that try to collectively negotiate price terms with health care payors even if the trade association is not clinically or financially integrated. The Act reaches a bit deeper than the Sherman Act and Clayton Act and is intended to protect consumers in other ways, such as deceptive advertising. Also, one emerging FTC power is protection of consumer privacy, which the FTC shares with the United States Department of Health and Human Services, Office of Civil Rights, the agency responsible for enforcing the Health Insurance Portability and Accountability Act of 1996 privacy rules.

C. **What Are the Federal Trade Commission Regulatory Powers?** The Act authorizes the FTC to bring actions against every trade practice which: (1) restrains competition in violation of the Sherman Act; (2) may lessen competition in violation of the Clayton Act; (3) is contrary to the public policy underlying the Sherman and Clayton Acts; (4) is contrary to broad principles of ethics or "fairness;" or (5) might deceive the public. Under the Federal Trade Commission Act, the FTC is empowered to (a) prevent unfair methods of competition, (b) seek monetary sanctions and other relief arising from conduct that injures consumers, (c) promulgate rules that describe specific conduct that is by definition "unfair" or "deceptive" and establish requirements intended to prevent such conduct, (d) conduct investigations related to potentially anticompetitive conduct of entities engaged in interstate commerce, and (e) provide reports and recommendations to Congress.

D. **How Does the Federal Trade Commission Work with the DOJ Antitrust Division?** Although there are no clear lines of delineation, because any violation of the Sherman Act is also a violation of the Federal Trade Commission Act and the FTC can act on matters that violate each Act, the FTC and the DOJ Antitrust Division work collaboratively through interagency protocols. However, only the DOJ Antitrust Division can prosecute criminal misconduct, although the FTC may assist the DOJ Antitrust Division with a criminal investigation.

VI. WHAT CONDUCT IS EXEMPT FROM APPLICATION OF THE FEDERAL ANTITRUST LAWS?

A. **What Conduct or Persons Are Exempt or Immune From Antitrust Law Enforcement?** There are various persons, actions, and situations that are exempt or immune from antitrust enforcement. Most exemptions are "express" and described in the federal antitrust laws. Some exemptions are created by judicial decisions and are described as "implied," but they are disfavored. The following is an overview description of several of the more important express exemptions or conduct that is beyond coverage of the federal antitrust laws.

B. **What Is the "State Action" Exemption?** Basically, the United States Supreme Court many years ago established the rule that the Sherman Act was not intended to restrain state actions or official action directed by a state. There are some state laws that directly restrain competition and create barriers for competitors to enter the market, but those laws are not subject to federal antitrust law enforcement. For example, some states have enacted "Certificate of Need" (CON) laws which permit the states to develop a "need formula" for the provision of health services and require providers of new institutional health services to obtain a "certificate" before proceeding with development of the health service. This clearly protects holders of CONs from competition if the need formula developed by the state indicates that there is no need for the service, even if the new service might lead to lower consumer prices, higher quality, and greater consumer choice. Also, some states have "Certificate of Public Advantage" (COPA) laws that permit hospital mergers that create monopoly power. However, what a state permits or approves is not subject to federal antitrust law enforcement.

C. **What Is the "Noerr-Pennington" Exemption?** Commonly called the "Noerr-Pennington" exemption after the two United States Supreme Court decisions that created it, it has long been established that the antitrust laws do not apply to private parties' petitioning the government for anticompetitive action, for example, through filing litigation (unless the filing is either fraudulent or a "sham").

D. **What Is the Federal Governmental Immunity Exemption?** The federal antitrust laws do not apply to the federal government and its agencies or agents.

E. **What Is the Labor Exemption?** Even though labor unions are cartels that fix the price of the labor that they sell, labor unions are exempt from federal antitrust law enforcement.

F. **What Is the Health Care Quality Improvement Act (HCQIA) Exemption?** To protect hospitals from damages in antitrust lawsuits arising from denials of physician medical staff privileges, the HCQIA exempts hospitals from antitrust damages, but not liability, arising from a hospital's denial, revocation, or suspension of a physician's medical staff privileges. The exemption is limited to "professional review actions" of "professional review bodies" in the course of "professional review activities" and does not apply to other forms of allegedly anticompetitive conduct, such as a hospital's entering into exclusive contracts for provision of services such as anesthesia, radiology, and pathology.

VII. WHAT ARE THE FTC AND DOJ STATEMENTS OF ANTITRUST ENFORCEMENT POLICY IN HEALTH CARE?

A. **When Were the FTC and DOJ Statements of Antitrust Enforcement Policy in Health Care First Published?** In 1993, just as managed care and development of integrated delivery systems was taking off, the FTC and DOJ issued their first joint health care antitrust statements that generally provided guidelines or "safety zones" that are intended to promote procompetitive conduct. The original "safety zones" were clarified and expanded in 1996 including guidance on clinical integration and multi-provider networks. In October, 2011, the FTC and Antitrust Division of the DOJ issued a joint Statement of Antitrust Enforcement Policy Regarding Accountable Care Organizations Participating in the Medicare Shared Savings Program that was intended to facilitate development of ACOs as described in the Centers for Medicare and Medicaid Services resolutions governing participation in the Shared Savings Program created under the Affordable Care Act of 2010.

B. **What Is the Current Status of the FTC and DOJ "Safety Zone" Guidance?** First, it should be emphasized that the FTC and DOJ joint statements promulgated in 1993, 1996, and 2011 merely constitute "guidance" and not enforceable law. Also, conduct outside of the "safety zones," like conduct outside of the federal Anti-Kickback Statute safe harbor regulations (which do have the force and effect of law), is not necessarily contrary to law. Consequently, because of their characterization as "safety zones," the health industry comfortably relied on the guidance and felt immune from prosecution provided that the conduct fell within the safety zone guidance or close to it. The joint guidance provided at least a degree of certainty regarding antitrust law enforcement. However, in 2023 the picture abruptly changed: DOJ, which has the power to prosecute alleged antitrust law violations in the courts, but not the FTC, which has the power only to pursue only administrative remedies, unilaterally withdrew its support of all prior joint statements. According to DOJ, because "the health care landscape has changed significantly" since the joint statements were issued "the statements are overly permissive on certain subjects, such as information exchanges." DOJ further stated that it does not intend to replace the withdrawn statements with new guidance but instead will use a "case-by-case enforcement approach [that] will allow the [DOJ Antitrust] Division to better evaluate mergers and conduct in health care markets that may harm competition." The FTC has not yet withdrawn from the joint statement guidance, but that may happen. Therefore, while, the "safety zones" do not have the value that they once had, an understanding of the guidance that was supported by both agencies for thirty years is a necessary backdrop for appreciation of how antitrust laws are applied to the health industry.

C. **What Is Covered in the Statements?** A wide variety of topics are covered, including mergers, consolidation, alliances, networks, group purchasing, and collective bargaining. Applicability of the statements to managed care contracting is separately discussed. The guidance provides that the following would be permissible:

1. **Mergers Among Hospitals.** A merger of two general, acute care hospitals if one (a) has fewer than 100 beds or (b) has an average daily inpatient census of fewer than 40 patients over the last three years. Mergers outside the safety zone are reviewed in accordance with DOJ/FTC Horizontal Merger Guidelines. Keys: Is the merger procompetitive? Are there cost savings? Would the merger eliminate a failing hospital?

2. **Information Exchanges.** Information exchanges among competitors are permitted under the safety zone guidance provided that (a) the exchange is managed by a third party, (b) the data is more than three months old, and (c) the data consists of information that is anonymized and aggregated, with the report including data from at least five participants and with no single participant representing more than 25% of the total data. This safety zone in particular was singled out by DOJ in its announcement regarding withdrawal from the joint guidelines, principally because today electronic data is so easily shared.

3. **Hospital Joint Ventures Involving High Technology or Other Expensive Health Care Equipment.** A joint venture among hospitals to purchase or otherwise share the ownership cost of high-technology or other expensive health care equipment if the cost of the individual purchase is financially unfeasible. Otherwise, joint ventures are suspect and will be analyzed under the Rule of Reason under the following analytical process:

    a. Define the "Relevant Market."

    b. Evaluate the Competitive Effects of the Venture.

    c. Evaluate the Impact of Pro-Competitive Efficiencies.

    d. Evaluate Collateral Agreements.

4. **Hospital Joint Ventures Involving Specialized Clinical or Other Expensive Health Care Services.** The belief was that most hospital joint ventures formed to provide specialized clinical or other health care services do not create antitrust problems and should be tested under the Rule of Reason as described above.

5. **Joint Purchasing Arrangements Among Health Care Providers.** Any joint purchasing arrangement when (a) the purchasers account for less than 35% of the total sales of the purchased good or service in the relevant market and (b) the cost of the jointly purchased products and services accounts for less than 20% of the total revenues from all products or services sold by each competing participant in the joint purchasing arrangement.

6. **Physician Network Joint Ventures.** Exclusive networks whose physician participants share substantial financial risk and constitute 20% or less of the physicians in each physician specialty in the relevant geographic market. For nonexclusive networks, the threshold is 30%. "Sharing of substantial financial risk" can mean capitation, global case rates, withholds, or other means.

7. **Multiprovider Networks.** Multiprovider networks are scrutinized for anti-competitive effect as described in greater detail in Section VIII regarding application of antitrust law principles to managed care contracting and collective fee negotiations.

8. **Accountable Care Organizations That Participate in the Medicare Shared Savings Program.** The DHHS Centers for Medicare and Medicaid Services' promotion and implementation of what became known as "value-based arrangements" began in earnest with Accountable Care Organizations that participated in the Medicare Shared Savings Program created under the Affordable Care Act of 2010. Consequently, because DHHS wanted to incentivize ACO formation, in 2011 CMS and the DHHS OIG promulgated fraud and abuse law waivers as described in Chapter One. However, ACOs also had to comply with antitrust laws administered by the FTC and DOJ. Consequently, on the same date that CMS and the OIG promulgated ACO formation rules including the fraud and abuse waivers, the FTC and DOJ promulgated a new "safety zone" for MSSP ACO organizations. The guidance included an expedited FTC and DOJ "business review" process that in practice is rarely used, a "safety zone" for ACOs that fall within certain "market share thresholds," and description of some forms of conduct by ACOs that the FTC and DOJ characterize as "problematic." In general, the ACO antitrust safety zone applies to ACO participants who provide the same "common service" and have a combined share of thirty percent (30%) or less of each common service in the primary service area. Higher market shares of physician services may still be "safe" if the primary service market is in a rural area. The FTC and DOJ identified the following as examples of potentially problematic conduct:

   a. "anti-steering," "antitiering," "guaranteed inclusion," "most favored nation," or similar contract provisions;

   b. tying sales of the ACO's services to a private payor's purchase of other services from providers outside of the ACO, especially providers affiliated with an ACO participant;

   c. exclusive contracting with ACO physicians, hospitals, ASCs, or other providers that may discourage or prevent those providers from contracting with private payors outside the ACO; and

   d. restricting a private payor's ability to make certain information about the ACO's cost, quality, and efficiency available to the payor's covered beneficiaries.

9. **Safety Zones for Value-Based Arrangements and Other Coordinated Care Payment Models.** As described in Chapter 1, in 2020 CMS and the OIG promulgated regulations for application of the Stark Law and the federal Anti-Kickback Statute to "value-based arrangements" that

became effective in 2021. However, although the FTC and DOJ Antitrust Division promulgated complementary antitrust "safety zones" when the original ACO/MSSP Stark and Anti-Kickback Statute waiver rules were promulgated in 2011, the FTC and DOJ did not expand the antitrust safety zones when the broader value-based arrangement rules were promulgated. Perhaps more importantly, while this may change because of DOJ's withdrawal from the joint antitrust law compliance guidance, antitrust enforcement against the different types of provider-controlled contracting networks does not currently appear to be an enforcement interest of either agency compared to the 1990s and 2000s when the vast majority of the FTC and DOJ antitrust enforcement efforts targeted provider networks. Together, the FTC and DOJ have filed very few actions since issuance of the ACO/MSSP antitrust safety zone, and the actions that have been filed were neither in the last several years nor against MSSP ACOs. This may be interpreted to be a recognition by the FTC and DOJ of effective clinical integration by operating provider networks that operate in the coordinated care payment economy. Provider networks are required to operate in a manner that checks all of the FTC/DOJ clinical integration boxes, and the antitrust enforcement agencies realize that proving that a provider network that pursues coordinated pay/financial risk contracts is not clinically integrated is virtually impossible. Therefore, as the market moves toward greater penetration of both private insurance and government reimbursement coordinated care payment models, there is less need for antitrust regulatory scrutiny of provider networks like there was when provider networks were relegated to relying principally on the messenger model.

VIII. WHAT ANTITRUST PRINCIPLES APPLY TO MANAGED CARE CONTRACTING AND COLLECTIVE FEE NEGOTIATIONS?

A. **Contracting Through Provider Networks.** The antitrust laws allow certain integrated networks to create price agreements which, absent such integration, might otherwise be illegal when the integration produces significant efficiencies that benefit consumers. In every case, the price agreement must be integral to the significant efficiencies that the integration is meant to achieve. There are two primary kinds of integration: financial integration; and clinical integration. According to the FTC Bureau of Competition, in the absence of such financial or clinical integration, collective negotiation by physicians simply results in an agreement between competitors on prices, which is *per se* illegal. For non-integrated IPAs and PHOs, this means that any evidence of collective negotiation might result in liability.

1. **Financial Integration Through Risk Sharing.** Financial integration may be achieved by (a) agreement by the network to provide services to a health plan at a "capitated" rate; (b) agreement by the network to provide designated services or classes of services to a health plan for a predetermined percentage of premium or revenue from the plan; (c) agreement by the network to provide a complex or extended course of treatment that requires the substantial

coordination of care by physicians in different specialties offering a complementary mix of services, for a fixed, predetermined payment, when the cost of that course of treatment for any individual patient can vary greatly due to the individual patient's condition, the choice, complexity, or length of treatment, or other factors; or (d) use by the network of significant financial incentives for its physician participants, as a group, to achieve specified cost-containment goals. Two methods by which the network can accomplish this are:

a. **Risk Withholding Programs.** Withholding from all physician participants in the network a substantial amount of the compensation due to them, with distribution of that amount to the physician participants based on group performance in meeting the cost-containment goals of the network as a whole ("Risk Withholding Program"); or

b. **Rewards Programs.** Establishing overall cost or utilization targets for the network as a whole, with the network's physician participants subject to subsequent substantial financial rewards or penalties based on group performance in meeting the targets ("Rewards Program").

c. **How Does a Risk Withholding Program Work?** The Risk Withholding Program establishes a fee schedule, but, under it, participants agree with payers that a certain amount of each fee will be withheld and only paid out at a later date if the physician group meets certain agreed-upon targets. The acceptable amount of withholding will vary in each case, but must be large enough to induce member physicians to modify their behavior in a way that improves quality or improves costs to meet the targets that trigger the withholding to be paid. Thus, the amount of withholding depends, in part, upon the starting point for the fee schedule because, if the fee is high enough, the physicians may have no incentive to ensure that they obtain the withheld amount. The FTC has allowed a withholding of 15% based on a fee schedule that was set around the 50th percentile of national rates and the 60th percentile of prevailing rates in the area. On the other hand, the FTC disapproved a 15% withholding for a PPO that set its maximum fee at the 88th percentile of fees regularly charged. The FTC noted that the second initial fee schedule was high enough that most physicians would be receiving full payment and the withhold was unlikely to provide a significant incentive to modify their behavior and create the efficiencies that the withhold was meant to induce.

d. **How Does a Rewards Program Work?** The Rewards Program is analogous to a reverse Risk Withholding Program. Instead of withholding a percentage, the plan negotiates discounted rates and then sets goals for reducing the payor's costs. The physicians then get a share of any reduced cost savings. For every group of fees in the set schedule there needs to be a corresponding cost reduction program. For example, the plan could project, based on historical data, the hospital costs for a covered population and share in any reduction. This program may not produce any efficiencies for certain outpatient procedures for which fees are set. Thus, other programs may be needed. A similar program could be established for a reduction in prescriptions or utilization of specialists.

2. **Financial Integration Through Direct Employment.** We are now in the second wave of health care delivery system integration through hospital acquisition of medical practices and direct physician employment by health care delivery systems. The first was the advent of "managed care," when hospitals believed it was necessary to acquire the services of primary care gatekeepers. However, managed care merely became "managed cost," hospitals overpaid for medical practice acquisitions, and the concept was a financial disaster. The second wave is being led by health system acquisitions of high end specialists in an effort to preserve the volume of inpatient, acute care procedures. Today, fewer than 30% of all physicians are employed by physician-owned, independent medical practices, and that downward trend is expected to continue.

3. **Clinical Integration.** Like financial integration, the purpose and result of clinical integration must be to achieve significant efficiencies. Such integration may be evidenced through an active and ongoing program to evaluate and modify practice patterns by the network's physician participants and create a high degree of interdependence and cooperation among the physicians to control costs and ensure quality. Like financial integration, the agreement and use of a set fee schedule must be reasonably necessary to realize the intended efficiencies. The program may include:

    a. **Monitoring Utilization.** Establishing mechanisms to monitor and control utilization of health care services that are designed to control costs and assure quality of care.

    b. **Measuring Quality.** Clinical protocols must be established to reward provision of best practices, evidence based medicine.

    c. **Selecting Efficient Providers.** Selectively choosing network physicians who are likely to further these efficiency objectives. This is, in essence, pay for performance.

    d. **Investment of Capital.** The significant investment of capital, both monetary and human, in the necessary infrastructure and capability to realize the claimed efficiencies.

4. **Can a Provider Network Rely on Clinical Integration Alone?** The market is moving toward development and acceptance of clinical integration models for joint negotiation of price terms and holistic management of health care costs. From 2000 to 2010, the FTC approved

three clinical integration models, and these determinations led to a new wave of clinical integration strategies.

a. **FTC and DOJ Analysis of Clinical Integration Arrangements.** Based on their joint experience, the FTC and DOJ have set forth the following questions that these agencies will ask when analyzing clinical integration strategies:

   i. What do the physicians plan to do from a clinical standpoint?

   ii. How are these activities designed to improve quality of care, reduce the cost of care, or produce other efficiencies?

   iii. How is the program designed to provide interdependence among physician participants?

   iv. How will the physicians be collectively motivated to achieve those goals and efficiencies?

   v. How significant will the physicians' investment (both monetary and in "human capital" form) be?

   vi. How will performance be monitored and measured?

   vii. What are the consequences of physician non-performance or sub-par performance?

   viii. Why is joint price negotiation reasonably necessary to achieve the intended benefits of the program?

   ix. What are the likely competitive effects of physicians' joint negotiations?

b. **First Business Review Letter.** In 2002, the FTC approved an arrangement involving an IPA that was located in a market where HMO and other managed care plans operated. The IPA consisted of 25% of the general practitioners and 20–35% of specialists, depending on the specialty. Most importantly, the IPA implemented a system to establish practice standards, protocols, and goals relating to quality, and appropriate utilization of services by IPA participants. The IPA engaged in case management, preauthorization of some services, and concurrent and retrospective review of inpatient stays. The IPA participants also made a significant investment in the information systems necessary to gather, analyze, and report the aggregate and individual information. There was also a significant investment in participants' and employees' time to establish and monitor standards, protocols, and goals. Based on its evaluations of both individual participant's and the network's aggregate performance, the IPA modified individual participant's actual practices where necessary. The IPA provided for remedial action, including expulsion, for participants failing to adhere to standards and protocols. As described above, clinical integration requires a significant commitment to creating efficiencies through establishing and imposing standards and protocols. The FTC found that the IPA's use of a single fee schedule in the previous example was reasonably necessary to achieve the goals of integration. Clinical integration, however, is probably most used in networks that are also financially integrated. Thus, any network that is clinically, but not financially, integrated should be ready to explain how, without financial integration, one member is truly concerned with the performance and efficiency of other members, and why the set fee schedule is necessary to achieve the established goals for improved efficiency.

c. **The GRIPA FTC Advisory Opinion.** In September, 2007, the FTC issued a thirty-page advisory opinion regarding a proposal by the Greater Rochester Independent Practice Association ("GRIPA") under which GRIPA would negotiate contracts, including price terms, with health care payors on behalf of its physician members in connection with the sale of a program of "integrated services" by GRIPA. GRIPA, an independent physician association incorporated in 1996, had approximately 630 physician members. Since its inception, it entered into "risk sharing" contracts, such as capitation arrangements with HMOs. Through these programs GRIPA used physician referrals and utilization data to implement case management programs to educate and monitor high risk patients. GRIPA also operated a credentialing program and case management, disease management, and pharmacy management for patients. When the market shifted to a PPO market, GRIPA told the FTC that it intended to collectively negotiate price terms of PPO payors implementing its existing programs, which GRIPA asserted was a "new product" in the market that would lead to cost effective provision of medical services. The FTC opined that this "clinical integration" model would allow GRIPA to engage in collective fee negotiations. The FTC also noted two critical mitigating factors: (i) membership in GRIPA was non-exclusive, and physicians were free to negotiate directly with payors; and (ii) it appeared that, using 35% of physicians in a particular specialty as a baseline, GRIPA could not exercise undue market power.

d. **Using Technology to Promote Clinical Integration: TriState Health Partners.** In April, 2009, the FTC approved a clinical integration program proposed by TriState Health Partners, a multispecialty physician-hospital organization (PHO) based in Hagerstown, Maryland. The PHO included both independent and employed physicians. A core part of the program is implementation of a web-based health information technology system as well as the more traditional physician performance targets, utilization and disease management, clinical protocols, and quality of care standards. The network is non-exclusive and payors are free to contract directly with any member. Based on the facts, the FTC drew three conclusions:

i. The program has the potential to create substantial integration among its participants, which creates efficiencies leading to improved quality of care as well as cost effective care;

ii. The joint contracting is related to the goal of delivering the coordinated care and achieving the quality and cost efficiency goals; and

iii. Since the network is non-exclusive, there is still open competition.

E. **Norman (Oklahoma) Physician Hospital Organization: Refined Clinical Integration Review.** On February 13, 2013, the FTC issued a favorable business review letter to the Norman Physician Hospital Organization ("Norman PHO") that described a business model based substantially on clinical integration that has become the model for achieving clinical integration. In essence, the Norman PHO had functioned as a "messenger model" independent provider organization since 1994, but it wanted to engage in collective negotiation of price terms under a clinical integration model. Under the new structure, participating physicians work collaboratively to establish clinical practice guidelines, create a high degree of transparency and visibility with respect to their practice patterns, and provide mechanisms for monitoring and enforcing compliance with Norman PHO's practice guidelines. These objectives are accomplished through:

- a Quality Assurance Committee that audits medical records and generates regular reports on individual and aggregate physician compliance rates on clinical measures as well as making recommendations for and overseeing necessary corrective action;
- hiring a Medical Director to oversee the clinical information program;
- engaging a Medical Informatics Officer who specializes in the management and processing of data, information, and knowledge;
- developing its own evidence-based clinical practice guidelines;
- investing time, money, and effort in developing an electronic platform by participating physicians, including an electronic clinical decisions support system, e-prescribing, electronic medical

records system, and an electronic health interface system, all of which is intended to enhance quality care and reduce medical errors;

- requiring each physician to satisfy credentialing and medical staff appointment requirements, pay a $350 membership fee and $150 annual dues, enter into and comply with a Participation Agreement, and commit to the clinical integration program;

- requiring each physician to acquire and maintain certain computer equipment, software rights or licenses, and training necessary for implementation of the electronic platform;

- requiring physicians to make ongoing "human capital" contributions to development of the clinical integration program;

- committing to retain only those physicians who effectively implement the clinical integration program; and

- being a non-exclusive network and permitting its participants to enter into direct contracts with any payors who do not contract with Norman PHO, but requiring all participating physicians to participate in any contract between Norman PHO and a payor.

As a result of the clinical integration, Norman PHO anticipates the following benefits will be created:

- for patients, improved quality of care and reduced medical errors;

- for payors, centralized credentialing and contracting, better satisfied beneficiaries, elimination of duplicative services, and lower costs of care; and

- for providers, reduced paperwork, more efficient scheduling, and the ability to focus more on quality of patient care.

Norman PHO is generally seen as the model for proper clinical integration.

B. **What Kind of Conduct By Non-Integrated Entities is Considered By the FTC and DOJ to Be "Safe"?** As described in Section VII, above, to assist providers in navigating through the assortment of permitted and prohibited activities, the DOJ and the FTC issued guidelines from which DOJ has now withdrawn setting out "safety zones" for joint conduct and describing how certain health care antitrust issues are analyzed. Under the guidelines, non-integrated IPAs and PHOs can contract using a "messenger model." In the traditional messenger model, a payor submits a fee schedule to the network, which then transmits the fee schedule to the member providers through an independent agent. The member providers then independently determine whether to accept or reject the proposed fee schedule. The network responds to the payor, and the payor contracts with those physicians who accept the offer. The guidelines also provide for certain permitted variations from the traditional messenger model, which are set forth below.

1. **Minimum Fee Solicitation.** A network messenger that is unaffiliated with any of the network members may obtain from each member individually a fee schedule or conversion factor (for example, a percentage of RBRVS) that represents the minimum payment that the member will accept from a payor. The network messenger may also be authorized to contract on behalf of the members with payors offering prices at or in excess of the individual member's fee schedule. The network messenger must not share one member's minimum authorized fees with other members. The network messenger must convey all payor proposals to the network members without regard to whether the proposal meets the fee schedule authorized by the individual network members. The network messenger must not negotiate price or price related terms with the payor.

2. **Authority of an Agent to Execute a Binding Contract.** If done under the limitations described above, a network messenger also may be authorized by individual network members for a specified period of time to bind the network members to any contract offers with prices equal to or better than those in a contract that the individual network member has previously approved.

3. **Aggregation of Price Information.** If done under the limitations described above, a network messenger may aggregate the price information of network members, develop a chart that sets forth the percentage of members in the network who have authorized contracts at various levels, and provide that information to payors at the payor's request.

4. **Direct Negotiation By an Agent Prohibited.** The guidelines specifically prohibit a network from hiring an agent to negotiate prices with payors on behalf of the network's members, even when the agent does not propose a fee schedule and relays the negotiated contract to each member for an individual decision to accept or reject.

C. **Recent Developments in Health Care Antitrust Enforcement.** Despite the FTC and DOJ guidance, it is exceedingly difficult to determine at what point conduct ceases to create efficiency by streamlining contracting and begins to become illegal anti-competitive conduct. The recent enforcement cases suggest that, in practice, networks frequently deviate from a permitted messenger model. In order to stay within permissible antitrust bounds, IPAs and PHOs should avoid the following conduct:

1. Forming an association in order to gain market power and increase fees from payors.

2. Adopting a fee schedule, even if the schedule is developed by an independent third party.

3. Suggesting a price level required in order to obtain full participation of the members.

4. Negotiating price or price related terms even if negotiations are conducted by a third party.

5. Refusing to messenger some payor proposals to members.

6. Expressing an opinion on payor proposals.

7. Causing members to terminate individual payor contracts.

8. Encouraging members to refuse to negotiate individually with payors or insist that contracts be through the network.

D. **Misplaced Reliance on Outside Advisors.** Recent cases also demonstrate that associations should be careful when relying on the advice of outside advisors. Some outside advisors are not well versed in the antitrust rules and the boundaries imposed on group negotiations. There have been a number of cases in which associations have engaged the services of outside advisors, including consultants, to handle contract negotiations with payors, and, at least in part due to the advice of the outside advisors, been determined by the FTC to have violated the antitrust laws. In *R.T. Welter & Associates, Inc.*, an outside consultant advised the creation of a "steering committee" composed of one member of each member practice to meet periodically to decide on strategy apparently to increase fees, conduct deemed illegal by the FTC. In *Aurora Associated Primary Care Physicians*, a consultant compiled a "Confidential AAPCP Play Book" in which the consultant advised physicians how to leverage their collective strength to get higher fees from payors. In *The Maine Health Alliance*, the network's lawyer and business agent sent a letter to the payor demanding that the payor retract its offers for direct contracts with network physicians, notify the physicians that the network's contract with the payor governs the relationship between the physicians and the payor, and "return, marked void, to the physicians any contract executed by the physician" in response to the payor's offer. The incorrect advice of outside advisors had serious adverse consequences for the associations as well as the individuals providing the advice. It is critical that networks select experienced and knowledgeable outside advisors and that outside advisors understand that the FTC will hold them accountable for the advice they give.

E. Integration Strategies for a New Health Care Economy.

1. **Demise of the Fee for Service Economy.** Many economists predict that the "fee for service" health care economy cannot survive. In short, the economy cannot afford to provide health care services to an aging population based on the number of procedures performed or services provided. Alternative payment methods must, by necessity, be implemented. Unfortunately, while much groundwork has been laid and there is near unanimity among academic and political leaders regarding the general nature of the necessary payment reforms, integrated clinical care will require the innovative creation of new care delivery systems, new organizational structures, new provider relationships, new quality measurement capabilities, and information technology that is far more capable than has been effectively implemented in today's market. Both governmental reimbursement programs and private payors will eventually abandon the traditional fee-for-service model and implement payment systems that require greater provider accountability through an increase in shared financial risk. Accordingly, consolidations, new integration agreements, new quality measurement approaches, and new health information technology systems will be developed and adopted. Long discussed and now expected to be implemented are payment systems that will replace traditional fee for service, including pay-for-performance; hospital-physician bundling for specific diagnosis-related group (DRG) codes; episodic bundling for specific DRG codes, including hospitals, physicians, home health agencies and nursing homes; and capitation or shared-savings models.

2. **Threats to Continuing Viability of the Medicare Program.** Given that Medicare is, in essence, the last bastion of indemnity insurance under which there are no limits on the amount of services a covered beneficiary can acquire, and given that control of Medicare costs will be a critical issue for federal deficit reduction and fiscal policy, changes are required if the Medicare program is intended to continue in existence without overwhelming the federal government budget.

3. **Accountable Care Organizations.** One response that could possibly address both private economy and federal budget concerns is the formation of Accountable Care Organizations ("ACOs") that can be organized to manage funds in a system that involves "shared financial risk." In essence, an ACO is a provider network that is involved in collective negotiation of fees for provision of health care services. Although an ACO can serve the dual purpose of competing for provision of health care services in both a coordinated care payment financial model and a traditional fee for service model (such as a preferred provider organization), the fundamental difference between the independent provider associations (sometimes called "IPAs") of the past and the ACOs of the future is the focus on competing in a coordinated care payment model in which the network of providers is compensated based on the ability

to deliver cost effective services to a population based upon performance and the ability to provide the spectrum of care without being compensated on the volume of services provided or procedures performed. Even though the ACA mandates the creation of ACOs through its Medicare Shared Savings Program, private payors and providers are also implementing experimental ACO programs.

4. **What Federal Regulations Govern ACO Formation?** CMS has promulgated federal regulations governing formation of ACOs for purposes of participating in the Medicare Shared Savings Program. The first regulations were promulgated in 2011. Because many ACOs failed to move to downside risk models, in 2018 CMS promulgated new rules that compel a "glide" toward downside risk. Today there are two categories of ACOs: ENHANCED, which is a two sided model in which there are both shared savings and shared losses; and BASIC, which has five levels labeled A through E and implement the "glide" from shared savings only to full shared savings and shared losses. The following are the fundamental elements required for ACOs that participate in the MSSP:

   a. The ACO must be a separate legal entity.

   b. At least 75% of the ACO governing board must be representatives of ACO participants, and at least one Medicare beneficiary attributed to the ACO must be on the governing board.

   c. Starting in 2020, the term of the ACO's MSSP Participation Agreement with CMS is five years. Previously, the term was three years.

   d. Originally, there were four different "tracks" for ACO participation. Track 1 had no downside risk, but the other tracks all put the ACO at risk for downside "shared losses."

   e. Physicians can participate in only one MSSP ACO at a time.

   f. To qualify for MSSP participation, the ACO must be responsible for managing the care of a minimum of 5,000 "attributed" Medicare beneficiaries. "Attribution" is generally determined by CMS by reviewing Evaluation and Management (E&M") codes on physician claims for payment. Beneficiaries are attributed to the physician who submits the bulk of a Medicare beneficiary's E&M coded claims for payment. Consequently, the pool of "attributed" Medicare beneficiaries is a constantly floating number. However, a recent rule change permits a Medicare beneficiary to select participation in a specific ACO.

5. **What Antitrust Compliance Issues Arise From Organization of ACOs?** Without antitrust law reform, ACOs will be required to comply with all of the standards governing clinical and financial integration described above. Consequently, the provider community is engaged in discussions with the FTC and the DOJ Antitrust Division regarding ways to facilitate the organization of ACOs without fear of violating antitrust law. In general, the FTC and DOJ have publicly stated that they will use their best efforts to review and approve ACOs that are designed to increase quality and cut costs, but there are always countervailing concerns that organization of ACOs will stifle competition or promote price-fixing. Some specific antitrust law concerns are as follows:

   a. **Market Power and Monopoly Concerns.** As we have discussed, inefficient markets consolidate. The private insurance market has been consolidating for quite some time, and some private insurers have substantial market power. Similarly, an ACO could integrate to the point of also having substantial market power. The issue, therefore, is to define when "monopoly" concerns arise.

   b. **Exclusivity.** The existing "safety zones" have specific limitations depending upon whether the provider network is exclusive or non-exclusive. The FTC and DOJ generally oppose exclusivity, but ACO development may require a different perspective on exclusivity.

   c. **Inter-Agency Conflict.** While CMS is generally in favor of ACOs and will likely relax enforcement of fraud and abuse laws to accomplish an ACOs purposes, the FTC and DOJ are not as invested in that process.

6. **Co-Management Agreements.** Co-management agreements are an alternative to complete financial integration involving direct employment of physicians by hospitals and health care delivery systems. Under this structure, the physicians and the hospital combine resources for the planning, management, and oversight of clinical service lines. Physicians can be compensated not only on a time of service basis for discrete services like a Medical Director but also for achieving clinical outcomes including attainment of specific quality metrics and operational efficiencies. Compensation is generally based on "pay for performance" programs under which a hospital engages physicians to improve an entire service line. Typically, remuneration includes a base fee that is a fixed payment that compensates for day to day time in managing and improving the clinical service line plus an incentive fee that is paid based upon accomplishing objectives.

IX. WHAT ARE THE PENALTIES FOR VIOLATING THE FEDERAL ANTITRUST LAWS?

A. **How Are the Federal Antitrust Laws Typically Enforced?** Although the FTC and the DOJ Antitrust Division have the ability to bring civil and criminal proceedings to enforce the federal antitrust laws, the overwhelming percentage of cases alleging federal antitrust law violation are brought by private plaintiffs, not governmental agencies.

B. **What Damages Can a Private Plaintiff Seek for Antitrust Law Violation?** The Clayton Act provides that a private party injured by any conduct that violates the federal antitrust law can sue to recover treble damages, costs, and attorneys' fees.

C. **What Can a Private Plaintiff do to Prevent Continuing Harm?** A private plaintiff can sue for injunctive relief against threatened losses and damages arising from antitrust law violations provided that the plaintiff can show irreparable harm; no adequate remedy at law (such as monetary damages); balancing the interests of the parties, equitable relief is warranted; and issuing the injunction will not harm public interest.

D. **What Criminal Sanctions, Civil Monetary Penalties, and Fines Can be Sought by Federal Antitrust Enforcement Agencies?** Violation of the antitrust laws can result in severe penalties: individuals may be convicted of a felony, with a maximum prison term of 10 years and a fine up to the greater of approximately $1,000,000 per violation or twice the defendant's gross gain or the victim's gross loss; a corporation may be fined up to the greater of $100 million per violation or twice the defendant's gross gain or the victim's gross loss.

X. HOW CAN YOU MITIGATE ANTITRUST RISK?

A. **Exercise Caution When Communicating With Competitors.** Any discussion among competitors, no matter how harmless it may seem at the time, may later be subject to antitrust scrutiny. You should assume that any conversation with a competitor, for example, at a trade association meeting, may later be the subject of testimony given under oath by your competitor and other participants in the conversation or meeting, who may be subpoenaed by government investigators to appear before a grand jury. The following topics should be strictly avoided in any communication between competitors:

1. Prices and pricing policies.

2. Terms or conditions of sale.

3. Credit terms and billing practices.

4. Suppliers' terms and conditions of sale.

5. Costs.

6. Profits or profit margins.

7. Advertising and marketing plans and practices.

8. Bids, including your intent to bid or not to bid for a particular contract or program, and the timing or amount of your bid.

9. Allocation of territories or customers.

10. Refusals to deal with a supplier or customer.

A. **How Is Antitrust Law Risk Managed in Horizontal Mergers, Acquisitions, and Consolidations?** As stated above, inefficient markets consolidate, and "horizontal" merger, acquisition, or consolidation of entities that are otherwise competitors in the market is a common integration or survival strategy. However, remember Baker's Rule of Business Transactions: Most Deals Don't Happen. If competitors engage in merger, acquisition, or consolidation discussions, at some point there must be an exchange of "price information" of a nature that might otherwise constitute a *per se* violation of Sherman Act Section 1. Consequently, parties are subject to strict scrutiny under both federal and state antitrust laws and must proceed cautiously to ensure antitrust law compliance. All communications should focus on the procompetitive aspects of the potential arrangement and if possible show awareness of and compliance with antitrust law. While the parties' legal counsel need to be involved and their advice followed, the following are suggestions on how to manage antitrust risk in horizontal mergers, acquisitions, and consolidations:

1. **Confidentiality Obligations.** Each person or entity participating in the preliminary discussions should be party to a confidentiality agreement that states that the confidential and proprietary information exchanged by the parties is to be used only to evaluate the possibility of a merger, acquisition, or consolidation of the subject entities and will be disseminated only on a strict "need to know" basis within each organization.

2. **Limitations During Preliminary Discussions.** At no time during the preliminary deliberations is it appropriate for the consolidating organizations to engage in discussions that contravene antitrust laws, including but not limited to: (a) discussions of prices charged by consolidating

organizations for the provision products or services; (b) discussions of mutually agreed upon limitations on the products or services offered by consolidating organizations regardless of whether those limitations are defined by product, by geography, by customer segment, or by any combination thereof; and (c) discussions of mutually agreed upon refusals to conduct business with certain suppliers or customers.

3. **Authorized Representatives.** Only designated representatives may prepare written communications, including, without limitation, e-mail and text messages, regarding the potential merger, acquisition, or consolidation.

4. **Joint Defense Agreement.** The organizations' legal counsel should consider entering into a "joint defense agreement" with respect to antitrust law compliance in connection with the transaction. Under such an agreement, the parties state that they will jointly strive to comply with antitrust law, with the joint defense agreement being terminable if the interests of the parties on antitrust issues become divergent.

5. **Involvement of Legal Counsel in Communications.** With respect to each communication from one party to the other, legal counsel should receive a copy. This gives an opportunity to characterize the communication as being "privileged" under the attorney-client communication privilege. It also gives legal counsel the opportunity to provide advice regarding how to proceed under the subject matter described in the communication in accordance with applicable law.

6. **Involvement of Legal Counsel in Meetings Between the Parties.** Legal counsel for each party should also be involved in formal meetings between the parties at which issues such as structure and strategy are discussed. Attendance can be by telephone conference call, electronic communication services, or physical presence. This provides the triple benefits of (a) permitting legal counsel to read an antitrust compliance statement before the communications commence, (b) providing legal counsel with an opportunity to stop any line of discussion that might implicate the antitrust laws, and (c) being able to assert attorney-client communication and attorney work product privileges related to analysis and advice provided with respect to the antitrust laws. It is in this context that a "joint defense agreement" has specific value.

7. **Tying Due Diligence Information Flow to the Status of the Negotiations.** Conducting due diligence and obtaining detailed information regarding a competitor in the market is a natural aspect of horizontal mergers. Because price and strategic information must be shared, policies and procedures need to be put into place that tie the flow of information to the status of the negotiations and restrict the information flow to a "need to know" basis. While it is impossible to state in advance what information must flow and when, the parties, with the advice of legal counsel, need to be sensitive to this overall objective.

8. **Term Sheet.** There is no sense in investing time, effort, and energy in a potential transaction if there are insurmountable obstacles. Also, if there are such obstacles, then the parties can go their separate ways without getting into deep due diligence that might implicate the antitrust laws. An effective way to ferret out potentially insurmountable obstacles is to develop a Term Sheet that outlines the fundamental terms and conditions of the transaction. One benefit of a Term Sheet is that it may describe fundamental terms and conditions that lead to an early decision not to proceed with the transaction, which may save the parties substantial time and resources.

9. **Engaging a Third Party for Purposes of Managing Price Information.** When price information begins to be exchanged, it may be beneficial to engage an independent third party, working with accounting and financial advisors, to assess the price information and prepare *pro forma* financial statements to predict what a merged or consolidated entity might look like.

B. **Maintaining Your Records.** The antitrust laws are concerned with substance, not form. Therefore, careful language will not avoid antitrust liability if the underlying conduct is illegal. On the other hand, conduct which is perfectly legal may become suspect if written documents are worded in a way that might be interpreted as indicating, contrary to fact, the existence of an antitrust violation. All documents should be written with the assumption that they may one day be required to be disclosed in connection with an antitrust investigation. In today's world, the greatest challenge is managing electronic communications, including electronic mail, text messages, and information sent through social media. If an arrangement provokes an antitrust law investigation, the Federal Trade Commission or Antitrust Division of the Department of Justice will engage in "e-discovery," permitting the regulators to perform an electronic search for "hot" words or phrases that might lead to antitrust compliance scrutiny. Consequently, all communications should focus on the pro-competitive aspects of the potential arrangement and if possible show awareness of and compliance with antitrust law.

1. **Personal Notes.** Personal notes which record personal impressions rather than the facts of what occurred in a meeting or conversation, or which are based on recollection rather than being made at the time of the meeting, can be particularly dangerous. If personal notes are taken and retained, they should be carefully written to avoid misstatements of fact, complete so as to prevent statements from being taken out of context, and dated.

2. **Drafts of Documents.** Drafts of documents, after a final version of the document has been completed, are no longer necessary and could be confusing or subject to misinterpretation if examined by a third person. This is also true of notes that are not dated, do not clearly set out the context in which they were generated, provide only partial information, or relate to a completed transaction. Therefore, the parties should consider implementing a document

retention policy that requires shredding of drafts and other documents once they are superseded. However, any document retention policy must be formally implemented and uniformly followed. This is what took Arthur Andersen down in the Enron scandal: documents were shredded in a manner that did not reflect customary practice, regardless of whether there was a written document retention policy.

D. **Is It Possible to Acquire Antitrust Insurance?** With the increased scrutiny by the FTC and DOJ, professional liability insurance that covers antitrust is becoming increasingly difficult to obtain. Insurers are often requiring minimum deductibles in excess of $100,000 for antitrust claims or are excluding antitrust from professional liability policies altogether.

E. **DOJ Business Review Letters and FTC Advisory Opinions.** Sometimes it is better to ask for permission than forgiveness, particularly when conduct is policed by powerful federal enforcement agencies. Recognizing that application of antitrust law is challenging and parties may be unwilling to engage in conduct if it will later bring antitrust law scrutiny, both the FTC and the DOJ Antitrust Division have developed protocols for obtaining pre-transaction permission to proceed. Under certain circumstances, an entity can request a Business Review Letter from the DOJ Antitrust Division or an Advisory Opinion from the FTC prior to engaging in conduct that might implicate the antitrust laws.

CHAPTER 9

UNDERSTANDING FUNDAMENTAL INTELLECTUAL PROPERTY LAW

I. WHAT IS "INTELLECTUAL PROPERTY"?

A. **Definition of Intellectual Property.** Land is called "real property." When you purchase a home or other real property in the form of land, title is passed in a deed, and the history of title to the land is recorded in a court. Material objects are called "personal property." You can see and feel personal property, and it can be possessed by only one person at a time. Under the law, original ideas, concepts, processes, and expressions are generally referred to as "intellectual property." One definition of "intellectual property" is "creative ideas and expressions of the human mind that have commercial value and receive the legal protection of a property right." These property rights arise from a person's intellect, and they are "property" even if you cannot feel or see it. The legal term for intellectual property is "intangible personal property." Like title to land, it is necessary to be able to trace the title to intellectual property so it can be protected from infringers. Unfortunately, many entrepreneurs unwittingly act in a manner that not only compromises ownership but results in a complete loss of intellectual property rights. For example, it is human nature to tell others about your great ideas, but even that simple act may have disastrously negative legal consequences. Also, every time a person or entity contributes to a business concept, intellectual property rights arise that may thwart a budding enterprise from implementing its business plan. Consequently, entrepreneurs need a fundamental understanding of intellectual property law before publicly disclosing the business plan to anyone.

B. **What Bodies of Law Protect Intellectual Property?** The American dream is founded on entrepreneurial spirit and rewarding ingenuity and initiative. The bedrock for promotion of entrepreneurial spirit is in the seminal document that our Founding Fathers created at the birth of this great nation. The Constitution of the United States of America grants Congress the power "*To promote the progress of science and useful arts, by securing for limited times to authors and inventors* *the exclusive right to their respective writings and discoveries.*" In common parlance, this provision is known as the "patent and copyright clause." Other bodies of law have arisen from the common law to protect confidential proprietary information and the marks used to distinguish goods and services in the marketplace. Within this framework, the law has evolved to include four flavors of intellectual property protection: trade secret; patent; copyright; and trademark. Think of it as chocolate, vanilla, strawberry, and pistachio. Each is important for any business venture and are generally described as follows:

1. **Trade Secrets.** Trade secrets protect confidential information from which a person or entity derives value or a competitive advantage.

2. **Patents.** A patent grants to an inventor an exclusive right to exclude others from making, using, or selling the invention if it is a new and useful process, machine, method of manufacture, or composition of matter, or any new and useful improvements thereof.

3. **Copyrights.** By contrast, copyrights protect the contents of original artistic or literary works and expressions, including books, magazines, newspapers, computer software, songs, and artwork.

4. **Trademarks and Service Marks.** Trademarks protect words, phrases, symbols, or designs that identify and distinguish the source of goods and services of one party from those of another. Examples of famous trademarks include MICROSOFT®, NIKE®, COCA COLA® and MERCEDES BENZ®. (NOTE: Technically, trademarks identify goods or tangible products, while service marks identify services. For ease of reference, the term "trademark" is used to identify both trademarks and service marks in this work.)

C. **Can More Than One Body of Law Apply to a Creative Work?** The ability to distinguish between the various rights can easily become blurred, particularly because several rights may be embodied in a single object. For example, the famous cartoon character "Mickey Mouse" is protected under copyright laws because it is an original artistic expression, but it also constitutes a trademark for Walt Disney's goods and services. Likewise, a golf club may be protected by patents for an element of the club that improves its performance (such as square grooves in the club face), while the club may also be identified by a trademark (like PING®).

D. **Why Is Intellectual Property Protection Important?**

1. **Every Business Enterprise Owns Intellectual Property.** Every business enterprise owns intellectual property, and every business enterprise should have an intellectual property protection plan.

2. **Intellectual Property Creates Value.** Intellectual property distinguishes business enterprises from their competitors, and it is frequently at the core of the value of a business. Conversely, failure to protect intellectual property devalues an enterprise and may prevent raising capital and implementing a business plan.

II. WHAT ARE THE FUNDAMENTALS OF TRADE SECRET LAW?

A. **What Is a "Trade Secret"?** It comes to you as if in a dream. There has to be a better way. There must be a product or service that satisfies a market need. You start sketching it out. You are excited. This will work. I know it. Even at this earliest stage in concept development, intellectual property rights arise. As long as you are the only person who knows the idea, it is a secret. "Trade secret" means information, without regard to form, including, but not limited to, technical or nontechnical data, a formula, a pattern, a compilation, a program, a device, a method, a technique, a drawing, a process, financial data, financial plans, product plans, or a list of actual or potential customers or suppliers which is not commonly known by or available to the public and which information (1) derives economic value, actual or potential, from not being generally known to, and not being readily ascertainable by proper means by, other persons who can obtain economic value from its disclosure or use and (2) is the subject of efforts that are reasonable under the circumstances to maintain its secrecy. Some businesses rely heavily on trade secret protection. Perhaps the most famous trade secret is the formula for COCA COLA®. Many competitors have tried to "reverse engineer" the Coke® formula, but none has been entirely successful. The safeguards on this trade secret are legendary.

B. **What Law Governs Protection of Trade Secrets?** Trade secret protection arises under the common law and is therefore principally governed by state and not federal law (although recent federal legislation described below provides some federal law trade secret protection rights). For example, under the common law, an employee must keep the employer's trade secrets confidential for all time, even in the absence of a written contract. An obligation to maintain trade secret confidentiality is usually held to be implied in independent contractor arrangements, but the best practice is to include confidentiality provisions in written independent contractor agreements. The common law of trade secrets has been codified in a "Uniform Act" called the Uniform Trade Secrets Act, which has been enacted in some form in every state or jurisdiction except three states: Massachusetts; New York; and North Carolina (although North Carolina law is very similar to the Uniform Trade Secrets Act). The Uniform Trade Secrets Act codifies the basic principles of common law trade secret protection, preserving its essential distinctions from patent law. As described in detail below, a valid patent provides a legal monopoly on certain "inventions" for a term of years in exchange for public disclosure of the invention, which, in essence, releases all trade secret rights. However, not all trade secrets are patentable, and, if the courts ultimately decide that the United States Patent and Trademark office (the "PTO") improperly issued a patent, an invention will have been disclosed to competitors with no corresponding benefit. In view of the substantial number of patents that are invalidated by the courts and the absence of a time limit for trade secret protection, many businesses now elect to protect commercially valuable information through reliance upon the state trade secret law.

C. **How Are Trade Secrets Protected?** Basically, trade secrets must be kept confidential and secret. The common law is well settled that an entity must undertake reasonable precautions under the circumstances to maintain the secrecy or confidentiality of the information. The Uniform Trade Secrets Act also requires as an independent condition of trade secret protection that the information "is the subject of efforts that are reasonable under the circumstances to maintain its secrecy." The nature of the information sought to be protected, the nature of the enterprise, the nature of the market, and the costs and benefits of each possible precaution will determine what efforts are necessary to meet the reasonableness requirement.

D. **What Remedies Are Available When Trade Secrets Are Misappropriated?**

1. **State Law Remedies.** If a trade secret is misappropriated, a business can either recover monetary damages (a "remedy at law") or obtain an injunction or restraining order (an "equitable remedy") by filing a lawsuit in state court. Litigation in the state courts is the most commonly used method to seek remedies for trade secret misappropriation.

2. **Federal Law Remedies.** Until 2016, trade secret remedies could be sought only in the state courts. That changed with the enactment of the Defend Trade Secrets Act of 2016 (the "DTSA"). The DTSA creates a federal cause of action for trade secret misappropriation similar to a state court action that can be asserted under the Uniform Trade Secret Act. However, the definition of "trade secrets" under the DTSA is generally more broad than under state law. The DTSA definition is as follows: all forms and types of financial, business, scientific, technical, economic, or engineering information, including patterns, plans, compilations, program devices, formulas, designs, prototypes, methods, techniques, processes, procedures, programs, or codes, whether tangible or intangible, and whether or how stored, compiled, or memorialized physically, electronically, graphically, photographically, or in writing if (a) the owner thereof has taken reasonable measures to keep such information secret; and (b) the information derives independent economic value, actual or potential, from not being generally known to, and not being readily ascertainable through proper means by, the other person who and obtain economic value from the disclosure or use of the information. Consequently, almost every type of information can qualify as a trade secret under the EEA so long as: (i) the information is actually secret; (ii) the owner took reasonable measures to maintain that secrecy; and (iii) independent economic value is derived from that secrecy.

E. **What Should a Business Enterprise Do to Preserve Trade Secret Rights?** Every person to whom the trade secret is disclosed should be informed about the value of the company's protected confidential information and that the information should not be disclosed to persons not authorized to have it. For W-2 employees, the duty to maintain confidentiality of an employer's trade secrets arises under the law, even in the absence of a written contract. For independent contractors, this is typically accomplished through a written "Confidentiality Agreement," which is sometimes called a "Non-Disclosure Agreement" or "NDA." Also, an enterprise should use reasonable physical security measures, for example by marking the written information as "CONFIDENTIAL." In the absence of executed NDAs, there is a risk of loss of trade secret rights when proprietary concepts, programs, processes, and ideas are disclosed outside of a relationship that protects trade secret rights. If there are no NDAs in place, one way to mitigate the risk of disclosure, at least for patentable inventions, is filing of a patent application.

III. WHAT ARE THE FUNDAMENTALS OF PATENT LAW?

A. **What Law Governs Patents?** Of the four major areas of law related to intellectual property (trade secrets, patents, copyrights, and trademarks), patent law is probably the most complex and confusing. Patents are governed exclusively by federal law; there is no common law of patents. Whoever invents or discovers any new and useful process, machine, manufacture, or composition of matter, or any new and useful improvement thereof, can obtain a patent from the United States Patent and Trademark Office(PTO) that gives the inventor an exclusive property right in the invention for a defined period of time.

B. **What Is the Purpose of Patent Law?** By giving the Congress the right to enact patent laws in the United States Constitution, the Founding Fathers intended to provide citizens with the incentive to innovate and publicly disclose their innovations in exchange for a period of exclusive ownership. When Congress developed the United States patent system, it did so, in part, to encourage the development of technology in the United States by granting inventors exclusive rights to their inventions in the form of a limited monopoly lasting for a period of years in exchange for disclosure of the technology of their inventions to the general public through the publishing of issued patents. Patent rights are exclusionary rights: a patent gives the patent owner the right to exclude others from using the patentable claims. Without patent law, innovations are more likely to be kept secret, which could be detrimental to both the economic health of the nation and society in general.

C. **What Is "Patentable"?** Patent protection can be obtained on new inventions and on new "improvements" to old inventions. An "improvement" generally is defined as adding to or altering an existing item resulting in an increased efficiency without destruction of identity. In other words, making an existing item better. To be entitled to patent protection, an invention or improvement must be: (1) new; (2) non-obvious; and, (3) useful.

1. **Definition of "New".** "New" generally means that the invention is not known, used, described, or patented by others.

2. **Definition of "Non-Obvious".** "Non-obvious" generally means that the differences between the subject matter sought to be patented and the prior art are such that the subject matter as a whole would not have been obvious, at the time the invention was made, to a person having ordinary skill in the art to which said subject matter pertains.

3. **Definition of "Useful".** "Useful" generally means that the invention will operate to perform a desired function to achieve an intended result.

D. **What Are the Types of Patents?** The United States Supreme Court has defined patentable subject matter as "anything under the sun that is made by man except "laws of nature, natural phenomena, and abstract ideas." There are three types of patents. "Utility" patents protect the physical structure of the invention (i.e., the "apparatus") or the function of the invention (i.e., the "process" or "method"). "Design" patents protect the ornamental appearance of an article. "Plant patents" protect distinct and new plant varieties.

E. **What Is a "Provisional Patent"?** Prior to June 8, 1995, the United States patent laws provided for only three types of patents and patent applications—the utility and design types previously described and the lesser-known "plant" type which protects new plants such as new roses or orchids. Since June 8, 1995, the less-expensive and simplified "provisional" patent application has been available to inventors and enables inventors to preserve their right to file utility and foreign patent applications within one year of the filing date of the provisional patent application.

1. **What Are the Advantages of a Provisional Patent?** The provisional patent application has a number of important benefits. First, it places domestic patent applicants on even footing with foreign patent applicants because the filing of a provisional patent application does not trigger the start of the 20-year patent term. Second, unlike a utility patent application and as described in more detail below, the provisional patent application has minimal legal and formal requirements. Third, the provisional patent application provides a mechanism whereby applicants can quickly and relatively inexpensively establish an early effective filing date and a constructive reduction to practice for any invention described in the provisional patent application. Fourth, the filing of a provisional patent application provides up to 12 months to further develop an invention, to determine its marketability, to acquire funding or capital, to seek licensing, and to arrange manufacturing.

2. **What Are the Disadvantages of a Provisional Patent?** While the provisional patent application is certainly of benefit to inventors, it is important to note that a provisional patent

application also has certain limitations. First, a provisional patent application cannot mature into an issued patent as it is not examined by an examiner at the PTO. The provisional patent application, once filed, merely sits idle at the PTO until it automatically becomes abandoned by law one year after its filing. Second, a provisional patent application is only available to disclose an invention which was formerly only the subject of a utility patent application. Therefore, an applicant cannot file a provisional patent application for an invention which should be the subject of a design patent application. Third, a provisional patent application is a regular national filing that starts the Paris Convention priority year (discussed below). Hence, international and foreign patent applications which claim priority on a provisional patent application must be filed within the 12-month period following the filing of the provisional patent application (unless they must be filed sooner due to sale, use, or publication of the invention prior to the filing date of the provisional patent application).

F. **Is Software or a Business Method Patentable?** Patentability of software-based inventions and business methods is in a state of flux. Historically, the PTO has issued "business method patents" as a form of utility payment provided that the underlying software performed an algorithmic function and actually processed data. At the advent of the "dot com" era in the late 1990s, the PTO was inundated with business method patent applications, many of which did nothing more than arrange information. As a result, the courts have struggled to define the line of patentability. The courts have said, for example, that patent law protects "functional and palpable applications in the field of computer technology, but a "method that can be performed by human thought alone is merely an abstract idea and is not patent eligible" subject matter. As a result, business method patents are vulnerable and have lost value.

G. **What If I Show My Invention to Others?** United States patent laws do not allow a patent to be granted, or issued, for an invention that has been on sale, in public use, or described in a publication for more than one year prior to the filing date of a patent application for the invention. Also, you will lose international patent rights from the moment of the first public disclosure. Therefore, maximum protection of rights requires that you must disclose what will ultimately become part of a patent application only if there is a confidential relationship.

H. **Who Can Claim Patent Rights?** Patent rights arise in individual inventors, and not in organized entities or enterprises such as corporations and limited liability companies. Therefore, an employer does not automatically own the patent rights to inventions created by an employee, even within the scope of employment, in the absence of a written employment agreement that assigns patent rights to the employer. This is in direct contrast to the "works made for hire" doctrine under copyright law described below.

I. **How Do I Start the Patent Application Process?** The patent process begins with a search of the "prior art." The purposes of the search include: (1) to ascertain whether the invention has been patented or disclosed previously (remember that if your invention is not new, it cannot receive patent protection); (2) to avoid filing a patent application and having it summarily rejected by the PTO because of an identical or substantially similar invention which would render your invention not new or not non-obvious; and (3) to allow the drafting of a better patent application by emphasizing those features of the invention not discovered in the search. The patent application is kept confidential for 18 months, which gives an applicant the ability to file a patent application and then abandon it if trade secret protection is preferred.

J. **How Is a Patent Application Prepared?** Unlike a copyright application, a patent application is not a simple form which can filled in and sent to the PTO. Instead, each patent application is a carefully-crafted original document, much like a research paper, which must follow certain organizational rules and contain specific types of information required by the PTO. In order to prepare a patent application, the drafter of the patent application must be supplied with a complete explanation of the invention, including, if possible and appropriate, drawings or sketches of the invention. It is also beneficial for the drafter and inventor to sit down and discuss the invention to enable drafting of a more coherent and precise application. In most cases, a working model or prototype of the invention is not required, although it can be helpful as an aid to the drafter.

1. **Utility Patent Applications.** A utility patent application includes a description of a problem, or problems, to be solved by the invention, a brief summary of the invention, a detailed description of the best mode of practicing the invention, a set of legal "claims" which define the metes and bounds of the protection sought by the inventor, and, if appropriate, a set of drawings which illustrate the invention.

2. **Design Patent Applications.** Unlike a utility patent application, a design patent application includes a relatively brief written description of the invention. On the other hand, a design patent application can require a larger number of drawings than a utility patent application.

K. **Duty of Candor and Disclosure.** While preparing a patent application and during the entire period of prosecution of the application, you have a legal duty of candor and disclosure with respect to the application in several respects. First, as noted above, there is a duty to disclose, in your patent application, the "best mode" of practicing the invention which is known at the time of filing your application. Second, you have a duty to disclose all "prior art" which is materially relevant to the prosecution of your patent application. The PTO requires that all materially relevant prior art known to the inventor and the inventor's attorney be submitted to the patent examiner in charge of the application. Such prior art includes all types of publications and other documents and things that disclose information which is pertinent to the invention. Third, the inventor and the inventor's attorney have a duty to disclose any known evidence or information showing any offers for sale or public use of the invention more than one year prior to the filing date of the patent application. Should the inventor or the inventor's attorney fail to make such disclosures to the PTO and should a patent issue from your patent application, a court may find your issued patent invalid in subsequent future litigation related to the issued patent.

L. **What Can I Do After the Patent Application is Filed?** Once your patent application is filed in the PTO, you can mark the invention (or its packaging if it is not possible to mark the invention itself) with the words, "Patent Pending" or "Patent Applied For." It is unlawful to use these words prior to filing of your patent application.

M. **What Happens If There Are Competing Applications?** For the entire history of United States patent law until passage of the Leahy-Smith America Invents Acts in 2011, the United States, unlike virtually all other industrialized nations, followed the rule that the "first to invent" had priority. The America Invents Act reversed that policy and, effective as of March 16, 2013, priority goes to the "first inventor to file," putting the United States in line with other industrialized nations.

N. **How Is a Patent Application Processed by the PTO?** Each examiner at the PTO is responsible for handling patent applications in a particular field of invention. The claims of most patent applications are "rejected" in the first substantive action (known as an "Office Action" or "Examiner's Action") by the PTO. To continue the process of trying to get an issued patent for your invention (i.e., the entire process being known as "prosecution"), a response must be submitted to the Office Action. The response can take the form of arguments as to why the claims are allowable, amendments to the claims which attempt to make the claims allowable, or both.

O. **How Long Does the Application Process Take?** Unless the application qualifies for prioritized examination, many months will likely pass before any substantive action regarding the application is received from the PTO. A number of factors contribute to this delay. First, unless special circumstances are present, patent applications are examined in chronological order based upon the date that they are received at the PTO. Second, a patent application, when received by the PTO, is assigned to an examiner responsible for the field of its invention, and, because more inventions are being made in some fields than in others (for instance, a plethora of inventions are being made every day in the fields of telecommunications, computer hardware, and computer software), some examiners have very large backlogs of applications to examine, whereas other examiners have smaller backlogs. The America Invents Act permits applicants to pay for expedited application processing, reducing the wait time for examination to months rather than years, but the program is limited to 10,000 applications per year.

P. **What Happens When a Patent is Issued?** When the PTO determines that the claims of your application are allowable and patentable, the PTO will issue a "Notice of Allowability," after which you have approximately three months from the date of mailing of the Notice of Allowability in which to pay the "issue fee" for your patent.

Q. **What Is the Duration of a Patent?** The length of time for patent protection is different for different types of patents. For "utility" patents, which protect the physical structure of the invention (i.e., the "apparatus") or the function of the invention (i.e., the "process" or "method"), the limited monopoly lasts for a period of 20 years from the date on which the underlying patent application was filed in the PTO. For "design" patents, which protect the ornamental appearance of an article, the limited monopoly lasts for a period of 14 years from the date of issuance of the patent.

R. **How Does United States Patent Law Relate to Foreign Patent Law?** The one year "grace period" afforded by the United States patent laws in which to file for patent protection after a prior offer for sale, use, or publication of an invention is not recognized in most foreign countries. Instead, the patent laws of most foreign countries have an "absolute novelty" requirement; that is, an invention must not have been on sale, in use, or published at any time prior to the filing of the foreign patent application. This distinction between the United States and foreign patent laws should be considered before offering an invention for sale, using an invention publicly, or publishing articles or advertisements describing an invention.

S. **What Is the Paris Convention Priority Right?** To mitigate the risk of disclosing patentable inventions and timely filing of patent applications, nearly all industrialized nations are parties to the Paris Convention for the Protection of Intellectual Property, which dates back to 1883. The Paris Convention provides the "Paris Convention priority right," which permits a patent applicant to use the patent applicant's filing date from one contracting nation as the effective date in another contracting nation provided that the applicant files subsequent patent applications within twelve months from the date of the first filing. The Paris Convention, with almost 180 members, covers most of the world, but there are some notable non-participants, such as the Republic of China (Taiwan) and Myanmar (formerly Burma).

IV. WHAT ARE THE FUNDAMENTALS OF COPYRIGHT LAW?

A. **What Is a Copyright?** Copyright is a form of protection grounded in the United States Constitution and granted by law for original works of authorship fixed in a tangible medium of expression. Copyright is an intangible personal property right that covers both published and unpublished works. Basically, copyright protects expressions. Copyright does not protect the medium in which the work is embodied. In other words, you can own a book, but you do not own the copyright in the book, or you can own a musical CD, but you do not own the copyright in the underlying musical work.

B. **What Body of Law Governs Copyrights?** Copyrights were formerly governed by both the states under the common law and federal law after the work was published. However, the federal Copyright Act of 1976 preempted all state laws, and, today, the Copyright Act of 1976, as amended, governs all copyright law.

C. **What Rights Comprise a Copyright?** Copyright is not a single piece of intangible property. Under the Copyright Act, a "copyright" is actually a bundle of rights that protects "original works of authorship fixed in any tangible medium of expression." There are five exclusive rights that comprise a copyright, each of which is individually conveyable by time, territory, or other manner, such as a specific medium, described as follows:

1. **Reproduction.** The right to make copies of a work.

2. **Distribution.** The right to distribute copies of a work.

3. **Derivative Works.** The right to create derivative works based on an underlying work.

4. **Performance.** The right to perform a copyrightable work.

5. **Display.** The right to display a copyrightable work.

D. **What Works Are Copyrightable?** The Copyright Act covers the following original works of authorship:

1. **Literary Works.** Works expressed in words, numbers, or symbols regardless of the material objects, including, for example, books, tapes, and disks, in which they are embodied. Computer programs and source code on which they are based are literary works.

2. **Musical Works.** Musical works, including any accompanying words.

3. **Dramatic Works.** Dramatic works, including any accompanying music.

4. **Pantomimes and Choreographic Works.** While not specially defined in the Copyright Act, it is generally understood that this category includes dance routines, ballet, and gymnastic routines, but the expression must be "fixed" (filmed or written down).

5. **Pictorial, Graphic, and Sculptural Works.** All two-dimensional and three-dimensional works of art (fine art, graphic art, and applied art), photographs, prints, reproductions, maps, globes, charts, diagrams, models, and technical drawings (including architectural plans).

6. **Motion Pictures and Other Audiovisual Works.** "Audiovisual work" is broadly defined as a series of related images that are capable of being shown by some device along with sounds that accompany the visual portion of the work. "Motion picture" is a specific type of audiovisual work in which the images, when displayed, give the impression of motion. Examples: movies; slide shows; video games.

7. **Sound Recordings.** A fixation of music, spoken information, or other sounds but not including sounds that accompany a motion picture or other audiovisual work.

E. **What Works Are Not Copyrightable?** Under no circumstance will copyright protect the following:

1. **Titles and Slogans.** Titles, names, short phrases, and slogans; familiar symbols or designs; mere variations of typographic ornamentation, lettering, or coloring; all of which are generally protected as trademarks.

2. **Ideas.** Ideas, procedures, methods, systems, processes, concepts, principles, discoveries, or devices, all of which are generally protected by patents.

3. **Commonly Known Information.** Works consisting entirely of information that is common property and containing no original authorship. For example: standard calendars, height and weight charts, tape measures and rulers.

4. **Business Forms.** Mere forms, without expression, are not protectable.

5. **Information That Can Be Expressed in Only One Way.** You cannot assert exclusive rights in information that can be stated in only one way, such as a mathematical algorithm.

6. **Domain Names.** Domain names are not copyrightable.

F. **How Is a Copyright Obtained?** Copyright arises in the author of the work upon the moment of creation.

G. **Who Can Claim a Copyright?** Only the author or parties that obtain rights through or from the author through a transfer of ownership can rightfully claim a copyright. However, under copyright law, the person who creates the copyrightable work may not be the "author" of the work.

1. **Works Made for Hire Doctrine.** When the "works made for hire" doctrine applies, the employer or other person for whom the work was prepared is deemed to be the "author" of the work. The works made for hire doctrine operates as follows:

   a. **Employment.** Materials created by employees within the scope of their employment are "works made for hire," and the employer is considered the "author" of the work, even in the absence of a written employment agreement. This rule applies only to W-2 employees: it does not typically apply to independent contractors.

b. **Independent Contractors.** There are only limited circumstances under which the entity that engages an independent contractor to create a copyrightable work is considered to be the "author" of the work. In the usual situation, the works made for hire doctrine does not apply to an independent contractor arrangement. Therefore, it is necessary to provide in a written agreement that the independent contractor transfers the independent contractor's copyright in the work to the entity that engages the independent contractor. This material difference is frequently missed by entrepreneurs and can create major missing links in the chain of title to an enterprise's intellectual property. For example, many business plans require the creation of computer software, a copyrightable work. Even if an enterprise pays for the computer programming, the programmer is considered the "author" of the software under copyright law unless the parties enter into a written agreement that transfers copyright ownership. These flaws are often discovered only when the enterprise reaches the point where it is necessary to raise private equity or in the event of a merger or acquisition. For example, before seeking private equity, it is necessary to disclose all "risk factors" to potential investors (because the misrepresentation or concealment of a material fact can lead to allegations of "securities fraud"). Consequently, an enterprise might need to disclose that a computer programmer may assert rights in software that is necessary for the business plan, which naturally devalues the enterprise and may make it impossible to obtain financing.

2. **Joint Works**. Whenever two or more persons contribute to a copyrightable work, it is a "joint work of authorship" which assumes that the contributions are intended to be merged into a single work. Unless there is a written agreement to the contrary, each "author" of a joint work has an undivided, equal interest in copyright ownership, and each co-author has the right to commercially exploit the work with only an obligation to account to all of the other co-authors for their percentage interest in profits derived from distribution of the work. Consequently, it is extremely important for any enterprise to enter into a written agreement with any person or entity that makes even an arguable contribution to a copyrightable work.

H. **Is a Copyright Notice Required to Preserve My Copyright?** No. A copyright notice or symbol was required on protected works prior to March 1, 1989. At this point, major changes in law occurred to make the laws of the United States consistent with the law of much of the rest of the world. The notice requirement was eliminated for all works after that date. However, displaying the copyright notice or symbol still remains an important incentive to a copyright owner wanting to maximize protection of an original work. The absence of a copyright notice does *not* mean a work can be copied freely. Generally, protected works display the following notice: (1) the word "copyright," or the abbreviation "Copr.," or the symbol © (except for recordings, which use a circled "P"); (2) the name of the copyright owner; and (3) the year the work was first published.

I. **What Benefits Can Be Derived From Copyright Registration?** Registration of a copyright with the Copyright Office is not required to protect or preserve a copyright, but registration has value and, therefore, increases the value of a business enterprise. The Copyright Office does not examine materials submitted with a copyright registration; it merely examines whether the material is a copyrightable work. Therefore, issuance of a copyright registration is only *prima facie* evidence of the validity of a copyright, and the validity of a copyright is challengeable. Advantages of registering a copyright include the following:

1. **Ability to File a Lawsuit for Infringement.** Registration is a prerequisite for filing a suit for infringement.

2. **Statutory Damages and Attorneys' Fees.** Registration will allow a copyright owner to recover damages regardless of the amount of actual damages as well as attorneys' fees.

J. **How Is a Copyright Registration Obtained?** Copyright applications are relatively easy to complete: with minimal training, a business enterprise can complete and file their own copyright applications. To register a work, the copyright claimant must send a properly completed simple application form (there are different forms for different works; Form TX for books, magazines, computer software; Form VA for videos, movies, etc.), and a filing fee of $35 to $55 per application if the work is registered online and $85 if mailed in hard copy, each of which requires a deposit copy or copies of the work. Completed applications are sent and reviewed by the Copyright Office, and if eligible, a federal registration will issue. The Copyright Office does not examine materials submitted with a copyright registration; it merely examines whether the material is a copyrightable work.

K. **How Long Does a Copyright Stay in Effect?** Generally, for 70 years after the death of the author, or in the case of a joint work, the death of the last surviving author. For works made for hire, the term is either 95 years from the date of first publication or 120 years from the date of creation, whichever expires first.

L. **Do I Always Have to Get the Permission of a Copyright Owner Before Using a Work?** Generally, yes. However, under the "fair use" doctrine, there are certain conditions when copyright law permits the use of copyrighted work without the permission of the copyright owner. You can generally use portions of copyrighted material for such purposes as criticism, comment, news, teaching (including multiple copies for classroom use), scholarship, or research and it is generally not an infringement of copyright. However, some restrictions apply to these cases as well. Anyone using a photocopy or reproduction for purposes in excess of "fair use" may be liable for copyright infringement. The following factors are used by courts to determine if a particular use is a "fair use:"

1. "The purpose and character of use," including whether such use is of commercial nature or is for nonprofit educational purposes.

2. The nature of the copyrighted work.

3. The amount and substantiality of the portion used in relation to the copyrighted work as a whole.

4. The effect of the use upon the potential market for or value of the copyrighted work.

There are also specific laws regarding use of computer software.

M. **Is My Copyright Valid in Other Countries?** The United States has copyright relations and treaties with most countries throughout the world, and, as a result of these agreements, we honor each other's citizens' copyrights. However, the United States does not have such copyright relationships with every country.

V. WHAT ARE THE FUNDAMENTALS OF TRADEMARK LAW?

A. **What Is a Trademark?**

1. **Identification of a Unique Source of Goods or Services.** Trademarks are marks or symbols that designate a source of goods or services and are recognized in almost every legal system. From the medieval ages, when guilds affixed their marks to silverware and glassware, to modern times, when companies spend millions of dollars to increase worldwide recognition of their business, trademarks have served a core role in our commercial society.

2. **Trademarks Represent "Good Will," and "Good Will" Represents Value.** "Good will" can be defined as an intangible asset valued according to the advantage or reputation a business has acquired (over and above its tangible assets) or an asset of a business based upon the business's established relationships with its customers. Although "good will" is intangible, standard accounting practices can be used to develop a monetary value of the asset.

B. **What Are the Functions of Trademarks?** In general, trademarks embody a business enterprise's reputation and perform four interrelated functions:

1. **Source of Goods or Services.** Trademarks identify one seller's goods or services and distinguish them from goods and services sold by others.

2. **Single Source of Goods and Services.** Trademarks signify that all goods or services bearing the trademark come from or are controlled by a single source.

3. **Quality.** Trademarks signify that all goods or services that are identified by the trademarks are of equal quality.

4. **Enhance Sales.** Trademarks help to sell goods or services. These functions are extremely valuable to the owners of such marks as GUCCI®, POLO®, and CHANEL®. However, these functions are also valuable even to companies that are not in the consumer brand business.

C. **What Are Trademark Formats?** Trademarks can assume almost any format that performs the four functions listed above. Most commonly, trademarks consist of letters, numbers, words, designs, or combinations of any of these. MICROSOFT®, ROLEX®, 7 UP®, GOOGLE®, iPAD®, the AT&T® Globe, and the NIKE® Swoosh are all familiar trademarks to world-wide consumers and serve to identify and distinguish their owner's goods or services. Likewise, slogans, such as JUST DO IT®, A DIAMOND IS FOREVER®, INTEL INSIDE®, and WHAT CAN BROWN DO FOR YOU?®, also function as valuable trademarks for their owners. Alternatively, trademarks can assume the form of color (OWENS-CORNING® "pink" insulation), music (the NBC chimes), product packaging (the COCA-COLA® bottle), or architecture (the McDONALD's® golden arches).

D. **What Distinguishes a Strong Trademark From a Weak Trademark?** Although trademarks can take different formats, they are not created equal. For purposes of trademark protection, this is known as the "spectrum of distinctiveness."

1. **Arbitrary Marks.** Arbitrary marks are strong marks. An arbitrary trademark has a common meaning, but the meaning is unrelated to the goods or services for which it is used. Examples of arbitrary marks are APPLE® for computers and electronic devices and MUSTANG® for automobiles.

2. **Fanciful Marks.** Fanciful marks are also strong marks. Absent marketing or sales to promote the connection, "fanciful" marks, such as EXXON®, KODAK®, and XEROX®, have no relation to the goods or services they identify or are coined specifically for the purpose of functioning as a trademark, and they, together with arbitrary marks, are generally afforded the greatest protection against other trademarks.

3. **Descriptive and Geographic Marks.** Descriptive marks are the weakest marks. At the other end of the spectrum are descriptive marks which immediately convey the nature or a characteristic of the goods or services they identify, such as AFTER TAN sunning lotion, BEER

NUTS salted nuts, or INTERNET banking services. Also, marks that describe a business enterprise by geographic location are weak (for example, CHICAGO STYLE PIZZA). In general, descriptive marks are not registrable unless they acquire "secondary meaning" as described below. This trips up many entrepreneurs. There is a tendency to want to describe the good or service by its function, but that is the least valuable mark and generally cannot be protected for exclusive use.

4. **Suggestive Marks.** Between these two ends of the spectrum lie "suggestive" marks which bear a relation to the identified goods or services, but which require a degree of imagination or "multi-step reasoning" between the product and mark to identify these descriptive qualities. Suggestive marks include 7-ELEVEN® convenience stores, SPRAY 'N VAC® rug cleaner, and CITIBANK® financial services.

5. **Generic Marks.** A generic mark cannot be protected as a trademark because it describes a specific category of product or service. Sometimes a previously strong mark becomes so associated with a product or service it comes to define it. For example, the term ESCALATOR to describe a moving stairway or ASPIRIN to describe a pain medication were once protectable trademarks but are now generic. Some marks require substantial monitoring and aggressive protection to keep a mark from becoming generic. Examples are XEROX® to describe paper copying and KLEENEX® to describe tissues.

6. **Secondary Meaning.** Classifying marks on this spectrum of distinctiveness is not without considerable difficulty and is often the subject of significant disagreements, the outcome which can be critical in trademark registration and litigation because courts will protect, and the United States Patent and Trademark Office ("PTO") will register, arbitrary, fanciful, or suggestive marks upon use in commerce as "inherently distinctive." However, descriptive marks are not eligible for registration or protection absent a showing of "secondary meaning;" namely, that the mark has become distinctive of the goods or services identified thereby through advertising, promotion, or sales. AMERICAN® airlines, PAYLESS® drug stores, and KENTUCKY FRIED CHICKEN® are examples of marks that would have been labeled as "descriptive," and therefore not initially protectable, but which have acquired "secondary meaning" reflecting that the public recognizes these trademarks as indicators of source, and not just descriptive words. In general, a mark must be in continuous use for five years to acquire secondary meaning.

E. **How Are Trademark Rights Created?** In general, you obtain trademark rights by using the trademark in commerce. The general rule is that the first to use an inherently distinctive mark in commerce is recognized as the party possessing superior rights in the geographic area where the party has used the mark.

F. **What Law Governs Trademarks?** There are separate bodies of state and federal trademark law, but federal law is dominant in practice.

1. **State Trademark Law.**

a. **Common Law Protection.** Use of the mark without a federal registration gives an enterprise common law rights under state law. But as with much of trademark law, there are several exceptions and conditions to this maxim, which is particularly complicated by the presumptions and rights afforded federal "use" and "intent-to-use" applications and registrations.

i. **What Trademark Protection Do I Get Under Common Law Rights?** Without a federal trademark registration, your trademark rights may only cover the geographic area in which the trademark is being used.

ii. **What Problems Arise From Relying Only on Common Law Rights?** A problem may occur when the territories of two common law trademark owners with similar trademarks on similar goods or services overlap. Most often, the owner that first used the trademark in the contested market will prevail and the other owner will be prevented from expanding into the overlapping territory. However, it is important to note that these situations are not categorical - the facts for each circumstance need to be examined to determine the outcome.

iii. **How Do I Put the World on Notice That I Claim Common Law Trademark Rights?** You can use the designations "TM" or "SM" without any kind of registration.

b. **State Trademark Registration.** For minimal fees, a business can register its trademark with the state in which the mark is used, usually with the Secretary of State. This is a simple and relatively quick process, and, after registration, it will appear in data bases used for trademark searches. However, state registrations do not require evidence of priority rights, and a state trademark registration is not very valuable in and of itself.

2. **Federal Trademark Law.** If a mark is used in interstate commerce, it can be registered with the PTO. Federal registration of a mark in the PTO conveys several important practical and procedural benefits, but no federal registration is required for creation of trademark rights. Marks are registered in different classes of goods and services. A relatively recent development in federal trademark law allows a party to file an "intent to use" application if it has

a *bona fide* intent to use the mark in commerce, which effectively reserves the mark in the PTO and, if registered, gives it a priority date back to the date of filing, but again, trademark rights do not arise until the mark is actually used in commerce.

a. **How Do I Start the Federal Trademark Registration Process?** You begin by determining whether there are any prior users of the mark by searching publicly available data bases. You must take reasonable efforts to determine your rights in the mark before proceeding with the registration process.

b. **How Much Does Federal Trademark Registration Cost?** PTO charges range from $225 to $400 per mark per class of goods or services, but there are additional costs related to the trademark search and the preparation of the trademark registration application.

c. **What Trademark Rights Do I Get With Federal Trademark Registration?** The primary benefit of obtaining a federal trademark registration is that it establishes nationwide protection to registered marks, regardless of the geographic areas in which the mark is actually being used.

d. **What Are Some Additional Advantages of Obtaining Federal Trademark Registration?** Trademark registration provides many legal and practical advantages, examples of which are as follows:

    i. An application or registration acts as a deterrent. By placing the mark on the register, you alert others who may want to use your trademark that it is already being used, and it shows the world you are serious about protecting your trademarks.

    ii. Enables you to use the registration notice "®" and notifies others of your trademark rights.

    iii. Safeguards future opportunities for nationwide expansion.

    iv. Provides access to federal courts to enforce trademark infringement rights and allows for the possibility of greater recovery of damages for infringement.

    v. Gives the registrant the ability to stop importation of goods that utilize infringing marks by depositing a copy of the registration certificate (and subsequent renewal certificates) with United States Customs.

vi. Your registration will show up in trademark searches, which may deter entities from even adopting a confusingly similar mark.

vii. The PTO will not permit registration of marks that are confusingly similar to your mark, and it will help police your mark from infringers for free.

viii. It creates value in your enterprise to the capital markets.

e. **What Is the Principal Register of the PTO?** The Principal Register is the register in which marks are provided with the fullest extent of trademark law protection. If you create an arbitrary or fanciful mark that is not confusingly similar to an existing mark, it will be registered on the Principal Register.

f. **What Can Be Done to Protect Descriptive Marks or Other Marks That Are Not Eligible for Registration on the Principal Register?** Marks that do not meet all of the requirements for registration on the Principal Register can be registered on the PTO's Supplemental Register. While this puts the world on notice of a claim of rights, registration on the Supplemental Register does not provide any rights greater than common law rights.

G. **What Is the Difference Between a Trade Name and a Trademark?** A trade name is merely the name of your business, and availability of a trade name does not give a business any trademark rights. In other words, just because the Secretary of State says a corporate name is available, and just because the business is incorporated under that name, does not mean that the business has the right to use that name in commerce as a trademark.

H. **Likelihood of Confusion: Cornerstone of Trademark Infringement and Unfair Competition.** For use of a mark to constitute trademark infringement of another mark, it is not necessary for the marks to be identical, and, even if the marks are identical, there may be no trademark infringement. Rather, likelihood of confusion, or, for federally-registered marks, whether a defendant's mark is "likely to cause confusion, or to cause mistake, or to deceive," are the tests for trademark infringement and its cousin, unfair competition. The following are samples of likelihood of confusion:

1. Resemblance between the sight, sound, and meaning of the conflicting marks.

2. Similarity of the goods or services identified by the conflicting marks.

3. Similarity of marketing methods and channels of trade.

4. Characteristics of purchasers or intended purchasers of the goods or services and the degree of care used in the purchasing decision.

5. The distinctiveness of the senior user's mark.

6. The junior user's intent in adopting the mark.

7. Actual confusion.

I. **What Is "Trade Dress" and How Is It Different from Trademarks?** Trade dress is the distinctive and non-functional physical detail and design of a product or its packaging, which indicates or identifies the product's source and distinguishes it from the products of others. In other words, it is the product's "total image" or "overall appearance." Trade dress includes color schemes, textures, sizes, designs, shapes, and placements of words, graphics, and decorations on a product or its packaging. A trade dress is non-functional if, taken as a whole, the collection of trade dress elements is not essential to the product's use or does not affect the cost or quality of the product, even though certain particular elements of the trade dress may be functional. Examples includes the "brown" theme for UPS® and the "orange" theme for HOME DEPOT®.

1. **Federal "Unfair Competition" Law.** In the usual situation, use of a symbol in commerce without federal registration would be subject only to state common law protection. However, there is a federal law that covers unfair use of "trade dress" under Section 43(a) of the Lanham Act, which provides protection for "any word, term, name, symbol, or device, or any combination thereof" used "on or in connection with any goods or services, or any container for goods."

2. **Federal Trademark Registration.** A product's trade dress can be registered on either the Principal or Supplemental Register of the PTO. The requirements for registration of a trade dress are the same as those for traditional word or logo marks. Also, like standard trademarks, the standard for determining trade dress infringement is "likelihood of confusion." To prevail on a trade dress infringement claim under Section 43(a) of the Lanham Act, the plaintiff must prove three elements: (a) its trade dress is inherently distinctive or has acquired secondary meaning; (b) its trade dress is primarily nonfunctional; and (c) the defendant's trade dress is confusingly similar.

3. **Trade Dress Rights and Other Forms of Protection.** Trade dress protection may also be available in connection with products, packaging, or business forms and stationery which are worthy of design patent, utility patent, or copyright protection. If these other forms of protection have expired or were never obtained, trade dress rights may nonetheless remain

available. Like protecting configurations, this area of the law, especially with respect to patents, is constantly evolving and varies from circuit to circuit.

J. **How Are Protection of Domain Names and Trademarks Related?** Reserving a domain name alone does not provide any trademark or service mark rights. Trademark law prohibits commercial websites from using a domain name that would cause a likelihood of confusion to consumers with respect to the parties' goods or services.

1. **How Are Domain Names Regulated?** The Internet Corporation for Assigned Names and Numbers (ICANN) is responsible for managing and coordinating the Domain Name System to ensure that every address is unique and that all users of the Internet can find all valid addresses. It does this by overseeing the distribution of unique IP addresses and domain names, and it also ensures that each domain name maps to the correct IP address. As a private-public partnership, ICANN is dedicated to preserving the operational stability of the Internet; to promoting competition; to achieving broad representation of global Internet communities; and to developing policy appropriate to its mission through bottom-up, consensus-based processes.

2. **What Are Typical Domain Name Issues?** Issues that commonly arise include the following:

   a. **Domain Name Already Registered.** Company attempts to register a domain name and discovers that it is registered by someone else.

   b. **Lapse of Domain Name Registration.** Company allows the domain name registration to lapse, and the domain name is registered by someone else.

   c. **Another Company Has Registered a Domain Name Incorporating Your Trademark.** Company discovers that someone else has registered a domain name that incorporates its trademarks.

3. **How Are Domain Name Issues Resolved?**

   a. **Cease and Desist Letter.** This is an informal way to put a party on notice of a domain name issue, but it has no legal significance.

   b. **ICANN Complaint.** There are three essential elements of an ICANN Complaint: (i) the domain name is identical or confusingly similar to your trademark; (ii) the infringing party has no rights or legitimate interests in the domain name; and (iii) the infringing party has registered and is using the domain name in bad faith (A) to try to sell it "for profit"; (B) if a competitor, to divert customers; (C) the mark is well known, so bad faith may be inferred; or (D) the party is not using domain name, so bad faith may be inferred. The ICANN decision is appealable for *de novo* review by a United States court.

c. **Federal Complaint Under the Anticybersquatting Consumer Protection Act.** You can file a complaint under the federal Anticybersquatting Consumer Protection Act, which requires essentially the same elements as an ICANN complaint.

K. **What Are the Dangers in Not Protecting My Trademarks?** As discussed earlier, trademarks = reputation = goodwill = value. If you allow others to use your trademark, or a mark similar to your mark, you run the risk of hurting your reputation and diminishing the value of the business enterprise. Does this other trademark user care about quality, service, or reputation? Do you want to trust your valuable name to others? Are you willing to risk lost sales from dissatisfied customers or from customers who have been diverted to a trademark infringer? Are you willing to risk lawsuits mistakenly filed against your company which should have been filed against another company? Are you willing to allow a diminution of value of your business enterprise to the capital markets? If the answer to any of these questions is "no," then you need to protect your trademark.

L. **What Should I Do Before I Use a Mark in Commerce?** Every business enterprise should access trademark and trade name data bases before commencing doing business. Failure to do so could lead to unforeseen expenses. A simple internet search engine inquiry is a good start, but there are other suitable data bases. Some are inexpensive and are suitable for "knock out" searches. Some are more comprehensive and should be accessed before filing an application for trademark registration with the PTO.

CHAPTER 10

OVERVIEW OF THE LAW GOVERNING PHARMACEUTICALS AND MEDICAL DEVICES

I. BUSINESS OPPORTUNITIES INVOLVING PHARMACEUTICAL AND MEDICAL DEVICE COMPANIES

A. **Why Is an Understanding of the Law Governing Pharmaceuticals and Medical Devices Important?** The health industry, which comprises almost 20% of the United States economy, has many component parts. Physicians are trained to provide professional medical services, which are complemented by institutional health care providers such as hospitals, ambulatory surgery centers, skilled nursing facilities, and home health agencies. The health industry also includes pharmaceutical and medical device companies, which directly intersect with the provision of health care services. Consequently, any guide to the law governing health care business transactions needs an overview of the law governing business transactions with pharmaceutical and medical device enterprises.

B. **Entrepreneurial Physicians.** For example, many creative physicians assess their surroundings and determine that "there has to be a better way." This results in inventions of medical devices such as surgical implants and tools used in the profession.

C. **Relationships With Pharmaceutical and Medical Device Companies.** Also, marketability of pharmaceuticals and medical devices requires clinical trials and testing, and physicians are required for these trials.

D. **How Are Pharmaceuticals and Medical Devices Regulated?**

1. **Food and Drug Administration.** The United States Food and Drug Administration ("FDA") is a scientific, regulatory, and public health agency that is part of the United States Department

of Health and Human Services ("DHHS"). The FDA is one of the nation's oldest consumer protection agencies. The FDA is responsible for protecting the public health by assuring the safety, efficacy, and security of human and veterinary drugs, biological products, medical devices, our nation's food supply, cosmetics, and products that emit radiation. The FDA is also responsible for advancing the public health by helping to speed innovations that make medicines and foods more effective, safer, and more affordable and helping the public get the accurate, science-based information they need to use medicines and foods to improve their health.

2. **Federal Trade Commission.** The Federal Trade Commission ("FTC") also has a role in regulating some activities of pharmaceutical and medical device companies. The FTC handles most matters regarding claims in advertisements for over-the-counter ("OTC") drugs and consumer medical devices, while the FDA handles most matters regarding the labeling and advertising of prescription drugs and medical devices. As with any other product, claims for OTC drugs and medical devices must be truthful and non-deceptive. Given the health and safety issues that can arise in marketing these products, advertisers should take care in substantiating their claims. Depending on the claim, advertisers may be required to back up their representations with competent and reliable scientific evidence, including tests, studies, or other objective data.

E. **What Other Laws Govern Relationships With Pharmaceutical and Medical Device Companies?** Business relationships with pharmaceutical and medical device companies are also governed by other bodies of law, including the Stark Law, the federal Anti-Kickback Statute, and the Physician Payments Sunshine Act (sometimes referred to as the "Open Payments Law").

II. HEALTH CARE REGULATORY ISSUES ARISING FROM ARRANGEMENTS WITH PHARMACEUTICAL AND MEDICAL DEVICE COMPANIES

A. **Overview.** Business arrangements between physicians and pharmaceutical and medical device companies raise many regulatory concerns. Many common business activities, including, for example, sales, marketing, discounting, and purchaser relations, may be perfectly legal in most industries but potentially implicate criminal laws, such as the federal Anti-Kickback Statute, when a pharmaceutical or medical device manufacturer is involved. Concern regarding the propriety of business arrangements between physicians and pharmaceutical and medical device manufacturers led Congress to require a public record of such arrangements under the Physician Payments Sunshine Act.

B. **Aggravating Circumstances.** The courts have identified several potentially aggravating circumstances that can be useful in identifying arrangements at greatest risk of prosecution. In particular, both physicians and manufacturers should ask the following questions, among others, about any problematic arrangements or practices they identify:

1. **Interference With Clinical Decision Making.** Does the arrangement or practice have a potential to interfere with, or skew, clinical decision-making? Does it have a potential to undermine the clinical integrity of a formulary process? If the arrangement or practice involves providing information to decision-makers, prescribers, or patients, is the information complete, accurate, and not misleading?

2. **Potential to Increase Costs.** Does the arrangement or practice have a potential to increase costs to the federal health care programs, beneficiaries, or enrollees?

3. **Disguised Discount to Circumvent the Medicaid Rebate Program.** Does the arrangement or practice have the potential to be a disguised discount to circumvent the Medicaid Rebate Program Best Price calculation?

4. **Increased Risk of Overutilization.** Does the arrangement or practice potentially increase the risk of overutilization or inappropriate utilization?

5. **Patient Safety.** Does the arrangement or practice raise patient safety or quality of care concerns?

6. **Risk Areas.** For example, although they are not exhaustive of all potential risk areas, the OIG has identified three major potential risk areas for arrangements between physicians and manufacturers of pharmaceuticals and medical devices: (a) integrity of data used by state and federal governments to establish payment; (b) kickbacks and other illegal remuneration; and (c) compliance with laws regulating drug samples.

C. **Inducements to Purchasers of Pharmaceuticals and Medical Devices.** Manufacturers offer purchasers a variety of price concessions and other remuneration to induce the purchase of their products. Purchasers include direct purchasers (for example, hospitals, nursing homes, pharmacies, some physicians), as well as indirect purchasers (for example, health plans). Inducements offered to purchasers potentially implicate the federal Anti-Kickback Statute if the purchased products are reimbursable to the purchasers, in whole or in part, directly or indirectly, by any of the federal health care programs. Any remuneration from a manufacturer provided to a purchaser that is expressly or impliedly related to a sale potentially implicates the federal Anti-Kickback Statute and should be carefully reviewed.

1. **Discounts.** Discounting arrangements are prevalent in the pharmaceutical industry and deserve careful scrutiny particularly because of their potential to implicate the Best Price

requirements of the Medicaid Rebate Program. Because the Medicaid Rebate Program in many instances requires that states receive rebates based on the Best Price offered by a manufacturer to other purchasers, manufacturers have a strong financial incentive to hide *de facto* pricing concessions to other purchasers to avoid passing on the same discount to the states. Because of the potential direct and substantial effect of such practices on federal health care program expenditures and the interest of some manufacturers in avoiding price concessions that would trigger rebates to the states, any remuneration from a manufacturer to a purchaser, however characterized, should be carefully scrutinized.

2. **Product Support Services.** Manufacturers sometimes offer purchasers certain support services in connection with the sale of their products. These services may include billing assistance tailored to the purchased products, reimbursement consultation, and other programs specifically tied to support of the purchased product. Standing alone, services that have no substantial independent value to the purchaser may not implicate the federal Anti-Kickback Statute. However, if a manufacturer provides a service having no independent value (such as limited reimbursement support services in connection with its own products) in tandem with another service or program that confers a benefit on a referring provider (such as a reimbursement guarantee that eliminates normal financial risks), the arrangement would raise kickback concerns. For example, the federal Anti-Kickback Statute is implicated if a manufacturer couples a reimbursement support service with a promise that a purchaser will pay for ordered products only if the purchaser is reimbursed by a federal health care program.

3. **Educational Grants.** Manufacturers sometimes provide grant funding for a wide range of educational activities. While educational funding can provide valuable information to the medical and health care industry, manufacturer grants to purchasers, group purchasing organizations ("GPOs"), pharmacy benefit managers ("PBMs"), and similar entities raise concerns under the federal Anti-Kickback Statute. Funding that is conditioned, in whole or in part, on the purchase of a product implicates the statute, even if the educational or research purpose is legitimate. Furthermore, to the extent the manufacturer has any influence over the substance of an educational program or the presenter, there is a risk that the educational program may be used for inappropriate marketing purposes.

4. **Research Findings.** Manufacturers often contract with purchasers of their products to conduct research activities on behalf of the manufacturer on a fee-for-service basis. These contracts should be structured to fit in the federal Anti-Kickback Statute personal services safe harbor whenever possible. Payments for research services should be fair market value for legitimate, reasonable, and necessary services. Post-marketing research activities should be especially scrutinized to ensure that they are legitimate and not simply a pretext to generate prescriptions of a drug. Prudent manufacturers will develop contracting procedures

that clearly separate the awarding of research contracts from marketing. Research contracts that originate through the sales or marketing functions or that are offered to purchasers in connection with sales contacts are particularly suspect.

5. **Other Remuneration to Purchaser.** As already noted, any remuneration from a manufacturer provided to a purchaser that is expressly or impliedly related to a sale potentially implicates the federal Anti-Kickback Statute and should be carefully reviewed. Examples of remuneration in connection with a sale include, but are not limited to, "prebates" and "upfront payments," other free or reduced-price goods or services, and payments to cover the costs of "converting" from a competitor's product. Selective offers of remuneration (such as offers made to some but not all purchasers) may increase potential risk if the selection criteria relate directly or indirectly to the volume or value of business generated. In addition, manufacturers may contract with purchasers to provide services to the manufacturer, such as data collection services. These contracts should be structured whenever possible to fit in the federal Anti-Kickback Statute personal services safe harbor; in all cases, the remuneration should be fair market value for legitimate, reasonable, and necessary services.

6. **Formulary and Formulary Support**. To help control drug costs while maintaining clinical appropriateness and quality of patient care, many purchasers of pharmaceutical products, including indirect purchasers such as health plans, have developed drug formularies to promote rational, clinically appropriate, safe, and cost-effective drug therapy. Kickback concerns may arise from remuneration that is intended to influence inclusion of a drug or pharmaceutical in a health plan formulary.

7. **Average Wholesale Price.** The "spread" is the difference between the amount a customer pays for a product and the amount the customer receives upon resale of the product to the patient or other payer. In many situations under the federal programs, manufacturers control not only the amount at which they sell a product to their customers, but also the amount those customers who purchase the product for their own accounts and thereafter bill the federal health care programs will be reimbursed. To the extent that a manufacturer controls the "spread," it controls its customer's profit. If a manufacturer purposefully manipulates the "Average Wholesale Price" to increase its customers' profits by increasing the amount the federal health care programs reimburse its customers, the federal Anti-Kickback Statute is implicated.

D. **Relationships Between Physicians and Product Manufacturers.** Manufacturers and their agents may have a variety of remunerative relationships with persons or entities in a position to refer, order, or prescribe, or influence the referral, ordering, or prescribing of, the manufacturers' products, even though the persons or entities may not themselves purchase (or, in the case of GPOs or

PBMs, arrange for the purchase of) those products. These remunerative relationships potentially implicate the federal Anti-Kickback Statute and other laws.

1. **Activities of Inducement.** Manufacturers, providers, and suppliers of health care products and services frequently cultivate relationships with physicians in a position to generate business for them through a variety of practices, including gifts, entertainment, and personal services compensation arrangements. These activities have a high potential for fraud and abuse and, historically, have generated a substantial number of Anti-Kickback Statute convictions. Whenever a manufacturer provides anything of value to a physician who might prescribe the manufacturer's product, the physician and the manufacturer should examine whether it is providing a valuable tangible benefit to the physician with the intent to induce or reward referrals. For example, if goods or services provided by the manufacturer eliminate an expense that the physician would have otherwise incurred or otherwise have independent value to the physician, or if items or services are sold to a physician at less than their fair market value, the arrangement may be problematic if the arrangement is tied directly or indirectly to the generation of federal health care program business for the manufacturer. Moreover, under the federal Anti-Kickback Statute, neither a legitimate purpose for an arrangement (such as physician education), nor a fair market value payment, will necessarily protect remuneration if there is also an illegal purpose.

2. **Identification of Regulatory Risk.** A provider should identify potential regulatory risk arising from arrangements with manufacturers by referring to the following checklist:

    a. **Nature of the Relationship.** What degree of influence does the physician have, directly or indirectly, on the generation of business for the manufacturer? Does the manufacturer have other direct or indirect relationships with the physician or members of the physician's group?

    b. **Manner in Which the Remuneration is Determined.** Does the remuneration take into account, directly or indirectly, the volume or value of business generated (for example, is the remuneration only given to persons who have prescribed or agreed to prescribe the manufacturer's product)? Is the remuneration conditioned in whole or in part on referrals or other business generated? Is there any service provided other than referrals?

    c. **Value of the Remuneration.** Is the remuneration more than trivial in value, including all gifts to any individual, entity, or group of individuals? Do fees for services exceed the fair market value of any legitimate, reasonable, and necessary services rendered by the physician to the manufacturer?

d. **Potential Federal Program Impact of the Remuneration.** Does the remuneration have the potential to affect costs to any of the federal health care programs or their beneficiaries or to lead to inappropriate utilization?

e. **Potential Conflicts of Interest.** Would acceptance of the remuneration diminish, or appear to diminish, the objectivity of professional judgment? Are there patient safety or quality of care concerns? If the remuneration relates to the dissemination of information, is the information complete, accurate, and not misleading?

f. **"Switching" Arrangements.** Is product conversion an intended consequence of the arrangement? As noted in the OIG's 1994 Special Fraud Alert, product conversion arrangements (also known as "switching" arrangements) are suspect under the federal Anti-Kickback Statute. Switching arrangements involve manufacturers offering physicians or others cash payments or other benefits each time a patient's prescription is changed to the manufacturer's product from a competing product.

g. **Consulting and Advisory Payments.** Manufacturers frequently engage physicians and other health care professionals to furnish personal services as consultants or advisers to the manufacturer. In general, fair market value payments to small numbers of physicians for *bona fide* consulting or advisory services are unlikely to raise any significant concern. However, compensating physicians as "consultants" when they are expected to attend meetings or conferences primarily in a passive capacity is suspect. Also of concern are compensation relationships with physicians for services connected directly or indirectly to a manufacturer's marketing and sales activities, such as speaking, certain research, or preceptor or "shadowing" services. While these arrangements are potentially beneficial, they also pose a risk of fraud and abuse.

h. **Payments for Detailing.** Recently, some entities have been compensating physicians for time spent listening to sales representatives market pharmaceutical products. In some cases, these payments are characterized as "consulting" fees and may require physicians to complete minimal paperwork. Other companies pay physicians for time spent accessing web sites to view or listen to marketing information or perform "research." All of these activities are highly suspect under the federal Anti-Kickback Statute, are highly susceptible to fraud and abuse, and should be strongly discouraged.

i. **Business Courtesies and Other Gratuities.** Companies and their employees and agents often engage in a number of other arrangements that offer benefits, directly or indirectly, to physicians or others in a position to make or influence referrals. Examples of remunerative arrangements between manufacturers (or their representatives) and parties in a position to influence referrals include: entertainment, recreation, travel, meals, or other benefits in association with information or marketing presentations; and gifts, gratuities, and other business courtesies.

j. **Educational and Research Funding.** In some cases, manufacturers contract with physicians to provide research services on a fee-for-service basis. These contracts should be structured to fit in the federal Anti-Kickback Statute personal services arrangement safe harbor whenever possible. Payments for research services should be fair market value for legitimate, reasonable, and necessary services. Research contracts that originate through the sales or marketing functions or that are offered to physicians in connection with sales contacts are particularly suspect.

E. **Industry Codes Governing Physician Relationships With Pharmaceutical and Medical Device Companies.** In addition to the statutes and regulations, both the pharmaceutical and medical device industries have implemented voluntary "codes of conduct" that are intended to mitigate regulatory risk associated with physician relationships.

1. **PhRMA Code of Ethics.** Effective July 1, 2002, the Pharmaceutical Research and Manufacturers of America (PhRMA) Executive Committee, which represents the major pharmaceutical manufacturers, voted to adopt a new PhRMA Code on Interactions with Healthcare Professionals. The voluntary code outlines guidelines for how sales representatives and others involved in marketing pharmaceuticals should interact with health care professionals. The main points of the code are as follows:

a. **General Interaction.** Interaction should focus on informing the health care professional about scientific and educational information and supporting scientific medical research and education to maximize patient benefits.

b. **Entertainment.** Interaction should not include entertainment. Interaction should occur at a venue conducive to providing scientific or educational information. Specifically, this means no "dine and dash," no entertainment, and no recreational events (for example, sporting events or spa visits).

c. **Continuing Education.** Companies can provide support to the conference sponsor but should not fund individual participants. For example, a company should not pay an individual's tuition, but could provide support to the event sponsor. That sponsor may in turn provide grants to individuals to participate or reduce the overall registration fees for all attendees.

d. **Consultants.** Legitimate consulting or advisory arrangements are appropriate, but token consulting arrangements should not be used to justify payments to health care professionals. Characteristics of legitimate consulting arrangements include the retention of professionals based on their expertise, not as a reward or inducement for prescribing, and retaining no more consultants than needed for the specific program. For example, it would be inappropriate to retain 10,000 physicians for a program that requires no more than 1,000, or to select them as a reward for high prescribing.

e. **Educational and Health Care Practice-Related Items.** Educational and practice-related items may be provided to health care professionals, but should be for the health care benefit of patients and of less than substantial value ($100 or less). Items for the personal benefit of the health care professional should not be offered or distributed. In short, nothing should be offered or provided that would interfere with the independence of the health care professional's prescribing practices.

f. **Mitigating Risk.** Even though the PhRMA Code is not law, the OIG has stated in its compliance guidance that, although compliance with the PhRMA Code will not protect a manufacturer or physician as a matter of law under the federal Anti-Kickback Statute, it will substantially reduce the risk of fraud and abuse by demonstrating a good faith effort to comply with the applicable federal health care program requirements.

2. **AdvaMed Code of Ethics.** The Advanced Medical Technology Association ("AdvaMed") Code of Ethics is also intended to provide self-governance of vendor-provider relationships, and its principles are very similar to the PhRMA Code. The AdvaMed Code of Ethics is based on the premise that medical device companies have a responsibility to make training and education on their products and medical technologies available to health care professionals. "Training" means training on the safe and effective use of medical technologies. "Education" means communicating information directly concerning or associated with the use of medical device companies' medical technologies such as information about disease states and the benefits of medical technologies to certain patient populations. Training and education programs include, but are not limited to, "hands on" training sessions, cadaver workshops, lectures and presentations, and grand rounds. In fact, the FDA mandates training and education to facilitate the safe and effective use of certain medical technologies. Medical device companies should adhere to the following principles when conducting training and education programs concerning medical technologies for health care professionals:

a. **Sales, Promotional, and Other Business Meetings.** Medical device companies may conduct sales, promotional, and other business meetings with health care professionals to discuss, for example, medical technology features, sales terms, or contracts.

Programs and events should be conducted in settings that are conducive to the effective transmission of information. These may include clinical, educational, conference, or other settings, such as hotels or other commercially available meeting facilities. Often, these meetings occur close to the health care professional's place of business. In some cases, it may be appropriate for a medical device company representative to provide training and education at the health care professional's location. Programs providing "hands on" training on medical technologies should be held at training facilities, medical institutions, laboratories, or other appropriate facilities. The training staff used by the medical device company should have the proper qualifications and expertise to conduct such training. Training staff may include qualified field sales employees who have the technical expertise necessary to perform the training. It is appropriate to pay for reasonable travel costs of attendees when necessary (for example, for plant tours or demonstrations of non-portable equipment) and/or to provide occasional modest meals and refreshments in connection with such meetings. However, it is not appropriate to pay for meals, refreshments, travel, or lodging of guests of health care professionals or any other person who does not have a *bona fide* professional interest in the information being shared at the meeting.

b. **Prohibition on Entertainment and Recreation.** Medical device company interactions with health care professionals should be professional in nature and should facilitate the exchange of medical or scientific information that will benefit patient care. To ensure the appropriate focus on an educational or informational exchange and to avoid the appearance of impropriety, a medical device company should not provide or pay for any entertainment or recreational event or activity for any non-employee health care professional. Such activities include, for example, theater, sporting events, golf, skiing, hunting, sporting equipment, and leisure or vacation trips. Such entertainment or recreational events, activities, or items should not be provided, regardless of: (i) their value; (ii) whether the medical device company engages the health care professional as a speaker or consultant; or (iii) whether the entertainment or recreation is secondary to an educational purpose.

c. **Modest Meals Associated With Health Care Professional Business Interactions.** A medical device company's business interactions with health care professionals may involve the presentation of scientific, educational, or business information and include, but are not limited to, the different types of interactions described in the AdvaMed Code of Ethics. Such exchanges may be productive and efficient when conducted in conjunction with meals. Accordingly, modest meals may be provided as an occasional business courtesy consistent with the following limitations:

- **Purpose.** The meal should be incidental to the *bona fide* presentation of scientific, educational, or business information and provided in a manner conducive to the presentation of such information. The meal should not be part of an entertainment or recreational event.

- **Setting and Location.** Meals should be in a setting that is conducive to *bona fide* scientific, educational, or business discussions. Meals may occur at the health care professional's place of business. However, in some cases the place of business may be a patient care setting that is not available for, or conducive to, such scientific, educational, or business discussions. In other cases, it may be impractical or inappropriate to provide meals at the health care professional's place of business, for example, (1) when the medical technology cannot easily be transported to the health care professional's location, (2) when it is necessary to discuss confidential product development or improvement information, or (3) when a private space cannot be obtained onsite.

- **Participants.** A medical device company may provide a meal only to health care professionals who actually attend the meeting. A medical device company may not provide a meal for an entire office staff where everyone does not attend the meeting. A medical device company also may not provide a meal where its representative is not present (such as a "dine & dash" program). A medical device company may not pay for meals for guests of health care professionals or for any other person who does not have a *bona fide* professional interest in the information being shared at the meeting.

d. **Educational Items; Prohibition on Gifts.** A medical device company occasionally may provide items to health care professionals that benefit patients or serve a genuine educational function for health care professionals. Other than medical textbooks or anatomical models used for educational purposes, any such item should have a fair market value of less than $100. A medical device company may not provide items that are capable of use by the health care professional (or his or her family members, office staff, or friends) for non-educational or non-patient-related purposes such as a tablet or other personal electronic device. A medical device company may not give health care professionals any type of non-educational branded promotional items, even if the item is of minimal value and related to the health care professional's work or for the benefit of patients. Examples of non-educational branded promotional items include pens, notepads, mugs, and other items that have a medical device company's name, logo, or the name or logo of one of its medical technologies. Medical device companies also may not provide health care professionals with gifts such as cookies, wine, flowers, chocolates, gift baskets, holiday gifts or cash or cash equivalents. This section is not intended to address the legitimate practice of providing products for evaluation and demonstration purposes.

III. WHAT IS THE PHYSICIAN PAYMENTS SUNSHINE ACT?

A. **What Are the Purposes of the Sunshine Act?** The core purpose of the Sunshine Act as originally conceived and finally passed is to eliminate physician and teaching hospital conflicts of interest involving FDA approval of medical devices and pharmaceuticals and ordering of medical devices and pharmaceuticals when the physician has a financial relationship with the medical device or pharmaceutical manufacturer by requiring publication of a public record of business arrangements between physicians and pharmaceutical and medical device manufacturers. This presents two clear sides to the potential conflict of interest: one involving the FDA approval process; and one involving inducements to order an item covered by a federal reimbursement program related to which the device or drug manufacturer with which the physician has a relationship receives remuneration directly or indirectly from the federal reimbursement programs. At its core, therefore, the Act is intended to protect the public and health care payors (including the federal reimbursement programs) from (1) proliferation of medical devices and pharmaceuticals that may not be as effective as touted and may in fact cause patient harm and (2) payment of illegal inducements that taint physician judgment in ordering items for which the manufacturer receives direct or indirect payment from a health care payor, including the federal reimbursement programs. In other words, if physicians or teaching hospitals are compensated for clinical trials, product development, or in any other manner by pharmaceutical or medical device manufacturers, and if physicians have the ability to order or prescribe devices and pharmaceuticals into the future after they have been remunerated by the device and pharmaceutical manufacturers in other forms of payment such as consulting agreements or lavish entertainment, the public has a right to know about the potential conflicts of interest.

B. **What Caused Congress to Consider and Pass the Sunshine Act?** Throughout the legislative history of the Sunshine Act, its principal sponsor, Senator Charles Grassley (R. Iowa), cited several examples of egregious physician conflicts of interest. At Stanford University, the Chairman of Psychiatry received a National Institute for Health ("NIH") grant to study a drug while simultaneously owning as much as $6,000,000 in stock in the company seeking FDA approval. Similarly, at Harvard University, three professors failed to report almost a million dollars each in outside income while heading up several NIH grants. Last, the Chairman of Psychiatry at Emory University failed to report hundreds of thousands of dollars in payments from a pharmaceutical company while researching that same company's drugs under an NIH grant. In a statement before the Senate Committee on Aging's meeting on Let the Sunshine In: Implementing the Physician Payments Sunshine Act on September 12, 2012, Senator Grassley stated, in specific reference to the Stanford and Harvard incidents, as follows:

These problems led to the Physician Payments Sunshine Act. The Sunshine Act establishes a nationwide standard requiring drug, device and biologic makers to report payments to doctors to the Department of Health and Human Services.

C. **What Does the Sunshine Act Require?** The Sunshine Act is merely a reporting statute. It does not create any new legal standards of conduct. Therefore, financial relationships between physicians and other enterprises will continue to be primarily governed by the two laws that focus on patient referrals and physician conduct: the Ethics in Patient Referrals Act (commonly referred to as the "Stark Law"); and the federal Anti-Kickback Statute. While other federal laws may come into play, these two laws, when complemented by the federal False Claims Act, will continue to define permissible and impermissible conduct. The reporting required under the Sunshine Act, however, might be used to provoke regulatory investigations of arrangements that might appear questionable to the United States Department of Health and Human Services, Office of the Inspector General, or the United States Department of Justice.

D. **How Is the Sunshine Act Implemented and Enforced?** Federal laws like the Sunshine Act are implemented by federal regulations. Regulations are substantially more detailed than the statutes they implement. The Sunshine Act is administered by the Centers for Medicare and Medicaid Services (CMS), and CMS has promulgated final Sunshine Act rules. The scope and reach of the rules are substantially greater than reporting on the obvious conflicts of interest that arise from the situations described by Senator Grassley. Consequently, the health industry is discovering that CMS is interpreting the Sunshine Act rules very broadly, and the reporting requirements are touching parts of the health care community that did not expect it.

E. **Reporting of "Transfers of Value" and "Ownership Interests" Involving "Covered Recipients".** The Sunshine Act and its regulations require (1) reports by device and pharmaceutical **manufacturers** regarding direct and indirect payments and **transfers of value** to **covered recipients** and (2) reports by device and pharmaceutical **manufacturers** and **group purchasing organizations** (GPOs) of direct and indirect physician **investment or ownership interests**. For purposes of this outline, we will focus only on device and pharmaceutical manufacturers, which are defined in the rules as "applicable manufacturers," because only applicable manufacturers are required to report "transfers of value" to "covered recipients," who are defined to be either "physicians, physician assistants, nurse practitioners, clinical nurse specialists, certified registered nurse anesthetists, and certified midwives" (and their immediate family members) or "teaching hospitals." The definition of "teaching hospital" includes any hospital that receives direct or indirect graduate medical education payments from CMS. CMS annually publishes a list of such hospitals.

F. **What Is an "Applicable Manufacturer"?** To fall within the definition of "applicable manufacturer," an entity must:

- Operate in the United States (meaning that the manufacturer has a physical location within the United States or otherwise conduct activities in the United States, either directly or through a legally-authorized agent); **AND EITHER**

- Engage in the production, preparation, propagation, compounding, or conversion of at least one covered drug, device, biological, or medical supply; **OR**

- Operate under common ownership with an applicable manufacturer and provide assistance or support to the applicable manufacturer in the manufacturing, marketing, promotion, sale, or distribution of a covered drug, device, biological, or medical supply.

  The definition does not include distributors or wholesalers (including, without limitation, repackagers, relabelers, and kit assemblers) that do not hold title to any covered drug, device, biological, or medical supply.

G. **What Is a "Covered Drug, Device, Biological or Medical Supply"?** "Covered Drug, Device, Biological or Medical Supply" means any drug, device, biological, or medical supply for which payment is "available" under Medicare, Medicaid, or the Children's Health Insurance Program ("CHIP") either separately (such as through a fee schedule) or as part of a bundled payment and which (1) for a "drug or biological," requires a prescription by law to be dispensed or (2) for a "device," requires premarket approval by or premarket notification to the FDA. A drug or medical device does not become "covered" until it qualifies for payment under the Medicare, Medicaid, or CHIP programs. Therefore, during the clinical research and pre-marketing phases of product development, the Sunshine Act does not apply. However, as soon as the manufacturer produces even one covered drug or device, the Sunshine Act reporting requirement begins.

H. **How Is "Transfer of Value" Defined in the Sunshine Act?** Payment or transfer of value means virtually anything of value and includes the obvious monetary compensation and ownership interests but also includes less obvious forgiveness of debt owed by a covered recipient to a manufacturer, loans of medical devices and supplies for ninety (90) days or more (called a long term medical supply or device loan), and payments for a covered recipient's ownership interest in an enterprise acquired by an applicable manufacturer. Generally, applicable manufacturers are required to report all payments and transfers of value, whether they are related to a covered drug, device, biological, or medical supply, or not. However, there are some exceptions. For example, applicable manufacturers that had less than ten (10) percent gross revenue during the fiscal year preceding the reporting year from covered products are only required to report payments or other transfers of value related to covered products, not all products.

I. **What Transfers of Value Are Excluded From the Reporting Requirements?** The following are excluded from the reporting requirements:

1. **Payments or Other Transfers of Value of Less than $11 and Less Than $110 per year in the aggregate.** The original statutory *de minimis* thresholds in 2013 were $10 per item and $100 aggregated annually. CMS began increasing the *de minimis* thresholds based on the consumer price index (CPI) for reporting in CY 2014, but, because the incremental increases are very small, it is advisable to continue to use the $10/$100 amounts for internal compliance assessments. Small incidental items that are under $10 (such as pens and note pads) that are provided at large-scale conferences and similar large-scale events are excmpted from the reporting requirements, including the need to track them for aggregation purposes.

2. **Educational Materials that Directly Benefit Patients or Are Intended for Patient Use.** CMS received many comments questioning the meaning of "materials" and "directly benefit patients or are intended for patient use" as used in the definition of this exclusion. CMS believes that anatomical models or wall models provided to help explain a procedure to patients would be considered educational material because they are ultimately intended to be used with patients. If educational materials are provided to a physician on a flash drive to be distributed to patients, the flash drive would be included in the exclusion (but not if the drive was provided as a gift alongside the materials). CMS states that overhead expenses, such as printing and time, should be included in the exclusion if directly related to the development of the materials that directly benefit patients or are intended for patient use. CMS does *not* consider items that are educational to covered recipients (such as medical textbooks and journal reprints) to fall within the exclusion, as they are not directly beneficial to patients.

3. **Existing Personal Relationships.** This includes payments or transfers to a covered recipient made solely in the context of a personal, non-business-related relationship.

4. **Discounts and Rebates.** Discounts and rebates that are permissible under the federal Anti-Kickback Statute are excluded.

5. **In-Kind Items for the Provision of Charity Care.**

6. **Product Samples.** Drug samples intended exclusively for distribution to patients are excluded from the reporting requirements.

7. **Short-Term Loans.** Loans for covered devices and devices under development, as well as supplies of disposable or single-use devices (including medical supplies) intended to last for no more than 90 days. For a single product, the total number of days for the loan should not exceed 90 days for the entire year, regardless of whether the days are consecutive. For longer loans, manufacturers should start reporting as if the loan began on day 91.

8. **Contractual Warranties.** Warranties that are universally provided are excluded from the definition of "transfer of value."

9. **Provision of Health Care.** A physician's receipt of payments for professional medical services is excluded.

10. **Nonmedical Professional.** This covers payments to a physician as a non-medical professional; it will not likely apply to many arrangements.

11. **Civil or Criminal Action or Administrative Proceeding Payments.** This covers deposition and expert witness fees.

J. **How Must the Required Reporting Be Organized?** Applicable manufacturers are required to categorize all reportable payments as falling within one of the following payment descriptions: (1) consulting fees; (2) compensation for services other than consulting, including serving as faculty or as a speaker at an event other than a continuing education program; (3) honoraria; (4) gifts; (5) entertainment; (6) food and beverage; (7) travel and lodging; (8) education; (9) research; (10) charitable contributions; (11) royalty or license; (12) current or prospective ownership or investment interest; (13) compensation for serving as faculty or as a speaker for an unaccredited and non-certified continuing education program; (14) compensation for serving as faculty or as a speaker for an accredited or certified continuing education program; (15) grants; and (16) space rental or facility fees (teaching hospital only).

K. **What Information Must Be Reported for "Transfers to Value"?** All reportable Sunshine Act "transfers of value" must include the information described on **Attachment 10-A**.

L. **How Must Food and Beverage Transfers of Value Be Reported?** Transfers of value in the form of food and beverage have special reporting requirements. When allocating the cost of food and beverage among covered recipients in a group setting where the cost of each individual covered recipient's meal is not separately identifiable, such as a platter provided to physicians in a group practice setting, applicable manufacturers must calculate the value per person by dividing the entire cost of the food or beverage by the total number of individuals who partook in the meal (including both covered recipients and non-covered recipients, such as office staff). The per person value of the meal must be reported as a payment or other transfer of value only for covered recipients who actually partook in the food or beverage. However, applicable manufacturers are not required to report or track buffet meals, snacks, soft drinks, or coffee made generally available to all participants of a large-scale conference or similar large-scale event.

M. **How Is "Ownership Interest" Defined in the Sunshine Act?** Ownership or investment interest means: stock; stock options; partnership shares; limited liability membership interests; and loans, bonds, or other financial instruments. The ownership interest may be direct or indirect and through debt, equity, or other means. The following are excepted from the definition: ownership in a publicly traded company; ownership that arises from an applicable manufacturer or GPO's retirement plan; stock options or convertible securities received as compensation (until exercised); an unsecured loan subordinated to a credit facility; and an ownership interest that the applicable manufacturer or GPO did not know about.

N. **What Ownership or Investment Interest Information Must be Reported?** All reportable Sunshine Act ownership or investment interests must include the information described on **Attachment 10-B**.

O. **How Are the Sunshine Act Reports Administered?** The reported information is maintained in the Open Payments program administered by CMS. Physicians and teaching hospitals can register to obtain access to the CMS Open Payments system, which provides alerts when any data regarding the physician or teaching hospital is submitted by an applicable manufacturer or group purchasing organization and allows the physician or teaching hospital to review and dispute the data before it is publicly posted.

P. **What Are The Critical Sunshine Act Dates?** The critical Sunshine Act dates are as follows:

- ***March 31 of Every Year.*** Reportable transactions for the immediately preceding calendar year must be reported by March 31 in each succeeding year.

- ***June 30 of Every Year.*** Reportable transactions for the previous calendar year are typically published by June 30 of the following year.

Q. **What Are The Sanctions For Non-Compliance?**

1. **Failure to Report.** Under the Act, each failure to report is punishable with a fine of up to approximately $10,000, with aggregate fines not to exceed approximately $150,000 annually.

2. **Knowing Failure to Report.** In addition, each knowing failure to report can be punished with a fine of up to approximately $100,000, with total aggregate annual fines of up to approximately $1,000,000.

3. **Maximum Aggregated Penalties.** The maximum penalty for all failures to report is approximately $1,150,000 annually. This and all of the fines and penalties described above increase annually based on a "cost of living" index.

4. **The Greater Possible Sanction: False Claims Act Allegations.** Although not expressly a part of the Sunshine Act and its regulations, the greater possible sanction is liability under the federal False Claims Act. The OIG and DOJ, as well as possibly third parties, can be expected to "data mine" the published information to determine whether, for example, proceedings based on the federal Anti-Kickback Statute (which, by law, implicate the False Claims Act) or against teaching hospitals for improper use of research funds might be brought against both the applicable manufacturers and the physicians and teaching hospitals that receive tainted "transfers of value."

IV. UNDERSTANDING THE FDA AND THE FDA APPROVAL PROCESSES

A. **FDA's Mission.** The FDA's mission is to promote and protect the public health by helping safe and effective products reach the market in a timely way, to monitor products for continued safety after they are in use, and to help the public get the accurate, science-based information needed to improve health. The FDA consists of eight centers/offices, including the Center for Drug Evaluation and Research (CDER), which regulates drugs and pharmaceuticals, the Center for Devices and Radiological Health (CDRH), which regulates medical devices, and the Center for Biologics Evaluation and Research (CBER), which regulates biologics.

B. **How Does the FDA Regulate Drugs and Pharmaceuticals?**

1. **What FDA Center is Responsible for Approving Drugs?** CDER promotes and protects the health of Americans by assuring that all prescription and over-the-counter drugs are safe and effective. CDER evaluates all new drugs before they are sold and serves as a consumer watchdog for the drugs on the market to ensure they continue to meet the highest standards. The center routinely monitors TV, radio, internet, and print drug ads to ensure they are truthful, balanced, and in compliance with federal law and FDA regulations. CDER also plays a critical role in providing health professionals and consumers information to use drugs appropriately and safely. CDER continues to facilitate development of new drugs and new uses for already-approved drugs that could be used as medical countermeasures.

2. **What Is a Drug?** Drugs are defined as: substances recognized by an official pharmacopoeia or formulary; substances intended for use in the diagnosis, cure, mitigation, treatment, or prevention of disease; substances (other than food) intended to affect the structure or any function of the body; and a substance intended for use as a component of a medicine but not a device or a component part of an accessory or device. Biological products are included within this definition and are generally covered by the same laws and regulations but drug and biological manufacturing processes differ. "Intended use" may be established in a number of ways, including:

a. **Claims.** Claims stated on the product labeling, in advertising, on the Internet, or in other promotional materials.

b. **Consumer Perception.** Consumer perception, which may be established through the product's reputation.

c. **Ingredients.** Ingredients that may cause a product to be considered a drug because they have a well-known (to the public and industry) therapeutic use.

d. **Deceptive Descriptions.** Companies risk FDA enforcement actions when they attempt to market products as lesser-regulated food supplements but use advertising claims that are associated with drugs. Similarly, device products sold using medical device claims will be classified and regulated as medical devices by the FDA.

3. **How Does the FDA Drug Approval Process Work?** Generally, drugs must either receive premarket approval by the FDA or conform to final regulations specifying conditions to ensure that they are not misbranded and are generally recognized as safe and effective.

a. **Pre-Clinical Development.** During a new drug's early pre-clinical development, the sponsor's primary goal is to determine whether the product is reasonably safe for initial use in humans and if the compound exhibits pharmacological activity that justifies commercial development. When a product is identified as a viable candidate for further development, the sponsor then focuses on collecting the data and information necessary to establish that the product will not expose humans to unreasonable risks when used in limited, early-stage clinical studies.

b. **Investigational New Drug Application.** The main purpose of an Investigational New Drug (IND) application is to provide the data showing that it is reasonable to begin tests of a new drug on humans. Also, federal law requires that a drug be the subject of an approved marketing application before it is transported or distributed across state lines. The IND is not an application for marketing approval. Therefore, because a sponsor will probably want to ship the investigational drug to clinical investigators in many states, it must seek an exemption from that legal requirement. The IND is the means through which the sponsor technically obtains this exemption from the FDA.

4. **Phases of a Drug Investigation.** A sponsor shall submit an IND to the FDA if the sponsor intends to conduct a clinical investigation with an investigational new drug. A sponsor shall

not begin a clinical trial until the investigation is subject to an approved IND application. The clinical investigation of a previously untested drug is generally divided into three phases, but current FDA procedures sometimes include a fourth phrase. Although in general the phases are conducted sequentially, they may overlap. The phases of a new drug investigation are as follows:

a. **Phase 1.** Phase 1 includes the initial introduction of an investigational new drug into humans. These studies are usually conducted in healthy volunteer subjects. These studies are designed to determine the metabolic and pharmacological actions of the drug in humans, the side effects associated with increasing doses, and, if possible, to gain early evidence on effectiveness. Phase 1 studies also evaluate drug metabolism, structure-activity relationships, and the mechanism of action in humans. The total number of subjects included in Phase 1 studies is generally in the range of 20 to 80.

b. **Phase 2.** Phase 2 includes the early controlled clinical studies conducted to obtain some preliminary data on the effectiveness of the drug for a particular indication or indications in patients with the disease or condition. This phase of testing also helps determine the common short-term side effects and risks associated with the drug. Phase 2 studies usually involve several hundred people.

c. **Phase 3.** Phase 3 studies are intended to gather the additional information about effectiveness and safety that is needed to evaluate the overall benefit-risk relationship of the drug. Phase 3 studies also provide an adequate basis for extrapolating the results to the general population and transmitting that information in the physician labeling. Phase 3 studies usually include several hundred to several thousand people.

d. **Phase 4.** Increasingly, as a condition of market approval, the FDA will require sponsors to provide post-market surveillance. Post-market surveillance means the active, systematic, scientifically valid collection, analysis, and interpretation of data or other information about a marketed device. This process allows the FDA to monitor a newly-marketed drug for safety and efficacy issues that might not have been identified in the Phase 1–3 studies. Post-market surveillance is often referred to as a Phase 4 study.

5. **Types of INDs.**

a. **Investigator IND.** An Investigator IND is submitted by a pharmaceutical company or a physician who both initiates and conducts an investigation and under whose immediate direction the investigational drug is administered or dispensed. A physician might submit a research IND to propose studying an unapproved drug or an approved product for a new indication or in a new patient population.

b. **Emergency Use IND.** Emergency Use IND allows the FDA to authorize use of an experimental drug in an emergency situation that does not allow time for submission of an IND. It is also used for patients who do not meet the criteria of an existing study protocol or if an approved study protocol does not exist.

c. **Treatment IND.** Treatment IND is submitted for experimental drugs showing promise in clinical testing for serious or immediately life-threatening conditions while the final clinical work is conducted and the FDA review takes place.

d. **Compassionate Use.** Emergency Use and Treatment INDs are also generally known as "Compassionate Use" INDs, but the term "Compassionate" is not in the IND regulations.

6. **New Drug Application.** The new drug application (NDA) is the vehicle through which drug sponsors formally propose that the FDA approve a new pharmaceutical for sale in the United States. To obtain this authorization, a drug manufacturer submits in an NDA pre-clinical (animal) and clinical (human) test data and analyses, drug information, and descriptions of manufacturing procedures. An NDA is typically a massive (hundreds of thousands of pages) and expensive undertaking for the drug sponsor. An NDA must provide sufficient information, data, and analyses to permit FDA reviewers to reach several key decisions, including:

   a. whether the drug is safe and effective for its proposed use;

   b. whether the benefits of the drug outweigh its risks;

   c. whether the drug's proposed labeling is appropriate, and, if not, what the drug's labeling should contain; and

   d. whether the methods used in manufacturing the drug and the controls used to maintain the drug's quality are adequate to preserve the drug's identity, strength, quality, and purity.

7. **Abbreviated New Drug Application.** An abbreviated new drug application (ANDA) is usually used when submitted by manufacturers who intend to market a generic version of a drug previously approved by the FDA.

C. How Does the FDA Regulate Medical Devices?

1. **What FDA Center is Responsible for Approving Medical Devices?** The FDA's CDRH ensures that new medical devices are safe and effective before they are marketed. Many of these devices are the first of a kind, such as a robotic arm that can operate a variety of surgical tools. Other high-tech devices are designed to prevent, diagnose, or treat cancer, heart disease, impaired vision and hearing, and other health problems. CDRH also monitors devices throughout the product life cycle, including a nationwide post-market surveillance system, and it assures that radiation-emitting products, including not only health care devices such as radiation and proton therapy for cancer treatment but consumer products such as microwave ovens, TV sets, cell phones, and laser products, meet radiation safety standards.

2. **What Is a Medical Device?** A medical device is any instrument, apparatus, or other similar or related article, including any component part or accessory, which is: (a) recognized in the official National Formulary, or the United States Pharmacopeia, or any supplement to them; (b) intended for use in the diagnosis of disease or other conditions, or in the cure, mitigation, treatment, or prevention of disease, in humans or other animals; or (c) intended to affect the structure or any function of the human body or in animals and does not achieve any of its principal intended purposes through chemical action within or on the human body or in animals and is not dependent upon being metabolized for the achievement of its principal intended purposes.

3. **How Does the FDA Classify Devices?** Medical devices are classified into Class I, II, and III. This classification system defines the regulatory requirements for a general device type. The FDA's regulatory control process increases from Class I to Class III.

    a. **Class I Devices.** Class I devices are subject to the least regulatory control because they present minimal potential for harm to the user and are often simpler in design than Class II or Class III devices. Class I devices are subject to what are known as "general controls" only. Examples of Class I devices include elastic bandages, examination gloves, and hand-held surgical instruments. Most Class I devices are exempt from the premarket notification and good manufacturing practices regulations.

    b. **Class II Devices.** For Class II devices, general controls alone are insufficient to assure safety and effectiveness and existing methods are available to provide such assurances. In addition to complying with general controls, Class II devices are also subject to special controls. A few Class II devices are exempt from the premarket notification. Special controls may include special labeling requirements, mandatory performance standards, and post-market surveillance. Examples of Class II devices include powered wheelchairs, infusion pumps, and surgical drapes.

c. **Class III Devices.** Class III is the most stringent regulatory category for devices. Class III devices are those for which insufficient information exists to assure safety and effectiveness solely through general or special controls. Class III devices are usually those that support or sustain human life, are of substantial importance in preventing impairment of human health, or which present a potential, unreasonable risk of illness or injury (for example, cardiac stents).

4. **How Does the FDA Medical Device Approval Process Work?** Unless exempt, a device must receive FDA clearance or approval to be marketed. Most Class I devices are exempt from 510(k) clearance; most Class II devices require 510(k) clearance; and most Class III devices require premarket approval ("PMA"). The FDA also has a *de novo* pathway to FDA clearance for low risk medical devices that might otherwise fall within Class III that avoids a full PMA filing. CDRH may also require post-market surveillance of some newly-approved medical devices.

a. **What Is "510(k) Clearance"?** A 510(k) is a premarketing submission made to the FDA to demonstrate that the device to be marketed is as safe and effective, and substantially equivalent to a legally-marketed device that is not subject to PMA. "Substantial equivalence" means that a device has the same intended use and the same technological characteristics as a legally marketed device or has the same intended use and different technological characteristics, but there is information in the 510(k) demonstrating that the device is as safe and effective as a predicate device, and the device does not raise different questions of safety and effectiveness. Applicants must compare their 510(k) device to one or more similar legally marketed devices that qualify as "predicate devices" currently on the United States market and make and support their substantial equivalent claims. Applicants must submit descriptive data and, when necessary, performance data to establish that their devices are substantially equivalent to a predicate device. The FDA regulations provide the FDA with 90 days to review a 510(k) application once it is deemed complete. In addition, the FDA charges a fee for medical device 510(k) reviews that is fairly nominal: less than $3,000 for businesses with less than $100,000,000 in annual sales and just over $10,000 for larger businesses. Under current federal law, FDA 510(k) reviews may also be obtained for many low to moderate risk devices using the third party review process. This allows a manufacturer or device sponsor to engage a private reviewer accredited by the FDA to obtain a more rapid marketing clearance decision. This process is designed to enable the FDA to use its own scientific review resources for higher-risk devices, while maintaining confidence in the review by third parties of low-to-moderate risk devices.

b. **What Is Premarket Approval?** Products requiring PMAs are Class III, high risk devices that pose a significant risk of illness or injury, or devices found not substantially equivalent to Class I and II predicate devices through the 510(k) process. The PMA process is more involved and includes the submission of clinical data to support claims made for the device. PMA is an actual approval of the device by the FDA. PMA is the most stringent type of device marketing application required by the FDA. The applicant must receive FDA approval of its PMA application prior to marketing the device. PMA is based on a determination by the FDA that the PMA contains sufficient valid scientific evidence to assure that the device is safe and effective for its intended use. An approved PMA is, in effect, a private license granting the applicant (or owner) permission to market the device. The PMA owner, however, can authorize use of its data by another. Although the review time is normally longer, the FDA regulations provide the FDA with 180 days to review the PMA and make a determination. In addition, unless the small business fee applies, the FDA charges a standard PMA review fee that is quite substantial (exceeding $200,000).

c. **What Is the *De Novo* Pathway to FDA Clearance?** When a manufacturer wants to bring a medical device to market but there is no precedent or predicate medical device currently cleared by the FDA for public distribution, the FDA automatically classifies the device in Class III, requiring full a PMA filing. However, some novel medical devices have low risk to human use, and a full blown PMA process for such low risk devices would be costly, time consuming, and unnecessary. Recognizing this gap and wanting to facilitate medical device innovation, the United States Congress enacted legislation in 1997 that introduced the *de novo* classification for a new medical device as an alternative pathway to the full PMA process. Manufacturers of low risk medical devices can ask the FDA for *de novo* status by submitting an application with supporting documentation that evidences how the manufacturer mitigates the risk of using the medical device and how the medical device, although novel, is the substantial equivalent of medical devices already cleared by the FDA. If approved as a *de novo* device by the FDA, the path to clearance is much less burdensome and time consuming.

5. **How Does the FDA Regulate Digital Health Products?** In general, "digital health" products are characterized as "medical devices" for purposes of FDA clearance and approval processes. In that regard, the FDA has developed a Digital Health Innovation Action Plan that outlines the FDA's efforts to reimagine the FDA's approach to ensuring that all Americans have timely access to high quality, safe, and effective digital health products. The broad scope of digital health includes mobile health, health information technology, wearable devices, telehealth and telemedicine, and personalized medicine, including, without limitation, software as

a medical device. Many such devices also are governed by the Federal Trade Commission ("FTC") and, if the app processes, uses, or stores an individual's "protected health information" as defined under HIPAA, the Department of Health and Human Services, Office of Civil Rights ("OCR"). For developers of any mobile health app that collects, creates, or shares consumer information, the FTC has created a website tool to guide the developer regarding whether the FDA, FTC, and OCR statutes and regulations apply.

6. **Foreign Manufacturers.** In addition to other criteria, foreign manufacturers must also meet all of these applicable regulatory requirements in order to import devices into the United States, even if the product is authorized for marketing in another country.

D. How Does the FDA Regulate Biologics?

1. **What FDA Center Is Responsible for Regulating Biologics?** CBER is the gatekeeper for many of the most exotic treatments, from cellular replacement therapies to animal organ transplants. CBER regulates biological products for disease prevention and treatment that are inherently more complex than chemically synthesized pharmaceuticals.

2. **What Is a "Biologic".** The FDA defines a "biologic" as any virus, therapeutic serum, toxin, antitoxin, or analogous product applicable to the prevention, treatment, or cause of disease or conditions of human beings. In addition to other biologics, CBER regulates the following:

   a. Human gene therapy designed to alleviate human diseases by transferring normal versions of genes into target cells.

   b. Xenotransplantation—the technique in which organs, tissues, or cells from animals such as pigs are transplanted into patients.

   c. Cellular and tissue transplants, including stem cell therapy, which offer the promise of new therapeutic treatments, including restoring damaged tissue.

   d. Transgenic plants and animals whose products will result in new biotech vaccines and therapeutics.

   e. Genomics, proteomics, and bioinformatics—techniques that will lead the way for new biological product discovery and patient management.

   f. Variant CJD and BSE—evaluation of methods for testing and removal from blood products of infectious particles that cause the human illness associated with BSE or "mad cow disease."

g. Nucleic Acid Testing—methods to detect known pathogens with ever greater sensitivity and to identify emerging variants of these agents.

h. Vaccines and allergenic products—vaccines against diseases like AIDS, TB, malaria, antibiotic resistant infections, and chronic illnesses.

i. Blood and blood products, such as plasma, blood-derived proteins including clotting factors for hemophilia—tests used to screen blood donors, and devices used to make blood products.

j. Protein-based drugs, such as monoclonal antibodies and cytokines that stimulate the immune system to fight cancer, and enzyme therapies that stop heart attacks.

3. **What Is the Biologic Approval Process?** The biologic approval process is substantially the same as the drug and pharmaceutical approval process.

V. CLINICAL TRIALS

A. **What Are the Purposes of Clinical Trials?** Clinical trials are the ultimate premarket testing ground for unapproved drugs and devices. During these trials, an investigational compound or device is administered to or used with humans and is evaluated for its safety and effectiveness in treating, preventing, or diagnosing a specific disease or condition. The results of this testing will comprise the single most important factor in the approval or disapproval of a new drug or medical device. Although the goal of clinical trials is to obtain safety and effectiveness data, the overriding consideration in these studies is the safety of participants in the trials.

B. **What General Terms Describe Clinical Trials?** The following terms describe the fundamental elements of clinical trials:

1. **Clinical Investigation.** Clinical investigation means any experiment that involves a test article and one or more human subjects and that either (a) is subject to requirements for prior submission to the FDA or (b) is not subject to requirements for prior submission to the FDA, but the results of which are intended to be submitted later to, or held for inspection by, the FDA as part of an application for a research or marketing permit.

2. **Investigator.** Investigator means an individual who actually conducts a clinical investigation under whose immediate direction the test article is administered or dispensed to, or used involving, a subject, or, in the event of an investigation conducted by a team of individuals, is the responsible leader of that team.

3. **Sponsor.** Sponsor means a person who initiates a clinical investigation but who does not actually conduct the investigation. A person other than an individual (such as a corporation or agency) that uses one or more of its own employees to conduct a clinical investigation it has initiated is considered to be a sponsor (not a sponsor-investigator), and the entity's employees are considered to be investigators.

4. **Sponsor-Investigator.** Sponsor-investigator means an individual who both initiates and actually conducts, alone or with others, a clinical investigation. The term applies only to individuals.

5. **Human Subject.** Human subject means an individual who is or becomes a participant in research, either as a recipient of the test article or as a control. A subject may be either a healthy human or a patient.

6. **IRB.** Institutional review board (IRB) means any board, committee, or other group formally designated by an institution to approve the initiation of and conduct periodic review of biomedical research involving humans as subjects.

7. **Test Article.** Test article means any drug (including a biological product for human use), medical device for human use, human food additive, color additive, electronic product, or any other article subject to regulation under the Food, Drug and Cosmetics Act or Public Health Service Act.

8. **Minimal Risk.** Minimal risk means that the probability and magnitude of harm or discomfort anticipated in the research are not greater in and of themselves than those ordinarily encountered in daily life or during the performance of routine physical or psychological examinations or tests.

C. **How Does an IRB Function?** In accordance with FDA regulations, an IRB has the authority to approve, require modifications in, or disapprove research. An IRB is also obligated to monitor those research activities that it approves to ensure compliance and safety.

1. **Purpose.** The purpose of IRB review is to assure, both in advance and by periodic review, that appropriate steps are taken to protect the rights and welfare of humans participating as subjects in the research. To accomplish this purpose, IRBs use a group process to review research protocols and related materials (such as informed consent documents and investigator brochures).

2. **Generic Term.** "IRB" is a generic term used by the FDA (and HHS) to refer to a group whose function is to review research to assure the protection of the rights and welfare of

the human subjects. Each institution may use whatever name it chooses. Regardless of the name chosen, the IRB is subject to the FDA's IRB regulations when studies of FDA regulated products are reviewed and approved.

3. **Registration Requirements.** The form FDA-1572 "Statement of Investigator" for a study conducted under an Investigational New Drug Application requires the name and address of the IRB that will be responsible for review of the study. IRBs that approve studies of FDA regulated products must be established and operated in compliance with FDA regulations.

4. **Institutional IRBs.** Although not required, institutions engaged in research involving human subjects will usually have their own IRBs to oversee research conducted within the institution or by the staff of the institution. FDA regulations permit an institution without an IRB to arrange for an "outside" IRB to be responsible for initial and continuing review of studies conducted at the non-IRB institution. Such arrangements should be documented in writing. Individuals conducting research in a non-institutional setting often use established IRBs (independent or institutional) rather than form their own IRBs.

5. **IRB Payment for Services.** FDA regulations do not preclude an IRB member from being compensated for services rendered. Payment to IRB members should not be related to or dependent upon a favorable decision. Expenses, such as travel costs, may also be reimbursed. An IRB member, however, must ensure that any payments received are in compliance with applicable state and federal laws.

6. **IRB Liability in Malpractice Suits.** FDA regulations do not address the question of IRB or institutional liability related to malpractice litigation. The FDA does not have authority to limit liability of IRBs or their members. Compliance with FDA regulations may help minimize an IRB's exposure to liability.

7. **Conflicts of Interest.** IRB regulations prohibit any member from participating in the IRB's initial or continuing review of any study in which the member has a conflicting interest, except to provide information requested by the IRB. When selecting IRB members, the potential for conflicts of interest should be considered. When members frequently have conflicts and must recuse themselves from deliberation and abstain from voting, their contributions to the group review process may be diminished and could hinder the review procedure.

8. **Physicians in Private Practice.** Physicians in private practice who are conducting research with an FDA regulated product are required to obtain IRB approval. The FDA regulations

require IRB review and approval of regulated clinical investigations, regardless of whether the study involves institutionalized subjects. An investigator may be able to obtain IRB review by submitting the research proposal to a community hospital, a university/medical school, an independent IRB, a local or state government health agency, or other qualified organization.

9. **Clinical Investigations of a Marketed Product.** Clinical investigations involving a marketed product also require IRB review and approval.

10. **Exceptions to IRB Approval.** Test articles given to human subjects under a treatment IND/IDE (Investigational Device Exemption) require prior IRB approval, with two exceptions.

    a. **Life-Threatening Emergency.** If a life-threatening emergency exists other procedures may be followed.

    b. **Waiver of the IRB Requirement.** In addition, the FDA may grant the sponsor or sponsor/investigator a waiver of the IRB requirement. An IRB may still choose to review a study even if the FDA has granted a waiver.

D. **Informed Consent.** One of the most important aspects of a clinical trial is obtaining the subject's informed consent.

1. **Obtaining Legal Consent.** Unless an exception applies, no investigator may involve a human being as a subject in research unless the investigator has obtained the informed consent of the subject or the subject's authorized representative.

    a. **Without Coercion.** An investigator shall seek such consent only under circumstances that provide the prospective subject or the representative sufficient opportunity to consider whether to participate and that minimize the possibility of coercion or undue influence.

    b. **Understandable Language.** The information that is given to the subject or the representative shall be in language understandable to the subject or the representative.

    c. **Exculpatory Language.** No informed consent, whether oral or written, may include any exculpatory language through which the subject or the representative is made to waive or appear to waive any of the subject's legal rights, or releases or appears to release the investigator, the sponsor, the institution, or its agents from liability for negligence.

2. **Extreme Situations When Informed Consent is Not Feasible.** The obtaining of informed consent may be deemed unfeasible when, before use of the test article, both the investigator and a physician who is not otherwise participating in the clinical investigation certify in writing all of the following:

    a. The human subject is confronted by a life-threatening situation necessitating the use of the test article.

    b. Informed consent cannot be obtained from the subject because of an inability to communicate with, or obtain legally effective consent from, the subject.

    c. Time is not sufficient to obtain consent from the subject's legal representative.

    d. There is no available alternative method of approved or generally recognized therapy that provides an equal or greater likelihood of saving the life of the subject.

C. **Basic Elements of Informed Consent.** In seeking informed consent, the following information shall be provided to each subject:

    a. **Purpose.** A statement that the study involves research, an explanation of the purposes of the research and the expected duration of the subject's participation, a description of the procedures to be followed, and identification of any procedures which are experimental.

    b. **Foreseeable Risks.** A description of any reasonably foreseeable risks or discomforts to the subject.

    c. **Benefits.** A description of any benefits to the subject or to others which may reasonably be expected from the research.

    d. **Alternative Procedures.** A disclosure of appropriate alternative procedures or courses of treatment, if any, that might be advantageous to the subject.

    e. **Confidentiality of Records.** A statement describing the extent to which confidentiality of records identifying the subject will be maintained and that notes the possibility that the FDA may inspect the records.

    f. **Special Consideration When Risks are More Than Minimal.** For research involving more than minimal risk, an explanation of whether any medical treatments are available if injury occurs and, if so, what they consist of or where further information may be obtained.

g. **Contact Information.** Identification of a person to contact for answers to questions about the research and research subjects' rights or in the event of a research-related injury to the subject.

h. **Voluntary Participation.** A statement that participation is voluntary, that refusal to participate will involve no penalty or loss of benefits to which the subject is otherwise entitled, and that the subject may discontinue participation at any time without penalty or loss of benefits to which the subject is otherwise entitled.

4. **Additional Elements of Informed Consent.** When appropriate, one or more of the following elements of information shall also be provided to each subject:

a. **Risks to Embryo or Fetus.** A statement that the particular treatment or procedure may involve risks to the subject (or to the embryo or fetus, if the subject is or may become pregnant) which are currently unforeseeable.

b. **Termination Without Subject's Consent.** Anticipated circumstances under which the subject's participation may be terminated by the investigator without regard to the subject's consent.

c. **Additional Costs.** Any additional costs to the subject that may result from participation in the research.

d. **Withdrawal Consequences.** The consequences of a subject's decision to withdraw from the research and procedures for orderly termination of participation by the subject.

e. **Significant New Findings**. A statement that significant new findings developed during the course of the research which may relate to the subject's willingness to continue participation will be disclosed to the subject.

f. **Number of Subjects.** The approximate number of subjects involved in the study.

g. **State Law Requirements.** The informed consent requirements in the FDA regulations do not preempt any applicable federal, state, or local laws which require additional information to be disclosed for informed consent to be legally effective.

h. **Emergency Care.** FDA regulations are not intended to limit the authority of a physician to provide emergency medical care to the extent the physician is permitted to do so under applicable federal, state, or local law.

i. **Documentation of Informed Consent.** In most circumstances, informed consent shall be documented by the use of a written consent form approved by the IRB and signed and dated by the subject or the subject's legally authorized representative at the time of consent.

E. **Required Financial Disclosure by Clinical Investigators.** Regulations require an applicant whose submission relies in part on clinical data to disclose certain financial arrangements between sponsors of the covered studies and the clinical investigators and certain interests of the clinical investigators in the product under study or in the sponsor of the covered studies. The FDA will use this information, in conjunction with information about the design and purpose of the study, as well as information obtained through on-site inspections, in the agency's assessment of the reliability of the data.

1. **Purpose.** The FDA evaluates clinical studies submitted in marketing applications for new human drugs and biological products and marketing applications and reclassification petitions for medical devices. The agency reviews data generated in these clinical studies to determine whether the applications are approvable under the statutory requirements. The FDA may consider clinical studies inadequate and the data inadequate if, among other things, appropriate steps have not been taken in the design, conduct, reporting, and analysis of the studies to minimize bias.

2. **Bias.** One potential source of bias in clinical studies is a financial interest of the clinical investigator in the outcome of the study because of the way payment is arranged (for example, a royalty) or because the investigator has a proprietary interest in the product (for example, a patent) or because the investigator has an equity interest in the sponsor of the covered study.

F. **"Off-Label" Use of Marketed Drugs, Biologics and Medical Devices.** The FDA is not authorized to regulate the practice of medicine *per se*. Good medical practice and the best interests of the patient require that physicians use legally available drugs, biologics, and devices according to their best knowledge and judgment. If physicians use a product for an indication not in the approved labeling, they have the responsibility to be well informed about the product, to base its use on firm scientific rationale and on sound medical evidence, and to maintain records of the product's use and effects. Use of a marketed product in this manner when the intent is the "practice of medicine" does not require the submission of an IND, IDE, or review by an IRB. However, the institution at which the product will be used may, under its own authority, require IRB review or other institutional oversight. The FDA broadly defines the term "approved labeling," applying it to all product advertising and promotional materials as well as the actual packaging and product insert information. Manufacturers and distributors of approved drugs and medical devices may not advertise or promote the sale of their products for off-label indications.

VI. CLINICAL TRIAL COVERAGE ISSUES

A. **General Medicare Coverage Criteria.** Previously, Medicare did not pay for items and services related to clinical trials because of their experimental nature. As a result, only a very small percentage of American seniors participated in clinical trials, although the elderly bear a disproportionate burden of disease in the United States. In 2000, the President of the United States issued an executive memorandum to "explicitly authorize [Medicare] payment for routine patient care costs... and costs due to medical complications associated with participation in clinical trials." In keeping with the President's directive, CMS is engaged in defining the routine costs of clinical trials and identifying the clinical trials for which payment for such routine costs should be made. Medicare now generally covers the routine costs of qualifying clinical trials as well as reasonable and necessary items and services used to diagnose and treat complications arising from participation in all clinical trials. However, Medicare does not generally cover the investigational item or service itself or items or services provided by the sponsor free of charge.

B. **Medicare Coverage for Medical Devices.** Medicare limits coverage of medical devices investigated in clinical trials, particularly when the devices have not yet been approved by the FDA for marketing, on the grounds that the safety and effectiveness of the devices (generally or for a particular use) have not been proven. If a manufacturer wishes to study a medical device in a clinical trial and the medical device has not yet received FDA approval or has not yet been approved for a particular use, the manufacturer must generally obtain an IDE from the FDA to use the device in the clinical trial. When the FDA grants a manufacturer an IDE for a device, the agency will assign a special identifier number to the device. The FDA will also place the IDE in one of two categories in order to assist Medicare coverage determinations. The two categories are Category A and Category B.

1. **Category A.** Category A experimental/investigational devices are innovative medical devices for which "absolute risk" of the device has not been established (that is, initial questions of safety and effectiveness have not been resolved and the FDA is unsure whether the device can be safe and effective). Medicare covers the routine costs of clinical trials involving IDE Category A devices.

2. **Category B.** Category B applies to a device for which underlying questions of safety and effectiveness concerning that device type have been resolved or it is known that the device type can be safe and effective because, for example, other manufacturers have obtained FDA approval for that device type. Category B devices may be considered reasonable and necessary and, therefore, may be covered if all other applicable Medicare coverage requirements are met. Medicare payment for a Category B device and the related services may not exceed what Medicare would have paid for a comparable approved device and related services.

C. **General Commercial Payor Coverage.** In general, insurance coverage of a service provided in the context of a clinical trial will depend primarily on the clinical trial participant's contract with his or her insurer and the provider's participation agreement with the payor, if any.

1. **Limitation on Denials.** Some states have laws that limit the ability of insurers to deny coverage for services provided in connection with clinical trials. The laws may either mandate coverage of clinical trial services or establish mechanisms for appealing denials of clinical trials coverage.

2. **Example of Georgia Law**. Under Georgia law, any state health plan or any accident and sickness insurance benefit plan, policy, or contract, by whatever name called, that provides major medical coverage for dependent children and which is issued, delivered, issued for delivery, or renewed in this state on or after July 1, 1998, shall provide coverage for routine patient care costs incurred in connection with the provision of goods, services, and benefits to such dependent children in connection with approved clinical trial programs for the treatment of children's cancer ("Children's Cancer Law").

VII. CLINICAL TRIAL REGULATORY ISSUES

A. **False Claims Act.** Inappropriate claim submissions to any governmental reimbursement program implicate the False Claims Act ("FCA") if the services are not Medicare covered services or the services are Medicare covered services but the sponsor has been paid for the services. The risk is potentially enhanced when payment by commercial or governmental sponsors under the clinical trial agreement is not linked to specific costs (for example, fixed payment per subject or percentage of cost payment) because it is difficult to ascertain what specific services are covered by the sponsor's payment.

B. **Federal Anti-Kickback Statute.** As described above, many arrangements between physicians and pharmaceutical or medical device companies have been scrutinized under the federal Anti-Kickback Statute.

1. **Clinical Trial Concerns.** A clinical study agreement will raise concerns under the federal Anti-Kickback Statute when:

a. the clinical trial has no value to the manufacturer (for example, the trial is not scientifically valid); or

b. compensation paid to the principal investigator/health care provider for conducting the trial exceeds the fair market value of the services provided.

2. **OIG Fraud Alerts.** In August of 1994, the OIG issued a Special Fraud Alert which targets the aggressive marketing practices employed by some prescription drug companies. The Fraud Alert cautions that, if one purpose underlying an incentive is to induce physicians or other practitioners to prescribe or recommend medications for which reimbursement may be made under the Medicare program, the federal Anti-Kickback Statute is implicated. One activity specifically described in the Fraud Alert is a sham research agreement, which the OIG believes occurs when pharmaceutical companies provide research grants in which physicians are given substantial payment for *de minimis* record-keeping tasks. Therefore, investigators should take steps to ensure that (a) any compensation paid to the physicians reflects fair market value for services rendered to avoid any appearance of impropriety of inducing the physician to enroll patients and (b) they are not directly or indirectly involved with payments or gifts from pharmaceutical companies or medical device manufacturers that are unrelated to payment of fair market value for research services rendered.

C. **Prohibition on Inducements to Beneficiaries.** Medicare laws and regulations impose sanctions against individuals or entities that offer remuneration to a program beneficiary that they know, or should know, is likely to influence the beneficiary's decision to order or receive items or services from a particular provider, practitioner, or supplier that are reimbursable by federal or state health care programs. Remuneration includes the routine waiver of all or part of deductible and coinsurance amounts as well as the transfer of items and services for free or for other than fair market value. The OIG has interpreted the federal Anti-Kickback Statute not to apply to incentives of nominal value ($15 or less per gift and no more than $75 per year but adjusted annually for inflation).

D. **Informed Consent and ABN.** The informed consent form provided to potential participants in a clinical trial should clearly specify any costs the participants may incur for services included in the protocol, including coinsurance payments. An informed consent form which states that the participant (or responsible third party payor) will not be charged for a particular service may render an otherwise billable service unbillable.

1. **ABN.** Under Medicare, an advance beneficiary notice ("ABN") or some other evidence that the beneficiary knew the services were not covered is required in order to bill the beneficiary when (a) the services provided by the physician are services generally covered under Medicare and (b) Medicare may deny payment in a particular case because Medicare deems the services provided not reasonable and necessary.

2. **Not Medically Necessary.** If a provider has reason to believe that certain services provided in connection with a clinical trial may be deemed medically unnecessary, the provider should obtain an ABN.

E. **Investigator Financial Conflicts of Interest.** Regulatory authorities have concerns regarding whether the investigators involved in the clinical research have a financial conflict of interest. Therefore, investigators should take appropriate steps to ensure conflicts of interest do not exist between the investigators and the sponsor company. Potential steps investigators could implement are as follows:

1. **Committee.** If an organization does not already have a Conflict of Interest Committee, the provider should establish one to review and analyze conflicts of interest.

2. **Investigator Submissions.** The provider should request that investigators conducting studies of FDA regulated articles submit to a person designated by provider (possibly someone on the Conflict of Interest Committee) the same information that the investigators must submit to the sponsors of the studies (that will, in turn, be submitted to the FDA by the sponsors on either FDA Financial Disclosure Form 3454 or 3455).

3. **Annual Review.** The provider should collect and review information from all investigators regarding their financial interests with commercial sponsors on at least an annual basis.

4. **Educational Programs.** The provider should establish educational programs on financial conflicts of interest as part of its educational requirements for investigators.

5. **Intranet or Internet Posting.** The provider should make its financial conflicts of interest policies, related documents, and forms readily available and post them on its internet site if possible.

6. **Policies and Procedures.** While providers must clearly have policies and procedures for managing conflicts of interest among its investigators, if the provider as a whole would somehow gain from the results of a clinical trial, then the provider should endeavor to manage its own conflicts of interest as well.

7. **Preexisting Agreements.** The provider should ensure that it does not have any preexisting agreements with the investigators that might supersede, affect, or apply to this particular research arrangement.

8. **Billing Prohibitions.** The provider should also be sure that the investigators do not (a) bill Medicare, Medicaid, or any other payor for goods or services in connection with which the investigator or provider will also receive payment through the pharmaceutical or medical device company or (b) bill for services or products that are subject to the clinical trial but are still deemed "experimental" and are otherwise not covered goods or services.

F. **FDA Conflicts of Interest Disclosure Requirements.** Although the FDA financial disclosure requirements do not apply to investigators or research institutions, the investigators must provide the sponsor with sufficient financial information to enable the sponsor to meet FDA disclosure obligations. Therefore, the provider must ensure that the investigators disclose the appropriate information to the sponsor. For each investigator who participates in a "covered clinical study," the sponsor must disclose to the FDA the following financial interests of investigators:

1. **Financial Arrangement.** Any financial arrangement between the sponsor and an investigator when the compensation to the investigator for conducting the study could be influenced by the outcome of the clinical studies (for example, payments which are higher for favorable study outcomes, including royalty payments for sales of the product or ownership interests in the study sponsor).

2. **Compensation Arrangements That are More Than $25,000.** Any other compensation from the study sponsor to the investigator or provider to support activities of the investigator that is more than $25,000 (not including the costs of conducting the study) and given while the investigator is conducting the study or within one year after completion (for example, grants for ongoing research, equipment, honoraria).

3. **Financial Interest.** Any property or financial interest in the tested product held by the investigator, including patents, copyrights, or licensing agreements.

4. **Ownership Interest in the Sponsor With a Value Greater Than $50,000.** Any ownership or other financial interest in the sponsor held by the investigator, the value of which cannot be easily determined by reference to public prices, or any ownership interest in a publicly traded company that exceeds $50,000 during the time that the investigator is conducting the study or within one year after completion.

5. **Steps to Reduce Bias.** Any steps taken to reduce the bias created by these disclosed financial relationships

ATTACHMENT 10-A

SUNSHINE ACT TRANSFER OF VALUE INFORMATION

For every "transfer of value" that is reportable under the Physician Payments Sunshine Act, the following information must be disclosed to the Centers for Medicare and Medicaid Services:

- ***Name of the covered recipient.*** For physician covered recipients, the name must be as listed in the National Plan & Provider Enumeration System (if applicable) and include first and last name, middle initial, and suffix (for all that apply).
- ***Address of the covered recipient.*** Primary business address of the covered recipient, including all the following:
  - Street address.
  - Suite or office number (if applicable).
  - City.
  - State.
  - ZIP code.
- ***Identifiers for physician covered recipients.*** In the case of a covered recipient who is a physician, the following identifiers:
  - The specialty.
  - National Provider Identifier (if applicable and as listed in the NPPES). If a National Provider Identifier cannot be identified for a physician, the field may be left blank, indicating that the applicable manufacturer could not find one.
  - State professional license number (for at least one State where the physician maintains a license), and the State in which the license is held.
- ***Amount of payment or other transfer of value.*** A payment or other transfer of value made to a group of covered recipients should be distributed appropriately among the individual covered

recipients who requested the payment, on whose behalf the payment was made, or who are intended to benefit from the payment or other transfer of value.

- ***Date of payment or transfer of value.*** The date of each payment or other transfer of value. For payments or other transfers of value made over multiple dates (rather than as a lump sum), applicable manufacturers may choose whether to report each payment or other transfer of value as separate line item using the dates the payments or other transfers of value were each made, or as a single line item for the total payment or other transfer of value using the first payment date as the reported date. For small payments or other transfers of value reported as a single line item, applicable manufacturers must report the date that the first bundled small payment or other transfer of value was provided to the covered recipient.

- ***Form of payment or transfer of value.*** The form of each payment or other transfer of value (cash, in-kind, stock, etc.).

- ***Nature of payment or transfer of value.*** The nature of each payment or other transfer of value (the categories for which are described below).

- ***Related covered drug, device, biological or medical supply.*** The names of the related covered drugs, devices, biologicals, or medical supplies, unless the payment or other transfer of value is not related to a particular covered drug, device, biological, or medical supply.

  - For drugs and biologicals, applicable manufacturers must report the name under which the drug or biological is or was marketed and the relevant National Drug Codes, if any. If the marketed name has not yet been selected, the applicable manufacturer must indicate the name registered on clinicaltrials.gov.

  - For devices and medical supplies, applicable manufacturers must report at least one of the following :

    - » The name under which the device or medical supply is or was marketed.

    - » The therapeutic area or product category for the device or medical supply.

    - » If the payment or other transfer of value is not related to a covered drug, device, biological or medical supply, but is related to a specific non-covered product, applicable manufacturers must indicate "non-covered product." If the payment or other transfer of value is not related to any drug, device, biological, or medical supply (covered or not), applicable manufacturers must indicate "none."

- ***Payments to third parties.*** If the payment or other transfer of value is provided to a third party at the request of or designated on behalf of a covered recipient, the payment or transfer of value must be reported in the name of that covered recipient together with the name of the entity that received the payment or other transfer of value (if made to an entity) or indicate "individual" (if made to an individual).

- ***Payments or transfers of value to physician owners or investors.*** The report must indicate whether the payment or other transfer of value was provided to a physician or the immediate family of the physician who holds an ownership or investment interest in the applicable manufacturer.

- ***The form of payment or other transfer of value.*** An applicable manufacturer must report each payment or transfer of value, or separable part of that payment or transfer of value, as taking one of the following forms of payment that best describes the form of the payment or other transfer of value, or separable part of that payment or other transfer of value:

  - Cash or cash equivalent.

  - In-kind items or services.

  - Stock, stock option, or any other ownership interest.

  - Dividend, profit or other return on investment.

    » ***Additional information or context for payment or transfer of value.*** The applicable manufacturer may provide a statement with additional context for the payment or other transfer of value.

ATTACHMENT 10-B

SUNSHINE ACT OWNERSHIP INTEREST INFORMATION

For every "ownership interest" that is reportable under the Physician Payments Sunshine Act, the following information must be disclosed to the Centers for Medicare and Medicaid Services:

- ***Name of the covered recipient.*** For physician covered recipients, the name must be as listed in the National Plan & Provider Enumeration System (if applicable) and include first and last name, middle initial, and suffix (for all that apply).

- ***Address of the covered recipient.*** Primary business address of the covered recipient, including all the following:

  - Street address.

  - Suite or office number (if applicable).

  - City.

  - State.

  - ZIP code.

- ***Identifiers for physician covered recipients.*** In the case of a covered recipient who is a physician, the following identifiers:

  - The specialty.

  - National Provider Identifier (if applicable and as listed in the NPPES). If a National Provider Identifier cannot be identified for a physician, the field may be left blank, indicating that the applicable manufacturer could not find one.

  - State professional license number (for at least one State where the physician maintains a license), and the State in which the license is held.

- ***Amount Invested.*** Dollar amounts invested by each physician or immediate family member;

- ***Value of Investment.*** Value and terms of each ownership or investment interest; and

- ***Payments and Transfers of Value.*** Direct and indirect payments or other transfers of value provided to a physician holding an ownership or investment interest and direct or indirect payments made to a third party at the direction of the physician investor. See **Attachment 10-A** for information reportable for "transfers of value."

CHAPTER 11

CORPORATE GOVERNANCE AND FIDUCIARY DUTY

I. FUNDAMENTALS OF CORPORATE GOVERNANCE

A. **Election of Officers and Directors.** A corporation is managed by its directors and officers. In a "for profit" corporation, shareholders elect directors, and directors elect officers. In a "non-profit" corporation, the Board of Directors can be either elected by "members" or appointed through a "self-nominating Board."

B. **Responsibility of Officers and Directors.** Generally, the Board of Directors is responsible for making major business and policy decisions, and the officers are responsible for carrying out the Board's policies and for making daily business decisions. While some corporations may involve their directors in day-to-day activities, the Board of Directors is not usually expected to participate in the daily business affairs of the corporation. Rather, most Boards generally delegate management functions for daily business affairs to the officers or to executive committees of the Board.

C. **Power and Authority of Directors.** The Board of Directors is statutorily vested with ultimate responsibility for control of all of the business affairs of the corporation and has the authority to exercise all of the corporation's powers. Specific duties of the Board of Directors typically include the following:

1. **Appointment of Officers.** Election, removal, and supervision of officers.

2. **By-Laws.** Adoption, amendment, and repeal of by-laws.

3. **Compensation Issues.** Fixing management compensation, pension, retirement, and other compensation plans.

4. **Financial Management.** Overseeing audits of the corporation's finances.

5. **Extraordinary Corporate Acts.** Initiating extraordinary corporate action (for example, amendments to articles of incorporation, mergers, asset sales, and dissolution) which may require shareholder approval.

D. **Actions of the Board of Directors.** Action by the Board of Directors must be taken in accordance with the applicable Business Corporation Code and usually involves a resolution, properly adopted at a meeting of the Board of Directors, setting forth the appropriate action to establish the corporate policy.

II. DUTIES OF OFFICERS AND DIRECTORS TO SHAREHOLDERS

A. **Fiduciary Duty.** Directors and officers are fiduciaries of the corporation and its shareholders, and as such owe them duties of loyalty and care. The duty of loyalty is a duty to act loyally, honestly, and in good faith for the sole interest of the corporation and its stockholders. The duty of due care is a duty to act prudently with the same amount of care which ordinarily careful men and women would use in similar circumstances. This is as true for deciding how to respond to an acquisition overture as it is for making routine decisions.

B. **Duty of Loyalty.** The duty of loyalty encompasses two core areas—conflicts of interest and corporate opportunities. These duties are intended to ensure that directors and officers will place the best interests of the corporation ahead of their personal interests.

1. **Conflicts of Interest.** On occasion, a corporation will enter into a transaction in which a director or officer has a direct or indirect interest. This type of transaction is considered a conflict of interest because it puts a director or officer in a position that may cause him or her to put his or her individual interests ahead of the interests of the corporation.

a. **Common Law Principles.** Under common law principles, it is essential that these types of transactions and conflicts are considered carefully by the Board to ensure that the transaction is fair to the corporation and disclosed to, and authorized, approved, or ratified by, disinterested directors or the shareholders.

b. **Fairness of the Transaction.** Disinterested directors reviewing the fairness of a transaction having self-dealing elements are essentially seeking to determine whether the proposed transaction is on terms that are at least as favorable to the corporation as might be available from other persons or entities and, if minority shareholders could be adversely affected, the directors should be especially concerned that the minority shareholders receive fair treatment.

c. **Pursuit of Other Business Ventures.** In general, officers and directors of a corporation are allowed to pursue business ventures and employment with other corporations as long as they uphold their fiduciary duties to both corporations.

d. **Federal Law Prohibition.** Under certain circumstances, federal law forbids officers or directors from serving on two companies that are competitors. Section 8 of the Clayton Act provides that no person shall, at the same time, serve as a director or officer in any two corporations that are engaged in whole or in part in commerce and are competitors. The reasoning behind this is simple: to eliminate the opportunity or temptation of interlocking officers from violating antitrust laws. The Clayton Act only applies when a person is simultaneously engaged with at least two corporations that are competitors, each of which has capital surplus and undivided profits of at least $10,000,000 (as periodically adjusted for inflation).

2. **Corporate Opportunity Doctrine.** In general, the duty of loyalty requires that a director or officer make a business opportunity available to the corporation before the director may pursue the opportunity for the director's or officer's own or another party's benefit. Under the common law, whether a corporate opportunity must first be offered to the corporation depends on the following factors:

a. **Awareness.** The circumstances under which the director or officer became aware of the opportunity.

b. **Significance.** The significance of the opportunity to the corporation and the degree of interest of the corporation in the opportunity.

c. **Relationship to Existing Business.** Whether the opportunity relates to the corporation's existing or contemplated business.

d. **Reasonableness.** Whether there is a reasonable basis to expect that the director or officer should make the opportunity available to the corporation.

C. **Duty of Care.** As a general rule, in the corporate context, the duty of care focuses on the exercise of diligence by directors in the execution of their respective official duties. Generally, this duty requires directors to attend meetings and to investigate matters presented to them prior to making decisions. However, when acting in good faith, a director is allowed to rely on information, opinions, reports, or statements, including financial statements and other financial data that is given to them by:

1. **Officers.** An officer that is reasonably believed to be reliable.

2. **Experts.** Lawyers, accountants, or other persons reasonably believed to be within their professional or expert competence.

3. **Board Committees.** A committee of the Board upon which the director or officer does not serve which is duly designated, acting within the committee's authority, and which the director reasonably believes to merit confidence.

D. **What Is the "Business Judgment Rule".** If a director adheres to the above-referenced standards for the "duty of care," the "business judgment rule" generally will shield the director from liability arising from his or her business judgments that prove to be erroneous so long as the director in question deliberated the matter in good faith at the time it was decided. For most actions by a Board of Directors, or a committee thereof, the business judgment rule is applicable. The rule is a presumption that in making a business decision the directors of a corporation acted on an informed basis, in good faith, and in the honest belief that the action taken was in the best interests of the company (in other words, in accordance with their fiduciary duty). When the business judgment rule is applicable, the burden is on the party challenging a Board's decision to establish facts rebutting the presumption created by the rule, thereby making it more difficult for a challenger to be successful and making it easier to dispose of challenges at an early stage in litigation or to discourage challenges altogether.

1. **Applicability of the Business Judgment Rule.** For the rule to be available, various conditions must be satisfied. Each condition must be met, and failure to meet even one will prevent the rule from being available. While each court case has a slightly different formulation of these conditions, the conditions generally require that:

   a. a decision be made;

   b. the decision be by a group of directors who are disinterested; and

   c. those directors use due care.

2. **Process and Procedure May Be More Important Than Substance.** As illogical as it may seem, making the correct decision may not protect you as well as following the procedures necessary for the business judgment rule to be available. The best example of this is the Delaware case

of *Smith v. Van Gorkom*. In that case, the Delaware Supreme Court reversed a lower court's holding in favor of directors and found directors personally liable for a breach of due care in approving a cash-out merger which had been negotiated by the corporation's management. The court found several factors significant to its finding that the directors were grossly negligent: (a) the failure of the directors to make meaningful inquiries into the circumstances that led to the negotiated transaction; (b) the failure of the directors to question senior management regarding the value of the company; (c) the Board's approval of the transaction after only limited consideration "without . . . the exigency of a crisis or emergency;" (d) the absence at the time of the Board's approval of written documents regarding the proposed transaction; and (e) the Board's failure to seek a fairness opinion from an independent financial adviser (although the court made it clear that there was no absolute obligation to obtain a fairness opinion). The merger under consideration could very well have been in the best interest of the corporation's stockholders, and the outside directors were all respected businessmen who were eminently well qualified to make that determination, but the directors did not satisfy the requirement of due care in the process that they followed to reach that conclusion and could not rely on the business judgment rule to dispose of the complaint. Instead, they had to defend their actions for the next several years and ultimately settled the claims.

3. **Evolution of "Bad Faith" Theory of Director Liability.** After the *Van Gorkom* case, the Delaware legislature eliminated the concept of "gross negligence" for outside director liability for violation of the duty of care. However, in its place, the Delaware Chancery Court has implicated that an outside director may be liable for proceeding in "bad faith," which is part of the duty of loyalty, not the duty of care, under certain circumstances when the director might rely on the business judgment rule.

4. **Meaning of "Disinterested".** Whether a director is "disinterested" has been interpreted as requiring not just that the directors who make a decision have no personal financial interest in the outcome of the decision (other than as a typical stockholder), but also that the directors not have a competing interest and possibly that directors not have a significant business or personal relationship with an interested person. A director needs to consider carefully the impact of a potential transaction on the director, the director's investments, and any businesses with which the director may be affiliated to ensure that the director does not have a personal or competing interest.

5. **Conflicts of Internal Management.** Delaware law provides some guidance regarding how to manage recusal of an interested director when a conflict of interest has been disclosed and the conflict of interest transaction is being considered by the Board. Simply excusing the director when a vote is being taken may not be enough to prevent a conflict of interest that can be alleged to be a breach of the director's duty of loyalty. The Delaware Chancery Court

has ruled that an effective recusal requires a director to avoid completely any participation in the transaction deliberations. Only disinterested directors should attend the meeting at which the potential transaction is discussed. Interested directors should not be present at the meeting when the conflict of interest transaction is discussed and then step outside only when the vote is taken.

E. **Advisors.** Directors and officers should liberally seek out the advice of experts. Many states provide directors and officers who act on the advice of experts with substantial protections. In any event, reliance is favored, and the courts have recognized it as one aspect of exercising the "due care" required by the business judgment rule. An important aspect of relying on advisors is selecting them with "due care" as well.

F. **What Is the "Entire Fairness" Standard of Review?** In the typical situation, Boards are protected by the "business judgment rule," which permits Boards to make reasoned decisions based on reports from management and outside advisors such as legal counsel, consultants, and accountants. However, facts and circumstances sometimes do not permit application of the "business judgement rule" and require application of the more strict "entire fairness" standard of review. The "entire fairness" standard is triggered when a majority of the directors approving the transaction are interested or when a majority stockholder or other controlling stakeholder has an interest in both sides of the transaction. Application of the entire fairness standard arises in the context of a judicial challenge to a transaction that was approved by the Board but does not qualify for protection under the business judgment rule. This situation most frequently arises when individual officers and directors negotiate their own deals with a prospective purchaser prior to substantive economic negotiations between the parties. If, for example, a Chief Executive Officer has a personal financial interest in a liquidity event, the conflict of interest might be a breach of the Chief Executive Officer's fiduciary duty to the enterprise stakeholders, requiring review under the "entire fairness" standard, even if the conflict of interest was properly managed. Once the entire fairness standard is triggered, the Board has the burden of proving that the transaction is inherently fair to the stockholders by demonstrating both fair dealing (the process by which the transaction was approved) and fair price.

G. **Fiduciary Duty During Times of Business Crisis.** The Board has enhanced fiduciary duty during times of business crisis. When the enterprise is in true crisis, standard deference to management might lead to allegations of breach of director fiduciary duty. Also, Board members have fiduciary duty to monitor and assess management's post-crisis resiliency efforts, which relates to long term financial and cultural resiliency challenges arising from truly disruptive events, such as the COVID-19 pandemic and public health emergency.

H. **Fiduciary Duty for Oversight of Corporate Culture.** There is an emerging body of law providing that Boards have fiduciary duty to exercise oversight of corporate culture. The trend is based on the concept that a positive organizational culture can be a material corporate asset because it either increases or preserves enterprise value by maximizing operational performance, developing internal human resources talent, and enhancing organizational reputation. If all of these items create or preserve enterprise value, then failure of a Board to administer proper oversight can be alleged to constitute a breach of fiduciary duty. Studies have shown that the most discussed Board topics include productivity, health and safety, and talent development and recruiting and that Boards that are highly motivated have stronger business performance, are better at promoting innovation, and are more prepared for a crisis. An example of this trend can be found in initial responses to the COVID-19 pandemic. In some instances management tried to fix the problems on their own instead of involving the Board in decision-making, which caused the public health emergency response to spin quickly out of control. The trend also applies to enterprises that may be sheltering toxic workplace discrimination. The continuing expectation is that the human resources function, like the regulatory compliance function, should have direct access to the Board if complaints are not being properly addressed by enterprise management.

I. **D&O Liability Insurance.** Many companies obtain directors' and officers' liability insurance. The coverage usually has various exclusions, including liability attributable to gaining "personal profit or advantage" or committing a "dishonest, fraudulent, or criminal act or omission."

J. **Indemnification.** Most states allow a corporation's articles of incorporation and by-laws to provide for indemnification of directors. The range of losses that are covered is broad and may include attorneys' fees, although there is no obligation to advance attorneys' fees and other expenses.

1. **No Indemnification If Director Does Not Act in Good Faith.** However, there is no indemnification for a claim if the director did not act in good faith and in a manner reasonably believed to be in or not opposed to the best interests of the corporation or, in the case of a criminal action, unless the director had no reasonable cause to believe the conduct was unlawful.

2. **Shareholders' Derivative Actions.** With respect to shareholders' derivative actions, there is also no indemnification with respect to claims when the director is adjudged to be liable for negligence or misconduct in the performance of his or her duty to the corporation unless and only to the extent that the court determines upon application that, despite the adjudication of liability but in view of all circumstances in the case, the person is fairly and reasonably entitled to indemnity.

3. **Other Restrictions on Indemnification.** In addition, there may be statutory and public policy restrictions on a director's ability to be indemnified.

III. DIRECTORS' AND OFFICERS' FIDUCIARY DUTIES TO CREDITORS

A. **Directors' and Officers' Fiduciary Duty to Creditors.** Under the law of most states, both officers and directors of insolvent corporations are charged with the duty of conserving and managing the remaining assets in trust for the creditors. For example, officers and directors of corporations may be held personally liable for corporate indebtedness if they make preferential transfers of corporate assets to themselves while the corporation is insolvent.

B. **When Is a Corporation Insolvent?**

1. **Insolvency Standards.** There are two primary standards applied by courts in determining whether a corporation is insolvent: (a) equitable insolvency; and (b) balance sheet insolvency. Equitable insolvency simply refers to a person's or corporation's inability to pay its debts as they become due, while balance sheet insolvency focuses on whether an entity's total liabilities exceed its total assets.

2. **Application of Insolvency Standards.** Most state corporation codes follow both equitable insolvency and balance sheet insolvency in setting the standard as to when a corporation may make distributions to its shareholders. In order for a corporation to make a distribution to its shareholders, it must (a) be able to pay its debts as they become due (equitable insolvency) and (b) have total assets in excess of its total liabilities (balance sheet insolvency).

C. **Delaware Law Governing Directors' Fiduciary Duties to Creditors and Other Constituencies.**

1. **Directors' Fiduciary Duties to a Corporation's Community of Interests.** Under Delaware law, once a corporation becomes insolvent or enters into the "vicinity of insolvency," a director's fiduciary duties run not only to the corporation but also to the corporation's "community of interests," including its creditors. This expansion in a director's fiduciary duties does not require a Board of Directors to place creditors' interests above any other corporate constituency. Moreover, Delaware law does not permit or require directors to conduct the affairs of an insolvent corporation "in a manner that is inconsistent with principles of fairness or in breach of duties owed to the stockholders." However, creditors have a right "to expect that directors will not divert, dissipate or unduly risk assets necessary to satisfy their claims." The director's duty to creditors has been characterized as a duty to "protect the contractual and priority rights of creditors."

2. **When Is a Corporation Insolvent or in the Vicinity of Insolvency Under Delaware Law?** Delaware courts, like most state courts, typically apply the equitable insolvency standard in determining whether a corporation is insolvent. Thus, under Delaware law, a corporation

that is unable to pay its debts as they fall due in the usual course of business is insolvent. In making this determination, Delaware courts consider the amount of cash or cash equivalents the corporation has on hand, the size of a corporation's accounts payable, and various other factors indicating that a corporation is unable to pay its debts as they become due.

3. **What Does "Vicinity of Insolvency" Mean?** Delaware courts and courts in other jurisdictions interpreting Delaware law have applied different standards for determining when a corporation is in the "vicinity of insolvency." In one case, the court reasoned that the vicinity of insolvency "seems to refer to the extent of the risk that creditors will not be paid, rather than balance sheet insolvency." Other courts have looked precisely at corporations' balance sheets in order to determine whether the corporation was in the "vicinity of insolvency." At least one court interpreting Delaware law has held that if a director is aware that a certain event or decision will render the corporation insolvent, the corporation is in the "vicinity" of insolvency even if the corporation is solvent at the time the decision is made. Because there is an absence of clear guidance as to when a corporation enters the "vicinity of insolvency," directors should be mindful of their potential fiduciary duties to creditors and other constituencies at the outset of financial trouble.

IV. DOES A SHAREHOLDER EVER HAVE FIDUCIARY DUTY TO THE CORPORATION?

A. **Delaware Law.** There is some authority under Delaware law for the proposition that a controlling stockholder may owe some fiduciary-type duty to other stockholders.

B. **Domination and Control by Less Than Majority Shareholders.** In the absence of majority stock ownership, a stockholder must dominate the affairs of the corporation through actual control of corporate conduct for a fiduciary duty to arise.

V. FIDUCIARY DUTIES IN PARTNERSHIPS AND JOINT VENTURES

A. **Presumption of Confidential Relationship.** In general, the common law presumes that a confidential relationship exists in partnerships. Confidential relationships do not necessarily arise, however, from contractual relationships between businessmen, even if the parties repose trust and confidence in one another. If a confidential relationship does exist, then the parties have a duty of utmost good faith, including the disclosure of material facts. Similarly, if a confidential relationship exists, then the suppression of a material fact may constitute fraud.

B. **Confidential Relationships Arise from Obligations Involving Good Faith.** Under the law of most states, a confidential relationship arises when, from a situation of mutual confidence between the parties, such as in a partnership, the law requires the utmost good faith. The relationship can arise from a contract, statutory provisions, or the circumstances of the business arrangement, and typically, a partnership does create a confidential relationship. A confidential relationship is never presumed, however, and the burden of proof is upon the party asserting the existence of the relationship.

C. **Duty to Disclose.** If a confidential relationship is found to exist, however, then the ordinary diligence required in a business transaction, such as the reading of the contract or the independent investigation of industry facts, does not generally apply. A duty to disclose may also arise when a confidential relationship exists, or if the particular circumstances of the case warrant disclosure. That same duty to disclose can give rise to a fraud claim as well.

D. **Self-Dealing in Partnerships.** In the case law in most states regarding partnerships, the courts have found a breach of the fiduciary duty of disclosure if one party engages in self-dealing that specifically harms the other party, withholds information about profits, or under-invests in the joint venture.

VI. INDIVIDUAL RESPONSIBILITY FOR CORPORATE OR ORGANIZATIONAL ACTS

A. **Evolution of the Law.** The law has evolved to make responsible officers, directors, and managers individually liable, both criminally and civilly, for organizational acts, even if the responsible officers, directors, and managers were not directly involved in the questionable conduct.

B. **Responsible Officer Doctrine.** In the context of submission of claims for payment to a division of the United States government that come within enforcement under the federal False Claims Act, courts have held certain managers and officers liable for criminal acts of an organization related to government contracts under the "responsible officer" doctrine.

1. **Managers Are Responsible for Corporate or Organizational Acts.** The doctrine may be applied to those who by virtue of their managerial positions could be deemed responsible for commission of an illegal offense. United States v. Park, 421 U.S. 658, 672 (1975).

2. **Knowledge Not Required.** No direct knowledge of the facts revealing the offense or active participation is required. United States v. Dotterweich, 320 U.S. 277 (1943).

3. **Willfulness Arising From Responsibility.** The willfulness or negligence of the actor will be imputed to him or her by virtue of his or her position of responsibility. United States v. Britain, 931 F. 2d 1413, 1419 (10th Cir 1991).

C. **Individual Director Liability for Corporate Acts Under *In re: Caremark International, Inc.* Derivative Litigation.**

1. **Standard of Conduct Applicable to Corporate Directors.** The Delaware Chancery Court considered the legal standard that governs a Board of Directors' obligation to supervise or monitor corporate performance in the seminal case of *In re: Caremark International, Inc.* The Delaware Chancery Court posed the question as follows: what is the Board's responsibility with respect to the organization and monitoring of the enterprise to assure that the corporation functions within the law to achieve its purposes? The court stated that this question is given special importance by an increasing tendency, especially under federal law, to employ the criminal law to assure corporate compliance with external legal requirements, including environmental, financial, employee, and product safety law as well as assorted health and safety regulations.

2. **The Role of the Federal Sentencing Guidelines in Determining the Standard of Care.** The court recognized that, in 1991, pursuant to the Sentencing Reform Act of 1984, the United States Sentencing Commission adopted Organizational Sentencing Guidelines (the "Federal Sentencing Guidelines"). As stated by the Delaware Chancery Court, the Guidelines offer powerful incentives for corporations to have in place compliance programs to detect violations of law, promptly to report violations to appropriate public officials when discovered, and to take prompt, voluntary remedial efforts. Ironically, the Federal Sentencing Guidelines provide corporations with the only proactive alternative to engage in action that may be potentially exculpatory for the corporation and its responsible officers and directors: implementing a Corporate Compliance Plan that conforms with certain elements set forth in the Guidelines. When the *Caremark* case was decided, application of the Federal Sentencing Guidelines to federal criminal proceedings was mandatory. Since the *Caremark* case was decided, the federal courts have ruled that the Federal Sentencing Guidelines are advisory only and that strict application of the Guidelines is unconstitutional. However, as discussed below, the Federal Sentencing Guidelines for organizational defendants continue to provide the platform for the structure of compliance programs.

3. **The Duty Under Delaware Law.** A decade after the Delaware Court of Chancery issued its seminal decision in *In re Caremark* establishing the conditions for director oversight liability under Delaware law the Delaware Supreme Court in Stone v. Ritter adopted the Caremark test and stated that it imposes liability under either of two "prongs": (a) when directors utterly fail to implement any reporting or information system or controls; or (b) when after implementing such a system or controls the Board consciously fails to monitor or oversee its

operations thus preventing the directors from being informed of risks or problems requiring their attention (commonly called the "Red Flags Prong"). In other words, a Compliance Plan is effective and potentially exculpatory only if it is effectively implemented and capable of detecting "Red Flags" that may be indicia of material wrongdoing. Accordingly, under Delaware law, corporate directors have a duty to assure that a corporate information gathering and reporting system exists which represents a good faith attempt to provide senior management and the Board with information regarding material acts, events, or conditions within the corporation, including compliance with applicable statutes and regulations. The *Caremark* court specifically notes the potential impact of the Federal Sentencing Guidelines on any business organization:

Any rational person attempting in good faith to meet an organizational governance responsibility would be bound to take into account this development and the enhanced penalties and the opportunities for reduced sanctions that it offers.

4. **The Danger of Misplaced Reliance on Prior Standards.** No longer may corporate Boards believe that their obligations are satisfied if they are reasonably informed concerning the corporation's operations without assuring themselves that information and reporting systems exist in the organization that are reasonably designed to provide the senior management and the Board itself with timely, accurate information sufficient to allow management and the Board, each within its scope, to reach informed judgments concerning both the corporation's compliance with law and its business performance.

5. **Expansion of *Caremark* Duties to Officers.** In the case of *In re: World Health Alternatives, Inc.*, a federal bankruptcy judge applying Delaware law ruled that a corporate officer is subject to the same minimum standards of supervision and monitoring applied to the corporate directors under the *Caremark* Delaware Chancery Court decision. Therefore, at least under Delaware law, corporate officers are now subject to the *Caremark* standard of conduct.

D. **Federal False Claims Act.**

1. **Qui Tam Actions.** Under the False Claims Amendments Act of 1986, private parties known as "relators" may bring a "qui tam" action, which is a civil lawsuit in the name of the United State government against those who submit false claims to the government. Private citizens may prosecute such actions either with or without the Department of Justice dependent on whether the Department of Justice exercises its right to intervene.

2. **Damages.** Damages can be as high as approximately $11,000 to $22,000 per claim (which increases annually based on a cost of living index) plus three times the amount claimed.

The private parties whose qui tam actions are successful can recover from 10% to 30% of the judgment or settlement of the lawsuit plus awards for attorneys' fees and expenses, with the balance of the recovery going to the United States Treasury.

3. **Whistleblowers.** Employees who bring a qui tam action are entitled to reinstatement, two times the amount of back pay, and other special damages, including litigation costs.

4. **Individual Liability.** Responsible officers can be held individually liable for False Claims Act damages.

E. **Intermediate Sanctions Against Tax Exempt Organizations.** Officers, directors, and managers of tax exempt organizations are also exposed to potential individual liability for organizational acts. For many years, the only sanction available to the Internal Revenue Service for acts that violate the laws governing tax exemption was losing exempt status. Recognizing that this "death penalty" may not serve the interests of the public or the organization, the IRS is now authorized to administer "intermediate sanctions" against tax exempt organizations and their managers.

1. **Purpose.** The "intermediate sanctions" legislation was enacted to discourage tax exempt entities from entering into certain transactions with private, taxable entities that do not reflect fair market value called "excess benefit transactions." In general, this is defined as any transaction in which an economic benefit is provided by an applicable tax-exempt organization directly or indirectly or for the use of any disqualified person, and the value of the economic benefit provided exceeds the value of the consideration received for providing the benefit. To prevent organizations from converting to taxable status to avoid penalties, the "intermediate sanctions" also apply to organizations that are not tax-exempt at the time of the excess benefit transaction.

2. **Individual Liability.** Under the "intermediate sanctions" regulations, officers and directors who authorize arrangements that violate the statutes and regulations governing tax-exempt organizations may be exposed to individual excise taxes.

3. **Disqualified Person.** A for-profit company will only be subject to penalty taxes if it is a "disqualified person." Generally, a "disqualified person" is any person who was in a position to exercise substantial influence over the affairs of an applicable tax-exempt organization at any time during the five-year period ending on the date of the transaction.

4. **Penalties.** Penalty taxes are imposed on the difference between the actual consideration paid and the fair market value (the spread).

   a. A tax is imposed on the tax-exempt organization's management equal to the lesser of 10% of the spread to a maximum of $10,000 that is adjusted for inflation.

b. An initial 25% tax is imposed on the spread against the for-profit organization.

c. The for-profit has a specified period to remedy the transaction if it transfers enough cash or property to the tax-exempt party to make up for the less than fair market value consideration it originally paid.

d. If the transaction is not remedied, then a second tax equal to 200% is imposed.

e. Common law applies if the tax liability cannot be satisfied by the organization. The IRS will come after disqualified persons.

F. **Forfeiture Provisions of Health Insurance Portability and Accountability Act of 1996.**

1. **Forfeiture Provisions.** A court, in imposing sentence on an individual convicted of a federal health care offense, can order the individual to forfeit any real or personal property that constitutes or is derived directly or indirectly from gross proceeds that are traced to the commission of the offense.

2. **Trust Fund.** After the payment of costs related to the liquidation of the forfeited assets, and notwithstanding any other provision of the law, the Secretary of the Treasury will deposit the net amount realized from the forfeiture of property into the Federal Hospital Insurance Trust Fund.

G. **Piercing of the Corporate Veil.**

1. **General Rule.** The corporate (or LLC or LLP) shell protects investors, officers, and directors from individual liability for corporate acts unless (a) an individual personally guarantees in writing to assume responsibility for a corporate debt, (b) the obligee can "pierce the corporate veil," or (c) the corporate trust doctrine applies.

2. **When the Corporate Veil May Be Pierced.** Under a broad principle of federal law, a corporate entity may be disregarded in the interests of public convenience, fairness, and equity. Each situation must be evaluated on its own facts and circumstances. Factors to be considered are as follows:

   a. Failure to observe corporate formalities.

   b. Nonpayment of dividends.

   c. Siphoning of funds by the dominant shareholder.

d. Non-functioning of other officers and directors.

e. Absence of corporate records.

f. Commingling of corporate and personal assets.

g. Distribution to the shareholders, directors, or officers when the corporation is insolvent.

3. **Corporate Trust Doctrine.** Analogous to a traditional piercing of the corporate veil, this doctrine holds that a corporation's assets are, by law, held in trust for the payment of creditors, and a breach of that trust could lead to individual shareholder, officer, or director liability.

4. **Key Element to Liability.** In the cases in which the Medicare program has successfully pierced the corporate veil or invoked the corporate trust doctrine, there is one core, critical fact: the dominant shareholder or officer repaid loans from the dominant shareholder or officer to the corporation and then the corporation ceased business with a debt to the Medicare program.

H. **Sarbanes-Oxley Act of 2002.** The Sarbanes-Oxley Act of 2002 imposes potential individual liability for corporate acts on an entity's responsible officers when the organization's stock is publicly traded.

1. **Rationale of Act.** The Sarbanes-Oxley Act of 2002 was enacted in the wake of the corporate scandals that reduced confidence in public company accounting procedures and financial information.

2. **CEO and CFO Certification of Financial Statements and Periodic Reports.** CEOs and CFOs, in their individual capacities, are required to certify the accuracy of each quarterly and annual report filed with the SEC, including financial statements filed therewith. This certification requirement applies to all public companies.

3. **Certification Requirements.** To meet the requirements, the CEOs and CFOs must certify that: (a) the signing officer has reviewed the report and, to the officer's best knowledge, it is accurate and does not contain any materially untrue or misleading statements; (b) to the officer's best knowledge, the financial statements and related information fairly present the financial condition and results of operations of the issuer; and (c) the company's internal controls are effective.

4. **The Role of Independent Directors.** Sarbanes-Oxley effectively ends the era of the "professional director" and requires publicly traded corporations to involve independent directors in critical committees of the Board, such as the Audit Committee and the Compensation Committee.

5. **Penalties.** A knowing violation by the CEO or CFO of the Act's financial statements certification requirement is punishable by a $1,000,000 fine and up to 10 years in prison. A willful violation is punishable by a $5,000,000 fine and up to 20 years in prison. If the issuer is required to prepare an accounting restatement as a result of a material noncompliance with the reporting requirements due to misconduct, the CEO and CFO will be required to return to the company any bonuses, other incentive-based compensations, and profits from the sale of issuer's stock for the 12-month period following each improper financial report. Persons who destroy property or falsify corporate records in an attempt to impede or obstruct an investigation shall be subject to fines and imprisonment up to 20 years. Persons who commit securities fraud shall be subject to fines or imprisonment of up to 25 years.

I. **Corporate Integrity Agreements.**

1. **Governmentally Imposed Compliance Plans.** After an organization or other entity has been accused of wrongdoing, and sometimes after the principals have either been convicted of crimes related to corporate acts or entered into a settlement agreement with the Department of Justice and Department of Health and Human Services, organizations are permitted to continue to operate only if they enter into Corporate Integrity Agreements. Such agreements require ongoing reporting to the government regarding organizational acts.

2. **Individual Responsibility.** These agreements require organizational employees, including both managerial personnel and lower level operations personnel, to certify individually that the corporation or other organization's operations are in full compliance with the statutes and regulations that govern the corporation (which sometimes can be quite complex).

J. **Inadequate Management; Failure to Supervise Corporate Affairs.** The law in many states has evolved to make individual officers and directors liable for damages suffered by non-shareholder third parties for alleged inadequate management and failure to supervise corporate affairs. Examples include the following: failing to detect misconduct by employees; negligently managing underwriting risks; and gunshot wounds to a mall patron after management reduced mall security to maximize profits.

K. **DOJ Directive to Pursue Individuals for Corporate Fraud.** As described in Chapter 1, the United States Department of Justice ("DOJ") erased all doubt that individuals are being targeted for acts of both civil and criminal corporate fraud when, on September 9, 2015, Sally Quillian Yates, then the DOJ Deputy Attorney General, issued a directive to DOJ division leaders and United States Attorneys to combat corporate fraud by seeking individual accountability for corporate wrongdoing in what is referred to as the "Yates Memo." According to the Yates Memo, which remains in effect, the DOJ intends to fully leverage its resources to identify culpable individuals at all levels in corporate cases. The directive identifies six key steps to strengthen the government's pursuit of individual corporate wrongdoing as follows:

- to qualify for any cooperation credit, corporations or other organizations accused of wrongdoing must provide to DOJ all relevant facts relating to the individuals responsible for the misconduct;

- criminal and civil corporate investigations should focus on individuals from the inception of the investigation;

- criminal and civil attorneys handling corporate investigations should be in routine communication with one another;

- absent extraordinary circumstances or approved DOJ policy, DOJ will not release culpable individuals from civil or criminal liability when resolving a matter with a company;

- DOJ attorneys should not resolve matters with a company without a clear plan to resolve related individual cases and should memorialize any declinations as to individuals in such cases; and

- DOJ civil attorneys should consistently focus on individuals as well as the company and evaluate whether to bring suit against an individual based on considerations beyond that individual's ability to pay.

L. **DOJ Compensation "Clawback" Policy.** As part of DOJ's promotion of voluntary corporate compliance and ethical corporate structures as well as DOJ's commitment to individual accountability for organizational acts, DOJ has implemented a "Compensation Policy" that incentivizes organizational voluntary implementation of compensation structures that impose material internal financial penalties on individuals who engage in wrongful conduct which, in essence, "claw back" compensation paid to the individuals. Although whether an organization's compensation arrangements include "clawback" provisions is entirely an internal decision, knowing that inclusion and enforcement of clawback provisions is potentially exculpatory for the organization and individuals who do not participate in misconduct induces organizations to implement "clawback" policies that shift the financial burden of wrongdoing to individuals.

VII. FEDERAL SENTENCING GUIDELINES: THE BIRTHPLACE OF CORPORATE COMPLIANCE.

A. **Creation of the Sentencing Guidelines.** As cited in the *Caremark* case, the Sentencing Reform Act of 1984 required federal judges to impose upon defendants convicted of violations of federal criminal statutes a sentence called for by sentencing Guidelines. The initial set of Guidelines drafted by the United States Sentencing Commission took effect on November 1, 1987, and has been amended several times. Effective November 1, 1991, the Sentencing Commission made the Guidelines applicable to business organizations. The Guidelines were revised in 2004 to include expectations regarding ethical as well as legally compliant conduct. Although initially application of the Guidelines was mandatory, it is now discretionary. However, as a practical matter, judges are required to consider the Guidelines when imposing sentences.

B. **Application of the Guidelines to Organizational Defendants.** Buried deep in the Guidelines are Guidelines for Organizational Defendants. Like the individual guidelines, the organizational Guidelines provide a scoring system for assessing fines, restitution, forfeiture, costs to prosecute, and even imposing a period of probation on an organization convicted of a federal criminal offense. There are four general principles underlying the Federal Sentencing Guidelines.

1. **Curing the Harm.** First, the court must, whenever practicable, order the organization to remedy any harm caused by the offense.

2. **Divestiture of Assets.** Second, if the organization operated primarily for a criminal purpose or primarily by a criminal means, the fines should be set sufficiently high to divest the organization of all its assets.

3. **Effect of Corporate Acts on Fines.** Third, the fine range for any other organization should be based on the seriousness of the offense and the capability of the organization, which will be determined by the steps taken by the organization prior to the offense to prevent and to detect criminal conduct, the level and extent of involvement in or tolerance of the offense by certain personnel, and the organization's action after an offense has been committed.

4. **Possibility of Probation.** Fourth, probation is the appropriate sentence for an organizational defendant when needed to insure that the company will fully carry out a sanction imposed by the court, or to insure that the business will take steps to reduce the likelihood of future criminal conduct.

C. **Mitigation of Sentencing Through Implementation of a Corporate Compliance Plan.** Under the Guidelines, sentences are imposed by assessing numerical points related to each charge or violation. However, points may be reduced based upon corporate acts, such as cooperation and effective implementation of a Corporate Compliance Plan. The Guidelines provide specific criteria for implementation of an effective Corporate Compliance Plan. Consequently, it is somewhat ironic that the entire compliance industry sprang from criminal sentencing guidelines.

VIII. CHARACTERISTICS OF CORPORATE COMPLIANCE PLANS

A. **Corporate Compliance Plans Are Necessary.** Corporate Compliance Plans, at a minimum, mitigate sentencing under the Federal Sentencing Guidelines. If the organization has a system to prevent and detect improper conduct by its employees and agents, commonly referred to as a "compliance program," and the court deems that program to have effectively deterred and ferreted out misconduct, the Guidelines call for a decrease in the business's culpability score. If even for this reason alone, every organization that is involved in the health industry, regardless of whether the organization is a provider or a supplier of goods and services, should implement a Corporate Compliance Plan in accordance with the Federal Sentencing Guidelines. However, implementation of an effective Corporate Compliance Plan is no longer discretionary. The ACA requires that, as a condition of enrollment in Medicare or Medicaid, providers and suppliers must establish compliance programs that satisfy requirements to be established by the Secretary of the Department of Health and Human Services in consultation with OIG. To date, there are no universal implementing federal regulations, but the message is clear: every business enterprise that relies directly or indirectly on revenue derived from governmental reimbursement programs should implement a Compliance Plan that conforms with the core elements described in the Federal Sentencing Guidelines for Organizational Defendants.

B. **Self-Assessment and Detection of Fraud.** Compliance Plans establish rigorous self-assessment systems intended to detect fraud within an organization and prevent the occurrence of additional incidents of fraud and abuse. In other words, it permits an organization to engage in meaningful self-assessment to detect and avoid compliance issues rather than having CMS or the OIG impose a self-assessment system.

C. **Culture of Compliance.** Compliance Plans instill a culture of compliance within an organization. This is critically important to effective implementation of a Corporate Compliance Plan. The Plan must be more than a document that is filed in a drawer or placed on a shelf: it must be a living, breathing part of every organization.

D. **Protection and Avoidance of Sanctions.** Compliance Plans may insulate an organization from activities of fraud and abuse by a rogue employee who fails to follow the procedures stated in the Plan. If allegations of fraud and abuse arise, then the existence of a compliance program may help an organization, and its responsible officers and directors, avoid sanctions. It may also reduce a long, drawn out inquiry to a short investigation.

IX. STARTING THE COMPLIANCE PROCESS: THE REGULATORY ASSESSMENT

A. **Assessment.** A Compliance Plan regulatory assessment is, at minimum, a review of the legal duties imposed on an organization, violation of which subjects the organization to federal criminal prosecution or violation of federal civil laws such as the False Claims Act. Regulatory assessments should identify conduct, reports, and the like which may put the organization at risk of violation of federal criminal or civil law and identify all material federal criminal or civil statutes which reasonably apply to the business. It is not, however, an "audit" to find all material loss contingencies.

B. **Review of Claims for Payment.** The assessment requires a baseline analysis of matters related to billing, coding, and the foundation for submitting claims for payment (especially to the government reimbursement programs).

C. **Relationships With Referral Sources.** The assessment should also cover other legal obligations, such as compliance with the Stark Law and the federal Anti-Kickback Statute.

D. **HIPAA Privacy and Security Compliance.** The assessment should also determine whether the organization has the policies and procedures in place to insure compliance with the HIPAA privacy and security rules.

E. **Employee Interviews.** Employee interviews should be aimed at gaining an understanding of the organization's operational logistics and ferreting out any unethical or illegal conduct.

F. **Documents and Records Review.** The assessment includes thorough review of an organization's records and documents, especially the organization's contracts and business arrangements with third parties, including referral sources.

G. **Attorney-Client Privilege.**

1. **Protection of Attorney-Client Communications.** Communications from clients to attorneys are usually privileged, including communications to consultants engaged by the attorneys.

2. **Protection of Attorney Work Product.** The attorney's work product is generally protected.

3. **Limitations on Attorney-Client Privileges, Including the "Crime-Fraud" Exception.** Arguably, work product is not protected unless there is a dispute or threat of litigation or some other

proceeding. Also, it can be argued that the work product was part of commission of a crime. Last, the DOJ and other prosecutors frequently require waiver of the attorney-client communication and attorney work product privileges when negotiating regarding potential health care regulatory sanctions.

4. **Duties and Obligations to Disclose Certain Information and Penalties for Failure to Do So.**

   a. **Law Prohibiting Concealment.** By law, if a provider, after receiving payment from a governmental reimbursement program, later discovers that it is not entitled to the payment, and the provider conceals this information with an intent to keep the money, then the provider has engaged in criminal misconduct.

   b. **The Rule of the Two D's.** The attorney-client privileges do not protect an organization from bad facts. If an anomaly is discovered, follow the Rule of the Two D's: Documentation and Disclosure.

   c. **Affordable Care Act Repayment Requirement.** In accordance with the procedure created under the Affordable Care Act of 2010 and implemented by federal regulations, any federal reimbursement program overpayment that is discovered must be repaid within sixty (60) days from the date the overpayment is identified (commonly referred to as the "60 Day Rule"). Failure to return the overpayment can be characterized as a "reverse False Claim," exposing a provider to substantial monetary damages. Additional civil monetary penalties may be assessed for late returns of overpayments.

X. REQUIRED ELEMENTS OF A CORPORATE COMPLIANCE PLAN

A. **Seven Requirements.** The Guidelines for Organizational Defendants set forth seven specific elements that must be set forth in every Corporate Compliance Plan.

1. **Standards of Conduct.** The organization must establish compliance standards and procedures to be followed by its employees and other agents that are reasonably capable of reducing the prospect of criminal conduct and that:

   a. contain specific ethical standards and policies;

   b. clearly advise employees of standards they are expected to follow and of the consequences for failure to do so;

   c. include all applicable laws and regulations; and,

d. is distributed to all officers, directors, and employees.

2. **Governing Body Oversight.** Specific individuals within high-level personnel of the organization must be assigned overall responsibility to oversee compliance with such standards and procedures.

3. **Delegation of Authority.** The organization must use due care not to delegate substantial discretionary authority to individuals whom the organization knew, or should have known through the exercise of due diligence, had a propensity to engage in illegal activities.

4. **Communication.** The organization must take steps to communicate effectively its standards and procedures to all employees and other agents by, for example, requiring participation in training programs or by disseminating publications that explain in a practical manner what is required.

5. **Monitoring and Auditing.** The organization must take reasonable steps to achieve compliance with its standards by, for example, instituting monitoring and assessment systems reasonably designed to detect criminal conduct by its employees and other agents and by having in place and publicizing a reporting system whereby employees and other agents can report criminal conduct by others within the organization without fear of retribution.

6. **Discipline.** The standards must be consistently enforced through appropriate disciplinary mechanisms, including, as appropriate, discipline of individuals responsible for the failure to detect an offense (adequate discipline of individuals responsible for an offense is a necessary component of enforcement; however, the form of discipline that will be appropriate will be case specific).

7. **Response and Prevention.** After an offense has been detected, the organization must take all reasonable steps to respond appropriately to the offense and to prevent future similar offenses, including any necessary modifications to its compliance program to prevent and detect violations of law.

B. **Formality of Compliance Plan Will Vary.** The size and complexity of the organization will dictate the formality of the Compliance Plan.

XI. IMPLEMENTATION OF A CORPORATE COMPLIANCE PROGRAM

A. **Implementation Challenges.** Once an organization has completed the self-assessment and created the Compliance Plan document, it will confront the challenge of implementing the Plan. This can be a painstaking and difficult process, so it should be carefully planned.

B. **All Compliance Programs Shall Include Written "Codes of Conduct".**

1. **Ethical Standards.** The Plan contain specific ethical standards and policies. A Code of Ethics was not a specific requirement of the original Guidelines, but, with the 2004 revisions, it is clear that ethics plays an important role in an effective Compliance Plan.

2. **Employee Notification.** The Plan should clearly advise employees of standards they are expected to follow and of the consequences for failure to do so.

3. **Description of Laws and False Claims Act Educational Requirements.** The Guidelines state that the Plan should include a description of all applicable laws and regulations. Separately, the Deficit Reduction Act of 2005 (the "DRA") has a specific educational provision that requires organizations that receive more than $5,000,000 of Medicaid funds annually to establish an employee education plan about state and federal false claims laws and whistleblower protections. As a condition of participating in a state's Medicaid program and receiving Medicaid funds, an entity subject to the DRA educational requirement must provide written policies that provide detailed information about four major topics: (a) the federal False Claims Act; (b) administrative remedies for false claims and statements; (c) any civil or criminal penalties under state false claims laws; and (d) whistleblower protections under federal and state law. The written materials must explain the role these laws play in preventing Medicaid fraud and abuse and describe the "entity's policies and procedures for detecting and preventing fraud, waste, and abuse." The DRA further requires that the entity's employee handbook contain a specific discussion of these topics. Failure to comply with this requirement exposes an organization to a false claims lawsuit or to exclusion from federal health care programs because the education requirement is a condition for participation in Medicaid. Consequently, this description of law will be a material part of any Corporate Compliance Plan for a covered organization.

4. **Distribution.** The Plan should be distributed to all officers, directors, employees, and other agents, including, for example, independent contractors. It may not be necessary to distribute the entire Plan to every person in the organization, so the organization may need to engage in specific educational programs as they relate to a person's function within the organization.

E. **Compliance Officers or Committee and Access to Upper Management.** The Compliance Plan should also identify the organization's Compliance Officers and the process for engaging upper level management in the compliance function.

1. **Description of Duties.** The Plan should identify Compliance Officers and their duties in writing.

2. **Continuing Assessment.** Compliance Officers should work with general counsel and outside legal counsel to monitor development of the compliance process.

3. **Access to Management.** The Plan should always provide access to the Chief Executive Officer and the Board of Directors.

4. **Appointment of Compliance Committee.** Depending upon the size and complexity of the organization, it may be appropriate to delegate compliance responsibility to a Compliance Committee.

E. **Government Audits and Investigations.** Although not a requirement under the Guidelines, every effective Compliance Plan requires a system to control an organization's interactions with regulatory and investigatory governmental agencies.

1. **Communications With Government Agents.** The Plan will educate the company's representatives regarding their rights when approached by a government agent and how to report any such contact through the compliance process.

2. **Reporting Outside Inquiries.** The Plan will include mechanisms for reporting outside inquiries received by the company's representatives.

E. **Internal Mechanisms for Reporting Suspected Misconduct.**

1. **Anonymity.** To the extent possible, the Plan will conceal the identity of reporting representative. This is very important to the DHHS OIG, but it may not be entirely possible in small organizations.

2. **Discipline.** Reporting cannot be the sole ground for discipline, but failure to report may be grounds for discipline.

F. **Corporate Document Retention System.** Although not required by the Guidelines, an appropriately administered document retention system promotes the compliance function.

1. **Retention System: Remember Arthur Andersen.** A system for document retention should include their creation, distribution, security in storage, and destruction.

2. **Cornerstone of Compliance.** Document retention is a cornerstone of compliance.

XII. OIG GOVERNING BOARD COMPLIANCE GUIDANCE

A. **OIG Practical Guidance for Health Care Governing Boards.** On April 20, 2015 the OIG, in collaboration with the American Health Law Association, Association of Healthcare Internal Auditors, and Health Care Compliance Association, promulgated Practical Guidance for Health Care Governing Boards on Compliance Oversight which clarifies the OIG's expectations regarding Board oversight of compliance program functions. Overall, it is clear that governing Boards must provide active supervisory oversight of the compliance function, and, conversely, oversight of the compliance function cannot be delegated entirely to operating management.

B. **OIG Expectations for Board Oversight of Compliance Program Functions.** The critical elements of proper Board oversight as described in this Practical Guidance include the following:

1. **Information and Reporting System.** The Board must ensure existence of a corporate information and reporting system that is adequate to assure the Board that appropriate information related to compliance with applicable laws will be brought to the Board's attention timely and as a matter of course.

2. **Baseline Assessment Tools.** The Board should use public compliance benchmarks, including the Federal Sentencing Guidelines, OIG voluntary compliance guidelines, and OIG Corporate Integrity Agreements ("CIAs"), as baseline assessment tools for identifying the elements of an effective compliance program.

3. **Duty to Review Adequacy of Compliance Systems.** Although compliance programs should be designed to fit the organization, all Boards are expected to put forth a meaningful effort to review the adequacy of existing compliance systems and functions.

4. **Formal Education Plan.** The Board should develop a formal plan to keep the Board educated and informed regarding regulatory changes and operations challenges so the Board can ask pertinent questions of management and make informed strategic decisions regarding the compliance function, including funding and resource allocations.

5. **Compliance Expertise on the Board.** A Board can raise its level of substantive expertise regarding regulatory and compliance matters by adding to the Board or periodically consulting with an experienced regulatory, compliance, or legal professional. By doing so, the Board sends a strong message about the organization's commitment to compliance, provides a valuable resource to other Board members, and helps the Board better fulfill its oversight obligations.

C. **Roles and Relationships.** The Practical Guidance also addresses expectations regarding roles and relationships within an organization as follows:

1. **Including the Compliance Function in Organizational Charts.** Organizations should define the interrelationship of the audit, compliance, and legal functions in organizational documents such as an organization chart that describes structure and reporting relationships between, for example, quality assurance, risk management, and human resources.

2. **Role of the Compliance Function.** The compliance function promotes the prevention, detection, and resolution of activities that do not conform to legal, policy, or business standards.

3. **Role of the Legal Function.** The legal function advises the organization on the legal and regulatory risks of its business strategies.

4. **Role of the Internal Audit Function.** The internal audit function provides an objective evaluation of the existing risk and internal control systems and framework within an organization. Internal audits ensure monitoring functions are working and identify where additional management or Board oversight is required.

5. **Role of the Human Resources Functions.** The human resources function manages the recruiting, screening, hiring, and educational training of employees.

6. **Role of the Quality Improvement Function.** The quality improvement function promotes consistent, safe, and high quality practices within health care organizations.

7. **Board Oversight of All Functions.** Boards should periodically evaluate the adequacy, independence, and performance of the different functions.

8. **Role of an "Independent" Compliance Officer.** With respect to "independence," the OIG restates its long held position that the Compliance Officer should neither be nor report to general counsel or the legal department in any manner. The functions should be separate but collaborative. The same rule applies to the internal audit function. This will require a balancing of attorney-client privilege with the goal of providing access to key individuals who are responsible for ensuring compliance as well as reporting and remediating any alleged instance of noncompliance.

9. **Board Oversight of Proper Access to Information.** The Board should have a process to ensure appropriate access to information for all functions. Organizations without the resources to permit formal separation should recognize the potential risks of such an arrangement and provide persons servicing multiple roles to execute each function in an independent

manner when necessary, including the ability to communicate directly with the Board and executive management.

10. **Board Responsibility for Assuring Coordination of All Functions.** The Board should have the separate management functions work together to identify compliance risks, investigate potential compliance breaches, identify and implement corrective actions, and communicate between the various functions throughout the process.

D. **Reporting to the Board.** The Board should set and enforce expectations for receiving regular reports regarding the organization's risk mitigation and compliance efforts, separately and independently, for persons responsible for audit, compliance, human resources, legal, quality, and information technology. Suggested ways to accomplish that objective include the following:

1. **Objective Scorecards.** The Board may request development of objective scorecards that measure how well management is executing the compliance programs, mitigating risks, and implementing corrective action plans.

2. **Investigation Reports.** Requiring management to report on internal and external investigations, issues raised in internal audits, hotline call activity, and allegations of management misconduct.

3. **Reporting Systems.** Assuring implementation of mechanisms for reporting suspected violations and taking corrective action.

4. **Regular Internal Assessment Reviews.** Regular internal reviews that provide a Board with a snapshot of where an organization is, and where it may be going, in terms of compliance and quality assurance.

5. **Board Executive Sessions Without Senior Management.** The Board may conduct regular "executive sessions" that exclude senior management with leadership from the compliance, legal, internal audit, and quality functions to encourage open communication.

E. **Identifying and Auditing Potential Risk Areas.** The Board should ensure organizational focus on the four areas of typical risk exposure: relationships with referral sources; correct submission of claims for payment; privacy and security of health information; and quality of care. Board guidance for identifying potential risk includes the following:

1. **Internal Audits and Hotline Reporting.** Use of internal sources, such as internal audits or employee hotline reporting.

2. **Using External Sources as Benchmarks.** Use of external sources, such as asking management whether processes are in place to prevent publicized failures in similar organizations.

3. **Risk Area Assessment and Corrective Action Plans.** Ensuring that management consistently reviews and audits risk areas and implements corrective action plans.

4. **Matching Compliance Initiatives to Changing Risks.** Assuring that compliance initiatives reflect changing areas of risk, such as risks arising from coordinated care payment models such as value-based purchasing, payment bundling, and global payments for maintaining and improving population health and individual patient quality of care.

5. **Reviewing Financial Relationships.** Reviewing financial relationships arising from industry consolidations (such as hospital-physician arrangements) necessary to compete in a changing health care economy.

6. **Reviewing Publicly Available Data.** Using information that is publicly available through an increase in transparency, such as Medicare quality and payment data and the Physician Payments Sunshine Act, to identify risk areas.

F. **Encouraging Accountability and Compliance.** Boards may assess employee and overall organizational performance in promoting and adhering to the compliance programs and then use financial incentives based on compliance and quality outcomes. The Practical Guidance suggests the following:

1. **Policy for Complying With "60 Day Rule" For Return of Overpayments.** Requiring management to develop a policy for identifying and returning any federal reimbursement program "overpayments" to assure compliance with the "60 Day Rule," which requires repayment of all internally identified overpayments within sixty days to avoid False Claims Act sanctions.

2. **Protocols for Identifying Potential Violations and Voluntary Self-Disclosure.** Asking management what protocols are in place for identification of potential violations and voluntary self-disclosure when problems are discovered.

3. **Encouraging Compliance Reporting.** Evaluating whether employees feel confident that raising compliance concerns, questions, or complaints will result in meaningful inquiry without retaliation or retribution.

4. **Reports from Management Regarding Compliance Responses.** Requesting information from management regarding how management responded to identified violations of either laws or internal policy.

G. **Summary of OIG Guidelines for Health Care Boards.** The OIG perspective is simply stated: every Board is responsible for ensuring that its organization complies with relevant federal, state, and local laws and regulations. This responsibility cannot be delegated or ignored by the Board. The Board should make efforts to increase knowledge of relevant and emerging regulatory risks, the role and function of the organization's compliance program in light of those risks, and the flow and evaluation of reporting potential issues and problems to senior management. In short, developing a structured culture of compliance is critical.

XIII. DOJ COMPLIANCE PLAN IMPLEMENTATION GUIDANCE

A. **Department of Justice Compliance Program Guidance.** As stated above, there is no absolute legal requirement for health care providers and suppliers and other entities that participate in the governmental reimbursement programs to implement Corporate Compliance and Ethics Plans. However, existence of an effective Compliance Program is definitely a mitigating factor if an organization is exposed to allegations of federal criminal and civil misconduct, and it is an absolute best practice. While federal agencies have published guidelines for structuring Corporate Compliance and Ethics Programs for many years, historically there has been little guidance on how a Compliance Program is expected to operate. All enterprises now have Compliance Program implementation guidance directly from the main governmental enforcement agency. The Fraud Section of the United States Department of Justice ("DOJ") published comprehensive guidance on "Evaluation of Corporate Compliance Programs" (the "DOJ Compliance Program Guidance") that is accessible on the DOJ web site and periodically updated.

B. **The DOJ Compliance Program Guidance Complements Other Compliance Guidance.** The DOJ identifies three fundamental lines of inquiry for determining effectiveness of a Compliance Program, each of which is followed by a series of specific questions for focused evaluation. Most of the questions dovetail neatly with the Federal Sentencing Guidelines as well as Compliance Guidelines promulgated by other governmental agencies such as the United States Department of Health and Human Services, Office of the Inspector General ("OIG") and statutory requirements for skilled nursing facility Compliance and Ethics Programs enacted through Section 6102 of the Affordable Care Act of 2010 (which for convenience are collectively described as the "Other Compliance Program Guidelines"). In addition, the DOJ Compliance Program Guidance reflects the growing emphasis on identifying individual persons who are involved in the compliance process as first expressed in the "Yates Memo" issued by former Deputy Attorney General Sally Yates that, in essence, directs DOJ to identify potentially culpable individuals as part of any DOJ investigation of an organization.

C. **Summary of DOJ Compliance Program Guidance In the Context of Other Compliance Program Guidelines.** Putting the DOJ Compliance Program Guidance into perspective, the Other Compliance Program Guidelines are prophylactic in nature and address what an organization should do to prevent allegations of wrongdoing in specifically identified risk areas, while the DOJ Compliance Program Guidance describes how DOJ determines whether the organization has in fact implemented an effective Compliance Program after an allegation of misconduct arises. Overall, the topics and questions that DOJ uses when evaluating the effectiveness of a Compliance Program are much more focused and detailed than the seven core requirements of a Corporate Compliance and Ethics Plan as described in the Federal Sentencing Guidelines and are much more process oriented than the more substantive Other Compliance Program Guidelines.

D. **The DOJ Three Prong Review Process.** The DOJ process involves three separate lines of inquiry:

- Is the Compliance Program **well designed**?
- Has the Compliance Program been **earnestly applied in good faith?**
- Does the Compliance Program **work in practice?**

In a nutshell, "design" addresses development of the Compliance Program, "earnestly applied in good faith" addresses whether the Compliance Program is adequately staffed and financed to permit the Compliance Program to function effectively, and whether the Compliance Program "works" asks why, if a Compliance Program is well designed and effectively implemented, it may have failed in detecting the wrongful conduct that is the subject of the DOJ fraud investigation. The following is a summary of some key points on each of the DOJ's three Compliance Program review prongs.

E. **Is the Compliance Program Well Designed?** Critical factors in evaluating any Compliance Program include whether the Compliance Program is adequately designed for maximum effectiveness in preventing and detecting wrongdoing by employees and other agents and whether corporate management is enforcing the program or is tacitly encouraging or pressuring employees to engage in misconduct. DOJ breaks the design analysis down into the following lines of inquiry:

- Risk Assessment;
- Policies and Procedures;
- Training and Communications;

- Confidential Reporting Structure and Investigation Process;
- Third Party Management; and
- Mergers and Acquisitions.

1. **Risk Assessment.** Because an effective Compliance Program begins with an organization's assessment of its regulatory risk, DOJ prosecutors are directed to determine whether the Compliance Program is designed to detect the misconduct most likely to occur in an organization's line of business and complex regulatory environment, the effectiveness of the organization's internal risk assessment and the manner in which the organization's Compliance Program has been tailored based on that risk assessment, and whether the risk assessment criteria are periodically updated to address compliance issues that have arisen over time. The questions under this topic relate to the Other Compliance Program Guidelines requiring a baseline assessment of regulatory risk and include inquiries regarding the following:

    - The methodology that the organization used to identify, analyze, and address its particular regulatory risks;
    - What information and metrics the organization used to help detect the misconduct in question;
    - Whether the organization dedicates sufficient resources to policing high risk areas rather than low risk areas; and
    - Whether the risk assessment is current and subject to periodic review.

2. **Policies and Procedures.** DOJ states that any well-designed Compliance Program has policies and procedures that give both content and effect to ethical norms and that address and aim to reduce risks identified in the organization's risk assessment process. As a threshold matter, DOJ prosecutors are instructed to determine whether the organization has a Code of Conduct that is accessible and applicable to all of the organization's employees and other agents and describes the organization's commitment to full compliance with relevant federal laws. DOJ Compliance Program assessment under this topic corresponds to the Other Compliance Program Guidelines requiring standards of conduct and communicating the standards of conduct to the organization's agents and include inquiries regarding the following:

- The process for designing and implementing policies and procedures, including responding to changes in the legal and regulatory environment;
- How the organization manages accountability for supervisory oversight of performance in accordance with the standards of conduct; and
- What guidance and training were provided to the "key gatekeepers in the control process" (likely Compliance Officers) regarding how to detect misconduct and when to escalate an internal investigation with reporting to upper management.

3. **Training and Communications.** Another hallmark of a well-designed Compliance Program is appropriately tailored training and communications. DOJ states that prosecutors should assess the steps taken by the organization to insure that policies and procedures have been integrated into the organization, including through periodic training and certification for all directors, officers, relevant employees, and, when appropriate, other agents and business partners. The questions under this topic relate to the Other Compliance Program Guidelines requiring effective communication of the Compliance Program standards and procedures to all employees and other agents and include inquiries regarding the following:

    - Whether the organization provided tailored training for high-risk and control employees that address the risk in the area where the misconduct arose;
    - Whether supervisory employees have received different or supplementary training;
    - How the organization measures effectiveness of the training;
    - What senior management has done to let employees know the organization's position on the misconduct;
    - What communications are generally made when an employee is terminated for failure to comply with the organization's standards of conduct;
    - What resources are available to employees to provide guidance regarding compliance policies; and
    - Whether the organization has assessed whether its employees know when to seek advice and whether they are willing to do so.

4. **Confidential Reporting Structure and Investigation Process.** A well-designed Compliance Program is expected to have an efficient and trusted mechanism by which employees can anonymously and confidentially report allegations of a breach of the organization's Code of Conduct, breach of policies and procedures, or suspected or actual misconduct. The questions under this topic relate to the Other Compliance Program Guidelines requiring responding to allegations of misconduct and preventing further similar offenses and include inquiries regarding the following:

    - Whether the organization has an anonymous reporting mechanism and, if not, why not;
    - How the compliance hotline or other reporting mechanism is communicated to employees;
    - Whether the compliance reporting mechanism has been used;
    - How the organization collects, analyzes, and uses information from its compliance reporting mechanisms and determined which complaints merit further investigation;
    - How the organization insures that investigations are independent, objective, appropriately conducted, and properly documented;
    - Whether the organization uses timing metrics to insure responsiveness;
    - Whether the organization has a process for monitoring investigation outcomes and insuring accountability for responding to the findings;
    - Whether sufficient financial resources are dedicated to the reporting and investigating mechanisms; and
    - Whether the organization periodically examines compliance reports for patterns of misconduct or other red flags for compliance weaknesses.

5. **Third Party Management.** In general, regulatory authorities distrust independent contractor arrangements under the theory that they are more susceptible to fraud and abuse. Accordingly, all Compliance Programs are expected to address the risks associated with third party management companies. The questions under this topic relate to the Other Compliance Program Guidelines requiring delegation of authority for implementing

the Compliance Program to qualified persons when an organization's operations have an independent, third party management company and include inquiries regarding the following:

- How the organization's third party management process has corresponded to the nature and level of the enterprise risk identified by the organization;
- Whether this process is integrated into the relevant procurement and vendor management process;
- The business rationale for using a third party management company;
- What mechanisms the organization uses to insure that the third party management company contract terms specifically describe the services to be performed and have appropriate payment terms, the described contractual work is actually performed, and that compensation is commensurate with the services rendered;
- How the organization analyzes the third party's incentive model against compliance risks;
- How the organization monitors third party management performance;
- How the organization has trained the relationship managers about what the organization's compliance risks are and how to manage them;
- How the organization has incentivized compliance and ethical behavior by third party management companies;
- Whether red flags were identified from the due diligence of the third parties involved in the misconduct and how they were resolved;
- Whether a similar third party has been suspended, terminated, or audited as a result of compliance issues; and
- How the organization has monitored situations to insure that compliance issues related to vendor relationships do not arise again.

6. **Mergers and Acquisitions.** Compliance issues frequently arise in acquisition due diligence. Consequently, DOJ expects organizations to include a comprehensive compliance risk

assessment as part of the organization's due diligence process. The questions under this topic relate to review of the compliance function in a specific setting and do not precisely fall into the requirements identified in the Other Compliance Program Guidelines and include inquiries regarding the following:

- Whether the misconduct or risk of misconduct was identified during due diligence;
- How the risk assessment due diligence was conducted and who individually conducted it;
- How the compliance function has been integrated into the merger, acquisition, or integration process;
- What has been the organization's process for tracking and remediating misconduct identified in due diligence; and
- What has been the organization's process for implementing compliance policies and procedures at new entities.

F. **Is the Compliance Program Earnestly Applied in Good Faith?** DOJ says that even a well-designed Compliance Program may be unsuccessful in practice if implementation is lax or ineffective because it is not adequately resourced and empowered to function effectively. Prosecutors are instructed to probe whether a Compliance Program is a "paper program" or one implemented, reviewed, and revised in an effective manner. DOJ breaks the effectiveness of implementation analysis down into the following lines of inquiry:

- Commitment by Senior and Middle Management;
- Autonomy and Resources; and
- Incentives and Disciplinary Measures.

1. **Commitment by Senior and Middle Management.** The DOJ states that, beyond compliance structures, policies, and procedures, it is important for an organization to create and foster a culture of ethics and compliance with the law. The effectiveness of a Compliance Program requires a high-level commitment by organizational leadership to implement a culture of compliance from the top. DOJ emphasizes that the organization's top leaders, specifically the Governing Board and executive officers, set the tone for the entire organization. The Governing Board is responsible for implementation of an effective Compliance Program, and that responsibility

cannot be delegated. In fact, the DOJ expects an organization's Governing Board to include a representative with compliance expertise. The questions under this topic relate to the Other Compliance Program Guidelines requiring specific high-level personnel to have overall responsibility for implementing the Compliance Program and include inquiries regarding the following:

- Whether compliance expertise is been available on the board of directors;
- Whether senior leaders, through their words and actions, encourage compliance, including the type of misconduct involved in the investigation.
- Whether senior leaders have demonstrated leadership in the organization's compliance and remediation effort and what specific actions senior leadership has taken in that regard;
- Whether the board of directors have held executive or private sessions with the compliance and control functions;
- What types of information the Governing Board and senior management examined in their oversight of the area in which the misconduct occurred;
- Whether managers tolerated greater compliance risks in pursuit of new business and greater revenue; and
- Whether managers encouraged employees to act unethically to achieve a business objective or impeded compliance personnel from effectively implementing their duties.

2. **Autonomy and Resources.** As evidence that a Compliance Program is more than a piece of paper kept in a drawer, DOJ instructs prosecutors to inquire into the sufficiency of the personnel and resources dedicated to the compliance function and in particular whether compliance officers have (a) sufficient authority within the organization, (b) sufficient resources, particularly staff available to undertake the requisite auditing, documentation, and analysis required of an effective Compliance Program, and (c) sufficient autonomy from operating management, such as direct access to the organization's Governing Board or the Board's audit committee. Prosecutors should also evaluate the resources the organization has dedicated to compliance, the authority and independence of the compliance function, and availability of compliance expertise to the Governing Board. The questions under this topic relate to the Other Compliance Program Guidelines requiring communicating compliance standards and procedures to all employees and other agents as well as requiring

specific high-level personnel to have overall responsibility for implementing the Compliance Program and include inquiries regarding the following:

- Whether the Governing Board established an information and reporting system that is reasonably designed to provide management and the Governing Board with timely and accurate information sufficient to allow them to reach an informed decision regarding the organization's compliance with applicable law;
- Whether the Compliance Program is an independent function reporting to the CEO or Governing Board (which is preferred under all Guidelines) or whether it reports to the legal department or business department (which is disfavored);
- How the compliance function compares to other departments regarding rank, titles, resources, compensation levels, and access to key decision makers;
- Whether compliance personnel are properly qualified;
- Whether the compliance officers had direct reporting lines to the Governing Board;
- How often do Compliance Officers meet with the Governing Board or the Board's audit committee and are members of senior management present for these meetings;
- How does the organization insure independence of the compliance function;
- Whether the compliance department received proper funding and resources; and
- Whether the organization outsourced the compliance function to an external firm or consultant and if so how that decision was both made and managed.

3. **Incentives and Disciplinary Measures.** Discipline is an obvious fundamental element of an effective Compliance Program. DOJ instructs prosecutors to assess the extent to which the organization's communications convey to all of its representatives that unethical conduct is not tolerated and will bring swift and consistently applied consequences, regardless of the position or title of the representative who engages in the misconduct (implying that disciplinary measures must apply as much to senior management as to mid or low level employees). As stated above, when confronted with a fraud investigation, the first response from an organization to mitigate potential consequences is frequently to inform the investigators that "we have a Compliance Program." Investigators sometimes attempt to validate the assertion by countering "then let me see your disciplinary records." DOJ also instructs prosecutors to

review whether the Compliance Program provides incentives for improving and developing a Compliance Program or demonstrating ethical leadership. Prosecutors are instructed to conduct the following inquiries under this topic:

- Who participates in making disciplinary decisions;
- When and how the reasons for discipline and disciplinary actions in response to the misconduct are communicated to representatives;
- Whether the organization has ever terminated or disciplined any person for similar misconduct;
- Whether disciplinary actions are consistently and fairly applied; and
- Whether the organization incentivizes engaging in compliant and ethical conduct.

4. **"Clawback" Compensation Structures.** As stated above, one way that individuals can become financially responsible for organizational wrongdoing is through "clawback" provisions that impose internal financial penalties on individuals who engage in wrongful conduct. The DOJ Compliance Program Guidance endorses that by providing that in determining the effectiveness of a Compliance Plan DOJ looks for compensation structures that clearly and effectively impose financial penalties for individual misconduct and at the same time provide positive incentives such as promotions, rewards, and bonuses for improving and developing a compliance program or demonstrating ethical leadership.

G. **Does the Compliance Program Work in Practice?** Prosecutors are required to assess the adequacy and effectiveness of the Compliance Program at the time of the offense that is under investigation and at the time of the charging decision. DOJ reviews the following in determining whether a Compliance Program works in practice:

- Continuous Improvement, Periodic Testing, and Review;
- Investigation of Misconduct; and
- Analysis and Remediation of Any Underlying Misconduct.

1. **Continuous Improvement, Periodic Testing, and Review.** DOJ says that one hallmark of an effective Compliance Program is its capacity to improve and evolve because actual implementation of compliance controls in practice necessarily reveals areas of risk and potential

adjustment. Every organization's business changes over time as do the laws that govern its actions, industry standards, and the general competitive environment in which the organization operates. Accordingly, DOJ instructs its prosecutors to consider whether the organization has engaged in meaningful efforts to review its Compliance Program and insure that it is not stale. In evaluating whether a Compliance Program works in practice, prosecutors should consider revisions to the Compliance Program in response to lessons learned. Prosecutors are specifically directed to determine whether an organization has taken reasonable steps to insure that the organization's Compliance Program is followed, including monitoring and auditing to detect potential misconduct and evaluating periodically the organization's Compliance Program. Inquiries under this topic relate to the Other Compliance Program Guidelines requiring monitoring and auditing the effectiveness of the Compliance Program and include inquiries regarding the following:

- The organization's process for determining when and how frequently the organization has undertaken an internal audit of the effectiveness of the Compliance Program;
- What kind of audits would have revealed the misconduct before it occurred, whether those audits conducted, and what were the findings of any such audit;
- Whether relevant audit findings and remediation progress have been reported to senior management and the Governing Board on a regular basis and whether senior management and the Governing Board have followed up;
- How often internal audits are generally conducted in high risk area assessments;
- What control testing the organization has generally undertaken;
- Whether the organization updated its risk assessments and reviewed its compliance policies, procedures, and practices;
- How often and how does the organization measure its culture of compliance; and
- Whether the organization seeks input from all employee levels to determine whether all employees perceive senior and middle management's commitment to the Compliance Program.

2. **Investigation of Misconduct.** DOJ prosecutors are instructed to determine whether the organization has a properly functioning system for the timely and through investigation of

any allegations or suspicions of misconduct by the organization and its employees and other agents. This line of inquiry relates to the Other Compliance Program Guidelines requiring organizations to "respond" to allegations of misconduct and take action to "prevent" further similar offenses and include inquiries regarding the following:

- Whether the organization insures that investigations are independent, objective, appropriately conducted, and properly documented;
- Whether the organization's investigations are used to identify root causes, system vulnerabilities, and accountability lapses, including among supervisory managers and senior executives;
- The organization's process for responding to investigative findings; and
- How high up in the organization the investigative findings are reported.

3. **Analysis and Remediation of Any Underlying Misconduct.** Under DOJ's internal rules, to receive full credit for timely and appropriate remediation of misconduct, an organization should demonstrate a "root cause analysis" and, when appropriate, remediation to address the root causes. Accordingly, prosecutors are instructed to consider any remedial actions taken by the organization including appropriate discipline of all employees and other agents involved in the misconduct, either through direct participation or oversight failure, as well as those with supervisory authority over the area in which the misconduct occurred. This is a common theme: DOJ expects effective discipline and accountability for senior management, up to and including the "C-Suite." Inquiries in this area include the following:

   - The organization's analysis of the root cause of the misconduct and whether the response revealed "systemic issues" (in contrast to an isolated incident);
   - Who was involved in making the analysis;
   - If policies and procedures should have prohibited the misconduct, whether they were effectively implemented and whether employees and other agents with responsibility for implementing the policies and procedures have been held accountable;
   - Whether there were prior opportunities to detect the misconduct, and, if so why the opportunities were missed;

- What specific remediation has addressed the issues identified in the root cause and missed opportunity analysis;
- Whether the organization took timely disciplinary action in response to the allegation of misconduct;
- Whether the organization considered disciplinary action for failures in supervision; and
- Whether the organization has ever terminated or otherwise disciplined any representative for the misconduct at issue.

H. **Using the DOJ Compliance Program Guidance for Self-Assessment.** Organizations now have a detailed template for understanding how the DOJ assesses existing Compliance Programs when there is an allegation of wrongdoing. It is therefore advisable for all organizations to engage in a self-assessment of the effectiveness of their Compliance Programs using the DOJ Compliance Program Guidance as a baseline for how Compliance Programs are expected to perform. While DOJ attempts to break its Compliance Program analysis into three prongs, each with detailed lines of inquiry, there is substantial overlap between the three prongs. Consequently, it is helpful to take a step back and identify some fundamental elements that can guide any organization regarding assessment of its Compliance Program. Reflecting on the content of this analytical framework, we see the following themes:

1. **Compliance Expertise Must Be Made Available to the Governing Board.** The Governing Board must actively oversee implementation of the organization's Corporate Compliance and Ethics Plan. This is consistent with the standard of conduct for directors of Delaware corporations established in *In re: Caremark International, Inc.*, which, in essence, provides that directors may be exposed to individual liability for breach of the duty of care if the organization fails to implement a Corporate Compliance and Ethics Plan that satisfies the seven elements described in the Federal Sentencing Guidelines for Organizational Defendants.

2. **The Governing Board Should Include a Director with Compliance Expertise.** The DOJ expects an organization's Governing Board to include a representative with compliance expertise.

3. **Senior Management Must Be Actively Involved In Supervision of the Compliance Process.** When an allegation of misconduct arises, DOJ can make senior management accountable, even if senior management is not directly involved in the alleged misconduct. This is consistent with both the "Responsible Office Doctrine" that has long been part of federal False

Claims Act law and the "Yates Memo" that focuses on making individuals responsible for corporate acts.

4. **The Compliance Function Must Have the Ability to Report Directly to the Governing Board.** This addresses the concern expressed in the Compliance Program Guidelines that compliance concerns reported to compliance officers through the organization's internal reporting system might be blocked by senior management (such as the chief financial officer, general counsel, or chief executive officer), whose performance may be implicated in the report.

5. **DOJ Distrusts Independent Contractors.** In general, federal regulatory agencies believe that there is more opportunity for misconduct through independent contractor arrangements than there is through *bona fide* employees, and the DOJ Guidance is consistent with that belief. For example, it is perfectly permissible for an organization to outsource the compliance function to an independent contractor, but, if so, then how and why that decision was made and how it was managed must be explained. This leads back to informed decision making by the Governing Board. Also, the DOJ dedicates an entire topic to Third Party Management, demonstrating that DOJ perceives third party management as a regulatory vulnerability. Although third party management agreements are also perfectly permissible, they are subject to intensified scrutiny when an allegation of misconduct arises. Once again, responsibility for oversight of the third party management agreement and accountability of third party vendors in general falls on the organization's Governing Board.

6. **The Organization Is Expected to Engage in Continuous Self-Critical Analysis and Regulatory Risk Assessment.** A Corporate Compliance and Ethics Plan cannot be a static piece of paper filed in a notebook in the organization's bookcase: it must become a living, breathing part of the organization. Resources must be allocated for active management of the compliance function and periodic assessment to identify potential regulatory risk.

XIV. THE ROLE OF BUSINESS ETHICS IN REGULATORY COMPLIANCE

A. **The Relationship Between Fraud, Compliance, and Ethics.**

1. **Relationship Between Compliance and Fraud.** Compliance and fraud are related only because they are opposites.

2. **Relationship Between Ethical Conduct and Compliance.** Ethics involves distinguishing between good and evil in a moral, not legal, context. Conduct that is unethical or immoral may not be illegal or technically non-compliant.

3. **Avoidance of Allegations.** To avoid punishment, we are compelled to act in accordance with a set of laws, mores, and standards, which involves both legal compliance and ethical behavior. Compliance and proper behavior take practice.

B. **Code of Ethics.** As stated above, development of a Code of Ethics is a critical element of an effective Compliance Plan.

ABOUT THE AUTHOR

Thomas William Baker was for over 30 years a leading national health care attorney and has over 15 years of experience as an Adjunct Professor in the Auburn University Physicians Executive MBA Program, for which he wrote this book. He received his A.B. degree in political science from Syracuse University in 1972, his M.B.A. from Georgia State University in 1978, and his J.D. from Vanderbilt University in 1981. Mr. Baker is also the Managing Member of Coronat Services, LLC (www.coronatservices.com), which provides educational, strategic planning, business advisory, and corporate governance services and is the Chairman and Chief Executive Office of Boncrest Resource Group, Inc. (www.boncrest.org), a mission driven charitable organization that operates senior living communities and provides a broad range of other services, activities, and programs for the benefit of populations and communities most in need.

www.ingramcontent.com/pod-product-compliance
Lightning Source LLC
LaVergne TN
LVHW062034101126
852251LV00025B/331
* 9 7 8 1 7 3 2 6 6 9 4 8 2 *